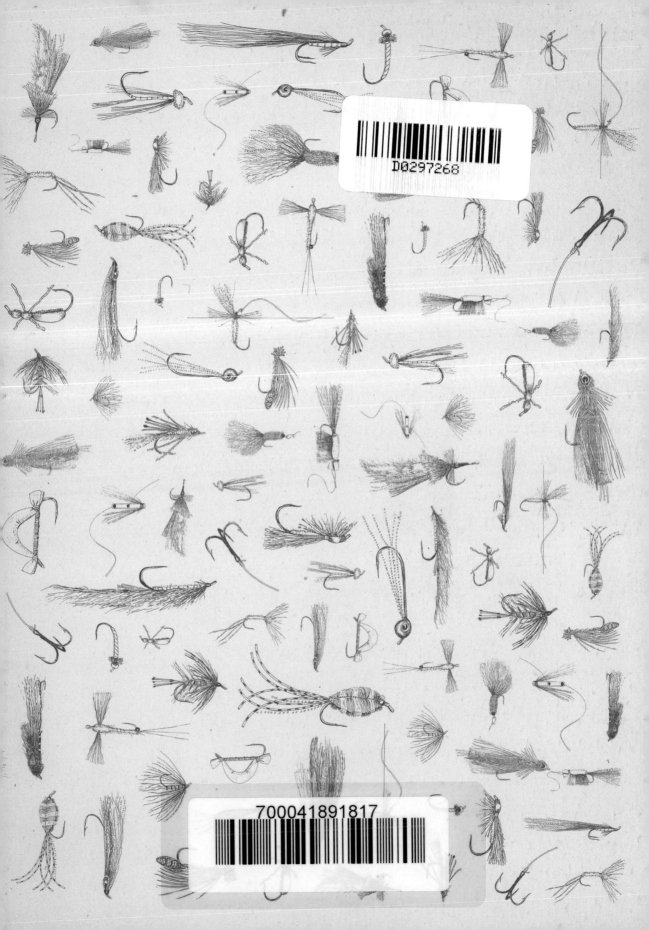

Flyfisher's Chronicle

In Search of Trout and Other Fishes and the Flies that Catch Them

WRITTEN AND ILLUSTRATED BY

Neil Patterson

Constable

London

CONSTABLE
First published in Great Britain in 2015 by Constable

A CIP catalogue record for this book
is available from the British Library.

ISBN 978-1-4721-1916-2 (hardback)
ISBN 978-1-47210-596-7 (ebook)

Typeset in Baskerville by Penny Mills
Printed and bound in Great Britain by Bell & Bain Ltd, Glasgow

Constable
is an imprint of
Constable & Robinson Ltd
Carmelite House
50 Victoria Embankment
London EC4Y 0DZ

An Hachette UK Company
www.hachette.co.uk

www.littlebrown.co.uk

For Doris and Robin,
who were always with me
when I wasn't there

~

In memory of Peter Lapsley,
my bestest friend,
& Sandy Scarth

~

The longer I fish,
the more I long for simplification
and lightness.

Dr Tom Sutcliffe, *Reflections on Fishing*

Contents

Preface: The Naked Flytyer

In praise of minimal flytying
(or life's too short to spend tying the wrong flies)

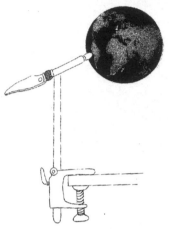

WHEN MICHELANGELO CARVED a horse out of a block of marble, someone asked him how he managed to create such a beautiful object from such a massive, shapeless lump. 'It's simple,' he said. 'I cut away everything that isn't a horse.'

Legs out of feathers, bodies out of fur, wings out of fluff. Flytying is an art, too: the astonishing art of creating something that looks like it's living, out of lumps of things that are lifeless. (Flytying is more than an art – it's a miracle!)

Now, there's a secret to every art. And there's a secret to the art of tying flies that fish can't resist clamping their teeth around.

It's this: Keep it simple.

But not everyone agrees. Too many flytying writers and commentators think flytying has to be difficult to be good. That it has to be complicated to convince the fish.

I'm not convinced. And neither, I believe, are a good many of the fish I chuck flies at; be they trout, bonefish, or dorado. In fact, anything with fins and fussy ways.

For these writers, their approach sells a lot of DVDs giving instructions on how to perform the impossible procedure they prescribe.

The message of this book is different: You don't have to be fancy-fingered to tie flies with supernatural effectiveness.

So, what is 'minimal' flytying?

It's not fishing with bare hooks. (Although one Florida guide checking out my saltwater fly box said it was like opening up a girlie magazine full of hookers with no clothes on.)

Minimal flytying is identifying the most critical and compelling features of the prey you are imitating. The 'clinch features', I call them: the bare essentials that confirm your fake's authenticity to a fish. No more than that. It's not about piling on as many features as you can fling on a hook. It's about stripping things back to the basics and then starting work. But, more crucially, it's about knowing when to stop. It only takes a hump to turn a horse into a camel.

For this reason, one mantra chimes through the pages you're about to read: the less you give a fish to question, the more likely you are to get the answer you were hoping for. The fewer tying procedures, materials and turns of thread you slap onto your creation, the fewer fish will find fault with your counterfeit and shout 'Fraud!' The result? The more fish you will catch.

This is the miracle of minimalism.

A flyfisherman once told me that if flyfishing didn't exist – if every fly-gobbling fish were to disappear off the face of the earth – he'd still tie flies.

This book introduces you to a series of flies that are a joy to tie, not a task. It's about flies that go for the filtered, rather than the full-strength; the cut-down, rather than the complicated; the clear, rather than the concentrated; the slender, rather than the stout.

None has been invented just to be different, or to demonstrate my digital prowess at the vice (this is non-existent). Instead, they are flies that have been designed to answer a particular brief, perform a particular job and pull off a particular stunt. Designed to be simple. All of them refusing to fall in line with what flyfishermen tend to automatically focus on: pattern, rather than performance.

They are flies that have been given a twist. A twist to their effectiveness – without you getting your fingers in a twist.

Finally, each and every one of them has undergone rigorous trials out in the field, up against the hardest criterion, winning the respect from the piscatorial assassins who have tested them. More than half of the flies have been in constant use for over twenty years; others, for over thirty years; one, for over sixty.

But this book is more than just a catalogue of flies that won't let you down.

I believe the best flies represent life. To me, they embody the best times of my fishing life.

Artificial fishing flies have accompanied me to Russia after brown trout never fished for before; to lonely beaches in Mexico patrolled by ghosts, the bonefish; to snake-infested waters in Argentina in search of El Dorado. They have accompanied me to Alaska after Arctic char in glacier streams you can only reach by floatplane; stream-born rainbow trout in South Africa among savage baboons; brook trout in Patagonia where locals carry Colt .38s; lake trout in Chile among volcanoes ticking like time bombs; tarpon four hours off the Cuban mainland; sea trout in Iceland, salmon in the Outer Hebrides; snooping on snook in fashionable Floridian shopping malls at midnight.

Flies are treasured memories. Opening up my fly box, I'm reminded of fish caught, fish lost. I see places, and I see faces. Faraway places I have explored with a four-piece fly rod where I have had to cast long lines. Faces of flyfishermen and crazy people I have met on my travels with whom I spent too short a time and exchanged too few words. Flyfishing adventures, unplanned and unexpected – but, above all, stories told.

Recollections of all sorts, wrapped round a hook with fur, feather and fluffy bits that, miraculously, bring these memories back to life.

Acknowledgements

TO LIST ALL THE PEOPLE who have played a part in this book would fill another book. But there are some to whom I am especially indebted, for without them there wouldn't be any book at all.

To John Goddard, who kicked my ass and told me I should spread my wings – and fly; flyfish other waters, other than the chalk stream at the bottom of my garden. To those who dared venture with me: Vincent Meade, Philip Thomsett, David Profumo, John Hotchkiss, Ron Clark, Theo Pike, Alan Black and Steve Edge.

To those who were there when I arrived: Michael and Benjamin Beale and Antonia, Diego Vigano, Jimmy Stewart, Luis and Carina Parsons, Sonia and Pedro Davila, who lent me their garden – and Guilly and Laura Boll, their swimming pool. To those who were still there when I got back home: Bill Parry-Davies, Charles Campion, Pierre Affre, Huw Williams, Lesley Scarth, Wegg Kimbell, Mike Davis, Jamie Birkmyre, John Colley, Jane and Charlie Robins, my sister Ann and Roger Doubal.

To those who stood in the background: the many editors, past and present, of magazines who gave me a chance to air my thoughts and who allowed me to publish some of those thoughts again in this book. But, in particular, the spectacularly brilliant Mark Bowler and his outstanding team at *Fly Fishing & Fly Tying*.

To those who stood on the front line: Editor of the *Flyfishers' Club Journal* and my dearest friend, Peter Lapsley, for his ceaseless encouragement. To Nick Lyons, my constant inspiration and support transmitted from so many miles away. To Tim Benn, for his relentless energy and for helping me prepare this book for take-off.

Finally, my eternal gratitude to Nick Robinson, who got it to spread its wings and fly.

Kintbury, Berkshire, England

Fishing should be the exercise of your skills –
and its rewards the places it brings you to.

Negley Farson, *Going Fishing*

Chile

Hotchpotch

Hook: No. 14–18
Thread: Brown
Body: Cream belly fur
Wing and Thorax: Brown Antron wool
Hackle: Ginger Cree

Circles in the Shadows

I WAS ABOUT TO TELL YOU ABOUT the man who kept thirty crocodiles at the bottom of his garden, in a shed in south London, but I have another jungle incident I need to get off my chest.

While the others were down at the lake pushing out their boats from the sheltered dock, I was still inside pulling on my underpants, sheltered from the weather outside, watching what was going on from my bedroom, bollock-naked.

Waves rolled ashore from an angry sea of grey water. The wind blew fierce and cold straight off the Ventisquero Yelcho Glacier forever gazing down at you, blue in the face.

It was not a morning for fishing.

Gales had woken me many times during the night, howling like wolves, shaking my windows and rattling them like a set of castanets. It was eight in the morning and there was still howling and windows shaking. But this wasn't all.

I had heard distant rumblings. and at one point, I thought I'd felt the room move. A glass had fallen off the shelf in the bathroom and smashed on the floor. Yes, it had been an earth tremor. But I had been told to expect this.

Chile is the home of two thousand volcanoes, and it was only six months since one of these volcanoes blew open after two thousand years of slumber, six miles from the town of Chaitén, a worrying forty-minute drive from the lodge.

It shot larva and volcano ash two miles up in the sky, depositing a layer of dust a foot deep in Futaleufú, fifty miles away – and an inch on the windowsills of the *cabaña* where I stay on the banks of the Rio Carrileufú in Argentina, eighty miles away as the ash flies. Cows woke up to toxic snow covering the fields, the children in Cholila spent two weeks wearing face masks and the fishing guides had lean bookings the following season.

Everyone was hoping Chaitén had erupted for the last time, that that was it for another few thousand years. Most of the four and a half thousand residents had been evacuated. The town was now surrounded by burned-out forests, the sides of the roads leading to it piled high with white ash like the approach to a ski resort. A few people remained. They must have felt the tremors, too, and got little sleep, like me.

The night before, one of the guides had been talking to a member of the security team monitoring the situation in Chaitén and the surrounding area. They had observed an increase in the size of a column of ash and smoke from the volcano. That same evening, the Deputy Interior Minister, Patricio Rosende, warned that one of the cones was about to collapse. 'This is more proof of the imminent risk in the area. It is a time bomb,' he announced.

But today, it was time to get the rod out. Once again, fishing had a certain frisson, one could say.

Adrian, my guide, said he'd be in reception waiting for me at nine. If, that is, *el lago* was fishable. At nine, he was there: on the button.

'Not a bit too rough out there this morning?' I said, shaking, and probably howling a bit internally, too.

No, a toss of Adrian's head told me, as he unhooked my rod from a rack in a corner of the rod room, which I had all to myself as I was the only fisherman with a room in the main building of the Yelcho en la Patagonia Lodge.

This room was simple enough, on the corner of the building, with a bench built in under two windows, allowing me to sit and look over the lake, and across to the *cordilleras*, way in the distance. The other fishermen, a party of eight from Santiago, were somewhere at the back of the lodge in little cabins dotted about.

They were very keen.

If Adrian hadn't showed, I'd planned spending the morning at the Termas de Amarillo. Located twenty miles east of Chaitén on the Carretera Austral, this is where you go to soak in abject bliss, in natural hot springs heated by that very volcano that had blown open – and could blow again at any moment.

Instead of all this, I was shortly being blown across waves topped with cream, hood up, back to wind, hands gripping the side of the boat, watching virgin forests flash by. If Adrian's little rower turned over, it was reassuring to know that the entire shoreline of Lago Yelcho in the Rio Futaleufú system is uninhabited. In only two places does a road touch the rim of this twenty-seven-mile-long blue eye, with depths in places close to two thousand feet, making it the deepest – and probably the coldest – lake in Chile. An ocean as deep as God's voice.

But then it also has some of the largest, meanest and most aerobatic rainbow trout in Chile. And this, I thought, would have to be compensation enough.

I had arrived at the Yelcho the day before, a primordial sense of adventure on slow build the moment I crossed the border at Trevelin. Thoughts of giant trout rolling for dry flies kept my mind from drifting off the road.

There had only been one car in front of me at the Argentine frontier post. I had planned a picnic sitting on a roadside rock looking down the Rio Futaleufú, but my cheese, ham and salami were confiscated by the Chilean border guards. When it came to smuggling forbidden food items into their country, I was Le Grand Fromage – *el Queso Grande*.

There is no paved road after the small border town of Futaleufú all the way to Chaitén, almost the entire width of Chile. And from now on there would be no telephones, no mobile signal and I saw no postboxes. But they had *empanadas* to refill my picnic basket.

The four-hour drive along skinny, dusty dirt roads, with cambers inviting you to roll off into the turquoise rivers rushing only yards away, was hazardous. But tunnelling through huge yellow gorse bushes and shoulder-high lupins, and bumping past fields manicured by grazing farm animals to golf tournament standard, made it a picturesque journey. A flock of vultures picking at a shattered hare in the centre of the road refused to get out of the way. Stopping the car, I climbed out and they only moved when I threatened them with a rod tube.

I longed to see another human being.

To forewarn of an approaching bend, every kilometre or so a road sign told me to *REDUZCA VELOCIDAD*. By the time I arrived at the lodge I was as chilled as I could ever hope to be. Speed reduced.

At the lodge, Juan Paulo, the manager, greeted me with a glass of Chilean Carménère and told me a guide had been arranged for me. That night, he roasted a freshly killed spring lamb, dripping hot chunks spiked on a long stake.

It would have been a wonderful evening to fish, but I didn't. I sat on the terrace until late, enjoying a gentle wind as soft as darkness, and a sky scattered with stars. Coming from inside through an open door I could hear the red *roble* logs crackling. They stood upright, stacked to attention in the fireplace. I could also hear the other fishermen sipping wine, sighing at the tales of the monster trout they'd lost, cheering the ones they hadn't.

My first day was a half day. In the morning there was no wind. Temperatures hit 28°C. The sun hung long and high in the sky as Adrian slid us across a glassy, flat surface to Cuba half an hour from the dock. Cuba, the name I gave this lonely area, looked more like a bonefish flat in mangrove country than a lagoon on an inland water. Here, the colour of the lake bottom shifted from amber to yellow to gold and back to amber again, suddenly shelving off into great ultramarine-blue depths. Ultramarine, coincidentally, being a blue pigment consisting primarily of aluminium, sodium and sulphates, all of which are to be found in abundance in the surrounding mountainsides.

After breakfast, I set up two rods on a table on the terrace outside the bar overlooking the lake: a 5-weight with a floating line and a 7-weight with a 300-grain sink tip.

'No,' a shake of Adrian's head told me, as he stored away the 7-weight: 300 grains was a might too Herculean for the delicate work we had ahead of us. He preferred the 5-weight, which he lifted carefully from the racks on the side of the boat, handing it to me with the reverence of a priest at communion. A 'yes' nod indicated my Damsel Fly Nymph would do the trick – but not all the various versions of them that I had tipped into the palm of his hand for inspection and his opinion; just the one with the ten-ton head. Let the fly do the sinking.

Not all bits of trout food give you carte blanche to keep your imitation nice and sweet and simple. But the Damsel Fly does. When I'm tying one up, I don't think about how complicated I can make the pattern. I just imagine I'm creating a character out of a Jules Verne adventure. It's that simple.

Whatever else I might think necessary for my artificial fly to take with it on its descent to the bottom of the lake, I never forget that the most important thing is weight. Nothing should conceal the plummeting side of your Damsel's personality. Bags of fluffy, woolly, feathery materials, frilly extras and unnecessary turns of silk that will impede its progress downwards should be left back up there on dry land, on your work bench. Better still, tucked away out of reach in a drawer.

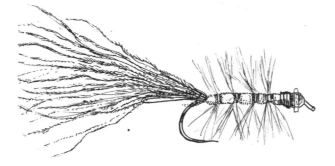

To ensure my pattern dives deep and fast, when it comes to prioritizing tying procedures, top of the list is the thing that's going to get my fly to the bottom. I start by sliding a gold-faceted tungsten bead to behind the eye of a #10 long-shank hook. Behind this, to hold it in position, I tie in a slip of an olive hen hackle with primrose yellow thread (two turns

15lb mono

prevents
wing-wrap

of thread only, please). Hen because cock hackles repel the water, but hen hackles appear to suck it in. (What other reason could there be for wet flyfishermen through the ages to prefer them?) Behind the bead, I tie in a small length of light green Supreme Plastic Hair, looped. This loop extends the barb slightly, preventing the small bunch of medium olive marabou tail – which I am just about to tie in – winding round the hook bend. I top this with a meagre bunch of golden olive marabou. At the bend, I tie in a length of hefty wire and a length of thin light green chenille which I wind to behind the bead. Finally, I palmer the hackle down to the bend (three turns only) and wind the wire back through the hackle back to behind the bead. I whip-finish with a length of lime green Glo-Brite thread. And here you have the fly that caught the guide – his approval, at least – long before it hit the lake and sank out of sight.

Adrian told me that in the summer it was all dry flyfishing. Dragonflies crowd the skies and the fishing gets impossibly hard. The water is so crystal-clear it's like air and the trout have the highest FlyQ of any you'll ever fish for. They see everything, miss nothing.

I quickly learned that it takes great skill and frustration to get a Yelcho rainbow to come anywhere near your fly before the game's up – in particular, your best-tied nymph imitation, as there is very little surface activity this early in the season. Racing towards it from what seems like fifty yards away and discovering it's a sham, rather than head for the aluminium-laden Andes, Yelcho trout fin-tap half-open mouths and yawn. The only fish I know that snore when they're awake.

Plonked at the other end of the boat from Adrian, who was sitting quietly picking at his nails, I leaned over the side watching trout react to my fly, as if looking into a goldfish bowl. It got me back to basics.

We all know why trout take our flies. They look worthy of being eaten. Progressive anglers know something else: the way a fly progresses can provoke the same reaction. Movement certainly rouses curiosity. Enough for a trout to want to investigate further – with their mouths. (You would, too, if you didn't have hands.)

Sometimes it's not the design of a fly, but what you do with the design, that matters. Inching my Damsel along the bottom at the same speed – and imitating the same movements of the ones I once kept in a tank – I got the reaction I was after: interest. But not what I was really after: the take. At least, not until I changed my Damsel's behaviour and started lifting up my rod tip and lowering it again in jerky movements. A sink and draw movement, making my Damsel not so much swim as stutter.

It looked crazy, but I could see my Damsel was driving the trout crazy, too – with more than curiosity. This unorthodox motion made the fly look injured, helpless and just asking to be pounced on. Stuttering along in fits and bounds, my Damsel was in distress – and, irresistibly, bound to be easy prey.

The key to this behaviour was in the design of the fly. It incorporated not just any bead head, but a tungsten bead head, the heaviest one I could get my hands on (or a crane to lift). I was happy to place an order at the Harland and Wolff shipyard, Belfast, if need be. Every cast I made, I feared for the brave few still in Chaitén, lest they read the arrival of my Damsel on the lake bed as another earth tremor.

'Look at these fish following my fly!' I yelled at Adrian as a five-pound Yelcho snapped at a two-pounder who had joined in the chase. Adrian just laughed and shook his head.

I was inching my Damsel along the ledge of an ochre drop-off that plunged into midnight blue. Raising my rod tip and letting the fly dive back down, I gave it a series of almighty stutters. Like some crazed aquatic Ceilidh dancer, the trout swirled and spun round a couple of times at the tail of the fly, before grabbing it, one-two-three, and gobbling it up.

'*Mosca tartamedeo!*' – 'Stutter fly', Adrian named it.

My Damsel in distress wasn't the only stutterer. Moses stuttered. So did Darwin, Churchill, John Lee Hooker, B. B. King, Tiger Woods and Bruce Willis. Not forgetting Marilyn Monroe and Nicole Kidman.

A famous line-up, but when did Nicole Kidman ever catch anybody a five-pound trout?

When bead heads first arrived on the market so many years ago (but not that many), the American publisher Nick Lyons said to me, 'Neil, jigging has now become an art form.'

Like Nick, I'm not Mr Bead Head's greatest fan. They flash, and truly wild trout see the ruse. With small nymphs, I usually rely on lead strips concealed in the dressing.

But that day on Lago Yelcho, when I watched how a strategically placed lump of deadweight could create such a beguilingly attractive stutter movement, I must confess, I was left speechless.

Back again to that storm-filled second day.

Adrian was all wrapped up, too. He was getting the spray flying up from the front of the boat, over my shoulders, straight in his face. His hood was pulled low over his forehead, joining up with his collar pulled high over his nose. His deep-sea eyes peering through a slit as thin as string told me that in his mind he was somewhere else.

He gave two boats anchored in the lee of the mountains a wide berth and kept on going. The wind was still in the tops of the *colehues* we passed.

Scrunched up inside my fishing jacket like a tortoise in a shell, I was able neither to see nor to know where we were going. All I could do was sit back and trust that it would be somewhere worth all the banging and slapping of the boat and the rearranging of my vertebrae. It was a good time for thinking and being still and alone. The noise of the outboard made conversation an impossibility.

Tucked up in the warm darkness of your fishing jacket, you can reflect on the life you're powering away from: the adventures, the agonies, the pleasures and the prices you pay to go fishing, now all gone, taken by the currents of a stream, sucked down and away in the slow, cold yawn of the waves turning over all around.

To get to this point in time, this place on a compass, I had had to work hard to earn the cash and find the time to be here. And now, with hands screwed up in tight fists shoved deep down in pockets, mouth tucked away behind the high flap of a breath-warmed collar, I raised an imaginary glass high up into the chilly Chilean air, closed my eyes, counted my blessings and drank to my incredible good fortune.

The fishing writer Roderick Haig-Brown tells us:

> We search in many ways and many places, each of us, I suspect, with some secret inward vision, subconscious as often as not, of what trout fishing really is. We settle for less,

often much less, and we may even find other, unexpected experiences more brilliant than the one we seek. I have many friends who never stop travelling in search of trout.

I could have been one of Haig-Brown's friends. Right now my unexpected experience was discovering just how cold it was on this lake, as opposed to the brilliant sun the day before, on my first day.

Now I could feel the pace slowing, the bow lowering, and see Adrian's windblown face glowing as we pulled out of the rough air and slipped, in creep mode, into a quiet water creased only by our boat.

At last I could pull back my hood and look around.

We were in grassland behind an island, with tall dried rushes to one side, a jungle on the other; an impenetrable woodland sending out shoots of willow and *arrayanes* in an attempt to claim new ground, stretching out to join hands with the water lilies and gain access to the shallow reed beds opposite.

The further we crept into this curious new land hidden away at the end of the lake, the narrower grew the distance between the reeds and the island, the shallower the water. Eventually, Adrian stopped the engine and started poling us silently towards the first of three pools that punctuated what, to all intents and purposes, was developing into something more like a stream than a mid-lake pond. A stream that joined the two sides of the lake. A stream with no current. If you have seen the film *The African Queen*, starring Humphrey Bogart and Katharine Hepburn, you'll recognize the scene I found myself in.

'Take off that fly,' Adrian said, shaking a finger at my Damsel. He was preparing me for something.

A fish moved. I didn't see it, but Adrian did. A circle in the shadows.

It was time for me to forget that I was fishing a lake. I was now in an overgrown creek demanding I pitch clever casts as close into the bank as possible between overhanging branches and fallen trees; places where a trout might be lying waiting for something to either fall off a branch, climb in or out of the water, or where minnows shelter in the tangle of underwater roots and decaying branches.

'Do you take all your clients here?' I asked Adrian, realizing that fishing was no longer a matter of slinging a fly out into open water, leaning over the bow of the boat and watching trout react to it. The bottom was as black as a motorway. Under the trees it was dark, full of lost whispers. It was impossible to see anything move unless it swam just under the skin of the water and tickled the surface.

'No, *nunca*,' Adrian replied, his eyes never leaving the water. I was privileged, it seemed. Or rather honoured, for none of his clients could handle it. It was too unfamiliar. I was beginning to wonder if I would be able to do any better.

There was a huge splash under the bank at the end of the pool, in a trickle that fed it; a tight area overhung with dead branches, bookended with a large root on one side, a fallen tree on the other. A fish was feeding under this canopy.

Adrian poled past it. He wasn't going to stop. The hole where the trout had leapt was no bigger than a handkerchief. We decided that, rather than feeding on something, a cruising trout had suddenly found itself lost in a jungle of underwater debris, and panicked. Either get the hell out, or die of claustrophobia. We were looking for excuses to avoid having to perform a truly impossible cast to get a fly to it.

Then the fish rose again. It turned on something small on the surface in exactly the same place, in that same handkerchief area.

Adrian kept on poling. But I just had to have a shot. Any shot. A wild shot, with no style would do. I had nothing to lose, only a fly up on a branch.

I ended up casting one of those casts you could never have executed (or wanted to, necessarily) had you not been feeling a bit wild and, as I say, had nothing to lose. Technique didn't come into it.

I had waxed up and tied on a small sedge, the Hotchpotch, my all-round, jack-of-all-trades sedge pattern that does just what I want a fly to do when I really don't know what I want it to do and when I really have no idea what fly to put on.

Soundlessly (and miraculously), the Hotchpotch morphed through a myriad of mid-air obstacles and landed in the handkerchief, an inch from the side of the stitching. It cocked beautifully, its body lying flat under the wing in the surface film. Adrian had stopped poling, so I let it float a while.

I was just about to pick up my line and cast again, this time a little closer to the bank, when it occurred to me that I would never be able to repeat that first cast with the same precision and get my fly to where I managed to get it in my wild days. So I let it be and went back to feeling like an Indian stalking a fish, the ambush set.

Suddenly, the handkerchief exploded and the Hotchpotch was lost in a cloud of crystals, shadows, darkness, lightning and tarmac. The trout didn't leap, it burrowed.

Sometimes the successful playing of a fish isn't so much to do with calculating the size and strength of what you have at the end of your line, it's calculating the size and strength of the line before you attach yourself to anything. It's about knowing your tackle is up to it.

With trout patrolling between lily pads and logs, I had upped the strain of my tippet to eight pounds. For this reason I began the fight with an advantage. I knew that I could probably land a tarpon if I wanted to with my set-up. I gave whatever was on the end of my line no slack. Whichever way my fish might have wanted to proceed, it could proceed either up or down but not across or to either side. I had my fish wrapped up in that handkerchief neater than Dick Whittington's belongings when he set off for London to seek his fortune.

My fish went down. I could feel him brooding beneath a ledge, wiping his nose in the mud somewhere in the handkerchief, planning his next move. The occasional tap confirmed he hadn't died on me, at least not totally.

Adrian poled the boat across the top of some lily pads that stood between the trout and us, parking in a narrow strip of clear water the shape and size of a trouser leg. Handkerchiefs, trousers: I was fishing in the men's department of a high street store.

Adrian had smoked a whole cigarette in the time it took me to decide that some lifting needed to be done. I put the pressure on. My trout co-operated – at least, to begin with. It started to surface. But seeing the lily pads up top, he decided that the stalks were much more interesting and started playing out my greatest fears. He dived into them.

Adrian wasn't having any of it. He poled the boat straight at the offending vegetation, mowing down lilies, trout and anything else that got in his way, without fear – or favour, for that matter.

The snowplough scam worked. The trout surfaced and flapped onto the top of the lilies, which started to sink under its weight, on contact. It was a brown trout. A big old *marron* with barely a mark on its body. A black-backed, yellow-bellied specimen of spotlessness. Six pounds, at least.

Adrian wet his hands, lifted him up, bent over, groaned under the weight and slid the grand old fish back between the lilies. Before it disappeared under the tarmac, I'm sure I heard the old soldier groan, too. How undignified this must have been for him.

An interview, without coffee.

At the dock, I let Adrian tie up the boat and walked straight up to the Yelcho lodge, taking up residence at the bar, stocking-foot waders and all. Gonzalo the barman's Bloody Marys were something to die for and I knew that he only had half a carton of tomato juice left until Friday, when the supply man arrived. I was the first man back.

'Mind if I smoke my pipe?' I asked Gonzalo.

'I think we've had enough ash around here for while,' he said, pointing at some books that had slipped over on a shelf and handing me my toxic measure. 'Do you feel tremors out on a lake in a boat?'

I told him we didn't feel anything. Just the tugging of an angry trout.

Earthquakes and volcanoes notwithstanding, I was thinking how great it is to be sitting here at the bar in my chest waders – with a big fish in my mind and nothing else. What could be better?

I told Gonzalo about my fly that had fooled the monster *marron*, the big bad brown. Now, I don't know if he was interested in this fly or not, but that's what barmen in fishing lodges are paid for: to pour drinks and look interested. At least the best ones are.

Gonzalo asked me if Adrian had been a good guide. I told him that he had been the very best, but that guides are called 'ghillies' in the UK – a Scottish word. Gonzalo seemed to understand me better than Adrian. Anyway, if he didn't, he did a first-class job pretending he did. I decided to tell him a ghillie, or rather a boatman, story. This was something I had wanted to tell Adrian during those silent moments, what with him being my boatman, or ghillie. Gonzalo's English was good, a lot better than Adrian's. But how good was his Irish?

I told him I'd never really fished in Ireland. I pootled about in a leaky boat on some still water down south near Skibbereen, County Cork. But only the once, and this was the extent of my Irish fishing ventures.

If I were to go there now, I don't think it would be for the fishing. My reason for this is very simple. When my friends come back from a fishing trip in Ireland, they spend five minutes talking about the fishing and an hour howling with laughter about all the mad things that happened to them.

One of my favourite stories comes from a ghillie called Villy. Villy the ghillie. That's funny before we start. Gonzalo flashed a knowing smile.

Villy was a boatman on Loch Conn – a great name for a lough that charges you a fortune to hire a boatman, only to come back at the end of the day not having caught or touched a fish. The Irish are funny even when they're being serious.

Villy tells a story, not about the fantastic trout fishing, but about the huge pike that haunt the lough.

'They be eating up all the lovely trout,' Villy tells you. But at certain times of the year, the lough has something else in abundance. 'It's the frags. There be frags everywhere. You go out wadin' and you wade through frags and even more frags.'

A lack of frogs doesn't seem to be much of a problem in the margins of the lough in the summer. 'And there's nothing them pikes like better than the nice frag.'

Villy and the other ghillies make good use of this period of plenty. They go down to the reeds at the side of the lough with buckets and collect as many of those frogs as they can. 'Y'see, them pikes will take a frag if you give it to 'em. They love the frags. And night time is when the big pikes come out looking for a frag for dinner.'

Villy tells you it's very important that you know how to mount the frog on the hook properly. 'You don't be going and pushing hooks into the frags, now. They be dying if you do that. What y'do is ye get a nice elastic band and wind it round the frag and the hook so it's nice and tight, like. Not so tight that the frag can't breathe, now. And not so slack. Them frags slips out.'

Clearly a great amount goes into this mount. But there was more.

'To stop 'em swimming away, y'ave a bung. You gotta have a bung. A nice big bung to keep 'em swimming around. Then we goes home and come back in the morning.'

This should be the end of the story, but when you ask Villy why he is no longer seen going to the reeds with his bucket to collect frogs, he'll tell you he doesn't use frogs as bait any more.

'No, I be putting out a live bait. Y'see, them big pikes like nothing more than a nice roach.'

Better than a frog?

'Oh, no. Not really.'

So why doesn't Villy use frogs any longer?

'Well, y'see, them frags are clever little dee-veals. That next morning, when we went down to see how many pikes we'd caught on the rods, not a pike had we taken on them lines.'

And why was that?

'Well, for sure, them frags don't like being eaten up by the pikes, and they knows that if they goes in the water for a swim, they'd soon be eaten up. So when we went looking for the frags and couldn't find them, we found them sitting up on the bungs, just as pretty as can be.'

Gonzalo laughed, and asked me if I wanted a magazine to read. In case I was going to tell him another story, in Welsh. I thanked him for the offer, but told him that I wasn't a great reader. Most of what I learned about riding bikes, blowing bubbles with gum, whistling with two fingers and flyfishing, someone showed me how to do it.

I picked up the idea of the Hotchpotch from something I saw in somebody's box, the simplicity of which overwhelmed me, and named it after John Hotchkiss, one of England's finest guides, whose guiding abilities also overwhelmed me. I was given one to try. And, more importantly, take home to my laboratory for closer examination.

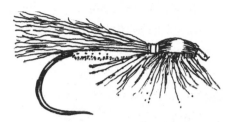

The sedge was tied on a #14 barbless hook. Armed with a scalpel, I picked away at it like some demented ophthalmic surgeon to reveal the tying procedures. Light brown thread had been tied in two-thirds of the way down the hook and wound to the bend. A deliciously creamy material from the flytyer's dubbing larder had been used to form a body that started at the bend and ended back at the starting position where the thread had been secured. Here a short length of light brown, camel-coloured Antron floss had been tied in directly behind the hook eye so that, once secure, it flopped over the top of the eye. The thread was then returned to the starting position. On the way, a light brown cree hackle was tied in, the tip lying shiny side up so that it also flopped over the Antron and the hook eye. The hackle was then wound back to the thread starting position and secured. The fibres on top had been trimmed. Finally, the Antron was folded back over the hackle and secured with a whip-finish where the hackle had been secured, at the starting position. The wing was trimmed so that it extended the hook bend.

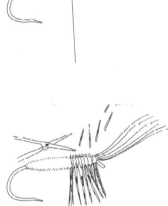

The design answered one of the trickiest questions. Put simply – and I like to keep things simple when I have a Bloody Mary in my hand – can there be such a thing as The Perfect Sedge Pattern? The answer is, yes, there is such a thing.

So, what is a perfect sedge pattern?

If Mr *Ephemeroptera*, the upwing fly, is the Francis Drake of the aquatic fly world, Mr *Trichoptera* – or Señor Sedge – is the Buzz Lightyear. Maximum motion. Bags of action. Sacks of buzz. No wonder that, when you hear a splash on an evening, it can only be a trout, sedge-bound. 'To infinity – and beyond!'

clip

In the past, a palmered body hackle has been light years ahead of any other method in imitating this 'buzz' a sedge displays when it finds itself hatched out, far from home, far from secure, too nervous, far too vulnerable – and freaks! For me, the body-palmered style of sedge hackling has design faults. It cleverly, but not too cleverly, lifts one of the most important parts of the sedge clean out of the menu-gazing vision of a hungry trout diner. The beef; the body.

A big, fat, juicy sedge body should be presented to the trout – in full view. After this, legs, wings, antennae and all the rest is just soup stock. So, if there's not going to be any pre-supplied, palmered 'buzz' in this design, where is the attraction in this serve-all sedge pattern?

With the Hotchpotch, the 'buzz' is where – and when – you want it. If, indeed, you need it at all, for I have found the body gets all the buzz I want, from a trout. Could this be the first super-seductive static sedge?

If you want buzz – or 'movement' – you can control it. It's at your beck and call. Static, the pattern is designed to keep the seductive body in full view of the trout, just like a fast-escaping sedge wishes it wasn't. The design sits this body on a soft mattress of hackle – rather, a platter. Not held high on a spiky bed of hackle nails. Out of sight, out of stomach. Twitch the rod tip to impart movement. The motion is more representative of the natural.

With the 'palmer' style, the fly pushes a wave out in front of the fly, like a bow wave of a rowing boat. With the Hotchpotch, lift the rod and the wing keeps low and trails a gentle wake behind it, like an outboard motor, forming an irresistible 'V', identical to that of a natural.

The sideways positioning of the hackles of the Hotchpotch makes it plane the water, lifting it up on its tail. It's here – at the tail, not the head or along the body – where the action really is.

Anything more to say about the design? Yes. Latter-day patterns miss out on important features displayed by the natural. One of these unmissable features, from a trout's vantage point, is the thorax. Look at a sedge from below, from the trout's view, and you will see the front part of the sedge (not along the sides) is all thorax and legs. These are perfectly imitated in the design of this pattern.

Finally, the design supports a theory I have had for many years now, that it's not always best to tie off your fly at the head. With the

Hotchpotch, you whip-finish mid-fly, behind the thorax where there's less room to make mistakes – and risk being banned by your local Fly Dresser's Guild for having an untidy head.

I hate trout. Eating them, that is. So I'm a catch-and-release fanatic. For my riverside neighbours, who watch me going down the track to the river from my home, catch and release means coming back from fishing with nothing to show for it. In a way, they're right. The cupboard (rather, their cupboard) is bare, but then the river isn't.

I like to keep score of trout I've caught or released (or neither) on a day. So, I bought a 'clicker', a little contraption with a knob you press that keeps count of every trout.

Foolproof? But, more importantly, lie-proof?

Well, no. Not if you sit up against a tree, or rub up against something, with this clicker in your pocket. At the end of the day, when you'd swear you'd only caught four trout, the clicker tells you that, in actual fact, you've caught four hundred. Well, what a surprise! And what an impressive entry in your record book!

So, nowadays, every time I release a trout (in other words, poke out a barbless hook with my rod tip), I snap off a twig or pluck a leaf and put it in my pocket. And when I get back up the track, and the neighbours ask me how many trout I've caught, I say, 'One twig, three daisy heads, a reed and a duck feather.' They say, 'Sounds like you've had a good day.'

In ancient times – in old angling literature, at least – the top-catching fly in a fly box, the fly that has caught the most fish, in the most locations, with consistency, is referred to as a 'sheet anchor'.

The dictionary defines a sheet anchor as 'a large strong anchor for use in emergency', suggesting that if things get desperate, you could do worse than trawl the depths with something huge and leaded. Surprising, then, to discover that my 'sheet anchor' fly of the year isn't weighted. Indeed, it's very dry. A fly design that, at the final tote, has caught me more twigs, daisy heads, reeds and duck feathers than any others. It's my Hotchpotch. And a variation of the Hotchpotch I call my Hyper Hotchpotch, which I've just got to tell you about, because this tinkering means the Hotchpotch now sports an even more interesting difference than the tying style. How much of a difference is hard to judge.

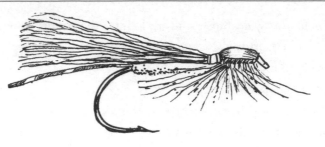

Hyper Hotchpotch

For progressive flytyers, the most successful flies are those that are a tad unorthodox, with 'attractor' elements designed into the fly to market them better to the trout, giving them an extra something that renders them more irresistible than the naturals sitting next to them. That makes them stand out in a crowd. Sometimes even when there's no crowd at all.

Newness creates interest, I say, for man, and trout alike. And there are no end of flashy new materials in the catalogues that can give your fly the Hollywood treatment. Synthetic materials that have imitations sparkling and twinkling as they Tinsel-Town their way down a river or across a lake with more gleam, glitter and glistening glory than Lady Gaga, dressed as Tinker Bell, on a Christmas tree.

Exaggerating a feature of the fly, or highlighting it with one of these new materials, helps your fly achieve the first thing any fly has to do: get noticed. 'Helps', I say. Over-use results in an adverse effect and has trout heading for the hills, which is why I'm no fan of gold bead heads. (Although I do use them, sparingly.)

Add a little Tinsel Town

For this reason, with the Hotchpotch style, I prefer to mount flashy materials under the wing, not on top of it. This way, the effect of 'flashy materials' is diffused, but not diminished. Here's why.

Under the wing, it is light that is reflected up off the water, not from directly above, that animates the materials. When light coming from the air strikes water, part is reflected and part is refracted but, more importantly, a large chunk is absorbed, giving your fly just the right amount of muted pizzazz to impart a true shiny, lifelike look. Enough to drive her Ladyship, the hungry trout, gaga.

So, why not the same for those flat-winged terrestrials, the reed smuts that parade down a river in the summer sun, wings reflecting light like crusader shields in the desert sun? Tied in the Hotchpotch style, except with a black body, white polypropylene wing and a strip of silver Holographic Tinsel as underwing.

So, here's today's flytying advice: Hide your flashy materials under a bushel. Even better, a wing.

TWO

Russia

Banana Fly

Hook: No. 14 (up-eyed)
Thread: Primrose Yellow
Thorax: Fluff from a yellow Cul de Canard plume
(tied behind the eye)
Hackle and Wing: Yellow Cul de Canard plume
(funnelled forward with two turns of thread tied over roots.
Trim small 'V' on top side)
Body: Fluff from a yellow Cul de Canard plume
Tail: Small bunch of cul de Canard fibres
(tied slightly round bend)

Where Reindeer Dare to Tread

IT WAS AT A TIME WHEN I had an office with a receptionist sitting out there taking my calls.

'There's a Peter Power on the line,' she said.

Now, when you're in advertising, you get lots of calls from people with crazy names. Ziggy Stardust? Peter Power? Sounded like a photographer to me. Another photographer wanting to come in and show me his book.

I asked if she could find out who he was and I put the phone down. It rang again, almost immediately.

'He told me to tell you that he owns two and a half million acres of Russia.'

'OK,' I said. 'Put him through.'

Peter Power was phoning to invite me to his estate near Eynsham in Oxfordshire. He'd heard that I was a serious trout-fishing buff and he had plans for me. He wanted me to explore the upper regions of three of his rivers on the Kola Peninsula that drain north into the Barents Sea: the Kharlovka, the Rynda and the Eastern Litza above the waterfalls, where the salmon can go no further. In July, the first week of the first season, to explore the wild brown trout fishing. I would have to pay my fare to Murmansk, he told me. After that, he'd provide everything else I needed so that I could scout around, assess the trout fishing possibilities and report back to him with a recommendation of what he should do with it all.

After an in-depth introduction to his fishings on video, we had lunch. Then he walked me round his goose park. He told me he had the largest and most comprehensive collection of goose breeds in Europe. I looked around, wondering who was eyeing up who: the geese, me; or me, the geese. Or Peter, studying my reaction to it all.

After his presentation, the stories of his battles with the Russian mafia, his success in outsmarting them, I was spellbound and filled with admiration – and my mind was on the Kharlovka. I was already there. I mumbled something about his geese shuffling all around me, but I wasn't aware of exactly what I had said, but it was complimentary, for sure.

'What I like about you advertising people', Peter said as we walked back to the house, 'is that you know exactly the right thing to say.'

The next month, arrangements were made through Roxtons in Hungerford.

It was 1,843 miles from London to Helsinki and my overnight stop. Finnair flight AY834 was a spanking new Airbus, just launched. The toilet flushed automatically when you finished. How it knew this, I just don't know. Most of the time, I don't know myself.

More impressive, back at your seat, overhead screens flipped down and a camera mounted in the nose of the plane showed you what the pilot could see. After a while, this got a bit dull. How about what the pilot was *thinking?*

I looked out of the window, wondering what he could be thinking. Looking back at the camera, I was given a clearer view. On the screen was the pilot, a ginger-haired man wearing thick glasses – with a girl on his lap. Then I snapped out of it. The nasal camera had switched off and the in-flight entertainment had started.

Viewed from the window of the plane, Helsinki looks like a string of Christmas tree lights dropped on top of an estuary. There's a two-hour time difference between London and Helsinki and the light does funny things. At midnight, it's still midday – and it was bedtime. With no time for sightseeing, I went straight to the hotel, checked in and hit the pillows. I had to be up at five o'clock the next morning to catch a 7.45 flight to Murmansk. In the rush, I left my hairbrush at the hotel.

Was this a sign?

On this hour-and-a-half flight, I sat next to a salmon fisherman on his first trip to Russia. He demonstrated that this wasn't the first time he'd flown by telling me that the landing at Murmansk was 'better than landing on Barra beach' in the Outer Hebrides, where you think you're going to land on the sea.

On the Road to Trout, you meet people you least expect to meet, in places you least expect to find yourself. Inside a saucepan, for example.

As bald as a stainless steel coot, the arrivals hall at Murmansk airport, twanging at the frosty 69-degree line north of the Arctic Circle, is a symphony of echoes. Like waiting for the hatch, they say that waiting for immigration to process the incoming Friday Flyfishing Finnair Flight from Helsinki is all part of that special Russian fishing experience. People were talking about records. Not salmon or trout records: waiting-time records.

'I waited four hours,' boasted one salmon fisherman in pink corduroys.

'That's nothing,' said Dick, an ex-advertising agency owner I had once worked with (never knowing that he was a flyfisherman). 'I waited four days.'

Classic comparative advertising, I remember thinking. Once an adman, always an adman. But Dick had sold up and now had his own lodge somewhere out in the tundra, on the Kanga.

'My lodge has just arrived from the US. The hillside is strewn with containers,' he told me in the same tone of voice I'd heard from people who had just bought furniture at IKEA.

We swapped addresses. His was somewhere in Monte Carlo.

At 3 p.m. we were still fogbound. As the hours slipped by, seasoned visitors remarked how much quicker things were getting. I used the time to try and identify the three other members of the two parties of flyfishermen fortunate enough to have been invited by Peter to the upper regions of his northern rivers.

One was a Czech called Frank, a member of the Czech flyfishing team. The other, a German called Nils. It had me wondering who I would be sharing a tent with. Unfortunately, we were not staying in one of the plush pinewood chalets at the base camp Kharlovka lodge, with bouncy beds, a sizzling sauna and hot and cold running Atlantic salmon. Once we were paired up, a helicopter was to fly me and my mystery partner out into the naked tundra to be dropped off in an area that had never been visited before, let alone fished; to live under canvas with Vasiljev Kiselev, a Russian guide who had just been on a crash course at Berlitz. (Not the same one as the helicopter pilot, I hoped.) As our guide and cook, I hoped Vasiljev had also attended the Roux brothers' summer school at the Waterside Inn.

No, our lot was to be the basest of base camps.

Right now, stranded in Murmansk, trout lepers in a colony of salmon fishermen shoaled in a sea of rod tubes, waiting to be dispatched up one or other of the Kola Peninsula's sixty-odd rivers, you'd imagine finding the other members of our discreet group would be a hard task. In fact, it wasn't: you go blazer and Alice band-spotting. This eliminates nearly all salmon fisherpersons instantly, leaving three unclassified: Nils, the German, wearing a hat with a bunch of feathers sticking out of it; Frank, with big brown, match-the-hatch eyes that stared out into the middle distance, at rivers we were yet to see; and only one other person, the hippy sitting on the haversack, busy taking air temperatures, barometer readings and checking his position on his GPS. This was my tent-mate.

Peter Wulff is a Swede who has trout-fished the Kola more times than any other man. Certainly for long enough to know that you don't get anywhere fishing in Russia unless you know how to sit around – and wait.

What I didn't know then was that my journey with Peter the Wulff man was to be an expedition that would redefine what the brochures claim to be the ultimate in adventure fishing, in the last of one of the world's true wildernesses; cocking a snook at wild brown fishing on the over-idealized New Zealand streams and the well-trampled Alaskan plains that I had turned my back on ten years earlier.

At 4.30 p.m. they told us the helicopter was ready for lift-off. But Peter had been here before. Lifting his head, he told us that it couldn't be ready as he hadn't heard one return from the Rynda.

'I don't trust the Russians,' he said, returning to his barometer and other techie things; things that don't lie. 'Visibility is 340. It has to be 350 to fly.'

Peter was right. At 9 p.m., after ten hours of waiting, we were still there, waiting. My techie things (my eyes) told me it was still light. I had camped out in a shop stall. Peter had spent the last hour feeding the sparrows flying around the airport. At least at Murmansk airport something could take off.

It was Justin Staal, the Roxtons tour guide, who finally informed us that our luggage had been taken off a helicopter. He had made arrangements for us to bed down at the Polarnie Zori in Murmansk, a hotel forty-five minutes away.

A grumpy prop forward with a square jaw made of sandpaper, who was wearing a camouflage jacket and camouflage trousers, broke cover and pushed his way through us, growling like a bear.

'I'm glad we've seen the back of him,' I said to Peter as we gathered up our stuff.

In fact, we were to see the back of him again the next day. He was the helicopter pilot.

The streets of Murmansk are poorly lit and dripping with depression. We went to a bar. Girls wearing long cloaks and home-made clothes and leftovers from the sixties were sitting in groups round tables. They were laughing and joking. I looked around and wondered what they could find to laugh about. But even in the cold fluorescent lighting, you couldn't deny the fact that whatever they were wearing they would still look elegant. Fashion wasn't the word, it was pride: pride in what little they had; pride in their appearance.

Built in 1973 and reconstructed in 1997, the Polarnie Zori is considered to be one of the best hotels of the city with 'a wonderful view of the Kola Bay'. Clearly my room faced the other way. As I closed the curtains, in the city half-light I could see the back of a derelict building across from the hotel. When I switched off my light, the darkness was absolute.

You can tell how happy a country is by its breakfast cereals. The next morning, the only cereal on offer was a bowl of what looked like brightly coloured earplugs. On the hi-fi Boney M. were singing: 'Man will live for evermore because of Christmas Day.' It was July.

Nils and Frank were sitting at a table tying flies. The Wulff man was nowhere to be seen. As I waited for the scrambled eggs that I had ordered an hour earlier, I made the ultimate enquiry: 'Anyone got a mouth organ?'

Back in my room, I looked out of the window and studied the bombed building opposite, in the cold light of day. There were curtains at the windows. Clothes were hanging out to dry. People lived there; people who had no electricity, otherwise I would have seen lights in those windows the night before.

I pulled the curtains shut again and remembered something that my good friend David Profumo had told me about when he'd done a similar trip the year before, on his way to the Ponoi River. 'Neil,' he'd said to me, 'Murmansk isn't exactly twinned with anywhere; rather it has a suicide pact with Grimsby.'

At 1 p.m. we had clearance. We piled aboard a helicopter fresh from the killing fields of Afghanistan, an Mi-8 medium twin-turbine transport helicopter that can also act as a gunship. It takes fourteen people and travels at about 10 mph. You have to look out of the window to check you're moving. Birds overtook us.

We arrived at the Rynda camp at 2 p.m. with just enough time for Peter Power to say a few words to us and for a mosquito to bite me on the nose. Nils and Frank were dropped off on a small island in the middle of the Rynda. I was all ready to get off, too, but the helicopter took off before I could get my ear protection muffs off, heading upriver to a spot Wulff man seemed to know, but Vasiljev didn't, which meant we had to circle for five minutes. Once again, our camouflaged helicopter pilot couldn't hide his grumpiness.

Eventually, we landed in the middle of nowhere, right on the middle of nothing. Our pilot decided that the best way to cure his crabbiness was to throw, rather than pass, our gear down to us. He was glad to see the back of us.

As the Mi-8 lifted off the tundra, the Wulff man and I lay on top of a heap of tents, sleeping bags, knapsacks, rod tubes, food containers, gas canisters, a cooking hob, a paraffin stove, an inflatable dinghy, a GPS and a satellite telephone (that was never going to work from the moment we landed until the moment we set off again), to stop everything being blown away by the downthrust.

Here, camped on the side of a track tattooed into the sphagnum moss by a thousand years' worth of relentless reindeer ploddings, was where we were going to stay.

Clearly, the tent I'd been given in which to brave the elements simply wasn't up to it. It was pure lingerie; Agent Provocateur's best. Peter put his lighter to it and it curled up and disappeared in seconds. He said I could bunk down in his High Sierra 4000, which would sleep three, secure in the knowledge that they would survive the night and, quite possibly, nuclear fallout.

From the foyer of the Kharlovka Hilton – Wulff man's canvas abode – you could see the river bow into a lake and narrow, before careering down through boulders, broadening out half a mile downstream to become a lake again.

Nothing here grows higher than a reindeer's antlers. It doesn't have the time to. The landscape is an icebox nine months of the year: spruce, mountain birch, sphagnum have only three months of summer to stretch up to a sun that never sets.

That night I slipped into my sleeping bag fully clothed and lay on my back, gazing up, mesmerized by canvas.

'It's starting to rain, Peter.'

'No, it's the mosquitoes trying to get in.'

I asked Wulff man if he'd ever fished anywhere else in Russia.

'Only the Varzuga,' he told me.

I asked if he'd ever bumped into a very good friend of mine, Steve Edge, because things had a habit of bumping into him.

The time Steve fished the Varzuga River, winter water was still coming down, along with huge blocks of ice which you had to avoid. But when Steve hooked up to a double-figure-weight salmon almost the same size as him, the only thing on his mind was avoiding losing it. And that's when he struck the iceberg. Or, rather, a block of ice the size of a small car struck him.

'I got the fish,' Steve told me on his return. 'I also got three broken ribs and a cracked jaw.'

Back home in Shoreditch, he visited his doctor for a check-up. The waiting area was crowded, but he signed in and made his way to the back of the queue where there was standing room only. He'd hardly got there when his name was called out. The doctor would see him now.

In the surgery, the doctor was studying his notes.

'Thanks for seeing me so quickly,' Steve said. 'Are all those people waiting to see you?'

'Sit down, Mr Edge. I had to see you straight away.'

Now Steve was anxious. Had his doctor spotted something nasty that the medical team at the Varzuga camp had missed?

'Your case is quite unique.'

Steve was really worried now.

'You see, I retire in two weeks, and in all my forty years as a doctor here, I've never treated someone hit by an iceberg in London.'

On our way to the river the next day, I considered death. I thought of this small 'window of survival' I had encapsulized myself into, so to speak.

Imagine a single day that lasts for months. If life here has only these few months in which to feed, blossom, grow and procreate before freezing over, surely sedges, stoneflies and ephemerids would all be in the same frenzied mood? And (my fly box began to rattle in my pocket) would not the rumbling-tummied trout be also?

I also felt I was going to a dinner party rather than going fishing. Every trout for themself.

I sat on a boulder overlooking the inlet where a river slid into a small, clear, beef consommé lake. My watch read eleven at night. The sky read eleven in the morning. I ought to have been feeling like going to bed, but I wasn't tired. If I hadn't already been up, I'd have felt like getting up.

The loneliness of the tundra was getting to me.

I was beginning to imagine things. A motor launch was coming at me across the water. It was heading for the rocks. I was about to stand up and wave it away when it exploded, sinking without a trace beneath a thick-rimmed circle the diameter of a Frisbee.

'It's TK time,' said Wulff man, who had crept up behind me. 'Huge, aren't they?'

Was he referring to the sedge that had so narrowly missed me? Or the trout that was chasing after it?

Wulff man tied something to my line. It was bushy, black and buzzy, with a woven pink fluorescent butt woven on at the end of the hook. A simple black gnat, with attitude. A pattern invented by Torill Kolb of Elverum, the legendary female Norwegian flytyer.

'I just love TK's woven bottom.'

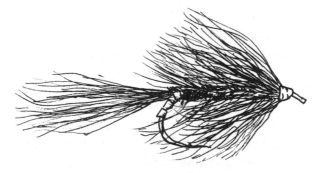

TK's Woven Bottom

Clearly, Wulff man and I had lots to talk about when we got back to the tent.

I kicked TK's sexy backside out in the direction of the rock, landing it just above where the last of the Frisbee circles were fast fading. A large dark shape lifted horizontally, back out of the water, like a slice of bread popping out of a toaster. A trout, in its head-to-tail entirety.

This was the last I was to see of it for fifteen minutes. The piece of toast burnt the full length of line from my reel – in a downward direction, head-butting the rocks.

When it lifted, it surfaced tail-first, at my feet. It was a gorgeous liquorice colour made up of a cluster of burnt sienna and umber spots with a sprinkling of scarlet specks. Its flat, coal-scuttle-shaped tail was disproportionally large for its size. It was fat. A little over four pounds.

'Lucky to catch one that size my first throw,' I said. Wulff man smiled back and made imaginary temperature-measuring gestures in the air. What he knew, but wasn't going to tell me, was that the tricky part is catching a trout under this size.

The trout in the Kharlovka grow big on a diet of snails and miniatures of themselves. The former, they chew off the rocks, like we do corn off the cob. The latter, they chase around until they corner them. This ferocity is something that they have learned from the many large pike that I was to meet on more than one occasion; on my dinner plate, as we ran out of food on our third day.

The light flattened, temperatures dropped, the wind shifted. My watch said 4 a.m.; the sun said 4 p.m. Vasiljev, who had just finished erecting the Hot House – a kitchen-cum-dining-room-cum-airing cupboard – knocked on the canvas door of the Kharlovka Hilton with a velvety paw.

'Lunch,' he said, forking imaginary juicy things into his mouth.

By now, if not geographically, I was in a time warp. Lost, in all sorts of tundra-like ways.

We fished on for twenty-four hours, the sun forever skipping along the skyline, which had the same effect on us as artificial daylight has on battery hens; except that we never laid down our rods. Every trout was over four pounds.

We collapsed at ten o'clock the next morning – not before dinner of pike and onions, in the Hot House.

The next day I didn't return to the pool where I had left a hundred trout rising. I had come to find unknown trout waters. There had to be more. We headed down rivers through mountain beech that grew horizontal rather than vertical, plaiting together to form basketwork fences that gave a gentle bankside stroll a new meaning. I passed evidence of a campfire. Had someone been here at the end of last season? Vasiljev put me right. It was scorched yagel moss that takes forty years to grow back.

'Thirty years ago, perhaps,' Vasiljev reassured me. 'Not even I have been here before.'

As he was the local guide, I didn't know whether I felt reassured or not. I was flushed with loneliness, with a guide who didn't know the area he was guiding. And with no satellite phone.

We broke through the jungle to get to a rock, the only place where you could cast a fly on a pool the size of a football pitch. The water here was deep, the colour of black coffee, fed by foaming cappuccino. We all squeezed on the rock. Sedge the size of small floatplanes took off and landed like a busy day at Anchorage airport. A gang of trout were feeding where the water flattened between two runs, sucking sedge pupae from the surface underskin, lifting it with their black skulls; flicking their shovel-shaped tails in the air, beckoning us to cast impossible casts in their direction.

Wulff man had one of those casts. He shot out his cul de canard pattern. One of the trout was so pleased to see it, it gave the fly a kiss, the couple disappearing in a tiny siphon of water. A trout well over five pounds.

After tea, which we shared with three million mosquitoes stabbing at our head nets with ever-increasing frustration, we continued our exploration. Undergrowth got deeper, thicker. The air got darker as the mosquitoes collected on our face nets, blocking the sun. We cut off through glacier crowfoot and cotton grass to a distant braid that sounded like a busy highway in the distance. On arrival, it was thunder. Foaming and boiling, it was white with movement. Stoneflies flung themselves out of the spray.

I flicked a Stimulator the size of my fist where the water lapped at the bank, inches from my feet. Before my jaw had time to drop, a trout turned and made off with my fly, leader and all the composure required to prevent me from screaming like a little girl in front of my camp companions.

A fish lay waiting at the inlet, all ready to catch whatever the lake belched out into the river. It snubbed my #10 Humpy; and a small deer-hair winged sedgeling. Then I noticed on the water a hatch of dull yellow flies with a large hind wing and three tails. *Potamanthus luteus*, or the Banana Fly; the name I gave them when I spotted them drying their wings on the rocks.

This time, Wulff man had the fly, tied parachute-style, with cul de canard wings. But with the trout so picky, I had suggested he tie it differently, using the upside-down style that I had developed in the tying of my Funneldun series; flies designed to answer the first question you need ask yourself if there's a hatch of duns and your pattern falls short of your expectations. When it is unceremoniously refused and the game is up.

Too big? The wrong shape? The wrong colour? Why worry if your imitation is lying belly-down on the surface with a great hook hanging under the water, alerting fish that something fishy's going on?

The Funneldun is base camp. It is designed to eliminate the problem of whether or not your slip of a hook is showing. Only when you know this is not the case can you start looking for faults in the pattern. But a 'pattern' is what the Funneldun is not. It's a design; a method of tying a dun, spinner, gnat, or any surface insect. Even one that looks like a banana. Any pattern or colour you like. And when you tie it, you put right all manner of design faults that afflict the traditional dry fly tying method. Two of which I drew to Wulff man's attention; both important in the tying of flawless, jaw-snapping bananas.

Firstly, in his window, a trout sees a highly distinctive thorax. This is clearly visible from an underwater vantage – and notably absent on the traditional duns. When tying the Funneldun, the first thing you do is to add that thorax behind the eye – and one behind the wing where it won't be missed.

Now, that hook. Because the finished hackle protrudes in front of the Funneldun, making it longer in profile than if you were to tie it by the conventional method, if I want to tie a #14 fly, I tie it on a #16; a #16, I tie it on a #18, and so on. This is a bonus, because the hook is smaller in proportion to the fly size. And with less iron, a Funneldun floats like balsa wood. So less weight and less hook for the trout to see. But why show trout the hook at all?

To tie the whole caboodle upside down, hook out of the water out of view, you need only do two things: at the whip-finish at the tail, tie the tail in a little way round the bend; and while still in the vice, clip the top off the hackle. This will be the underside of the fly when you chuck it on a saucer of water and it flips upside down, making the same imprint on the surface as a spinner's outspread wings.

Wulff man flicked out his inverted banana and it appealed. The fish took it immediately, turning back down Thunder Alley and away to join the other trout. For this trout, having an earring through the lip had suddenly become rather fashionable in that part of the river.

The next day, the Mi-8 returned to whisk us away to the Eastern Litza. With one eye each on the map, and the other peering between the pilots' heads out through the cockpit, Wulff man and the helicopter navigator decided on a campsite. As they were wearing earmuffs to dispel the roar of the engine, all this was done using an internationally understood sign language: a profusion of pointing-down movements.

We had the tents up in the time it takes to get dressed. It was late. We knew this because Vasiljev had made chicken soup. Chicken soup and vodka meant it was evening; porridge and tea, morning. I had swapped my watch for a menu.

Vasiljev dragged the orange rubber dinghy to the lake and rowed it to where the river was fed by braids. He made for the one with the most foam: our trout-spotting abilities had reached new technical heights.

With a wading staff that he'd fashioned from the branch of a birch, Wulff man strode off to an island across a snarling fast shallow with boulders that stuck out like teeth. I sat looking at the enormous sky.

Vasiljev returned in the pike-filled dinghy to pick me up and go round the island to collect Wulff man. The water was mirror calm. Sedge speedboats zipped across the surface and a trout rose ten yards away, rocking the rock. I covered it with a small deer-winged sedge. A hole appeared in the black treacle water and it was sucked down into it. The trout was too large to land in the dinghy – it could have sunk it – so Vasiljev rowed me to a handy boulder where I pulled it on top of a shelf to measure it. Fifty-six centimetres, or twenty-three inches. A fat six pounds.

We repeated this procedure twice more; each time the trout were the same length. And so it went on – or could have done, but I had had enough. Fish numbers mean nothing to me. It was someone else's turn, except that there was no someone else there, so I sat on a rock while Vasiljev went to find Wulff man. Whatever trout he'd been catching, they sounded big. We could hear a lot of whooping.

Knee-high in starry saxifrage gazing up at me with pale, wide-open faces, I looked across the silent water. It was the first time that I had stopped to think things over: the desolation, the remoteness, the hundreds of shapes we'd seen in the pools we hadn't fished. At times we could have walked across the river on their speckled backs. I was shrouded in a strange guilt; that I shouldn't be here; that I was intruding on the wild trout's last frontier.

Too tired to fish, Wulff man and I left the outlet with Vasiljev on the oars, rowing across the lake in a flat golden light. Suddenly, a huge trout leapt behind Vasiljev. It jumped in one of his ears and out the other, or so it seemed from my low angle. Wulff man had a fly out in its direction before the water had stopped washing over the side of the dinghy. Up it came again. It twisted on the fly, heading off, its huge dark blue back dipping and now waving like a harpooned whale towing our dinghy behind it. Having made the necessary run-up, the fish sounded and threw itself high up out of the water, inches from me. I could have touched it but my hands were soldered to the rubbery side of the dinghy in a life-preserving position.

Wulff man's rod straightened and the tippet returned, flyless.

'That's what I call bad luck,' Wulff man said, shaking a finger at his tippet, scolding it. With our chins virtually resting on the surface of the lake, the camera angle couldn't have been more dramatic.

With the lake flooded in golden light, the lighting couldn't have been more spectacular, either.

'That's what I call a Hollywood trout,' was my consolation. The fish was a veritable eighty centimetres. Huge poundage.

'I look forward to seeing the repeat,' Wulff man replied.

But there wasn't to be one that trip. When we returned to base camp at the lodge, the quiet Czech told us about a seventy-eight-centimetre that had swallowed his streamer. This failed to relieve the numbness of losing the trout that made off with the Wulff man's diminutive dry fly.

We didn't talk about it again.

To this day, I still go to sleep thinking of the Hollywood trout. Once asleep, I dream of it. You see, it's a dream that can come true because I know that fish is still there, getting bigger – and bigger.

The Wulff man had worked this out, too.

The next day was our last. Wulff man and I stood in a humming cloud of blackfly, waiting for the helicopter to fly in. Praying for mosquitoes to fly out.

I had time to think.

There are times in the tundra (and on the west coast of Scotland, for that matter) when you can't fish because fishing is just too uncomfortable. There's no comfort to be had when the gauze mask protecting your face from mosquitoes is so covered with blackfly you can't see the mosquitoes. At times (but I couldn't see to confirm this observation) I was convinced that the smutting trout snaffling up something that was coming down like a huge surface soup were doing their bit, not just to fill their stomachs, but to rid the world of blackfly, trapped in the surface film.

Now blackfly are even smaller than smuts and I wondered if I had a pattern in my box that was micro enough. One that didn't mean I'd have to swap my fingers for microscopic space-age equipment to tie up a pattern devised by an exceptional flytyer with wire-thin fingers (and huge, googly bluebottle eyes, recently laser-treated) who was determined to demonstrate to the world that if he wasn't a flyfisherman, he'd get a job as an ophthalmic surgeon.

This got me thinking (the helicopter was going to be another hour arriving) of an article I had read on the merits of large and small flies written by the legendary English flyfisherman and flytyer, Richard Walker.

'The dictionary definition of the term "lure",' he writes, 'is not much help in an angling context, but to define it in our sense is rather difficult.' He went on to do just that:

> To most anglers, a lure is a device that makes no attempt to imitate any kind of insect; that is usually from $1\frac{1}{2}$ in to as much as 4 in long.

He wrote this back in the sixties, a time remembered as the Stillwater Revolution by English flyfishers; a time that pulled people who had never touched a fly rod before off their sofas and down to one of the many stillwaters sprouting out all over the place.

I had a theory why these first-timers took to stillwater flyfishing and flytying so effortlessly. It was because of one thing: lures. These were flies on a large scale that didn't require complicated finger-twisting and eye-popping movements to tie. Whip 'em up. Bung 'em out. Strip 'em in.

Why shouldn't all flytying be this uncomplicated? Why shouldn't flies tied in minute sizes also be tied in a minute – essential flies required to fool trout feeding exclusively on insects the size of a full stop? There's no reason why this shouldn't be so. Not if you share the same line of thinking as I do, which is the following: the less chance you give a trout to question the validity and authenticity of your imitation, the better the chances of that trout shutting its mouth on your sham. For this reason, lure or little 'un, I try and fish as small a fly as I can so that the trout doesn't get a very good look at it in a critical inspection parade. This factor puts the odds heavily on the side of the flyfisher with a diminutive fly on his tippet.

But what about the flytyer who has to tie up that titchy thing?

The fact is, the smaller the fly, the less detailed the imitation needs to be. And as long as you keep clear of flytying writers who encourage tricksy procedures to show off their flytying prowess – rather than to tickle the taste buds of some tricky trout – you should be fine. With small flies, for instance, you needn't add wings. The hackle represents those.

So what is this simple small fly system?

It's a style of tying small flies that was tested years before its creator,

Guy Plas – a flytyer and breeder of high-quality cocks – first introduced it to the French flytying aficionados, thirty or more years ago.

Of course, as a hackle trader and a businessman, Plas uses just the one material in his X-traordinary X fly. Would you believe – cock hackles? Two per fly. Double the profit.

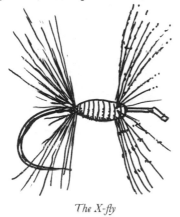

The X-fly

Cynicism aside, the way Pays constructs his X fly and positions his hackles on the hook intrigued me greatly, leading me to think of another benefit this style has, apart from catching basketfuls of trout hardwired into taking tiny flies in the streams Plas fished in the Limousin region in central France.

Plas's fly, like my Funneldun, plays mind games with the trout. With my Funneldun, the hackle is funnelled forward over the hook eye. This creates a footprint in the trout's window in front of the eye, making it the first thing the trout sees. Not the hook, if you go the conventional dry flytying style. The illusion is of a larger fly on a small, less noticeable hook. With Plas's fly, it's the opposite. The illusion is of a smaller fly. The centrally positioned X-shaped hackles conceal the fact that it's tied on a larger hook.

For those of you still perspiring profusely at the thought of tying tiny flies, rather than on #6 longshanks, here is the X Factor. Plas's style allows you to tie titchy flies on hooks you can actually see! See for yourself.

In the centre of a #20–24 hook, wind on three turns of black thread. Tie in a black cock hackle so that it lies over the hook bend, shiny side up, and wind on two or three turns. Now wind turns of silk over the

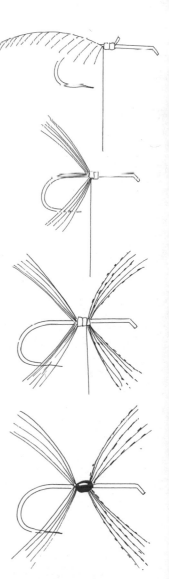

roots to ensure hackles point towards the bend. Wind silk back towards the centre of the hook, leaving a small gap. Now do the same with a grizzle hackle, the hackle pointing to the eye. The two hackles form an 'X'. Whip-finish in the gap, varnish whipping with black Cellire Varnish. Now where's that helicopter?

THREE

South Africa

John Lennon

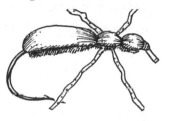

Hook: No. 16
Thread: Dark brown
Shellback Fore and Aft: Strip of tan closed-cell foam
Bodies Fore and Aft: Tan polypropylene dubbing
Legs: Light brown Sili Legs

The Beetles' Greatest Hits

I TURNED AND LOOKED AT James with a face as long as a pole. Sincerity streamed out of my eyes along with perspiration that had been welling up there in the African sun.

'This isn't flyfishing, James. This is thigh fishing.'

The overland trek to get to our fishing beat had been challenging. When we arrived, the river was carpeted with orange stones webbed with bright green weed as fine as old ladies' hair.

Rock-hopping required Olympian feats of balance if I was to avoid breaking limbs. Like satellite-directed turbine engines that hold cruise ships in position so that anchors don't damage the coral, my little leg muscles had been working overtime to hold me steady and stop me being destroyed too.

This was classic 'pocket-fishing'. House-to-house, hand-to-fin combat. Attacking small pouches of water topped up by trickles fed from the overflow from a puddle above.

'One cast per pool,' James recommended. 'Then move on to the next.'

Fishing in this way demands a lot of disco dancing. Rocking and rolling on the balls of your wading shoes. Bending double to stop your outline filling the sky. It was like fishing for someone's precious goldfish in a pond in their rockery without the owner spotting you through his French windows.

A curl broke the surface in a pool the size of a bedspread. Bushes on all sides and a mess of currents didn't make life easy. The hatch was coming to an end and this was probably my last chance at a feeding fish.

'Aim for that bubbly run!'

My fly drifted under a bush and a rainbow trout shot up and out, turning like a mirror in the sun. A pound and a quarter, it had more freckles than Kate Moss.

'I'm impressed!'

Praise indeed, from James. And the fact that he also hugged me suggested that it was more than guide talk with a hefty tip in mind.

Was he telling me that I had caught a good fish for these parts and I should savour the memory? Or was this a warning that things were going to get even tougher now that the sun hiding behind the mountains was about to open fire on the stream, baking the trout into inactivity like porcelain in a kiln?

South Africa is one of the most perfect places on the planet. If, that is, it's December in the UK and you want to shoot a television commercial where the action opens in an English country garden in July, and your budget is minuscule. The shoot for the film I'd written was three days, but I put in for six so that I could shoot off and do three days' fishing up north.

In a recent BBC poll, Cape Town was voted number five in the Top Ten destinations chosen by British tourists. Surprising, really, considering the news pages never fail to mention that South Africa offers more than its fair share of hazards for residents and tourists alike. For this reason, Cape Town takes some getting used to. Not just the change from winter to summer. It takes some time adapting to the lifestyle. You can't help but notice that every house has more burglar alarms on the outside than windows. Driving about, you're advised not to stop (even if you run someone down). Carjacking is a national sport. Leave a door unlocked and someone's likely to jump in and drive off, without you inside.

Don't let this put you off. Only an hour and a half's drive away from the Victoria and Albert Waterfront – Cape Town's largest shopping mall, situated in its liveliest nightlife district – are swooping valleys bristling with prickly bushes, alive with aloes and slithering with snakes. These are dream valleys, with streams filled with wild rainbow trout, hungry for the flies in your fly box.

But first, you must get there.

James Warne, Cape Town's most celebrated fishing guide, collects you from the hotel in the town centre at 4.30 a.m. prompt. When he's clear of the city he picks up a sandwich lunch in the first service station heading north-west on Highway N1.

After that painless drive – and just when excitement is starting to peak – the boring part kicks in. You have to burrow your way through the two-mile-deep De Toits Mountains, Cape Town's Andes. Two centuries ago this took the first Dutch Huguenot pioneers two months to hike over in horse and cart; it now takes two minutes, through the Huguenot Toll Tunnel.

The journey ends on the other side, in what looks like a Sainsbury's car park, except that there are no trolleys – and no cars. And instead of a supermarket there are supernatural escarpments of vast, castle-like, sky-scraping mountains stacked high with scrub, stone and serpents: the De Toits Mountains, the Wemmershoek and, most notably, the Klein Drakensteins.

'Does it matter that I have no vampire bat imitations in my box?' I asked James, glancing up at the eerie peaks.

Togged up in thick socks and wading boots – with pockets filled with all I needed (very little) – I checked that James was carrying bottled water (a lot). The temperature was already in the thirties.

After a two-minute scramble through a concrete subway under a motorway booming with lorries, you are lost in scenery, the scent of dried flowers, silence – and then, suddenly, when the first puff adder pokes its fangs out from under a stone, thoughts of serum, which James has aplenty in his bag, along with the water.

It's a long, dusty, thigh-tightening trudge across yellow earth, rough gorse and burnt-out tree stumps as you follow the leopard-patrolled mountain trail teeming with curious, yellow-toothed baboons, high above the river you are about to fish, the Elandspadkloof. It's a beautiful view, if you are able to see through the sweat pouring off your brow. It was like driving in a rainstorm with no wipers.

The steep descent into the cool of the river valley was more hair-raising than the climb. No path, just James's dust tracks. He was on the lookout for a marker. A fish painted on a board pushed into the dirt somewhere. This indicates the number of the beat and where it starts. Its whereabouts had James parting bushes, turning over rocks, crossing eyebrows and whistling uncontrollably through gritted teeth.

The start of Beat 3 looks like an explosion in an Egyptian temple. Blocks of stone are strewn everywhere. A trickle that looks as if it's gushing from a burst water main's leaking pipe is the river.

It's December: the height of the summer dry season in the Cape. During the winter wet season, from April to September, rivers swell and run coloured. But in the summer season, from October to March, streams are little more than a drip. Even so, between the rocks, there is still plenty of rough water to hide the fish and conceal the angler. Fishing the pools and the runs is highly profitable.

Crystal clear water demands the utmost skill in the approach and presentation. It's at this time that the Western Cape flyfisherman comes into his own – and he has developed his own style of dry flyfishing. Something that he has taken to a fine art. This technique is known as *Stuck-in-the-Surface* or *In-the-Surface Dry-Fly Fishing*. I was anxious to find out more.

Six a.m., and here I was, the early bird, standing at the head of the queue awaiting my first lesson in 'Stealth Education'. Without which, I had been advised, any credibility I might have as a half-decent dry-fly dude would not survive a single morning, let alone a day. And I was booked in for three.

But with my Christmas presents packed before I left, I had all the time in the world.

The stinky, hot, steaming and sultry summer had left the Elandspadkloof sunken-cheeked and shallow. And the contents, much the same. Clouds of black upwing flies blew off in their thousands. These tiny flies were more akin to the family of *trico* flies I had found in Montana than any other *ephemera* you were likely to meet in UK. The size of black gnats, they had every fish in the stream to the surface.

Fishing an eight-foot, #4, four-piece travel rod, a twelve-foot leader and a two-pound tippet, I had to select my fish, spot the biggest and then make sure that it wasn't one of the many small-mouthed bass that haunt this stretch.

'Hardly worth the bother, my fly is so small,' I commented to James. I was fishing a #20 gnat, tied in the X Fly style. I had a hundred strikes, ending up with twenty trout. All around the pound. All before the sun appeared.

It was testing fishing, but not that testing. It certainly didn't require any special techniques.

'I hope that's got that out of your system,' James shouted across to me from a bone-white boulder, mid-stream, as I returned my last fish. 'Because that's the end of it.'

The hatch was over. The sun was up. My flesh was starting to sizzle.

'Now it's time to get cute!' James said, pulling a fly box from his haversack. 'You guys have your Beatles. And we have ours. A band of insects that get big hits this time of year.'

Cape flyfishers have great respect for their beetles. They say they must be God's favourite creatures. Why else should there be more different species of them than any other creature on earth? Some 35,000 of them worldwide. And in the Cape, like chocolates, they come in all shapes and sizes. And, like chocolates, they sweeten the gums of the sourest-mouthed trout in a shy, dry-season mood.

James handed me a foam-bodied pattern on a #14, designed to sit half in, half out of the surface. It had a shellback and silly legs – or Sili legs, as they're known in the trade. It felt heavy in my palm.

'It's an imitation of the shiny golden-brown beetle that reaches plague proportions in the summer. When it hits the water, it's a ten-ton ant. Every trout in the area knows that something interesting has arrived – not just the trout lying directly underneath it. Sure, they can flee. But where to, in this thin water? No, it pays to advertise.'

He had no name for his beetle pattern, but I did. I called it the John Lennon.

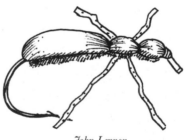

John Lennon

The pattern is simple enough. James winds dark brown thread onto a barbless #16 hook, tying in a strip of tan, closed-cell foam to act as the shellback. He then dubs to halfway up the hook with a tan polypropylene dubbing and folds the foam over the body and secures it at this point. He then ties in two small lengths of light brown Sili Legs, lying flat on top of the hook shank, winding the dubbing through these legs so they sit comfortably in a criss-cross position. He then folds the foam over this. Finally, he dubs the remaining area up to the eye and folds the foam over this, whip-finishing and varnishing to complete the fly. But only when he has trimmed the legs so that they are shorter than the body.

'The colour of the pattern should match the natural beetles in the area,' James went on. 'Normal variations would range from light tan through to dark brown to black. A good option is to use the lightest colour possible – tan – and keep a few marker pens in your fishing vest. That way any colour can be matched while fishing.'

James was determined to give me the whole upbeat beetle rundown while I tried to tie his bug on my leader. My fingers were slithering round the nylon like a puff adder on an ice rink. He had all the time in the world.

'The best surface fishing time is early morning and late evening, due to the intense heat. A foam beetle extends your fishing time.'

Beetles are found on the surface all day. Unlike Mayfly and caddis, they have no scheduled hatch times. They thrive during the hottest time: mid-afternoon. In the swoon of the day, they snooze off after lunch, dropping off their perches.

'And because trout don't need to break the surface to feed on these morsels they are happy to make an appearance in this sun.'

He went on to tell me that as the water warms during the day the fish swim up to the oxygenated water, at the head of the run. 'Like this one,' he said, squinting his eyes in the direction of the fizzing water at the neck of the pool.

'Standard dries get drowned in this water. But the foam beetle allows you to shoot a fly into broken water, because it rises back to the surface in the slack water. It's often taken while submerged.'

John Lennon now hung limply on the end of my tippet. I turned to invite James to be at my shoulder and direct me and John Lennon to the trout place of his choice. Instead, he turned round, flicked some sticks off the top of a boulder and sat down, patting the place next to him.

'Sit down. It's time to reveal to you the *real* secret of *in-the-surface* dry flyfishing. In ten seconds' time you'll be an expert.'

Ten seconds was too long. I couldn't wait.

'It's not the length of your rod, the size of your tippet, a sexy new knot . . . a tricksy casting style. It's not even your fly.'

Shaking with anticipation, I moved to sit closer to him, expecting that he would prefer to *whisper* The Great Secret in my ear. Instead he bawled the house down:

'IT'S YOUR ASS!'

I landed on mine with a thud, next to him – the sound of bum on

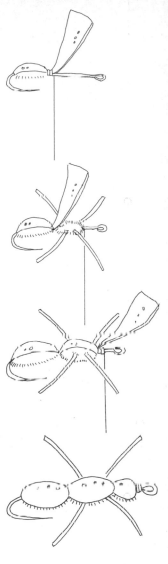

boulder following hot on the heels of James's revelation as it reverberated round the mountains.

'It's not his action, it's his lack of it. This is what makes a Cape flyfisher an expert at this time of year.'

I may have brought my rod to South Africa, but I had left my head at home. He was telling me what I already knew, but wasn't putting into practice. I have written a dozen times about what I call 'The Shooting Stick Philosophy'. I like to quote from my book, *Chalkstream Chronicle*:

> Tails, fins, snouts poking out of weed-beds, silver patches where scales are missing against gravels, pinky warts. The more exacting flyfisherman looks into the river and asks himself: When is a trout not a trout? He looks for imaginary trout and takes away the tail, the fins, the gills, the body, the head – hoping something in the tight area he scans holds one or more elements of a trout. Only then can he conclude that a trout is not a trout – when it was never there in the first place.

The stream-walker – the man not sitting quietly – misses all this. And along with it, probably his only chance of a fish.

After twenty minutes squinting into the glare, my eyes started to hurt.

'Help me, James! I'm beginning to imagine things. I thought I saw a crab!'

'You did.'

He went on to tell me that the Elandspadkloof has a healthy freshwater crab population and that, unlike newly hatched upwing flies and other terrestrials such as the acrobatic grasshopper, trout take beetles unnoticed. They take beetles close to the bank, sheltered by grass or an overhanging bush, never disclosing their whereabouts. You need to watch for a long time before a rise is detected. You must stop looking for the obvious – ever-spiralling rise forms – and start to register changes of light on the surface, inverted dents, shimmers, nervous water. The smallest dimple becomes an eruption and the gentlest flicker in the film becomes an opportunity.

'Oppressive summer heat enforces a lazy attitude in the flyfisherman. These periods of idleness should be used to full advantage. They give you time to upgrade your eyesight – and your earsight. You're not just looking for dimples. You're listening for sucks.'

A probable lie can be calculated by tracing a line of drift along its meandering course, until it strikes a likely place, then fixing the eye on the spot.

'The most interesting thing is that beetles strictly follow these drift lines, which they observe with more regularity than other insects. Mainly because, once on the water, they lose all power to direct their destiny. They are unable to move the slightest inch independently.

'Unlike upwing flies, they sit low. Their round shiny backs are shaped like bicycle helmets. The wind just slipstreams over them. A gust can't shift them across the flow. And as paddles their stumpy legs are useless.

'In short, the beetle on the water is a pathetic sight. They are there for the duration and have no option but to stay for tea. And snacking trout take them with a matching mood: quietly and unobtrusively.'

Just as trout get lethargic as the day heats up, so also do Cape flyfishers. Another advantage of the foam beetle is that it doesn't need to be treated to keep it performing at its optimum.

'And if you can't get them up to take your beetle, get on down to them. The foam beetle can be used as a very effective strike indicator. You can fish a nymph as a dropper underneath it.'

∼

By now, I had spotted a likely trout lie. A thin channel slid round a rock, turning everything it carried into a spin. Giddy blades of grass circled by the rock. A woozy leaf reeled in the slack.

I let John Lennon fall on the rock. Just before the current took my leader, I pulled him onto the conveyor belt, leaving as little slack as I dared.

Half in, half out, John made no more than a slight dent in the surface film. A tiny whirlpool appeared underneath it, inverting this dent and slightly enlarging it. That was all the indication I got.

'That fish sucked my beetle in through a straw,' I shrieked at James as the rainbow trout with John Lennon in its jaw tried to dive back into the hole from whence it had come.

'She loves you! Yeah, yeah, yeah! Now you're fishing like a Cape expert.'

As I slid the astonished trout back into the run, I felt strangely effective. It appeared I had found the fly for the worst-case scenario. The fly for every occasion. The only fly I need ever use. The universal panacea.

'Who needs a hatch of fly?' I declared to the world.

'Who indeed?' I answered myself, thinking of the chalkstream in the Berkshire Downs that I would soon be returning to – and the worrying year-on-year decline in river fly-life.

Who'll need it indeed?'

These days it's no longer possible to admit that you possess certain furs and feathers that you use to create things designed to tease innocent creatures that roam (or rather, swim) this planet, let alone any that could be made into a coat. If you do it's bound to upset some pressure group or other, whose members will scamper about, waving their arms in the air, calling for you to be shot, or skinned, or turned into a hat.

As a twenty-first-century flyfisher, conscious of just how delicate the environment is – and how valuable water of the same clarity and abundance as sun-sucked Elandspadkloof is to my happiness – I do what I can to avoid contributing to global warming.

Which is why I want you to know something about fly rods. In particular, those new carbon rods. Owning one, apparently, is the equivalent of doing your weekly shopping in a Harrier jump jet while repeatedly beating a polar bear with a stick and blowtorching a glacier.

These days, I only fish with my trusty split-cane rod. (Greenpeace prefers Greenheart.) Thus I was doing my bit for the world. Until someone told me just how many forests they have to cut down to grow the bamboo. You just can't win!

But I had to make amends. I thought of strapping a wind turbine to my casting arm. But I decided to see if I could balance out my carbon rod footprint by earning carbon points in other ways. And there, in a cupboard, I found myself face to face with one of the world's top destroyers of the environment. No, not my car (or my Harrier jump jet). It was my flytying kit.

All those carbon-based synthetic materials had to go. And what about all those bits of the animals and birds whose 'emissions' (methane and other greenhouse gases) a United Nations report recently identified as the greatest threat to the climate and which are to blame for a host of other environmental crimes, from acid rain to the introduction of alien species, from producing deserts to creating dead zones in the oceans, from poisoning rivers and drinking water to destroying coral reefs? So now you know why I keep flytying to the minimum number of movements possible. And materials? I keep a small cock cape. The smallest in the box. My thinking is that, being very, very super-tiny –

threatening only the most minuscule of ammonia emissions (one of the main causes of acid rain) – there is very little chance of it ever causing an ice cap in Antarctica to recede by a mile. At least, not in the next month or so. And how much better I feel for it all!

In fact, what my conscience got me doing is what a great deal of flytyers need to do. Reduce the size of their flytying materials. Is this a new idea? No, it isn't.

Now my flyfishing hero is Dr J. C. Mottram. An international, out-there campaigning eco-warrior? No, he was a Director of the Pathology Department at Mount Vernon Hospital, in Middlesex, working mainly on cancer research. He died on 4 October 1945.

His book *Fly-Fishing: Some New Arts and Mysteries* (The Field c.1913) is one of the most innovative books written in the last century. He introduced the factor of transparency in dry fly dressing ten years before J. W. Dunne, used marabou in his fry patterns fifty years before it became common, invented swimming and resting nymphs and a midge larva.

He was the first to design a midge pupa pattern that suspended just under the surface, using strips of cork. (Fifty years later, my Suspender pattern incorporated a floating material wrapped up in my girlfriend's tights. A corker, too.)

In the summer of 1935, Mottram wrote an article in the *Flyfishers' Club Journal* called 'Simple Flies'. It changed my life.

'There is no doubt,' he wrote, 'that the making of trout flies has gradually become very complicated, more to display the flytyer's art than to please the trout.'

Reading this, I sat down, buried my head in my hands and wept. My conversion was biblical.

Thirty years after J. C.'s words were delivered to me from Mount Sinai, I still hold my head in my hands, but this time with dismay when I see just how more complicated flytying has got, just how many more materials there are, just how far away we have come from tying flies for trout and not fingers into knots.

Mottram discovered 'how excellent dry flies can be made out of a single material: cocks' hackles. For me, with just the one black cock cape and a bobbin of thread sitting in front of me, reading this was a real stroke of luck. A godsend.

I immediately got to work. On page 45 of his later book, *Thoughts on Angling,* in a chapter entitled 'Some Notes on Artificial Flies', there's a diagram indicating what shape to trim a single hackle to create the correct body shape for Bumbles, Duns, Spinners, Smuts and Sedges.

As the trout's eyesight seems to improve at the same rate that mine deteriorates, my favourite is the Smut. Especially in June when flies get smaller and shorter – and the days get hotter and longer. And wild trout, warier.

'I welcome smutting trout,' Mottram tells us. 'It is very satisfying to kill a fat trout on hooks down to the smallest size. I think No.18 is the smallest made.'

His publishers, Herbert Jenkins, never dated their editions, but based on earlier published material we know that Mottram advocated smut patterns and the use of small hooks over a hundred years ago. Long before you could get your hands on #20, #22 and #24 hooks.

But, more importantly, long before the more cautious wild trout got to hear about Specsavers, prompting the need to tie flies capable of withstanding eye-squinting scrutiny.

Mottram's fiddle-free, fat-fingered one-hackle design goes to prove he was far from short-sighted.

On our last day on the Elandspadkloof, we arrived to find trout nuzzling the surface in a large flat area no more than nine inches deep. I waded in carefully behind one of the more constant risers to find out what was interesting him. Glued to the surface were tiny black smuts, but not in any great number, so I started casting out the 'paraloop'-style black gnat I had used the day before, that had interested several trout just before the sun lifted over the mountains to the screech of sun-blasted baboons and the popping of the skin on my face. But today the trout weren't having any of it.

'Let me have a look at your box,' James said, wading out to rescue me.

A confident finger poked a hole in among the other flies in my box to reveal one of my Simple Smuts, tied with just the one hackle.

'Complicated little feller, that one,' James said. 'But uncomplicated enough for that trout to come and give it a little inspection.'

Simple Smut

I told him the smut was tied using just the one hackle feather. I simply pull back the hackle fibres of a small, black cock hackle and shape them so that three-quarters of the hackle – from the hackle tip up – is clipped very short so that when wound up on the hook it forms the body. The remaining quarter, I keep long. As long as I want the hackle at the head to be. With black tying silk, I tie in the tip of the hackle at the bend of a #22 or #24 hook and bring the silk up to behind the eye. I then wind up the clipped short hackle, ending with the longer, uncut hackle fibres at the head.

'And that's all?' James said, as I cast my Simple Smut to the native rainbow still nuzzling away there at the end of a twenty-yard cast, not a care in the world. He slurped at the smut first cast and ran off with it.

'Yes, that's all,' I said to my highly accessorized guide, my face just starting to pop at the sun lifting over the mountain to the wails of baboons.

But for the progressive flytyer in search of the simplest and smallest smut, your work is never done. Because progress is about making things simpler, not more complicated, you're always taking this procedure out – without adding another in.

So, before you go away, let's take a close look at another fly designed to hide its true identity. A fly I call The Speck – the result of finding out that I needed specs to tie the flies required to fool trout with microscopes as eyes.

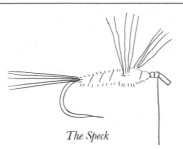

The Speck

More than a few years ago, when it was time to refill those gaps in my fly box, I decided to cheat. I rummaged in boxes I'd discarded years ago to see if I could blow the dust off flies I could reuse.

It was here that my troubles started.

Flies I tied twenty years ago were so much smaller than the ones I tie now. Some so small, I thought they were the dust I couldn't blow away. Tiny flies that once had chalkstream leviathans cowering in the corner.

It was when I began tying them up that I realized why things had changed. Nothing to do with tactics, patterns or revolutionary new thinking. I'd quite simply lost it. My fingers could no longer get round the intricacy of it all. Why should this be?

The answer was staring me in the face. And all I could see was a blur. Quite simply, my eyes are no longer what they used to be.

And so, top of my Wish List was one of those magnifying glasses you clamp to your bench, with little lights all around the rim, that looks like the mirrors they have in an actor's changing room. A piece of kit I thought was useful to help you see, but something you'd never see me using.

Well, that was then – now I have one. And when I examine flies I'd been tying pre-magnifier, they resemble something put together inside the bag of a vacuum cleaner.

The nutty thing about all this is that for years I'd been preaching the 'Go Small' gospel. The less you give trout to argue about, the less they can find fault with. Less, therefore, is more acceptable. But when it comes to looking at some of my flies, they might just as well have been tied by Ray Charles.

Blindingly obvious as the discovery of my super-duper magnifying glass may have been, it wasn't the whole story. I wasn't going to use my new sharp-sightedness to magnify the complexities of flytying. The reverse. I needed a minimal tying design.

Looking back over my diaries, I was reminded that once upon a time, when I could see, I had the great American flytyer, Dick Talleur, staying with me in my house by the river. And it was here, sitting at my kitchen table, that he taught me what he called 'The Simple Art of Diminution'.

Here's what he said:

'As difficult as it is to imitate very large insects convincingly, it is easy with tiny ones. Most anglers break into a cold sweat at the prospect of having to fish, and especially tie, minuscule flies. But not', he went on to say, 'if you keep it simple.'

These days we have tippet materials down to the meekest poundage: sensitive, fast-tip graphite rods; super-smooth drag reels; threads finer than the proverbial; hooks you're in danger of breathing in; tiny hackles; special 'jaws' for vices – and now (sorry, no excuses), Big Bench-Hugging Mummy Magnifying Glasses.

What we still have, though, are professionals trading mind-numbing, ego-boosting procedures to tie small flies. (The Gospel of simplicity is the other thing that gets me up on my pulpit.)

Well, wipe away all those DVDs that the digital digit acrobats dream up to complicate our lives so that they can make a fast buck when they should be out there earning an honest living, and listen to how Big Dick gets it on.

First he forgets about the wing. He lets the hackle do this. But, he says, hackles interfere with hook-engagement. The generically produced feathers with stiff, sit-up-and-beg, short-barbed hackles are too dense and prevent the point of the hook making contact.

He overcomes this problem by trimming a V out of the bottom of the hackle, rather as in the tying of my Funnelduns.

On hook-engagement, he spent more time talking about hooks. Once he used any old down-eyed dry fly hook. Then he read Vincent Marinaro's *A Modern Dry-Fly Code*, where Marinaro suggests offsetting the barb a little.

In search of the perfect 'hooking hook', Dick went round the houses. (Not mine.) He tried up-eyed and straight-eyed hooks, because both eliminated gape blockage. In the end, he came home to a down-eyed hook with a short point and a small eye, with a moderate turn-down. His preference was the Partridge K1A Marinaro Midge Hook, with a 'conservative' offset, built in at the factory.

Now some flytyers have had a big influence on my flytying. Only one has had a small influence. For this, Dick, a big thanks.

Here's how to tie up a small, light-coloured olive that hatched out every lunchtime on the Elandspadkloof; typically, just as we had started to get our teeth round one of those doorstep sandwiches we'd buy in the garage at six o' bleary clock every morning when things just had to be big if you were to see anything at all. Just adapt materials to match the hatch.

Vice a #20–24 hook and tie in primrose non-slip Spiderweb thread behind eye. Select a few stiff barbs of a ginger hackle. Tie in place to form the tail. Also tie in a few small strands of cream poly yarn. Wind thread forward to halfway up hook. Tie in small blue dun hackle. Cut V on the underside. Wind the poly yarn up the hook to behind the hackle. Pass this through the V to the front of the hackle. Wrap over and back again forming thorax. Secure, and whip-finish.

To tie, the Speck takes a sec.

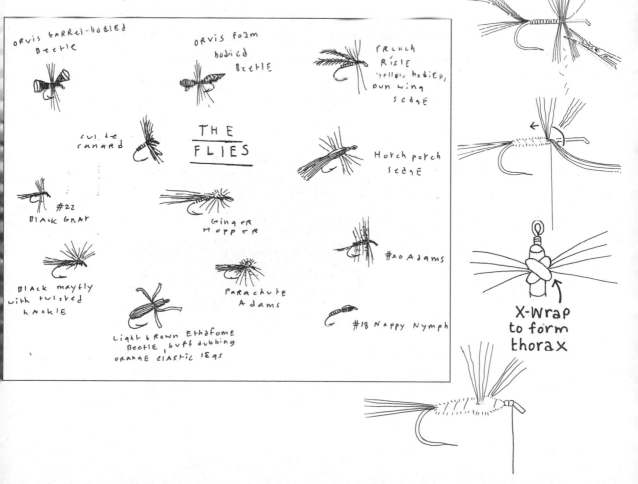

On our way back to the Huguenot Tunnel, down the road that runs alongside the river, we passed a car parked on the hard shoulder. Thinking it a bit risky leaving a car unattended in South Africa, I asked James if it was OK just to park there and go down to the river and fish.

'There's not much trouble out here. Well, not usually . . .'

I pondered those last few words for a mile or two, not really wanting to know more about the 'not usually' part.

'What do you mean, "not usually"?' I asked James, not able to hold myself back.

'Oh, last week a guy came fishing and parked back there. A couple of guys broke into the car and took his camera and a rod, you know, that sort of thing.'

Well, I thought, thank God it was only that sort of thing. That could happen anywhere. Even on the A303, just outside Stockbridge on the Hampshire Test. I told James I was relieved to hear that was all that happened.

'Well, it wasn't exactly all that happened.'

Here we go again. Another 'not usually'. This time I didn't hold back.

James went on to tell me that the guys went down to the river looking for the fisherman, and when they found him they took his rod and reel and his waistcoat, tied him to a tree and stoned him.

The next day, I kept unusually close to James.

FOUR

Montana

Shuck Sedge

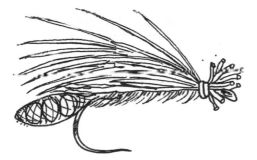

Hook: No. 14
Thread: Dull green
Pupa shuck: Four small dark-green embroidery beads
threaded on 4 lb monofilament and sheathed in Antron fibres
Body: Three turns of grey-green dubbing material
Wing: Deer hair. Clip butts directly behind the eye
to form small muddler head

Foam, Foam on the Range

IT WAS IN THE MID-SEVENTIES when I changed my childhood American cowboy hero, John Wayne, for another American. This time, it was the flyfisherman and angler-writer, Sparse Grey Hackle.

I was introduced to Alfred Waterbury Miller in 1978, at the Anglers' Club of New York. 'Sparse', as he called himself, became one of the best-known and best-loved storytellers and commentators on flyfishing of a generation. Sadly, not my generation. But, over the years, I've managed to go back, read up and catch up on a lot of his stuff.

As an active crusader against a town that ran its sewer into his favourite stream – and fearing that he'd 'turn up floating in the river with my head caved in', he invented the name Sparse Grey Hackle, a name he stuck with.

Whoever he was, he was my kind of fisherman. His humorous, 'fishless' writings redirected my thinking on flyfishing. Not on how I fished, but on what else I could get out of roaming around with a fly rod in my hand. Things other than catching trout.

'The true purpose of a fly rod', Sparse once wrote, 'is to prevent its bearer from being arrested for vagrancy.' He went on, 'For the delight of trout fishing is not the full creel but things seen and people met. A roughly dressed man idling with a rod in his hand is an angler; without it he is a vagabond.'

And so it came to pass that, last summer, I set off to Montana with my two American heroes in mind. John Wayne, because I had always dreamed of riding out on the plains with the cowboys (even though I'd never ridden before). And Sparse? Well, I felt I was heading off with him, too, with new things to be seen and new people to meet – perhaps, even a trout.

It's one of those things that need no explaining. Like swimming with dolphins, or boating down the Thames on a lazy summer afternoon. So, when I told my friends I was going horseback riding in America, nobody asked, 'Why?' What they said was, 'But you don't ride.'

This was not quite true. I used to ride a bicycle to work. But horses are well known for having minds of their own and don't respond well to spanners.

So it started as a family riding holiday at the Heaven on Earth Ranch. But it didn't end up quite that way.

The gateway to Heaven is Gatwick. It's a gentle eight-hour flight direct to Minneapolis, 'where all the quiet people go', a characteristic they shout from the rooftops. Then to the nearest town, Great Falls, it's a two-hour hop. Or rather, belly flop. Our descent was spectacular, if you like scary things. It wasn't so much horizontal (at a slight slant), more vertical (with more than a slight amount of screaming). We bumped straight down through the clouds like a knife slicing through the different layers of a cake.

'Now I know why they call this place Great Falls,' whispered the guy

'Honeymoon cabin' overlooking the Smith

sitting next to me, who'd run out of fingernails to chew. 'The plane falls. At great speed.'

'And the rain,' I said, making a dash for the terminal.

Waiting for me there, with a convoy of pick-ups the size of small buildings, were the cowboys. Gary Anderson, the ranch owner, stuck out an enormous hand to greet me. His Stetson rested on huge brows that sat above his large brown eyes like fluffy clouds over mountains.

'If you don't like the weather in Great Falls,' he said, 'just wait a minute, because you'll soon get the weather you want.' This said, in blinding sunshine we set off to the cowboy supermarket. Suitably equipped with cut-price Wranglers, cowboy boots and hats, we headed south-west to the ranch, an hour away.

'So, where are all those magnificent mountain views you promised?' I asked Daryl, Gary's lifelong neighbour, as we drove across prairies resembling Salisbury Plain under a heavy fall of custard.

'You won't see anything today. Forest fires in the Glacier National Park.' This explained why the forecast in the local newspaper read, strangely, 'Smoky'. 'That's overcast, in these

parts,' Daryl enlightened us, warning us that lighting up anything should be avoided in these bone-dry lands. 'Won't affect the fishing any. Could even improve it – if you like smoked trout.'

The Heaven on Earth Ranch is set on the banks of the Smith River and lives up to its name. It's Heaven. It's on Earth. And a divine river runs through it, which, as anyone who has been to the movies will know, is what all the best Montana streams do.

Gary Anderson and his eyebrows walked us down to the river to our cabin. 'We give newcomers the Honeymoon Cabin,' he said.

This cabin was so close to the Smith, Gary recommended taking a rod to bed with you, all set up. 'Roll out of bed and you're fishing.'

The bedspread thrown over the huge bed was embroidered with the image of a trout jumping out of a stream surrounded by pine trees.

'Any complaints, just let me know, 'Gary said, lifting a snow-capped eyebrow. 'Had none yet, but there's always a first. I was kinda expecting to hear something from the couple in here last night.'

I thought, how could anyone complain about this?

'Ted Turner and his lady, Jane Fonda, were here. But they were as sweet as apple pie.'

All night I lay in my apple-pie bed, wondering which side Turner had slept on.

Thankfully, the Smith River ran past – not through – my accommodation. Rainbow trout, brown trout, brook trout and native cut-throats did that. All the way along this five-mile length of river. At breakfast the next day, I broke the news to the cowboys. I couldn't ride. Gary was quick to impart to me the very essence of the art of western-style riding:

'Just git on that horse an' ride!'

With a Western saddle, you don't mount a horse, you collapse into it. It's the nearest thing to an IKEA sofa. The only difference being that when you jump up onto the back of your nag, it's already assembled.

That afternoon my companion, Jamie – with Gary and his son, Vic – rode the length of the river, pointing out prime places.

The next morning, I was up at six with the sound of water gurgling in one ear and out the other. Thoughts of casting a fly on the river

were running through me. Through the cabin window I saw antelope
with their faces deep in mist, searching for the youngest, freshest grass
shoots.

The meeting and eating area in Heaven is on a high gallery that sticks
out over the side of a cliff overlooking the river far below. All around,
crags half a mile away are peppered with bald-headed eagles. The
distance messes the mind. You feel you could stretch out and scratch
them like you can the end of your nose.

Jamie had his nose deep in a cup of syrupy black coffee. It had been
a late night. A night of extreme excitement at having private access to
so much fishing. And a night of 6 x 5 x 4 dice. To a man, we were both
sober. But, to a wife, we had enough alcohol on our breaths to take the
varnish off our rods.

Shorts and wading shoes, and you're fully equipped, sartorially;
emotionally, though, you are unprepared for first footing into the arctic
Smith. Fortunately, I had drunk enough to keep my radiator from
freezing all winter.

A ten-minute walk away, a riffle cuts under a cliff a hundred yards
high. In the mammoth shadow cast by this cliff, the air was filled with
dust. A million tiny *Trico* spinners, upwing *Ephemeroptera* the size of our

smallest *Caenis*, filled the sky, giving the landscape a pointillist look that Seurat would have envied.

Now there's a time and a place for everything. The time was 7.26 a.m.; the place was a small scramble of rocks that dizzied the flow, causing long, mirror-smooth runs to glide silently in all sorts of directions. It was here that the *Tricos* had opted to dump their eggs. A place where they would rest safely below a continuous, health-giving fizz. And it was here that the trout lay at forty-five-degree angles to the surface, ready to siphon in spent spinners.

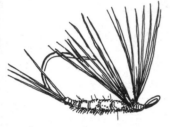

The first two small rainbows I had with ease. Then a brown at fourteen inches. On the end of a two-pound leader I had knotted a small fly I had developed for such occasions: the Patterson Flipper. They seemed to like it.

Years ago, Theodore Gordon said, 'Cast your fly with confidence.' Years later, I'm still saying, 'Cast a fly that gives trout confidence.' The most important thing to build into the design of any fly is assurance.

Design is stripping down to the basics; giving the trout nothing to question, in shape, colour, or size. All the time, avoid giving the game away; for instance, by showing them a hook. Do this and you may as well stick a microphone into a 200-watt Marshall PA bought second-hand from Pete Townshend, stand atop a twenty-step ladder and scream, 'Coming to get you!' So, after simplicity, presenting a trout with nothing it can argue with is top of my design list.

Over the past thirty years, in the pursuit of this principle, I've been asking flytyers: How can you expect a trout to take your perfect imitation if it has a clunky great hook sticking out of it? It's why I developed my upside-down fly, the Funneldun. And, no, I don't apologize for getting gushy about this subject again, because with dry flies there is no excuse for letting trout know your intentions.

But I never believe I've found the ultimate answer to any problem. For this reason, I didn't stop with the Funneldun design. I kept experimenting to see if I couldn't make the design even simpler.

Now, the biggest flytying challenge for me isn't making big flies easier to tie. It's tying small flies; with smaller movements and fewer materials. Imitations of the sort of gnatty *Trico* morsels even those wily Wild West wildies under them-thar willows were supping away at ever so cautiously, as they floated by at glacier pace on inspection parade. They say that with something smutty trout are putty in your hands. Nothing could be smuttier than the Flipper.

I don't mind admitting, weaselling out of awkward, unnecessary flytying procedures is, in my book, an important thing to learn. So, my Flipper is a fiddle-free fly: simple in design and so easy to tie you'll want to tie up all your small-size dries using this system, which is exactly what I do. The Patterson Flipper is a template. I match the colours of materials to the natural. The fly here is the Trico Flipper, tied on a #18–22 down-eyed hook. (For Funnelduns I prefer an up-eyed hook, but here down-eyes perform better.) I wind black silk behind the eye to just round the bend, tying in three or four black hackle fibres en route to form a stubby extended body, tips bending towards hook point. I dub the silk with black poly-dub or the like, to form the body, finishing off with two turns of silk behind the eye. I then tie in a small white or blue dun hackle, shiny side facing hook, and wind two or three turns and secure. I turn the hook over in the vice, bend uppermost. With thumb and forefinger, I pull all the hackle fibres upright, leaving no fibres sticking out below. I split them to form a pair of upright-standing wings, making sure they bend towards the hook point. I secure this hackle position with a whip-finish in front, and varnish.

'Sparse,' I thought (my Flipper, rather than my hero, in mind). What would he have done now? He'd have gone back for a hearty breakfast, happy just to have been here.

I'd seen two black bear cubs scampering about in the morning mist. An eagle had spent two hours circling us with eyes and wings wide open. And we'd enjoyed sight and sound of no other human.

Of course, fishing at Heaven on Earth is like football. It's a game of two halves. There's the tiny Tricos at daybreak, and there's sedge at last light; large, big-deal sedges, and trout that were an even bigger deal to fool.

Arriving on the Smith River for the first time, you just have to use what you have in your box and hope that you have patterns that, if not in every which way, at least are the same size as the sedges you are used to seeing – or, should I say, *used* to see – flying in of an evening on your river back home.

I had plenty of artificial sedge patterns the same size as the ones

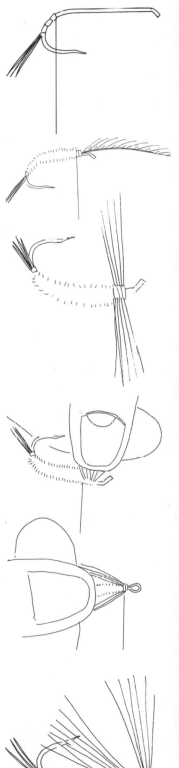

hatching out on the Smith. One we call the Caperer. Flight *Halesus radiatus*, from Latin Land. A sedge now in a speedy decline, thanks to another species with a Latin name: *Pacifastacus leniusculus*, the signal crayfish, from Yankee Land, designed to strip our streams of insects. We call these crayfish the Genghis Khan of southern streams, quite simply because the decline in our sedge population coincides with its arrival and its increase in numbers. And, you know what really bugs me? Even though I know crayfish are bugging my river bugs, there's bugger all we seem to be able to do about it.

The Shuck Sedge is the name I gave a pattern with no name, introduced to me on the Collon Cura, a big river in Argentina, similar in size to the Smith. The *pelmazo* with whom I shared a boat on a downriver float trip was not my kind of fisherman. He talked fishing non-stop. He had you sticking your fingers in your ears singing sea shanties. Half an hour of him and I was looking for a tree to hang myself. But his fly? Well, string it up, cast it out and – give me strength! – the surface rose up on the backs of fish herniating to get to it.

The most fun was when I put it to work on my river back home on those clammy September afternoons that cast a spell of nothingness. When it's back to the hut for tea – and prayers for a rise that evening. But not if you have that Bore from Buenos Aires's pattern in your *caja*. Sling it out over a comatose trout staring at the backend of a weed bed and watch the sparks fly.

I was anxious to see if it had the same effect on the know-it-all trout on the Smith when we set off for an hour before dinner, just before the hatch really began.

Of course, on any river – the Smith included – you may not see anything on the surface pre-hatch, but late afternoon things are starting to warm up. Under the surface, flights of sedge in pupa form

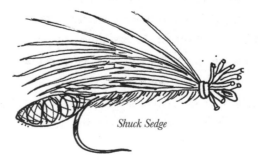

Shuck Sedge

are lining up for take-off, and the secret behind the Shuck Sedge is all about lining up.

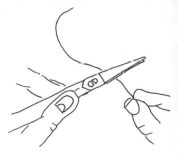

The Shuck Sedge is a semi-sedge. Half sedge, half pupa. The design incorporates a trailing shuck made up of beads threaded on a monofilament loop and encased in a translucent Antron sheath. The weight of the beads ensures the rear of the fly sinks below the surface film like the emerging natural.

Clear beads give the impression of an empty shuck. Beads that match the colour of the body give the appearance of an insect pulling free from the shuck – a sedge at its most helpless and vulnerable.

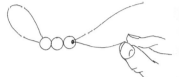

I tie my Shuck Sedge on a #14 hook. I flatten the end of a 6 in. (15 cm) length of 4 lb monofilament and tie it at the bend of the hook. Now I thread on four small dark green embroidery beads and thread the free end back through beads forming a loop behind the end bead. I clip a small bunch of antron, separate the fibres and insert into the loop. Pulling the free end of mono traps the Antron behind the end bead. Now, secure. Pulling the Antron forward over the beads forms a sheath. Now secure this, too.

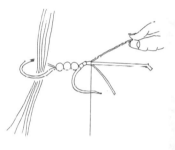

Dub a greyish-green synthetic dubbing material onto the thread and wind three to four turns in front of the shuck. Tie in a deer-hair wing, sloping over the body, making sure it extends the shuck a little. Finally, clip the deer-hair butts behind the eye to form a small 'muddler' head. Whip-finish and varnish, as only you know how.

Back at breakfast with our families, we planned our day. With nothing doing on the river, I cornered Gary. The ranch only takes on parties of friends. They don't book multiple groups, so we had the entire place to ourselves.

'And those trout of yours like to keep themselves to themselves, too,' I said to Gary, who had watched us set out early that morning.

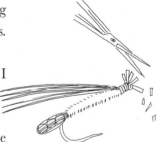

'You should have hung on for the Hopper Hour.'

That afternoon, we went riding again, with the sun high in the biggest sky I have ever seen. The plains smoked. Not with fire, with grasshoppers. Clouds of hoppers billowed up in front of us. Hoppers of all shapes and sizes. Small, moth-like ones on springs. Others rose up out of the grass in slo-mo, like something out of *The Matrix*, with huge black-tipped wings and freaky flight patterns.

'Do fish eat . . . these?' I inquired, pointing to a hopper casting a shadow on the grass the shape and dimensions of a bearskin rug.

'Sure. If it doesn't eat the fish first.'

This was the Hopper Hour Gary was talking about. It was also round-up time. I emulated my other hero, John Wayne. Walking Beauty, my fifteen-hand ride, towards the river, I got her to round up a bunch of hoppers, just like I had seen Wayne round up cattle in the movies, using the horse's hooves to corral them down to the riverside. And when we got there, I watched them hop their last hop – right into the river. Sitting high in the saddle, I watched them flop on down, marking out the trout as they went.

Tomorrow, I'd be back – not with a horse but with a hopper. A whopper hopper.

Melissa, our bubble-permed Girl Friday, jumped out of her dungarees when Jamie dropped his whopper on the kitchen table. It looked more like lunch than a fishing fly.

'It's a Club Sandwich. A killer in these parts', Jamie declared, pulling it away lest we should eat it.

'It would be a killer. If you dropped it on your foot,' I told him.

This hopper consisted of layers of yellow, coffee, vanilla and white foam

Club Sandwich

strips bound onto a #6 long-shank hook. It looked more like it had been constructed from an idea of Ben & Jerry's at the Swan Hunter shipyard than on some local tyer's vice. As I turned it round on the end of my fingers, its big black eyes staring back at me, I realized it was me who was being given the once-over. It was spooky, and I quickly put it back on the table.

It looked unnatural. I wanted a hopper that looked like it was living, not stuffed.

'Don't leave my hopper lying around!' Jamie shouted. 'The birds will get it!'

'They can have it,' I thought, getting out my hand-vice and wrapping a hopper round a hook that, if it didn't hop off the vice, sure looked like it might crawl off it. The main ingredient wasn't foam, it was deer hair. The other ingredients were a floating yarn and rubber legs, my only concession to a Plastic Age. No great flytying shakes, but I like to think the vultures circling overhead had their eyes on it.

Patterson's Hopper

The hardest part of hopper fishing, as I discovered during Hopper Hour the following day, is trying to cast one without bursting out into hysterical laughter. You can't believe any self-respecting trout would want to rise up and waffle a fly that looks more like a piece of furniture than a morsel of food.

I fished a 4-pc Sage Discovery travel rod, nine foot, taking a # 4 line. My tippet had risen from two to six pounds. The sound of Jamie and I casting our hoppers backwards and forwards sounded like the scene in *Apocalypse Now* when choppers attack a Vietnamese village.

I found myself alone and made my way upriver to the stretch where I had marked down a string of likely hopper-hungry trout.

I swung my hopper and a pile of loose line high above the stone where I had seen the first trout, into a snake basket of currents. As I lifted my rod tip on a high arm to hike my line and make immediate contact with my fly, the hopper rolled at my command, just in front of where the fish would have been lying, if he had not been lying elsewhere. To my chagrin, all the other trout were absent also.

The secret of hopper fishing is to be aware of the hugeness of the pattern you are asking a trout to believe in. The larger the fly, the more exaggerated the faults. The more obvious the deceits. The more transparent your intents. Which is why my scaled-down imitation, unlike the pattern bought at the sandwich bar, went for the non-obvious. The trademark of smaller flies.

My pattern gave the trout less to argue about. A *soupçon*. Something they could mindlessly snack on while they awaited the whoppers following on after them. They are taken, not as the main course, but as a matter of course. And because of this, because they are not taken seriously, they appear to offer no serious threat. But nothing could be further from the truth.

Sparse said, 'I laugh when I hear a doctor approving fishing as light recreation for a heart patient, without finding out what sort of fishing it will be.'

Hopper fishing takes it out of you, physically, if not mentally. And even these smaller hoppers were no mean feat to throw.

But right now my hopper wasn't taking anything out of anywhere. Where were all those fish I had seen yesterday?

Now Sparse also said, 'Fish are indispensable to the angler.' And he was right. Having fished a stream myself for a good long time, I know how demoralizing it can be for someone to come to a river for the first time and not find fish that are supposedly there. Local knowledge wins hands down. With no guide, I had to think like a trout.

In actual fact, although the fields were rattling with hoppers, with no wind there were few on the water. Now I was not only thinking like a fish, I was thinking like a grasshopper.

As Mr Trout for a moment, this thinking led me to the conclusion that if there is very little food coming my way, the best place to plonk myself isn't out in the middle of a piece of flat water the width of the Champs Elysées. I should be where the river narrows – where everything is concentrated.

This took me to the area where the river transformed itself into a fabulously, frothing foam. To where cream, whisked up in the tumbling shallows, had been skimmed off the surface and was wrapped round the shoulder of a corner of the river as snugly as a mink stole and, with it, every other surface item not liquid enough to dissolve into the raging current and follow the main flow. Like the occasional hopper.

Now, as Mr Angler for a moment, this was fishing I liked. Parked at this hopper-stopper, all I had to do was gaze mindlessly into the frothy head of a pint of ale. Something I do a lot. No need to practise.

You may not be able to see the fish in the dark water below, but every now and again a circle appears; a circle that remains imprinted in the surface foam like a shamrock in a pint of freshly poured Guinness. This is a fish; a fish in a mood to review your grasshopper.

Reaching these tell-tale shamrocks was no easy matter. I had to cast across a raging current and get my fly to remain stationary on a surface the same consistency as bubble wrap. Standing directly opposite a shamrock, I cast my fly high up into the air directly above where I wanted it to land. With it I threw up as much slack line as I was able to control – or rather not control – for then I pulled my rod back behind me, then I pushed it back forwards, leaving yards of slack line hanging in the air with no alternative but to drop back down into the torrent in a heap.

While the current tried to straighten out this Boy Scout's Field Day, my fly sat motionless in the foam for just enough time for a waiting trout to pounce on it. Nifty.

No sooner had my hopper alighted on the foam than it was sucked under by a rabid rainbow trout of sixteen inches that dived to the deeps with frothy white lips. No questions asked. The pattern's imperfections were disguised in foam wrap.

Luckily, a foam-feeding trout clears the area, hitting the fast water just as fast as it can, leaving any remaining trout unaware that there are devious goings-on afoot. I went on to catch over half a dozen trout from this pint-sized pocket.

Upstream, Jamie fished a deep run – with his imagination. When he found he couldn't bring the trout up to snack on his Club Sandwich, he tied a nine-inch length of six-pound line to the bend of the hook and knotted on a small Hare's Ear bead-head nymph and trotted it down the length of the pool using his hopper as a float. A 'Hopper-Dropper', he called it. And why not? He had his largest fish, a brown of eighteen inches, this way.

When times get tough; when the sun is high, the water crystal clear; when there is no hatch and only a dribble of terrestrials; when fish are super-skitty, fishing the foam can be the only way of ensuring a trout might just take a fly.

I confess I could have been a little more inventive, like Jamie. But I caught plenty of trout – browns and rainbows up to twenty inches – and a sack of white fish.

Now, would I have enjoyed myself any better if I'd gone and stayed at a dedicated flyfishing lodge, rather than a farm? This depends who you take fishing with you. With no guides, or regulars whose brains I could pick at Liar's Hour, I had to work everything out for myself. This was new territory for me, pioneering stuff, so the John Wayne in me enjoyed himself.

The black bear that strolled into our cabin; the raccoons that came to dinner; riding horseback across the river with the water up to your knees; the sky at night a broken net of stars above you; every trout well earned. This was good, honest fishing, so the Sparse in me relished it.

FIVE

Mexico: Yucatán

Burrowing Crab

Hook: No. 4 sea hook
Thread: Pink or white monochord
Eye: Set of dumb bells, to desired weight
Legs and Tails: Six thin white rubber legs and wisp of Flashabou
Body: Tan and Cream wool rug yarn
(tied one after another, figure-of-eight style)

Permit Have Scutes, Don't They?

TO THIS DAY, MY WIFE still can't understand why I let my six-year-old son swim in a cove filled with highly poisonous sea snakes. (I didn't tell her about the barracuda that hightailed it out to sea when he saw me standing on the rocks.)

Yes, I'd seen the serpent slither speedily away the moment everyone got into the sea. But it was terrified – of us – so why cause pandemonium?

I was more worried about the scorpion that had lost its grip on the thatched palm-leaf ceiling in our hut the night before and fallen on our bed. What if I'd been lying there, mouth wide open, snoring? (Which I'm told I do.) And what about that scorpion in the basin? Lots of questions, the biggest being: Where are all the bonefish on the west coast of Mexico?

Have they all been netted out by the sun-ravaged local *pescadores*? Have the hordes of surfers scared them off? Or did the relentless pounding of surf move them on?

71

Were they ever there to begin with?

Later I was to discover that the latter was the case. They had never been there. At least not around the area I was looking for them. This was at Puerto Escondido and the other beaches on the west coast of Mexico, accessible from Oaxaca, where we had been staying before we decided to hit the beach huts on the Singing Sands of Scorpions and Snakes, or whatever that place was called.

I learned from an old man who was sitting on a rock skinning his muscles that on the west the fishing is all bluewater, the Baja Peninsula offering opportunities to target dorado, marlin, roosterfish, various tuna species, snook and sailfish up to fifty kilos, plentiful from June to September. But no bones.

And this, *mi amigo*, is why I never went back to the west coast with a box of bonefish flies. But the east coast is another thing.

Another thing entirely.

That winter, my company had been working with Kuoni, the upmarket travel company. We'd given them sound marketing advice and shot them a TV commercial. In return, they gave me and the other directors a free flight to a select list of destinations.

I went for Cancún, on the east coast of Mexico. Not that I wanted to go anywhere near this utterly charmless holiday destination. A developer's dreamboat, an endless ribbon of hotel complexes, with people asking for money on every corner. I just wanted a flight to Cancún so that I could head off in the opposite direction and explore the Yucatán peninsula; anywhere south of Cancún, where there were bonefish beaches and the best chance you are ever likely to have of catching a permit.

So when our Britannia flight via Orlando descended through steely cobalt-blue skies and landed at Cancún airport, the tourists went one

way, I went the other. But, whereas everyone else on the flight knew exactly where they were staying, for my part, there may have been blue sky, but I hadn't the foggiest.

I had nothing booked. Not even a car. Blinding brilliance.

But with no queues at the Budget desk, within half an hour I was off in my Geo Tracker 4WD, the wind in my hair, pedal on the metal. There'd got to be a more economical way of fishing the salt, and I was about to find out.

The ocean ran parallel to the road, somewhere behind the jungles on my left. Every signpost pointing in that direction was of interest. But it was an hour before I espied anything that really caught my eye. This was a driftwood sign, hand-painted in what looked like blood, pointing down a track to a place called Punta Bete, a track that put my Geo through its paces. After fifteen minutes, and still in jungle, I started to worry-wonder where I was heading.

I was about to turn back when I heard the thunder of the sea, the jungle disappeared and I parked beside a white beach in front of three small *cabañas*, a palm-leaf-roofed restaurant and a stack of rocks alive with iguanas beside a turquoise ocean.

This was Frederico's Xala-Coco Resort.

Frederico was a retired bricklayer from Canada with a German accent. He and his wife ran the place along with Roger, a Mexican, the barman and cook.

I took one of the *cabañas* on the beach for £16 a night, and after a Dos Equis, or *dos*, at the bar, I went and had that sleep I'd tried to have on the plane.

I woke up the next day just in time to stop the ants lifting up my bag and throwing it out the door onto the beach. This place was clearly their place. I got Frederico to move me to another *cabaña*, one I could call my own. And there I stayed for four days.

During those days, I learned a lot. Mainly from the only other person staying there, an aged professor of marine biology, long retired, from Berkeley, with a big brown face that looked like a crumpled blanket and crinkly, tissue-paper skin. He'd come over on the *Mayflower* by the look of him.

We met at breakfast my first day, and every day after that – no matter what time I got up. For this reason I concluded he was always there, having breakfast, tying up flies and drinking coffee, his vice clamped to the table, bits of feather in the butter.

A thalidomide victim, he only had three vestigial fingers. This made his flies really interesting to look at. They were on sale in reception. Disabilities apart, he knew the shore like the back of his paper hand and he didn't mind telling me all about it.

'Let's walk. I'll meet you in the restaurant after breakfast,' he told me. I was curious to discover what time that might be.

It was lunchtime before he reappeared.

I had spent the morning watching a school of small permit, silver tails wagging at me in the sunlight, working their way between two rock crops further down the beach at the Captain Lafitte Resort, which I must have passed on my first day, driving from the airport. I tried for a snook (or was it a barracuda?) by some moored boats, and chucked at

half a dozen garfish that ripped my fly to shreds and made me promise
not to bother them again.

An active a.m.

'You got a lot to learn,' Breakfast Man told me at breakfast (at
lunchtime). 'Those permit you saw aren't permit. Did you catch one?'

I told him I'd caught two. One after the other.

'Size?'

'A couple of pounds.'

'*Trachinotus goodei,*' he said, sounding as if a piece of toast was stuck in
his throat. 'Palometas. Same family. Not the same fish.'

As we walked the beach, he told me how to tell whether I'd caught
a palometa or a permit. If you manage to hook and land it, odds are it
isn't a permit. A small palometa and a small permit look pretty much
the same, but permit are a lot harder to fool. Other than that, the
differences are subtle.

The palometa's fins are longer, their bodies more diamond-shaped.
The yellow on the underside is nearer the mouth. And you rarely catch
a palometa over a pound.

'Then there's the pompano,' the professor continued.

A member of the same family, the Florida pompano is more
streamlined than a permit or a palometa, with smaller, less angular fins.
They go to six pounds.

Pointing at the horizon, Breakfast Man told me that out there permit
go to forty pounds. He'd seen, but not caught, permit up to twenty
pounds finning along the beach.

'And none of them have scutes.'

'Scutes?'

'Hey, I thought you said you wanted to stay clear of guides,' Breakfast

Man said back at the breakfast table (at teatime). 'I'll send you my bill.'

After four days, it was time to move on. I paid up and headed south, past roadblocks and the military. It was only as I was giving the ancient town of Tulum, one of the best-preserved coastal Maya sites, a miss that I realized: (a) what a terrible tourist I am, but more importantly, (b) I'd forgotten to ask Breakfast Man what a 'scute' is.

Later that day, with the sun hanging low on one side of me, jungle on the other, and the unknown dead ahead, I decided to book into the first place I came to. This turned out to be the Osho Tulum, set in an idyllically peaceful, palmy cove (if the crash of a deafening ocean didn't bother you). Conical-shaped designer huts with thatched roofs and walls made of rock sprouted out of the dazzling white sands like mushrooms.

Osho turned out to be a yoga centre populated by spirituals. Skinny white-fleshed men strolled around, gazing heavenward, deep in thought. Gorgeously curvy, high-bronzed, shiny black-haired girls slalomed in between them on their way to the sea, or maybe to a hammock strung between two palm trees, a massage or the communal bathroom, a good place to hang out.

I slept in a bed strung from the ceiling on ropes, waking up with the inside of my mosquito net spangled with blood-filled mozzies.

The road south to Punta Allen through the Biosphere Reserve had more bumps than I had bites on my body. I say road, but anything remotely like a road (everything was remote from now on) stopped an hour after Osho. It was twenty miles of pure dust.

I passed only two other cars, both VWs. The roads in Mexico are paved with VWs. But there were other things to see. Iguanas flopped in front of me, foxes dived into the bushes and even a *tigre*, the jaguar that features prominently in Mayan and Aztec mythology, made a surprise appearance in mine.

I passed by the Boca Paila Fishing Lodge without giving it so much as a by-your-leave, got two hundred yards down the road and decided to reverse back.

The guides were having lunch. The lodge wasn't busy. Antonio told me he could give me a guide, if I wanted. $250 a day. But I remembered what I'd said to Breakfast Man and what he'd said to me. I told Antonio that I might drop in on my return.

Back in the Geo again, I began to think. Adventure apart, I really didn't know how I was going to get on, fishing on my own. No guide, no boat, no nothing. Just me, a beach, the wide-open ocean, a rod and a box of flies. Where do you start fishing two miles of blinding white beach that just goes on and on?

And why hadn't I asked one of those know-it-all guides at Boca Paila what a 'scute' is?

As luck would have it, the next place I decided to rest my head was another fishing lodge on the east coast. A lodge with a difference. Apart from a large slab of cork filled with flies that hung on the wall, and a flytying vice in the corner, Pez Maya could have been a seaside hotel. A seaside hotel with a difference. It had no guests. I had the place to myself.

I chose the yellow and green *cabaña* with its own bathroom right on the sea front. Here I could roll-cast through the window into the surf. Each of the half-dozen *cabañas* was named after a fish: Sábalo, Macabi, Tuberon. I went for Palometa.

Dinner in a large, echoing, decrepit hall filled with chairs and empty tables was like a scene from *Last Tango in Paris*, without Maria Schneider and the accoutrements. Only one table was set, with a napkin wrapped round a knife and fork and some chilli sauce. My table.

'*Un guia, para mañana?*' Sonia the cook and waitress asked me.

'*No, gracias.*'

'*Entonces*, I tell Enrique to meet you here at breakfast.' Then she disappeared.

Eh?

Back in my straw hut I got my tackle together for some serious beach fishing the next day. That night, instead of dreaming of blood-sucking mosquitoes, I dreamed of crazy Charlies.

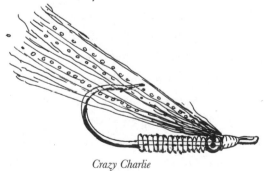

Crazy Charlie

Enrique joined me at the breakfast table. I said hello. He said *hola*. I sat. He stood, with a cup of coffee. He told me he was my guide. I told him I didn't want a guide. He told me, no problem, he would be my guide.

Eh?

He said he was happy just to walk with me along the beach. He had nothing else to do. This, of course, was a perfect arrangement. I had a guide, but I didn't have a guide. My guide wasn't a guide. So what was Enrique?

That morning I was to discover what he was. He was what I needed the most. A guide.

Whereas Breakfast Man could tell me all about the fish, Enrique knew where to find them. He could read a beach like a book. And, to him, the seashore was a library of different books. The sea rolling onto the beach was like pages turning over, from one chapter to the next, and I was to find out exactly what Enrique really was.

Enrique was a hunter, searching out places where he knew fish would be, and where they wouldn't. Looking for things that shouldn't be where they are (and shouldn't be doing what they are doing). Dark shapes that moved. Ripples among the calm. Sudden splashes. Shadows where there were no clouds or objects to cast them.

I quickly learned the secret of flyfishing on beaches. The trick is to get the sea to do the fishing for you. To get your fly moving naturally, the sea is by far and away the best way to do this, naturally.

For this reason, the first challenge was to find a rip, a fast-moving current that runs out from the beach. Or a sweep, which does the opposite. Here is where fish lie, waiting for the sea to bring food to them.

It's such a lazy life by the seaside.

The way to tell the difference between the two is to cast over the moving water. A rip pulls your line out to sea. If you want to get that fly further out than you can shoot it, just wiggle a heap of loose line out of the top of your rod and let the rip carry it to where you want your fly to go, over a sandbar to a drop-off, where a shallow area quickly falls away into deeper water.

On the other hand, a sweep washes the line back to your feet. Sweeps tend to move parallel to the beach. Once you've found out which way the undersea food lanes are travelling – out, in or shaking all about – the next thing you want to do is get into the gutter.

Gutters are troughs where piggy *pescados* stick their snouts, grovelling for food between the beach and a bank. Banks are shallow, sandy areas with deep water on all sides. Here waves rise up to form crests, breaking the surface and forming white water. This turbulence gives a fish cover and stirs up a stew of anything edible hiding in the thin sand. Fish are constantly moving in and out of rips and sweeps on the lookout for food – and these gutters, where they will find it.

Now, gutters come in all shapes and sizes – and colours. The colour of a gutter indicates its depth. The darker, the deeper. If a gutter is in a sweep running parallel to the beach, all you need do is cast your fly into this gutter and walk it along the shore, like a dog on a lead, making sure it stays in there. Letting your fly go with the flow. Getting the sea to do the fishing for you.

'The ocean's a better fisherman than we'll ever be,' Enrique said with a smile. 'She'll take you to where the fish are.'

A flock of snowy-white terns whirled angrily around a small area where a pelican had dropped from the sky on a shoal of baitfish it had spotted in a large V-shaped gutter in a bank that stretched out into the ocean at a forty-five- degree angle. A second bank, on the far side, acted as backdrop. When the wave dropped, it was like looking across into a goldfish bowl.

Enrique became animated. 'Cast into that sweep.'

The Burrowing Crab

I had my wool-bodied 'burrowing' crab on a #4 hook at the end of my line, with a small bunch of thin rubber legs and a wisp of Flashabou protruding out at the bend end, a set of dumb-bells at the eye end, with tan and cream wool rug yarn tied one after another, figure-of-eight style, across the hook to form a body. Arriving on the seabed, this pattern tips up leg first, dumb-bells down, allowing the elastic tentacles to squirm, like a crab digging for its life.

I cast at the gulls, watching my crustacean sink to the bottom. When it got there, I held it still, allowing the sea to sweep the legs from side to side, in a most seductive way.

A dark shape turned on something deep down near my crab. I half-lifted, half-struck into whatever was down there.

'A palometa,' Enrique confirmed after a short run; and the fish on the end of my line twisted in the wave.

Further down the beach, a snook came nosing about just beyond the beach break, where the waves collapse at your feet, and the backwash, where it spills back out into the sea again, exhausted. The snook turned and rushed a wagging strand of weed, somersaulting in the salt, virtually beaching itself in the process.

Enrique pointed to a wave licking the beach twenty yards ahead. As the foam cleared and the wave receded, we saw a shadow. Then,

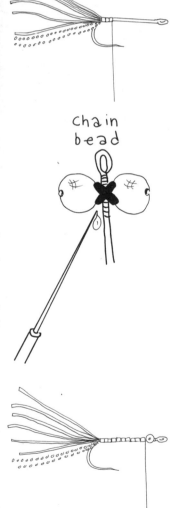

chain
bead

on closer inspection, the opaque shape of a fish that disappeared into the turbulence of churning sand thrown up when the receding water collided with the next incoming wave.

We quickened our pace to see if we could catch sight of it again, wading into the sea to get a better look. Shuffling along the shallow bank of the gutter like a couple of geisha girls, we disturbed the snook we'd overtaken in the beach break.

Permit, like jacks, keep up a good pace until they see something worth stopping to pick up, like a crab.

'A jack?'

'No. Permit.'

Just beyond a narrow point of sandy land that jutted out from the beach, the water shallowed. The gutter turned into a drain no more than a foot deep. Standing on a spit like this is a good place to spot any fish hunting along a shoreline.

Right enough, the permit crossed the sandy shallows, the tips of its dorsals and tail cutting the unruffled surface. It was bigger than any fish I had seen on a beach. How big? I was about to make a guess when it withdrew into the darker water of another gutter, at top speed. The surface erupted as it plucked a small fish or a shrimp, in passing.

On the clear face of a breaking wave the permit appeared again, riding in on the wave, then sweeping off to one side just before the sea smashed onto the beach. Enrique slapped my arm and tapped on my rod. It was time to get fishing. He rushed ahead, beckoning me to follow.

He pointed to a large, round, deep hole with white water on its outer edges. Permit can't resist paying a melon hole like this a visit. These potholes are snack bars for travelling permit, serving up potted shrimp and crab cocktails.

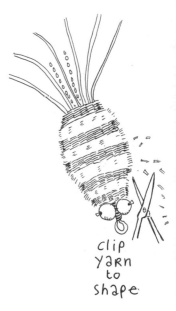

Enrique was getting frantic. He was stabbing the air in the direction of this honey-hole. I waded out up to my shorts so I could get my fly in place with a single cast, giving my 'burrowing' crab maximum time to sink and start that sexy squirming on the seabed. This pothole was the perfect spot for a potshot at that permit. When it arrived; if it arrived.

The best-laid plan was lying quietly on the seabed.

My heart was hammering in my chest when the permit finally caught up with us, nose-down, rooting around in shallow water and heading straight for the melon hole.

When it dropped in, I couldn't believe it didn't see my crab as it pushed up puffs of sand around where the crab was lying there motionless. Realizing that the permit could probably only see a few inches in front of its nose – and fearing that the weight of dumb-bells had sunk the crab too deeply into the thin sand – I gave my line a tug, lifting the crab and dropping it back down again. This time, the permit pounced.

A short strip with my left hand and the permit was on, thrashing about in the shallow water, taking a lift on the first rip out to sea, zigzagging its way to a channel fifty yards further out. And that was the last we saw of it.

There were only two ways the permit could go. Straight out. Or straight out via the only limestone rock on the beach – the way the permit opted to go. It couldn't have done a better job on my twelve-pound tippet had it pulled out a pair of scissors.

'That was no palometa,' I said, reeling in my line, teasing the baitfish chasing the tip of my leader as it skimmed back through the waves.

'For sure!' Enrique howled, rolling in the sand, screaming in despair. 'Otherwise you'd have caught it!'

Brian Jones, the lodge manager, bought me a beer. We talked until midnight. He'd had many businesses, including Blakeys on the Yorkshire Moors, where he'd slung out the Rolling Stones one raucous night. He'd opened an English pub just up the coast at Isla Cozumel and married a Mexican girl called Doris. Sarah, his daughter, was the only Mexican girl I was to see with ginger hair. Brian liked fishing the beach for bones.

'I catch them on dry flies,' he told me. But his favourite was a fly he called 'That's All'. A plain hook, a couple of Krystal Flash fibres and a split shot pinched behind the eye. I showed him one of my Wishbone Worms and he asked if I would swap half a dozen of them for a copy of *The Bonefish* by George Reiger, given to him by the Yellowstone outfitter George Anderson, with instructions to pass it on to someone who would appreciate it.

'You don't need a guide around here. Not with a beach like that,' he said, nodding out of the window in the direction of the ocean.

But I was beginning to think differently.

The next morning I walked down the beach to Sea-Clusion, where Enrique was camped out. What I hadn't realized was that neither lodge was on the mainland. They were both perched on a giant sand dune, on a causeway leading south. On one side, the Caribbean, on the other long, narrow lagoons rimmed with mangroves. Here, the water was only a foot or two deep in places. Bonefish roamed these shallows, with tarpon and snook patrolling the tangled roots in the deeper parts, closer to the mangroves. But more importantly, this was where permit came onto the shallows, probing into the soft mud between concrete marl.

To get there I needed someone with a boat.

Enrique was sitting at the end of the jetty wearing a T-shirt telling me to shut up and fish. I didn't need to say much. He knew what I wanted.

I looked up at the overcast sky. Enrique looked up, too, fingering the air. He wasn't happy. The wind was blowing off the sea at about forty knots. The wave action in the lagoon could make spotting permit troublesome. But we had no time to waste. With the tides as they were, permit, bones, jacks, everything but the small barracudas and boxfish were off the flat by 11 a.m., like someone had cleared the table.

We piled into a wood-caged pick-up and very soon we were bouncing across white-capped waves in a foaming sea in Enrique's emerald green, flat-nosed dugout heading for the lagoon half an hour away. The dugout ground to a halt in the lagoon in water barely nine inches deep, in a grove of small, single-stem mangroves. I watched a large bonefish amble slowly across the flat like a drunk, fifty yards away, pushing up the surface of the water as it went, like a snowplough. Enrique climbed out of the boat, telling me to take off my flip-flops and follow him.

This part of the flat was carpeted with tiny shells, grainy silt and stingrays, so I kept close to Enrique; in fact, right behind him, walking in his footsteps. With feet as flat and broad as dinner plates, Enrique floated. I sank.

Shoals of bonefish were tailing upwind, making casting to them difficult. To have the wind at my back, I had to get ahead of them.

Then the rain came down.

We sheltered in some mangroves, watching it whip the water to froth. We'd been there ten minutes when I noticed a golden eye staring up at me through the peppered surface. With the flick of a wrist, I threw my crab at it. The bonefish grabbed it, shot off, spitting it out on the way.

The sky cleared, the sun reappeared and wading started to get uncomfortable. The crunchy seabed changed to soft mud. Step into a crab hole and you were up to your thighs in sticky custard.

But this was the 'permit place'. On the side of a drop-off just below the bridge where you cross to get to the lodge. This was where they came to feed; here, where there was nothing to grab hold of to pull yourself out. There I stood in two feet of yellow mud, rod in one hand, crab pinched between thumb and forefinger in the other, with that sinking feeling. I was being sucked so slowly into the mud, it was hard to tell if I was sinking at all; but I was. I thought to myself, now I know what Venice feels like.

A small school of permit turned the corner about sixty feet away, beside some mangroves to my right. I blinked, opened my eyes to find they'd populated the flat, feeding in about two feet of water. One darted off after something, another stopped to blow up mud, and another waved a big forked tail at me as it sucked at a crab hole like an anteater. I dropped my crab as close to this permit as I could. This was several yards ahead of where I judged it would soon pass. The permit continued feeding, head down, getting on with it.

Just as it was about to reach the spot where my crab lay squirming, legs akimbo, I gave my line a small twitch and the permit lunged forward, as if to catch something falling off a table. Sea, sand, water exploded and my permit was in and out of that drop-off as I gave it space, and it took it back from me. It was a tug-of-war. But there was one tug too many. A tug too hard, and the permit was off under the bridge and back in the ocean.

'So?' Brian asked me back at the lodge.

So I asked him. 'Maybe you can tell me? What's a "scute"?'

Brian squinted, thought a moment and enlightened me.

'It's a kind of skin, isn't it? Like turtles and crocodiles have.'

'Do permit have scutes?'

'Why?'

'Because that permit today got away by the scute of its teeth.'

SIX

England

The White Sock

Hook: No. 12 (up-eyed)
Thread: Black
Tail: Three black horse hairs
Body: Strand of white polypropylene
Rib: Black floss
First Hackle and Thorax: Black cock
Second Hackle: Large Iron Blue, or teal dyed dark blue

Sock It to Me

'I'VE GOT THIS THING AND IT'S fucking golden and, uh-uh, I'm just not giving it up for fucking nothing. Unless I get something real good, shit, I'm not leaving the river.'

Darrel had a new, class pattern he wanted to test and nothing was going to get in the way of him giving it a whizz. It was going to catch the biggest trout in my river. He was swearing on it.

When John Goddard used to fish the beat on the River Kennet, just down the track from my house, all sorts of famous flyfishermen used to arrive at my front door, either to say hello, spend the night, or ask me to show them round the river because John couldn't get down, or was running late. Datus Proper, Dick Talleur, Garry Solomon, Lefty Kreh, Nick Lyons (a muddy bum-print is still there on the wall from when he returned after a serious fall-in) and Denmark's most famous flyfisher, Preben Torp Jacobsen, 'the naughty Dane', who kept visiting me with or without John, largely on account of the fact that my Danish wife was a tad prettier than Goddard in his sexiest wellies. Now Preben is no longer with us. And I never found out why he was known as the 'Naughty Dane'.

Of all these eminent flyfisherman, the angling writer and fabuloso flytyer from the US, Darrel Martin, was the man who arrived on my doorstep with a more serious mission than lunch. Darrel had this pattern he wanted to try out, and he was on the river with more electricity than a five-bar heater, hot on the heels of the biggest trout he could extract.

For me, watching him at it was life-changing; for any trout that caught his eye, it was life-threatening.

When he left, the following morning, after an overnight stay, having proved to himself that even the most tight-lipped trout in a southern English chalkstream can be made to suck, if perhaps not exactly snap, at an artificial, it was as if a tempest had rushed in through the stable door leading down to the river, whirled round the rafters in my hall, whooshed through the bedroom and out the front door to his car. No damage inflicted, only my sense of speed altered, on just how fast mind and limb can travel.

On that Grand Prix Day, when blackness finally ended his whirlwind foray, I did manage to sit him down in front of a late-summer fire and we got to talk things over. That night I gave Darrel a damn good listening to, well into the next morning.

Two weeks after his departure, when pot plants had returned to their usual upright position, having been bent over by the passing human hurricane, a parcel arrived from the States. It was from Darrel, thanking me for storm shelter (and the fishing). Inside, he had sent me three items I still cherish so many years later. The first, a portable screw-in flytying vice that unscrews into two pieces, fitting snugly into a leather pouch. The second, a set of stencils for drawing hooks, wings and other flytying paraphernalia. And the third, a signed copy of his flyfishing masterclass book. He was later to include my upside-down Funneldun pattern in a follow-up book. The only fly he chose to include – and in colour.

Apart from his talent and energy, what was different about Darrel was that he came outside the best time of the year to be a visitor on my

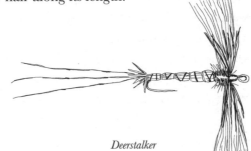

river. For, unlike the Test, the Itchen and all the other grand old southern chalkstreams, my beat gets mighty tough in the summer months, the time he chose to come. This is largely the reason why it has inspired and challenged some of the finest flyfishermen from all over the world during the thirty years I've lived there, and been featured in such films as *The Educated Trout* and *A Passion for Angling* – and Goddard's book *The Trout and the Fly*, in which he was able to experiment and share all his observations, thoughts and findings.

So when is the best time? Any time between 15th May and the second week in June. It's then that the one insect that seems to shrug off all the worst things the modern world can throw at it via our waterways pokes its ugly mug from out of the silt to drive fish and fishermen stir-crazy for two weeks plus. *Danica vulgata*: the Mayfly.

For many years now, I offer all my Mayfly guests, be they Tim from Timsbury or Tim from Buktu, a pattern that John once listed in a magazine article as one of his Top Three Mayfly Patterns. Now those of you who have opened a fly box in front of John will know that this is a very dangerous thing to do. He crawls all over it like an Olympic drug tester. If one of your flies hits this Trout Hit Man's hit list, you can be sure that you're on to something, so it was most reassuring to discover that one of his recommended killers was also one of the top killers in my box, too – not surprisingly, as it was one of my patterns.

This fly of mine was, or rather still is, a standard on many a southern chalkstream; in particular, where I developed it and have been testing it, year after year after year, on the beat I fish, just a Spey cast away from my house.

It's a pattern I call the Deerstalker because, in order to represent a female Mayfly egg-layer in the final death throes, lying face down in, not on, the surface film, the body is formed by strapping hollow strands of white deer hair along its length.

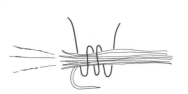

Deerstalker

This, as John was quick to note, gives it the seaworthiness and buoyancy that boasts the same highly attractive qualities as a haemophiliac in shark waters.

So, why don't I just stop here, where John left off, and say, job done – this pattern can't be beat?

There's a great flyfishing truth: no matter how good your fly, there's always someone who has a better one, and he's catching more trout as a result. For this reason, I never stop trying to improve on my improvements. Well, almost never, for there is one fly that I have no desire – or need – to improve on further. It's a Mayfly spinner pattern I fish when my Deerstalker doesn't earn its keep. It's called the White Sock, for no other reason than, if you think it doesn't look like a Mayfly spinner, this is the nearest thing it does look like.

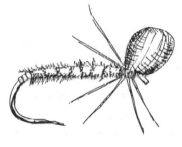

The Suspender Nymph

The Deerstalker was developed at a time when I was playing around with a flytying concept so mind-numbingly obvious it was starting to hurt. This was: if the main purpose of a dry is to float, then shouldn't we be tying them with floating materials?

Deer hair floats. The Deerstalker ticked boxes. A good deal of other interesting patterns came out of my thinking at this time. Perhaps the most enduring is my Suspender nymph that I originated, developed and named back in the late seventies and which John Goddard went on to adapt and publicize.

It was in the search for floating materials where John helped most in the early development of the Suspender. In early prototypes, I filled the nylon stocking sack at the head of the Suspender with little plastic balls from the impact-proof envelopes of that time. John suggested I use the

foam he used in the construction of one of his more popular fly boxes, trimmed to shape and size.

One of the first floating materials I considered for the Suspender was polypropylene yarn rolled into a ball. Unsinkable, accessible and easy to handle, it seemed the perfect answer. But the nylon 'sack' used to keep the Suspender 'suspending' had to be as small as I could make it. In small quantities, polypropylene yarn just didn't have the buoyancy power required to hold the head of the fly in the surface film. The amount of polypropylene required to keep things high and dry made the Suspender top heavy. My delicate little nymph looked like it was about to hatch out into the Elephant Man.

But the material continued to intrigue me. It had to be good for something.

I considered it for body material for the Deerstalker. The successful high-float of the deer hair was due to more than the fact that it was hollow. Strapping it down the hook lengthways with thread, rather than winding it round the hook, trapped air. This formed little bubbles all the way along the hook, like little lifebuoys. Do the same thing with polypropylene, and the air slips through the fibres. Winding it round the hook wasn't the answer, either.

But by taking a strand and 'hanging' a small hook from it, the yarn could keep the hook from plummeting to the riverbed. So, as long as I didn't mind having to abandon a #10 long-shank Mayfly hook – the size I use to tie Deerstalkers – using #12s, or #14s instead, floatability was possible.

Sometimes restrictions set free the most interesting solutions – and new concepts. Necessity, we're told, is the mother of invention. (The mothers who got stuck with glue that didn't stick know all about this. What did they do? They invented Post-it notes.) Being stuck with the challenge of tying a large Mayfly spinner on a small hook led me to think back to Frederic Halford and his Detached Badger pattern. Here, rather than tying the body *round* the hook, he tied the body *independent* of the hook.

This is what I decided to do with my strand of white polypropylene that looked so like a Mayfly body (or a sock).

This restriction pleased me greatly because it led me to consider

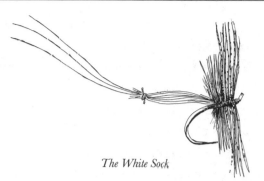

The White Sock

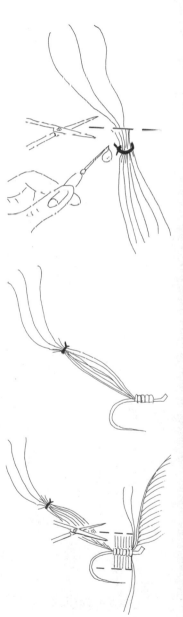

another blindingly simple flytying concept that still guides me today: the less you give a trout to question, the less likely it is to argue with your pattern – and the more likely it will be to accept it. In other words, the smaller the hook, the less likely it is that the trout will notice it. And the fewer the inhibitions it will have about wolfing it down.

So, to tie my Mayfly spinner pattern, you begin by tying the body *independent* of the hook. Before I put hook to vice, I take a 2 in. (50 cm) strand of white polypropylene and rub in three thin horsehairs so that they stick out at one end. I then knot them in at the end with a thick length of black Pearsall's Marabou silk. This I secure with a dot of superglue the size of this full stop. (Well, nearly.)

When dry, I clip off the butts of the silk and trim the polypropylene yarn underneath the tails so that it protrudes just enough to support the weight of the tails.

Next, I put the hook in the vice and tie this body a quarter of the way down from the eye of a #12 up-eyed hook, leaving enough room for two hackles: the first, a medium black cock; the second, a large iron blue.

I wind the black hackle over the roots of the body that I have already tied in. I then trim and shape three-quarters of this hackle – to represent a thorax – leaving a couple of turns at the head. Finally, I wrap three turns of the large iron blue hackle in front of this, to represent wings.

Easy-peasy to tie, light, unsinkable and freakily lifelike, the White Sock need only be squeezed in a handkerchief after a fish has snaffled it to make it float again. (Watch the share price of Mr George Gehrke's Gink plummet.)

One last thing before you get to work: a regular iron blue cock or hen hackle will do fine for wings. But if you're dead keen and a stickler for detail, dye some medium-sized teal breast feathers iron blue and use these. They represent wing veins superbly.

I was lucky. Recently, I was in a junk shop and I found a lady's hat that looked like it had been through two world wars. It certainly dated back that far. Attached to the side was what I can only describe as 'decoration', a badge made out of feathers containing a flush of teal breast feathers dyed a deliciously soft blue-grey. Just the job. They say, if the hat fits, wear it. I say, if it doesn't, to hell with it – tie a fly out of it.

But that's just the Mayfly spinner. With the Mayfly dun, after the first ten days, the trout start to wise up to the hatch and the smarter trout, pricked and caught and returned a few times, soon get to know what all the larger, hairier patterns look, feel and taste like.

Flytying instructions for mayflies famously start: 'Take hook. Put in vice.' The instructions for the Mayfly dun pattern I fish when the trout start turning their noses down, rather than up, at the artificials that have served me well for the first week or so, start: 'Take old pan.' What am I on about? Well, let me tell you.

In winter, when I can't get down to the river to fish, I have other ways of living it up. I dye. I love dyeing feathers. This means that when I reach for a shade of feather or fur, I have a colour range I would never be able to find in any catalogue or shop. Namely, the colour *I* want. In one short session, I can create a lifetime's supply of feathers that perfectly match the faint grey of a Spurwing's wing, the sooty blue of an Iron Blue, the slate of the Large Dark Olive and the metal blue of the B-WO. A wide range of shades, all by just leaving feathers in the dye for different lengths of time. Short, for light. Longer, for dark.

One of my most successful patterns when trout may or may not take your favourite Mayfly is a product of those winter days. An emerger pattern with a yellow green wing you whip up in minutes.

My Ten-Day May is designed for the ten or so days into Mayfly, when the trout have worked out exactly what the squidgy manna from heaven up top is. And, more importantly, the danger an angler's imitation can bring.

It's the simplest of flies. And here lies its effectiveness: it breaks all the rules. By doing so, it offers the best chance of breaking the fast of tight-mouthed Mayfly guzzlers that only part their lips to yawn – or giggle

The Ten Day May

– as they watch Gray Wulffs and other 'Big Hair' imitations float past, sporting more tresses and grizzly tufts of hair than a West End wiggery. Hair in hanks.

As a fly designer, I ask: Do Mayfly patterns have to be so hair heavy?

Of course they don't. And as long as wily trout keep refusing these full-fat, industrial-strength Mayfly patterns time after time, so the opportunity arrives to be super-sly: to parade something a little more pasteurized past their eyes. If only to break the boredom.

The Ten-Day May requires only five materials. For the wing material made of duck feather, you need to get the pan out. It's all in the instructions further on, so let's talk about the fly.

This pattern is designed to do everything most flyfishers don't want their Mayfly to do: keep a low profile. So low you might wonder where it's gone. But everything you can't see, the trout can. Isn't this what you'd prefer?

The Ten-Day May sits in the film, not on it. In size, it leans on the smaller side of the natural. It goes for the trim, not the tubby. The feather method, rather than the hairstyle. Just remember to grease the wing only; and that's really all there is to it.

In his book *Reflections on Fishing*, Dr Tom Sutcliffe says, 'The longer I fish, the more I long for simplification and lightness.' For this reason, when trout are on a fussy Mayfly stropathon, my Ten-Day May is just what the doctor ordered.

So how do you get that perfect Mayfly hue? Here's what you've been dying to know.

Take that old pan. Bring 1 litre of water to boil. Add 1 tablespoon of vinegar. Add ¼ teaspoon of Veniard Insect Green dye. Put small de-greased teal breast feathers in pan. Simmer and stir until colour penetrates. Check quill for colour. For lighter shade remove sooner

than for darker. Rinse in cold water. Remove. Dry in paper towel. Place feathers in cardboard box. Use hairdryer to bring feathers back to life.

Finished dyeing? Now the tying. Here's how you bring that fly to life.

Start by snipping off the barb of a #10 hook. With primrose silk, tie 0.5 mm yellow foam strip behind eye, pointing over it. Bend back, secure. Tie in three pheasant tail fibres to form: (1) three short tails round bend; (2) two bands at rear. Dub on cream mohair wool. Wind to behind foam thorax. Now lay one of those small dyed teal breast feathers over body, stalk parallel to hook shank. Secure stalk. Wind three turns of cream badger cock hackle dyed Insect Green behind thorax. Whip-finish behind eye. Varnish.

Now all that's left to do is give Darrel a call and tell him to come next Mayfly. Using this method he might just have caught that monster he deserved to catch.

If you're reading this, Darrel, you're always welcome. My house by the river is still stanvding. Just.

Darrel didn't managed to catch the biggest trout in the river – but only because no one knows how big the biggest trout in the river is. He certainly had one of the largest so far that season. I guess, on that mysterious 'fucking golden, uh-uh' fly of his.

The PTN

After dinner he found my collection of flies, some of them tied by their originators. Flies tied by Lefty Kreh, Frank Sawyer, Vincent Marinaro, Lee Wulff, Richard Walker – all the greats; all framed and signed. He was keen to rummage methodically through them.

The GRHE

To me, a Gold Ribbed Hare's Ear – perhaps one of the easiest flies to tie, using up only two materials – is just a pile of fur. To Darrel it's everything he believes a fly should be when it comes to selecting an effective pattern. It must look 'alive'. For him 'life' should be the body and soul of every fly you tie. Above all else. Because how do we distinguish between something that's alive or dead? Answer: if it's alive it moves. So the most important *initial* feeding trigger of any pattern is movement.

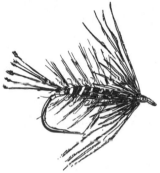

The Leggy Claret Bumble

He liked my Leggy Claret Bumble tied by Stan Headley. Very much alive and kicking, its springy appendages suggest a fly putting up a struggle. 'Like a wounded antelope to a lion, helplessness is a key feature to initiating a trout attack,' he told me. Sure enough, in the palm of your hand the sheer grubbiness of it makes it looks like it could give you a nasty nip.

The Parachute Adams

He was pleased to see I had an Adams in my box, a pattern that 'vibrates'. It's almost eighty years since Charles Adams first whipped up this all-round trout snatcher. Darrel directed me to what he wrote about it in one of his books: 'Its value lies in its variegated, but neutral colours. The banded grizzly-point wings suggest the vibrant fluttering of an insect attempting to fly.' 'Gray and funky and a great salesman' is how Thomas McGuane described it.

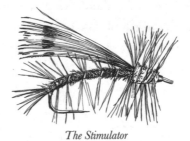

The Stimulator

He selected the Stimulator, a fly that caught me all those wild, black-backed trout up to ten pounds on the upper regions of the Kharlovka. Tied by its originator, Randall Kaufmann, it was designed to swing easy in the breeze. The blur of colour and moving light patterns are the feeding triggers.

The Grey Wulff

My Grey Wulff, tied by Lee Wulff, was the last one he tied before his fatal plane crash. 'A bulky, beefed-up, butcher's van of an imitation', it's designed for fast water where trout have no time to distinguish between a twig and a food item. Standing on tall, vertical wings, the Wulffs rock and roll, a stunt lighter-dressed flies just can't perform with any of the necessary drama.

I was hoping Darrel would go on and tell me about that 'fucking golden, uh-uh' dream fly of his.

But, uh-uh, in your dreams! It was time for bed.

~

Two miles downriver from my house, Tom Stoppard, the playwright, fished with his friend, the famous actor Sir Michael Hordern, who once said he preferred fishing to acting.

I eventually got to meet Michael when casting in a different way. He was to feature in a TV commercial I had written, playing the part of the chairman of a make-believe Weather Forecasters' Club who was introducing the new clubhouse cooker to his board of directors. He predicted that it would be just like every other cooker which, of course, the commercial was claiming it wasn't. The commercial ends with him saying that, because the weather was going to be good, he had organized lunch on the lawn. At which point the heavens opened up.

It was a three-day shoot, so there was plenty of time for Michael and me to chat about fishing.

We shot the commercial at Shepperton Studios. During a film break I went for a walk to nose around this famous studio. Tucked away at the back behind some other studio buildings I came across a small pond. Dark fishy shapes glided idly between streaks of sunlight.

The next day, I smuggled a Hardy Smuggler rod, some nylon and a small tin of nymphs onto the set. At first break, I told Michael about my find and we decided to skip lunch and head off to our *lago escondido* behind the huts.

Some of the larger chub we saw might have gone to a pound. But the fact that they had been slipping and sliding out of the limelight and preferring to stay in the wings of the shade – an uncharacteristic feature of most of the people who slip in and out of such a world-famous studio – intrigued both Michael and myself. At last, their moment had come. And for twenty minutes, at least, they had been noticed and had centre stage.

With such high production budgets at stake, film shoots are run like military operations. No time for prima donnas, or prime-time piscatorial activities. So, by the time we'd got the Smuggler up and Michael had climbed up the rod like a monkey threading the line, we only had half a dozen chucks each.

Even so, they were valuable minutes that have stuck in my memory and that's why, from that day on, I always have a Smuggler stuffed away somewhere at hand, wherever I go; whatever I do.

That day, we ended up with a couple of chub each and a rosy-red finned rudd or two, all on a little pheasant tail nymph.

'Who could have predicted that?' Michael said on the way back to the Weather Forecasters' Club.

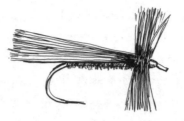

SEVEN

Norway

Czar Fly

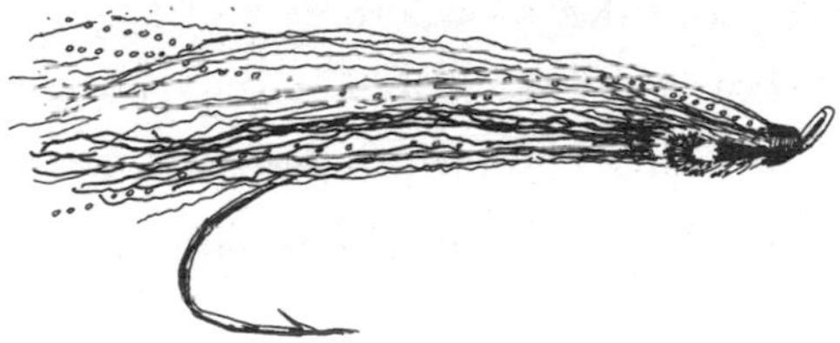

Hook: No. 2/0 Gold
Thread: Black
Wing: Yellow calf hair
(**Optional:** two strands Krystal Flash)
Cheeks: two Jungle cock cheeks

The Expert, the Inexperienced and the Executioner

'WELCOME TO OH-SO-SLOW AIRPORT,' John spluttered, having just dragged a rod case the dimensions of a Greek Doric column along mile upon mile of unmarked steel and laminated corridors of Norway's principal airport. Free trolleys there were.

'But *free* flippin' miles away – at the other end of the hall!'

David was beginning to share the same frustrations as John.

Oh-so-slow airport was ever-so-messing the minds of two impatient flyfishermen.

Oslo airport is not designed for men in transit with nothing else on their minds other than to get to a river for the second week of the season – and the early June run where, at this time of year, no salmon leaves the sea smaller than twenty pounds.

When they hit a second check-in queue, the calming effect of the nuclear soup (a lager called *Hansa*) that they had sipped on landing (at £6 a pint) finally wore off.

As the only member of the party carrying nothing heavier than the floss in my soap bag, I tried to clear the air.

'You salmon experts carry too much gear.'

No one was under any illusion about where I fitted into this *ménage à trois*. I was the one with no knowledge, no expertise – and no gear. And no worries. Written loud and clear in the brochure: all equipment is on offer, for-the-use-of, rods, reels, lines, nylon, waders, jackets, waistcoats. Everything, in every shape and size. And flies. Our Danish host, Jan Daugaard, is the largest supplier of ready-tied flies in Europe. So, what to bring?

Well, I had nothing to declare other than my incompetence in salmon-shaped things. Something I dearly wanted to correct. Accompanied by two of the UK's *salar supremos*, I guessed I was well on the way to catching my largest Atlantic salmon from a European water, on fly. From the Stjordal which, along with the Namsen and Guala, is one of Norway's, nay Europe's, most eminent salmon rivers. A river that is treated with such sacred reverence, the hackles on your flies fall on one knee and bow on entry.

'Everyone looks so tanned, so blonde and so beautiful,' I ventured, in an attempt to calm my crowd of two with thoughts of pretty things.

'How do they manage it? Two weeks of sun a year – and they're black.'

But not as black as the clouds hanging over the heads of my twosome audience. The sun was burning high in the sky. It had been for over a week. And it was there, sitting waiting for the departure of Flight SK 1530 to Trondheim, that I quickly learned my first lesson in salmon fishing.

A little rainwater, good. A lot of sun, bad.

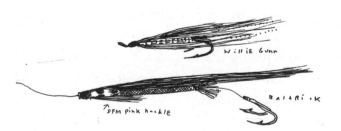

At Trondheim, the Old Lady was standing waiting for us, bathed in sun. She had undergone a total makeover. Gone were the flies stuck into the drapes that hang loosely from her. No bottles of Aquavit, hidden away, clinking at her every move. No ash piled high on the floor all around her, from the in-built wood-burning stove. No, the Old Lady, Jan's mobile home, had been upgraded since I was last transported in her, five years earlier, when John, Jan and I were shooting *The Take*, a series for Sky Sports.

Jan's farmhouse, due east, in the village of Ingstad, is a cornfield away from his mile of Stjordal fishing. No distance.

This was his thirty-eighth year here. In that time he had turned a rusty-red, pine-panelled farmhouse and the other rusty-red, pine-panelled barns that formed a quadrangle around a grass courtyard, into a summer fishing lodge and, for three weeks a year, a flyfishing school. This is his summer work. In the winter, he shutters up and returns home to Sweden. Spiriting my bag and John and David's cargo away, he sat us round a table and then disappeared into the farmhouse – for spirits.

I looked around. No need to check the Trade Descriptions Act. Chest waders and waistcoats in every conceivable size hung like curtains in the barn porches. Along the walls, fully made-up rods stretched out, like wires at a telephone exchange.

'Whose is all this gear?' I asked Jan as he returned with a tray.

'Yours,' Jan said.

I strolled over to the farmhouse. In the hall was a picture taken in the 1880s of a family standing in the farmhouse courtyard. Little had changed.

'Welcome, gentlemen,' Jan said, raising his glass. 'Tonight, we have herring with elderflower schnapps, moose in blackberry and juniper berry sauce and fried potatoes. And, tomorrow, whale.'

Jan hadn't changed much, either. And he never let us forget that as well as being a champion salmon fisherman he had once cooked for the Swedish king.

'Come see my *fangst*,' he said, leading us back to the farmhouse. He pointed to a piece of cardboard pinned to a rusty red pine wall at the foot of the stairs. The *fangst* is where all fish must be recorded.

'We ended last season with a hundred and sixty-six,' Jan said. As we stared blankly at the cardboard's blankness, the *fangst* revealed itself to be nothing more intimidating than a cereal packet opened out and reversed.

This was the second week of the season and no salmon had been caught yet. Was the run late? Whatever the reason, Jan had left plenty of room for us on the *fangst*. And, apparently, plenty of cereal.

'Breakfast is at eight. But you can fish all night, if you like. There's always a fire and coffee by the river – and the guides will serve you as much food as you like.'

Three weary travellers stood staring blearily at one another, with eyes that had first opened that morning at 4 a.m. Without a word spoken, we followed one another up a rusty-red staircase the same colour as our eyes – to bed.

David had been up bright and early to scout. Over a breakfast table groaning with tubs of berry jam, cold meats, yoghurts and herrings he delivered his report.

'The river is low. But a good height for a Scottish river.'

Jan's right-hand guide, Jorgen, a young Swede – my guide for the day – shook his head. His silence spoke volumes. As the beginner, I was given the best guide – and the best beat, at the top end, where 90 per cent of the season's salmon are taken.

Yellow Bucktail
Black Squirrel tail
Yellow Flash above

CZAR FLY #0/1 - 6

The CZAR, crowned

I might not have the casting and salmon-seeking skills but I had the fly. A huge gold hook, on a 2/0, a yellow calf hair wing and two jungle cock cheeks. The Czar Fly – sublime in its simplicity. And a favourite on the Varzina, so I have been informed, for I have only trout-fished in Russia.

I tied it up for the trip because I love the look of it. Not a philosophy I take with me to a trout stream, but certainly one I take with me salmon fishing. If nothing else happens, a fly you like can guarantee happiness.

I held it out to Jorgen on the palm of my hand for his approval. He looked at it enviously. Handing me a thirteen-foot and a slow-sink shooting-head, he looked down at it once again. His nod spoke volumes.

The water on the top beat was too thin to fish. We fished a hundred-yard stretch of fast water below it, roiling and rolling over rocks the size of small cars. Letting the Czar hold a while in front of each boulder, and then allowing it to parade ceremoniously round the side and swing into the ballroom at the back, where I let it dance a while. That morning, not an inch of river was spared an Imperial visit.

After two hours, I returned to Jorgen, who was sitting on a stone, carving a piece of wood.

'Not a fin,' I told the Swede.

Back at the farmhouse, I discovered I wasn't the only one who had not caught, touched, risen – or even had any sight of one of these guaranteed twenty-pounders.

Jan smiled and reminded us that if you are a true salmon fisherman, even on the finest salmon beats – at the prime time – catching one is a bonus. Everyone agreed. One salmon taken from the Tweed at the end of a week's hard slog beats a salmon every five minutes at a Russian camp.

'It's women who catch all the salmon. And the biggest,' said David.

'No, it's trout fishermen, like Neil, who just gets lucky.'

'Well, that's the end of me,' I said, feeling any good fortune that I

might have possessed drip down the side of my leg and seep into the grass in the courtyard.

Then it suddenly occurred: 'If this is so, why bother becoming an expert?'

After a second salmon-free day, and a third, it rained on the fourth night. A little, but not e nough. I had spent the morning fishing an area the size of a groundsheet, a bald, flat slither of water on the far side of a fast shallow that roared past with the sound of a train. It almost had me over twice, wading at ankle depth.

This was the 'Golden Triangle'. If you could get a fly to swim, dragless, through this deep, slow pothole, you raised your chances of catching a salmon, anywhere on the river, by a huge percentage.

I rose nothing all morning and returned early to the Gabahuk – the log fishing hut with a bird's-eye view of the biggest salmon pool on the beat. Jan's two other guides, Steffan and Morten, both students from a Swedish guide school – and Danes – were poking at the embers under a boiling, tar-coated kettle.

'There's a salmon in the pool. We saw it jump an hour ago,' Steffan told me as I clambered up from the river.

'*The* salmon,' Morten said, laughing. Steffan was more serious.

'All twenty silver pounds of it, rolling just . . .' – he pointed to the back of the pool with his poker – '. . . there. Have a go.'

No, I thought. To be honest, I was scared. I didn't know how to even start fishing this huge, swirling pool, so big it had a postcode. And, heaven forbid, I might just catch it. What then?

Over lunch, David described how he might try it from all angles. Even getting Steffan to row him across to the other side to try from there. Then, as if the knowledge had been delivered down to him from on high, he decided upon the exact spot where the salmon would be lying. And from where he would cast.

'Right there,' he said, biting into his fish paste sandwich with a vengeance and pointing to a lucky lupin that had managed to find a crack in the rock face with enough earth to accommodate its tender roots. 'That's where he'll take.'

David had studied that pool with a knowledge I didn't understand. With the clinical skill of an ophthalmic surgeon, selecting a microscopic vein to inject.

'I'd Dick it, David,' was John's contribution. John had been sorting through his fly box marking down the fly for the job with the same degree of expertise that Dave had been applying to marking the spot.

John lifted out a Red Francis (known as 'Dick', after the author Dick Francis) tied on a copper tube, with whiskers the length of a tigress's.

'Need any help lifting that, John?' I asked.

'Keep your hands off it, mate.'

No problem. It looked like it might bite me. Even worse, it might drop on my foot.

'What does that do?' I asked John, pointing at the striped hackle stems sticking out at all angles. 'Tickle the salmon to submission?'

'It's your turn, Neil,' David told me. 'Go get your rod. If anyone's going to catch it, it'll be you.'

Believe me, I tried to resist.

Now, I know when I'm not going to catch a fish. It's when I push my luck too far. In this case, my beginner's luck. But I decided to give it a try.

I didn't cast my Czar, I flicked it. I fished as feebly as I could, hoping that the salmon would sense my inexperience and grab it. Just to keep a tradition going.

Not feeling at all comfortable with this, I tried Tactic Number 2. I thought of Mrs Ballantine and her sixty-four-pound salmon from the Tay, Mrs Morrison's sixty-one-pounder from the Deveron and Doreen Dovey's fifty-nine-pounder from the Wye and I started to cast as a woman might cast, just to try and make the salmon think I was a girl.

I was searching my mind, not for tactics, but for tricks. I remember

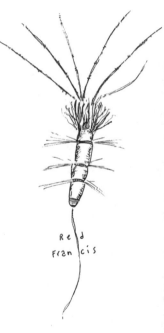

Red
Francis

meeting one man on the riverbank who salmon fished wearing his wife's bra. 'They can smell a woman,' he told me.

I considered an underarm cast.

'Stop poncing about, Neil. Give John a shot.'

I've never been so relieved to be relieved.

John declined. 'It's yours, David. I have the fly, but you know the lie,' he said, helping David lift the Francis from his fly box and wind it on his line.

Back at the Gabahuk, I sat back with a fish egg and smoked salmon sandwich to watch how the experts do it. But I wasn't there for long. Second cast, David's rod bent over.

The reel screamed. Or was it Jorgen? Everyone was screaming! The reel, the guides, the seagulls – and the salmon, screaming down out of the pool with David hot on its heels.

Twenty minutes later, I discovered what all the fuss is about with salmon fishing. One minute silver, the next lilac, David's eighteen-pound hen fish, forty hours from the sea, still crawling with lice, now lay at rest in the lupins, flashing its motionless beauty in the sun. I was all agog.

The Hardy Jameson Flask was taken down from a nail in the Gabahuk to toast David, the season's first serial killer. Jan's *fangst* was no longer blank.

Thinking back, that salmon we took wasn't caught, it was executed.

I say 'we' because, in a sense – and David would be the first to agree – we all played a part. It wasn't a fishing expedition, it was a trial. A trial by a jury of three.

There was me, representing the never-to-be-underrated traditional 'luck' element; John, with his enviable salmon sense, representing the need for exactly the correct fly selection; and finally David and his almost mystical understanding of where the salmon would lie, how the fly should travel and how it should behave, representing the execution of the plan – and, as a direct result, of the fish also.

But what made the week so interesting was the fact that there weren't scores of salmon in the river to be caught; there was only one in that most unusual, even freakish, early June week on the Stjordal. That was the challenge. And we got it.

Of course, the day after we left, the heavens opened and the river was filled with the fish we had rushed to catch. Fish that were there that first week. Only further down the river, waiting in the fjord.

But a tale such as this may be a thing of the past. Orri Vigfússon tells me that the river owners of the Stjordal, the Gaula, the Orkla and the Verdal, along with the North Atlantic Salmon Fund (NASF), are organizing a five-year pilot scheme to buy out the in-fjord nets, so days like the one we had, when one salmon was enough to feed the imagination, talents, good fortune and memory cells of three anglers, may be gone for ever.

Well, almost. Not even Orri, with all his energy and influence, can make The Big G turn the rain taps on and off by request.

So, did I learn anything from my trip?

Well, I can now throw a half-decent Spey, and I think I've got a better understanding of where salmon might lie and, more importantly, where they might take.

But even though I believe that there are two kinds of expert – those who don't know, and those who don't know they don't know – I am now convinced that you catch a salmon because you *know how* to catch a salmon. In short, you learn to catch a salmon. You don't just go to Russia and haul them out.

Expertise – and the help of those who know about it – is required. With, every now and again, a little luck and lingerie thrown in.

So, expertise. How does one become the right sort of expert – the one who *knows how* – in flyfishing? Or in anything else for that matter? What matters?

Let's ask the experts. Or, at least, let's observe one of them.

Not everyone fishes to catch fish. Does this sound strange? Well, let me tell you. No one likes to catch a fish more than John Goddard. He'd caught more than his fair share to prove this point. He'd spent his whole life catching fish all over the world and written about how he manages to be so successful at it.

If you know John, you'll know that no one would argue with you if you told them he was an expert. Except John.

Fishing with him at his small private syndicate lake in Surrey, where there's only one boat so you have to get there early – not that we've ever seen anyone else there – an interesting thing occurred. And, looking back, it could help in understanding how John might have developed his expertise.

As usual, John wanted me to row to the far corner of the lake so that we could fish past the sand-washing pump, the musical soundtrack of our day. We managed to catch nothing all morning.

After lunch, John asked to be rowed to the other far corner, on the other side of the lake from the sand-washing pump. (Still the same soundtrack, but at a distance.) Two hours went by and we'd caught nothing.

John was sitting at the end of the boat fishing some pattern or other. I had been sitting at the other end fishing everything I had in my box, reassured by the fact that John was probably doing the same.

'Pretty dead, John,' I commented, looking across the wide expanse of clay-coloured water. 'Any ideas?'

'Have you got one of my Tadpollys with you? That usually does the trick on days like today.'

Yes, I had one. John's tadpole imitation was tied on a long-shank, down-eyed, wide-gape #10 hook, using black silk, with a brass bead of desired size and weight at the head, a good tail of black marabou at the rear and a body of black wool all ribbed round with gold tinsel in between.

'Well, put one on. It's my sheath anchor.'

On it went. And almost immediately, I had a trout hanging on the end of my line.

'Told you so,' John said, with his little giggle, tying one on himself. Almost immediately, I was helping John land his first fish of the day, too.

In between the next two or three fish I took on his Tadpolly I could see John fiddling around at the other end of the boat, tying on different flies, new – and perhaps better – patterns and ideas. He was quite happy to be back catching nothing again. He had cast his sheath anchor overboard, proved to himself its effectiveness, hoisted it back up again, determined that whatever else he might have on his line would, perhaps one day, be another sheath anchor too.

Which is what I mean when I say, not everyone fishes to catch fish.

And that is why they become experts, in the process. And why they catch more fish, in the end.

If, and when, they choose to do so.

I visited Scotland several times on my own after my first trip to Norway with experts John 'The Hotchpotch' and David. But I stopped going. Mainly because my casting never got any better, but also on account of my last trip there and the salmon fishermen I had shared the river with. Each one saying how much they hoped they'd catch The One.

Long descriptions of The One were given, and endless protracted discussions entered into about The One's canniness, size, fight, silvery beauty, freshness; everything from the magnificence of its kype to the number of sea lice it carried with it, and the flocks of seagulls following it upriver waiting for them to drop off.

So many different and varied elements of distinction – practical and poetical. Too many, it seemed to me, making The odds of the One ever really being 'The One' remote – by hyperbole.

For this reason, when John invited me to go back to Norway again where I was assured that I might catch 'My' One – The One for me – all these discrete elements that make The One 'The One' I made secondary. For all I was really looking forward to was snow-zapped mountains, foaming white-bearded waterfalls, river water the clarity of honesty, and wild fish – in the company of friends, all far greater experts in the art of casting a salmon fly than I could ever aspire to be, so that I might learn something.

So, how did I feel when I put the phone down after our conversation? Very chuffed, is what I'd say. (Does anyone say chuffed these days except me?) John had invited me to join him and a small party of buddies to fish a river I'd never heard of before, the trip organized by Harald Oyen, renowned for being notoriously knowledgeable on Norway matters.

The Arctic river Harald had arranged for us to fish was situated snugly, but perhaps not so smugly, a tad north-east of the super-exclusive Alta, the two rivers differing only in how quickly you are able to get your tongue round the names. To pronounce the river I was to fish took some practice standing in front of the bathroom mirror.

The Lakselva – easy to say now, but not as easy as saying 'Salmon River', for this is what it means – had been given other names over the decades, all alluding to one feature. All incorporating the words 'salmon' and 'big'.

But My One salmon wasn't going to come straight away. Indeed, it was to be the 'Last' One.

On our way north from Bardufoss airport, John, David Profumo, Colin Bradshaw and Max Sardi – the above-mentioned party of buddies – and I stopped for two days to fish the Mälselva, staying at The Rundhaug. Garlanded with pink flowers, this historic, recently refurbished *gjestegaard* has pictures of salmon hanging everywhere. Some of these salmon are bigger than the people holding them. Here we were to rest our heads where Kings of Norway rested their crowns in the past – and continue to do so. Royalty – and generals. In the reception, the forever cheerful Reidun Nilsen, the hotel director, pointed out a photograph of Field Marshal Montgomery, standing at the entrance clad in beret and trench coat, looking thoroughly lost. Deserted, rather.

Strategically positioned midway up the Mälselva River, our lodgings were where the best fly water starts. And the next day we were to fish one of the best of the five beats where the hotel can arrange fishing. Last year a sixty-pounder had been taken there. Apparently, the water level dropped when it was scooped out – in a net large enough to park your car in.

On the Nymo beat, Colin started proceedings the way we all wanted to start proceedings. He hooked into a salmon as silver as his hip flask, which was quickly whipped out when our guide, Bjorn Nilsen, declared it to be just under thirty pounds. We were so delighted for him, as you can imagine, quickly scurrying off to tie on exactly the same fly that had taken his fish, whipping the surface of our respective beats to foam. And imagine how doubly delighted we all were when he got a picture of himself and his beloved salmon on the front page of the local newspaper the next day!

The journey north to Roar Olsen's Reisastua Lodge – with access to nineteen 'zones' on the River Reisa – takes you up the coast, snaking along fjords; mirrors in the calm and sunlight. Our transport – a school bus affair – was a lesson. We quickly learned just how much our legs had grown since we last travelled in one.

The Reisastua is situated on the banks of the Reisa River that weaves sixty-five miles through the wild and untouched nature of the Reisa Valley.

When you first step into the lodge, you think you've just walked into a zoo and turn around and walk out again. Until, that is, you discover that the vast array of animal life chilling out by the window, on the floor and halfway up the walls, is all stuffed. (The brown bear that looked like it had never flossed made me jump every time I entered the room.) The sign by the rug saying, 'Please do not walk on the Polar Bear' was to be a sign of colder things to come.

Over dinner on our first evening, we heard how world-class Spey caster, teacher and rod designer Scott Mackenzie – who had visited the lodge the week before – had been yanked head first into the pool by a salmon of 'inestimable size' when his reel overran and seized up.

The river was hot, hot, hot.

But that night temperatures plummeted – and stayed plummeted. From between 12 and 14° C – temperatures that make Reisa salmon want to dine out ferociously – to 8° C, which makes them consider anorexia a good idea. The chances of hooking into one of the several thirty-pounders that had been taken the week before melted away, like an ice cube.

However, that day many prospective 'Ones' were seen, turned, moved, rolled, teased, annoyed and tormented. Hooks acting more like toothpicks than clamping irons. John took a handsome grilse which spun up in the air, landing back down in the drink with such a crash it cleared the surrounding mountainsides of nibbling reindeer.

But the Reisastua allowed us to discover what those thirty-pounders grassed the week before had enjoyed grazing on. A vast array of flies was laid out on the table and discussed at incredible length, which some of them incredibly were.

The one most likely to catch The One, we decided, had to be at least four inches long, incorporating black and blue.

We arrived at the Lakselva at nightfall.

Back in that school bus, we'd talked 'tackle' all the way north to the Alta and beyond into the wildlands of Finnmark. This time it was me talking about The One. What other rod, I asked Max, other than a salmon rod, could boast of having the all-important, unique, indispensable, brand-separating 'One' added to it?

I was talking about The Sage, fifteen foot 'One' inch, lent to me by my good mate Steve Edge for the trip. This was 'The One' for me, apparently, although the feeling wasn't always mutual. It can't have been fun for the Sage to have a student at the command-end. Indeed, as we made our way across the narrow bridge to the woodland leading to the Kairanen beat – recommended to us by hawk-eyed river manager Egil Liberg – David confessed that watching me cast a salmon fly was like peering into the window of a washing machine. I couldn't argue, of course. This is what friends are for.

But when a temporary, short-lived morning mist caused by the spray and froth of my first cast eventually cleared, I was able to see the run I had just cast into. The tip of my line jarred and dipped. A silvery grilse had snatched my Black and Blue Sunray – in a pool David had pulled his fly out of five minutes earlier.

Of course, I thanked David for 'gingering' up the run. He accepted this graciously, whereupon he came up behind me and reaped the rewards of my tactical gingering, 'tailing out a tide-bright, sea-liced twenty-four-pound beauty'.

Now that's what friends are for.

~

After six days' fishing – with the possibility of fishing twenty-four hours of those days – every Spey-casting sinew of my body had surrendered. This was the second week of July. Sea trout don't normally enter the system until August. All the same, I'd packed a nine-foot seven-weight, so I put The One-inch rod aside and spent my last morning fishing the one rod I knew how to cast. I decided to riffle-hitch a small bit of Biro tube with some tail of stoat wrapped round the neck – my Riffler – to see if it could change my fortunes.

Finding a smooth run requiring only short roll casts to get the fly to where you needed to get it, a ceremony of various flies followed. During this time, a fish turned twice at the end of the run and my instincts changed.

No longer was I just thwacking out some monstrous make-believe into blank water, taking two steps down and repeating the process. I was now happily back in 'trout fisherman mode'. All good and proper, save for one thing. What if I got a fresh-run thirty-pounder on the end of my toothpick?

My bit of Biro got no reaction. Neither did a Sun Ray riffled across the surface. I tried a slightly larger Riffler. Then I tied on a small Stoat Tail on a double, set at an angle with a Portland hitch. I even lined up a Green Machine. But, first, I wound on a Jambo. A sea trout surface lure I'd skidded across the top of the River Towi at Abercothi one summer night last season. 'Do interesting things and interesting things happen to you,' I thought to myself.

By now, anyone with lesser determination and more sense would have backed off and rested the pool. Bombed out and bewildered, any salmon still lying there with fins folded over the top of its head must surely have been considering ways of evacuating the pool to escape the blitzkrieg. Attached to my missile was not an option.

Whether it was fear, frustration or fury, as my Jambo skated out of the pool and across the golden gravels of the shallows, a sinister inky black outline of a salmon came out after it like an Underground train out of a dark tunnel. And it kept on coming. Lifting slightly, its belly all but squeaking on the gravels, it took, turned and tore off.

Satellite silver, decorated with a rash of long-tailed sea lice, it required the combination of the many skills of David, Colin, Max and John to

land my fish, later estimated to be near enough to thirty pounds for me
– and my rod, thank you very much. 'The One', I conceded. Thanks to
'The Many'.

Just as there's more to fishing than catching fish, there's more to Norway
than catching salmon. There's grayling.

Normally, fishing lodges leave forms in your bedroom for you to fill
in, asking you to comment on your stay. The food, facilities, you know
the sort of thing. But there's one question no lodge ever asks: What
would the resident fish say if they were asked to comment on the river
the lodge takes you to?

Don't laugh. I know a lodge that did exactly that. And here's the
remarkable fact. The fish enjoyed their stay so much they couldn't wait
to come back.

The Glomma Grayling Lodge is situated on the banks of the River
Glomma. On the Kvennan beat at Tynset, near Telneset, a three-hour
drive north of Oslo; or two and a half hours south of Trondheim.

Three hundred and fifty miles long, the Glomma – or Glåma,
meaning 'thunder' – is the largest river in Norway. Its drainage basin
covers over ten per cent of Norway, all in the southern part.

Quite remarkably, apart from the occasional trout – and burbot
which find their way up there (the locals go after them with clubs
in the winter, stunning the ones they find lying under the ice)
– the river is populated almost exclusively by some of the largest
grayling in Europe. Perhaps the world. Grayling over twenty inches
(fifty centimetres) are there to be caught. Weight? Well, a twenty-
inch bonefish weighs four pounds. But grayling in the food-rich
Glomma can grow from one and a half to three inches (four to eight
centimetres) a year and specimens of up to two feet (sixty centimetres)
are taken every season. Not surprisingly, this is where the Norwegian
record was winched in.

For this reason, the Glomma Grayling Lodge is one of the most exclusive destinations in Europe. And not just for the flyfisherman.

Just recently, in order to assess the migration patterns of the massive grayling population and the general condition of the stretch of river in front of the lodge, Børre Dervo of the Norwegian Institute for Nature Research (NINA), which researches the behaviour patterns of wildlife in the area, and river keeper Hein van Aar radio-tagged a hundred and sixty grayling and released them twenty-five miles (forty kilometres) downstream. In three days, they had returned. Forms filled in, comments made, radios bleeping; happy to be back.

And the fishermen? Will they want to come back? Well, allow me to bleep for myself.

It was late August. I was picked up at Oslo airport by Barry Ord Clarke, one of Europe's most skilled flytyers and photographer supreme. Married to a Norwegian girl, he's lived in Norway for over twenty years in an area stiff with rivers, lakes and seashores. He needs only to cast out of the bathroom window to hook some fish or other.

The lodge is a converted farmhouse, a timber-framed, wood-panelled building with accompanying outbuildings only a minute's walk from the river through a field of lush grass. The main building accommodates up to twenty people, but Barry and I had rooms to ourselves, with en suite bathrooms. A cook can be provided, but Barry wasted no time revealing another of his many talents. That night, Ole Bjerke, who had organized the trip, and I tucked into Barry's Bang-Bang Chicken while Gudmund Nygaard of Fishspot banged on about the fishing he'd arranged for us. A noisy affair.

Within minutes of getting to know Gudmund, you wish there were more people in the world like him. An angling action man, he was once the Fisheries Manager of the Lakselva, one of Norway's finest arctic salmon rivers.

He's the man who started Fishspot, dedicated to the preservation and protection of the fishing between Oslo and Trondheim. Gudmund calls his crusade 'destruction management'. His mission was to open up unique, well-managed fly-only grayling zones in the area. 'Fishspot countries', they're called locally. Here rod numbers are restricted and the beats are fiercely policed so flyfishers can expect some of the highest-quality grayling fishing in Europe.

With six miles (ten kilometres) of fly-only, catch and release, easy to wade 'n' walk river to roam around (no boats allowed) – with a real chance of catching a nuclear-powered grayling of a lifetime – it's no wonder the Lodge and the Kvennan beat is the jewel in the crown of the Glomma. Once patrolled by G. E. M. Skues so many years ago, today this flyfisherman's paradise still attracts some of the finest flyfishermen and flytyers around.

That night, Marc Petitjean arrived.

In August the air is chilly at the beginning and end of the day. But daytime temperatures average between to 16 to 22°C. On our first day, we had planned walking down to the river before breakfast. But at 6 a.m., the mist was porridge thick and I decided to check out what fly-life I could expect to see.

Hatches are profuse on the Glomma. Pale Wateries and Small Dark Olives head the list at this time, padded out with Blue-winged Olives and maybe a last showing of yellow May Duns. Needle flies are a-plenty, with wind-blown crane flies and Hawthorns (they make a late appearance in Norway) and Medium Sedges in the evening.

Chironomids are abundant all season and I suspect they constitute the bulk of the grayling's diet, in pupa form.

The most-used fishing technique is the dry fly. But Gudmund advised us to go deep with heavy nymphs and strike indicators. Or with Czech nymphing techniques in the deeper runs and pools. Regulars fish nine-foot rods with floating three- to five-weight lines. The river can be 170 yards (160 metres) wide, the depth ranging from one to fifteen feet (half to five metres). If you want the freedom to roam up, down and across the river – and many do – bring a wading staff.

Barry had packed tiny dries, #18s to 22s. When Marc lifted the flap on his famous Petitjean waistcoat and flipped open one of the fly boxes that he slid out like drawers, the sight of so many cul de canard patterns, in all different sizes, colours and designs, had my glasses steaming up and my eyes popping out. In comparison, my fly box is an eye-rolling, shoulder-sagging affair.

The mist de-porridged after breakfast. Marc and Barry waded halfway across the river in front of the lodge to where the river splits in two and nudges round an island. The nearside split runs deep and fast. Marc opted to take his fully-stocked waistcoat – literally, his chest of drawers – across to the far split where the water shallows over crisp gravels.

Taking it steady my first morning, I decided to sit quietly upriver just below a bend, eagle-eyeing a deep-blue run of about a hundred yards that rubbed shoulders with a high bank. Here's where I'd be waiting to be fed, were I a grayling.

Back for coffee in the midday sun outside the lodge, we regrouped. Marc had taken thirty. I had taken, well, none. I hadn't cast a fly. I had sat there waiting for a rise that never came, as is my chalkstream flyfisherman way. I was soon to learn that on the Glomma, only one thing is more critical than the fly you have on the end of your line: this is to have it on the water.

Back on my bend, I fished one of Marc's small cul de canard olives, indiscriminately. Without cause, rhyme or reason. No sooner had the fly landed in the water than a grayling had it. 'Rising to the occasion'. The occasion being nothing more than my fly's arrival. So obliging, those Glomma grayling.

But not so when the hatch started in earnest just after lunch. A dragged dry is shunned. Patterns designed to be more in − rather than parading royally outside the surface − are accepted more freely. The reason why Marc's soft-hackled, surface-hugging patterns proved to be so effective.

I asked him about his C de C patterns and the extraordinary revolution he had started. The minimum materials, the minimal tying movements required and the magical tools Marc designed in order to tie them. His Magic Tool for mixing different feathers, his easy-to-load bobbin, his hackle pliers that look like a Japanese *nunchaku* chain weapon designed to grip up to three feathers at a time, and his Swiss Vice that allows for highly flexible extension arm positions. Finally his range of high-quality, hand-selected C de C feathers in sixteen shades.

These cul de canard feathers are found just a little north of a duck's arse. *Sur la face dorsale de croupion* − at the base of the tail feathers. Here lies the Texas of preening oils: the uropygial gland, surrounded by a dozen or so downy feathers of a surprising lightness that float better than any other. The reason for this is self-evident. Ask any duck that forgot to preen itself one morning − and sank. And so the same works for a dry fly tied using them.

Because they are 'so alive they jump out of the box and find themselves up a tree', Marc tells you that his flies shouldn't take more than three minutes to tie. His supply of feathers comes from farms in France and Hungary where he has special on-site 'pluckers' standing in the production line selecting and collecting feathers just the right size and quality. On average, a duck provides twenty or thirty of the larger feathers Marc believes make a better fly. Tied in Switzerland, mainly by women, between two and three hundred thousand flies are created every year. Any particular duck? 'The Rouen duck is best for larger feathers,' Marc will tell you.

Marc was philosophical when I asked him if anyone had ever tried to steal his ideas or the designs of his Magic tools. He reminded me of an old Indian saying: *Always sit downstream of your enemies on the Ganges. Wait for their ashes to drift by*.

Mark adds, 'And while you're waiting, do some fishing.'

The prime season on the Glomma starts at the end of may with the early hatches of mayflies: Large Dark Olives, Iron Blues and the slightly larger Claret and Sepia Duns. Dark stone flies also appear at this time, best tied on #10 and #12 hooks. Caddis hatches begin at this time also and continue into the autumn until the snow arrives when you can expect a second generation of mayflies. Autumn fishing starts in September when the mornings are crisp, the water crystal clear and the colours kaleidoscopic.

The stone road bridge at Telnaset is a place for dreamers. The water is crystal clear. To see grayling of a lifetime, just poke your head over, if you can stand it.

Just below this bridge, the river turns a bend and widens before another island splits the flow in two. The shallower water is on the other side of the river, so we waded across to fish the deeper, faster-flowing water that tumbles over a natural weir just above the island.

Marc handed me one of his parachute flies with a Coq de Leon hackle fibre tail, an olive C de C body, a pink 'post' wing and a light grey C de C thorax doubling as a hackle.

In the rush of water, it rode the waves like a Californian surfer, soon disappearing as grayling after grayling picked it out from a hatch of tiny olives too small to spot on the cartwheel of water they were riding.

Later that afternoon, when the hatch died down, Marc handed me a caddis pattern he had tied using just three C de C feathers, thread and a hook. I fished this in a slick of slack water that slid off the back of the island.

Earlier, Gudmund had taken a grayling of over seventeen inches (forty-five centimetres) from there on the same fly. I had to make do with one at fifteen inches (thirty-eight centimetres) and another at sixteen (forty centimetres). Both over three pounds.

I was curious to know why Marc had picked out these two flies in particular from the huge selection he had boxed away in his dresser.

'They catch fish,' he told me. 'I want you to know these flies so you can use them on that chalkstream you fish.'

'But you showed me how to tie them last night,' I said.

'Yes, but that was after a very fine dinner. You'll have forgotten everything,' Marc said.

I was confused.

'With these flies, you can see how to tie them when you're sober.'

I was intrigued.

'. . . On YouTube.'

How to tie these two patterns might be on YouTube, but there were certainly no flies on Monsieur Petitjean. Having shared many a towels-off sauna with him before we departed, Barry, Ole and I can vouch for that.

EIGHT

Cuba:
Las Islas De Los Jardines De La Reina

Wishbone Worm

Hook and Body: No. 4–6 Gold
Thread: Yellow
Eye: Bead chain. Metal or plastic, to desired weight
Head: Epoxy
Wing: two strands of Krystal Flash

A Bone in the Bush

THESE DAYS, SUPERMARKETS HAVE IN-STORE bakeries. The smell of freshly baked bread makes people hungry and this encourages them to buy food. In some fishing stores they have videos playing all day. Why not the smell of fresh pine where they lean their double-handed salmon rods; salty aromas in the sea tackle section; meadow flowers near the trout fly cabinets? For me the smell of coconut in the saltwater flyfishing area inhabited by the Abels, the Billy Pates, the Turissics, the Sages, Loomises and the Crazy Charlies would get me putting my hand in my pocket. For, every time I smell coconut, I think of Cuba.

But it wasn't coconuts, videos, or a deep-down urge to salsa that inspired me to take my very first trip to Cuba; it was a bus. The number 9 Roadster that I hopped onto outside Waterstones in Piccadilly. It was a bus that dumped me in Havana.

It was at this bus stop where I ran into David Profumo, waiting for the same bus as me, on the way to have his hair cut. In the time it took us to get to Knightsbridge, he had sold me the idea of joining him on a trip to Los Jardines de la Reina off the south coast of Cuba.

In one short bus journey to his hairdresser, he had me by the short and curlies.

The sustained high-pitch note, like the crackling of a faulty electric fire element, was the sound of the air overheating, melting my earwax to the consistency of pure alcohol. A splash and a thrash from the direction of the mangroves on the far side of the sandy drop-off we were patrolling broke the infernal hum.

''Cuda,' I said, in a way that was neither a statement nor a question. I didn't really know, but wanted to.

'Tuberon,' Ramon breathed back in his characteristic hushed whisper, like a wave rolling under his twelve-foot blue and white skiff, as he poled in the direction of the commotion that, he confirmed, was made by a shark.

Upfront on the stern, I was standing motionless and barefoot, the midday sun hot on my heels and the tops of my feet. Quartering the

water, and then studying every inch of it from a fifty-yard distance, then close to, I was sorting fingers of weed from fin shapes, dark arms of coral from shadowy bonefish outlines. My eyes were popping.

Ramon pushed the bamboo pole into the marl to hold it in position. His eyes were fixed on something under the mangroves. Folding away the ripples, pulling back the curtains of reflected light, I followed his line of vision.

''Cuda . . .?' I whispered again, with even less confidence this time. But Ramon was in no doubt.

'*Sábalo*! Kwik! Kwik!'

I was not prepared for a tarpon. I only had my seven-weight bonefish rod with a fifteen pound tippet. Looping on a shop-bought shock tippet of eighty pounds that I keep in my bumbag, I attached to this the largest fly in my box – a deer-hair crab pattern – hoping my rod would have the spine to deliver this heavyweight item, with dumb-bell eyes the weight of shot-puts, to the sleepy tarpon sunning itself in the shade.

If nothing else, it would wake it up when it hit the water.

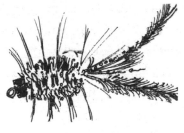

Deer-hair crab

My cast was awkward. The heavy-eyed crab made the sound of a Revenue and Customs spotter plane as it flew backwards and forwards over the skiff, eventually dive-bombing the mangroves. The splash was guaranteed to spook every bonefish from here to Havana. However, it relayed quite a different message to the tarpon lying three yards from where it crash-landed – and to a second, even larger, tarpon that I had not spotted, which materialized out of the mangroves to join in the high-speed chase to snaffle it. It signalled, 'Grub up.'

No starters ordered. The race began for the main course: crab *au gratin*.

The bigger of the two tarpon reached the table first, its mouth opening up like a cupboard door, sucking in the crab with a gallon of seawater. My left hand swung down, pulling my rod back to set the hook.

Whatever I had set into, to begin with, it didn't feel fishy. It felt architectural, huge and monumental. Bricks and mortar moving slowly in my direction, thankfully, and not back into the bushes.

The tarpon had bitten into steel and was well on. Throwing itself into the air to prove the point, it spewed out gillsful of water as it rose. As I bowed my rod tip to match the leap, the crab remained securely claw-pinched to the prehistoric monster's aluminium inner cheek. I slipped it out twenty minutes later, at the side of the skiff. My crab had done the trick and my rod hadn't snapped. Not for the first time during my stay on the *Tortuga* I'd been caught off guard. At the *Tortuga* you never know what's going to happen next.

'Tortuga' means 'turtle' in Spanish. A good name for the flat-topped, shell-like houseboat bobbing gently in a quiet corner of a deep-water lagoon tucked away privately in Los Jardines de la Reina, an archipelago made up of hundreds of tiny islands and cays – some miles long, others yards – a five-hour boat ride from Jucaro, which is a small port on Cuba's southern coast.

Here, nestled between mangroves, our small fishing party was to be marooned for six days in a maritime national park with fish of every imaginable species: wahoo, dorado, barracuda, shark, grouper, jacks of all shapes and sizes and, of course, tarpon, permit and bonefish. Each and every one of them protected from fishing vessels by something much more powerful and permanent than some decree invented by local

protectionist fishermen. Because Fidel said so. No fishing was allowed, except by the half-dozen staying in the houseboat.

The next day, in broad daylight, those 'shapes in the night' that the guide, David and I had collectively pulled out of the blackness in one fumbling, frenzied, midnight hour – on fly, then later on shrimp – were on display in the kitchen: the snapper and a grouper over ten pounds in weight. They were all to appear again that evening, restyled. Sushi'd or roasted with olives and dried tomatoes, on our dinner table.

As the days went on, the *Tortuga*'s position and her fish continued to demonstrate her uniqueness as a saltwater fishing location – in all manner of different ways. Where exactly did David's huge permit appear from? Compass hands had a habit of unscrewing, as we tried to figure out one cay from another. And that tuna that had appeared out of the sea from beneath a cloud of gulls; below them, the jaws of a sinister whale shark, twice the length of our skiff, that had sulked beneath us in a serene, single-minded way, filled with serious intentions towards the plankton it was stalking – and, fortunately, not us.

So, with such variety, what tackle? For Señor Sábalo, go light; go simple. Although news got back to us that a tarpon of well over a hundred pounds was boated shortly after we left, a ten-weight rod for permit and jacks can double as a tarpon pole, but only just. A twelve-weight is recommended.

I fish #2/0 and 3/0 circle hooks, but many experienced tarpon fly-rodders go for smaller sized hooks. They say the bigger the hook the easier it is for a tarpon to 'work' the hook out of its mouth.

But don't always follow the crowd when it comes to choice of fly, and fish standard long-nosed style, with a bunch of carnival-coloured feathers or fur sticking out over the hook bend at the back of the fly. Serve them something they would buy in a supermarket – a crab. And why not the same crab that you might chuck at a permit? The Chernobyl Crab, an easy-to-tie pattern – if, that is, you can spin deer hair Muddler Minnow-style – is worth considering. If it doesn't take, it's your presentation; or else it's time for a long-nosed attack.

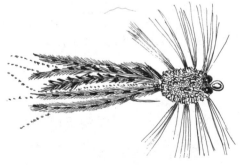

Chernobyl Crab

For Señor Macabi, your other rod should be a #7 or eight-weight, with a floating line. Fly selection is something else that doesn't require you to go overboard; whether you stay stern-bound, or wade.

The bonefish on the flats tend to be cautious and scary, rather than carefree and scatty. The water they slide in and out of tends to

be thin and shallow. Tailing bonefish are plentiful in the bays and
narrows between the mangroves at low tide. For this reason, lightly
weighted flies are recommended. A handful of non-weighted, plastic-
eyed shrimp patterns is worth consideration, although I confess that
I found myself opting for patterns with the lightest of silver or gold
bead-chain eyes.

Shop-bought Ultra Shrimps and Pop's Bitters fished well
for David, but I followed my normal flytying philosophy, one
I adopt wherever I am: the less you tie on a hook, the less the fish can
find.

My adaptation of a Gorell's Shrimp, a hugely underrated fly designed
with high chalkstream-imitation principles, rather than flats ones, works
well. It looks so much like a shrimp, I can taste the mayonnaise. And,
like a shrimp, with little bulk it lets light shine through it. It slips under
the water rather than dives into it. It glides downwards, rather than
sinks.

But if I had to fish one fly for bonefish – and one fly only – let me tell
you about the fly I'd use – and why I use it.

They say the bonefish is the 'ghost of the flats'. If you're a poet, that
is. If you're a dyed-in-factor-fifty flats fisher, you see Señor Macabi
differently: 'Dustbin of the flats' comes to mind, for no fish is more
opportunistic. A belly-rumbling bone, under stiff competition from its
other mates in the marauding pod, will gobble down anything that's
put in front of it, if it can get there first; if the flat-footed, flat-creeping
flyfisher presents his imitation correctly; and if the fly on the end of
his hard nylon tippet has been designed to help him execute perfect
presentation.

So, what's on the macabi menu?

Well, there's snapping shrimp, mantis shrimp, brown shrimp and white shrimp, for starters. Then there are mud crabs, green reef crabs, cusks, clams and *mojarras* (baitfish). Is that it?

Peek into any salter's fly box and it screams out, yes, that's it! But look in mine and you'll see we've left one out. This is a food form that is often buried deep, but not in 99 per cent of flats flyfishers' fly boxes. Yet in Florida, Mexico, the Christmas Isles and now in Cuba, when I show my box to my guide, asking his advice, my imitation of this food form is the one they always pick out, hold to the sun and say, 'Ahh!' Or even, 'Whoah!' (And my guides aren't easily excited. Not even at the price I cough up to hire them.)

This fly is my Wishbone Worm, tied on a golden or red hook, with bead chain behind the eye, with two strands of Krystal Flash tied in, the lot covered in epoxy.

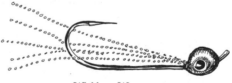

Wishbone Worm

Forget all the techie-talk about sea worms hatching at new and full moon tides. Certainly, spring to early summer is spawning time for the *nereis* and *palolo* worms. But this is like saying you only see earthworms after a shower of rain. Bung a worm in front of a fish any time, and he'll grab it: same with mad, munching Mr Macabi.

It's true that, during times when worms haunt the warm water flats in thick swarms, fishing can be tough. For this reason, the best time to fish them is when there's not a worm in sight. I also have another theory: my Wishbone Worm is just a great general bonefish pattern because the design concentrates on the most important feature of any saltwater pattern: weight. The wondrous, weighty worm allows you to vary the sinking rate, by adding or subtracting the bead chain or dumb-bell content – and the amount of the epoxy. Just as with shot on a coarse fisherman's line, you can play all sorts of games.

This gives you complete control of your fly, getting you to just the right depth, in just the right time. When worked skilfully with hand and rod tip, my worm imitates just about any mouth-sized morsel; the side-winding shrimp, the crawling crab, the meteoric *mojarra* and, well, the wandering worm.

The design gives the gum-rubbing bone nothing to question. Reasons for this? It's not overdressed. It is all weight – and movement. The colour, largely gold or red (worms tend to be this colour, although my favourite colour is gold), is all in the hook. A few Krystal Flash stems, a bit of epoxy and that's all. And because of its slimline shape, it cuts, rather than scary-splashes, its way down from surface to dinner table.

Lastly, you can whip up my worm in seconds. The longest part is waiting five minutes for the epoxy head to harden.

It's the Sawyer nymph of the salt, frankly. So, how about hook size? Saltwater fly-rodders tend to use hooks that are too big, which hit the water hard and make penetration into a bony bonefish mouth even harder. They also use hooks that are too small. Large bones scream off with a #6 or #8 and rip free after a few yards as they offer little purchase. So, use nothing smaller than a #4. And nothing larger.

Ramon and I were not after bonefish when I took my last bone of that trip.

After lunch, we had set out in search of permit reported to have been haunting some deep blue water an hour's ride from the houseboat. Ramon was on to them like a ferret on a rabbit. I threw

crab after crab, but my luck was not as great as David's; he had managed to boat one. That afternoon, at least, the elusive permit remained elusive.

Wanting to change location, I concocted a pile of broken Spanish to let Ramon know my intentions.

'*Vamos a movar al otro bajo*,' or 'Let's move to another flat, matey,' I told him.

Now *bajo* is a funny word. You must be careful when you say it, so that it doesn't sound like *baño*, which means something else entirely. Pronounced one way it means 'flat'. The other way it means 'bathroom'. I couldn't guarantee my pronunciation, but on receipt of this poorly rehearsed command, Ramon sped off in the direction of the flats, not back to the boat or the nearest bush, so I must have got it right.

It had been a long, slow, burning day. The tide slid out, pulling the bedcover off a tempting flat, three flats removed from the houseboat. A silver flashbulb glinted in the distance and Ramon swerved the boat in the direction of a shoal of tailing bones. To the theme tune from *The Sweeney*, playing in my head, we embroidered our way through endless alleys of mangroves, across ankle-deep water, finally arriving in a small clearing. Ramon shut down the motor and pulled his pole out like a sword from its scabbard and thrust it onto the marl.

Hemmed in by clumps of mangroves, here the seawater formed streams, braids, avenues of water. You needed a street map to find your way about. On all sides, bonefish were appearing round corners, cruising like hooker-seeking pimps in a bad part of town on a Saturday night. It was on one of these street corners where I planted my Wishbone Worm, laying it seductively next to a mangrove stalk sticking out of the water like a lamp post, and there it lay, soliciting.

A bone coasted close by and I immediately lifted my worm and got her to flash a strand of one of her Krystal legs to the finny kerb-crawler. He fell for it, hook, line and – well, just hook and line. The bone pounced on my moll, sucking her in with one huge, wet, rubber-lipped kiss. Swooping my hand down with the line, once, twice, thrice, I pulled the hook home.

It set; and off set the bone with my hooker at top speed, heading not for the open water but for the thousand open doorways of the mangroves where, once inside, he bust down roots, spines, branches; in fact, everything that got in his way. I stood watching his progress, the tips of the terrorized mangroves indicating his movements.

Then he stopped as dead as dead. I thought he'd had a heart attack.

Ramon didn't wait to think or call an ambulance. He wasn't a-wondering, he was a-climbing. Knotting the skiff to a mangrove shoot, he swung into the bushes like a squirrel, disappearing as instantly as the bonefish had done, leaving me, rod in hand, holding a slack line tethered . . . to a forest.

I thought it better to stay on the boat. Nothing to do with the crocodiles in the swamp, you understand; just in case the bone broke out of the mangroves and hit the street again. Then the top part of Ramon appeared out of the leaves, holding a six-pound bone.

'*Aquí, señor!*' my scratched, bleeding guide said, pointing in the direction of the bone he held in one fist, handing it to me, still hooked.

'Where was he heading for?' I asked Ramon, relieved that I didn't have to wet my tippy-toes in its pursuit. Ramon took the opportunity to reveal that he could speak much better English than I could Spanish.

'I think he needed to go to the *bajo*.'

For the first three days at La Tortuga, I shared a skiff with a Canadian, the owner of an outdoor shop outside Toronto. Everybody in his party called him Fridge.

Why 'Fridge' I cannot tell because I never asked him. Contrary to his name, he was warm, friendly, great company on the boat, and when we were staked out in the Gulf of Mexico waiting for tarpon to appear in temperatures nearing 100° F, he always had a story to tell. And it was good to have a fridge aboard to cool you down, if only psychologically. Now, when we joined up with two skiffs for lunch on a small archipelago crawling with iguanas, you could tell Fridge was longing to break the ice with some tale or other. The opportunity arrived when we'd munched our way through sandwiches the size of *War and Peace* hardbacks and he turned down the offer of coffee, asking his guide for a beer.

'Coffee's just no good out of a flask. It has to be hot. Hot, hot, HOT,' he said, cueing in a story about when he'd gone exploring the Miramichi River with a friend, deep in the wild and wooded heart of New Brunswick.

'In the lodge where we stayed there was a sexy girl called Rita who did all the cooking, the cleaning and the waitress stuff. More than this, if you ordered breakfast in your room, Rita brought it up to you. Every day I had the same. A muffin and coffee. Rita just loved coffee and, if you offered, she'd stay for coffee and a chat.

'One morning I ordered breakfast, and when Rita brought it up, I said, "Hey, how about a little coffee?" She said, "Love to," and I locked the door. I didn't want the coffee to get cold.

'Just as I was about to dunk my muffin, there was a knock on the door. It was the lodge owner.

'"Is Rita in there?" he shouted.

'I panicked, but I had the answer. My friend was in the next room and there was an adjoining door. I knocked on the door and, when my friend opened up, I pushed Rita in, shut the door and let the lodge owner in. Looking around and seeing no Rita, he growled a little and left.

'When he'd gone, I tried to open the adjoining door, but it was locked and my friend wouldn't give me back my Rita. So I had another idea. I phoned downstairs and told the lodge owner that if he wanted to know where Rita was, she was next door in my friend's room.

'Minutes later there was a knock on my friend's door, the adjoining door opened up and Rita was thrown back. But this story has a sad ending.

'In the meantime my coffee got cold.'

Fridge left our lodge the next day, after breakfast. But before he did, there was a knock on my door and there he was. He wanted to say goodbye and handed me an enormous bush knife in a leather sheath.

'Hey, mate, it was fun. Every time you use this, you'll think of me.'

'Yes,' I said.

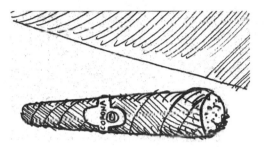

NINE

France

The Mole Fly

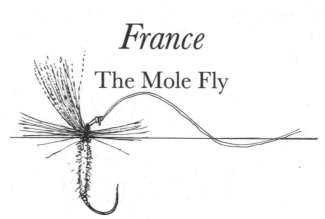

Hook: No. 16–14
Thread: Primrose Yellow
Wing: Teal breast feather fibres dyed grey
(Slope at 45 degrees over eye)
Hackle: Light grey cock hackle
(wind four turns over roots of wing)
Body: Hare ear fur lightly spangled with pale olive seal fur
(wind silk to bend and whip-finish at bend)

Flies that Feed Families

PEOPLE LOVE VISITING FRANCE, FOR ALL sorts of reasons.
Some love the Mediterranean, the sun and the beaches. Some love Paris, the galleries, the cafés and the shops in the Boulevard Saint-Germain. Others love French food, their wines and their cheeses.

I love their flies.

It's no secret that the French like eating – and not just frogs and snails. They eat trout. Fishing commercially for trout in rivers in France was still common practice until the sixties when a law banned the resale of wild salmonids. This coincided with the growth of trout farms providing low-cost rainbow trout for the pot and put the professional inland fishermen who harvested the stream and rivers for markets and restaurants out of business. It also said *adieu* to a generation of flyfishermen who discovered that the deadliest weapon of mass destruction was not the worm, the minnow, the net or the spear, it was the fly rod. These fishermen fed their families, not out of the fruits of their labours, but the fruits of their flies.

And it's these flies that I enjoy fishing most when I visit the Risle, Charentonne, Andelle, Crevon and Obiquet rivers in Normandy. Occasionally I also visit the Loue and the Doubs in the French Jura, on the other side of the Alps from Switzerland, the home and happy hunting ground of a doctor who lived in Besançon and who collected, collated and recorded these flies in a book entitled *Répertoire Des Mouches Artificielles Françaises.*

Jean Paul Pequegnot published this paperback bombshell privately, as a limited edition, in 1975. I have number 1435. Printed on blotting paper, it's the sort of book that, if you like to read before you go to sleep, requires you to take a knife to bed with you to cut the pages open.

Just as people can remember where they were when they first heard about John F. Kennedy's assassination, I remember exactly where I was when I first heard about a fly prescribed in the doctor's directory – the Cul de Canard, the 'duck's arse' – and the first time I fished it. And the very first fish I was to catch using it. Indeed, I can even tell you the exact date, and hour, give or take ten or twenty minutes.

And the river I caught it on: *l'Orbiquet.*

L'Orbiquet

Even before I had reached this stream on my first morning, things were definitely going downhill when the hire car rolled down a slope and ran over my guide's dog. It had been under the car, sleeping. How was I to know the mutt was there? It was instant death. More than this, I don't want to say. Other than that, for the rest of the day, my guide had little time for me, or anyone, or anything else for that matter. He was in mourning, so I was fending for myself.

Dogs have always bugged me when I'm fishing. They've kept me from places I would have gone and fished if there hadn't been a farm nearby, with a dog howling horrifics.

I can't handle them. But Vincent, my oldest friend and my guide on the second day, can.

Living in Paris, he has a small 'weekend' beat out in Normandy, the sort of chalkstream you imagine flows through heaven. Every ten yards is a new piece of water. There's a wide flat, about the width of a main road. There's a deep run on the far side of a meadow, where you mark a rising trout by how close it is to a cow. There's a deep black pool that runs below a mill. There's a fizzing riffle that sparkles like a necklace. There's a poplar tree for shade. But that morning Vincent had decided that we were to give this beat a rest and visit another stretch, an even more intimate stream, a short walk away. After a coffee.

A word about Vincent. Anything can happen when you set out for a day's fishing with him. Often I have seen him spend a day's fishing lying in the grass reading a book, or just sitting under a tree never even getting his rod out. His eating habits are just as strange. If he eats bread, he only eats the crust. He takes Ryvita biscuits in his pocket, which he nibbles when we eat in some of the most prestigious restaurants on the Rive Gauche. So, when he ordered coffee and a glass of Calvados with two lumps of sugar to dunk in it, as is the tradition, and slipped them in the top pocket of his shirt, I realized we were off for a long adventure and he might need the extra energy later on.

Over coffee, we talked about how much the Normandy streams had changed. In the main, they had been fished out. The contents of the streams taken out, taken home and eaten. Worse were the farmers: dairy and trout don't mix. Effluents from the many milk- and cheese-producing businesses up and down the river valleys were taking a heavy toll on the insect life of the rivers. But we were off to a more pleasant land, Vincent assured me, pointing to a clump of trees where he said the big fish lie.

My paced quickened . . . and then slowed as I started to hear horrific howlings being emitted from the farm we were approaching, which stood between the big trout and us.

It all happened so fast. I'd have missed it had I blinked. I didn't even have time to scream. A large shaggy dog appeared from nowhere. Travelling at great growling speed, it arrived ready-aerialized at knee level, heading straight for the first available fleshy object it could sink its teeth into which, it so happened, was Vincent.

Vincent clasped his heart. I thought he was about to have a cardiac arrest. Instead he held his hand out like a rugby player pushing off a tackle and the dog collapsed on the grass, a whimpering ball of fur. As it rolled onto its back, Vincent approached the hound, as if to administer the last rites. Instead he went further, and put what looked like his hand into the dog's mouth, its teeth gleaming in the bright Normandy summer afternoon sun.

It was then that I realized what the sugar in his top pocket was for – and that local knowledge isn't always a matter of knowing where the fish lie. It's knowing where the dogs are. And, more importantly, knowing how to make the fierce ones lie down.

The beat we were heading for was at the source of l'Orbiquet at La Folletière-Abenon, the banks ankle deep in buttercups. But we weren't the only people heading that way. A man came walking across the field in our direction dressed like a frogman, wearing black rubber tubing right up to his chin. He was accompanied by my friend Pierre Affre, *pêcheur extraordinaire*, Charles Ritz's casting protégé, who had just come back from fishing some weird fish in Somalia, or hooking into monster tarpon in a faraway place where nobody had ever caught a tarpon before. At least, not on a fly. Nick Lyons, who first introduced me to Pierre, once told me that he didn't know whether to envy or feel sorry for him. He still doesn't. And neither do I. And neither do dozens of other people.

Pierre and Frogman joined us to go and check out the beat we had all planned to fish. We inspected it, grunted a little and nodded to one another, agreeing that it would do just fine. By now, though, it was lunchtime and we had booked a table at L'Auberge de la Truite nearby, where we'd had coffee earlier, with its anaesthetizing, dog-snuffing apple brandy. At lunch, we drank a bottle of Margaux, a Chateau Palmer. We spent some time discussing whether the chateau on the label was Buckingham Palace.

Earlier that morning, before we met up, Pierre had had good fishing further downstream. I asked him what he had been catching his fish on.

'What I always use. Ze only fly I ever use!' he told me. 'Ze Cul de Canard.'

Cul de Canard

After lunch, Frogman slept, Vincent read his book and Pierre went back to Paris. I had the short beat below the source to myself. Despite the wine, I managed to catch seven trout that afternoon. All on the Cul de Canard. A Cul de Canard tied in the simplest of ways.

The hook is a #14–18, normally barbless. Behind the eye, I tie in a length of primrose yellow silk which, tied along the hook, is the body. Then, also behind the eye, I tie in a light grey duck down feather, tip first. I wind this away from the eye, securing and clipping off the butt. With thumb and forefinger, I pull the hackle forward and wind over the roots so the hackle slopes slightly forward. Finally, I wind the thread to the bend, whip-finish and varnish.

If you were to ask me what fly I'd choose if I was only allowed to fish one fly for wild trout, I would tell you the Cul de Canard. These days, this fly is no longer buried away on pages 30 to 31 of Pequegnot's rough-paged *Répertoire*. Hardly a flyfishing magazine hits the newsstands without mentioning a new 'C de C' pattern, or an adaptation. It's one of flyfishing's great success stories. So, is there a reason for this?

When it comes to dynamism and originality in flyfishing products, forget about rods, reels, lines and action wear. Cast away brands such as Orvis, Hardy, Sage and Simms. One name heads the list. That name is Petitjean: Marc Petitjean of Petitjean Fishing Equipment SA. The man who built a business round a duck's arse.

The first writings about the C de C came from the quack himself, Dr

Pequegnot, who alerted the flyfishing world to strange happenings that had been going on in the twenties, in the town of Vallorbe in the Swiss section of the Jura. In Franche-Comte, where a fly with a duck down hackle called the *Mouche de Vallorbe* – or the *Cul de Canard* – was being used to super-effect by local flyfishermen. Petitjean heard about this and for years now, as one of the true originators and inventive flytyers of a generation, he has been turning ducks' rears head over heels. The result: midge pupae, Mayfly nymphs, shrimps, spinners – even a hunchbacked hawthorn incorporating these feathers.

I was once the proud owner of a set of Marc's original flies in a presentation case, his name engraved on the lid. I never wasted them on trout, much preferring to use them to make people gloat. They were exquisite. Dick Talleur, the American flytyer, once visited me at my house by the River Kennet and I pulled out the box. Flicking back the lid, I presented him with . . . a row of bare hooks. A moth had dined out royally.

Today, feathers are dyed in all sorts of colours using a secret dyeing process. A special floatant is available – just for duck down.

But Petitjean wasn't the first there with a production line. Aimé Devaux, France's most eminent commercial flytyer, had a Cul de Canard on his lists. Indeed he perfected an entire series of flies 'in which the head hackle is duck down and the wings cock-hackle points'. Other famous French anglers were at it, too. Henri Bresson 'satisfied himself with duck down fibres slanted back a little', with no tails. While Pequegnot opted for a 'head hackle of duck down supported by a gray cock hackle palmered'.

So, which version fills that fly patch of mine?

As prescribed earlier, I stay with the pattern Pierre introduced me to that lunchtime in L'Auberge de la Truite. The style he fished when Petitjean was knee-high to a duck's egg. With it, he has 'performed miracles on catch-and-release waters', so writes Datus Proper in the introduction to the 1987 English translation of Pequegnot's tome, published by Nick Lyons in New York.

I believe that simplicity in fly design can be hugely advantageous when you are up against wary wild trout. But, as with anything in design, this can go too far. Successful merchandizing depends on creating a problem, and then creating the solution. Whether or not there's really a problem to begin with. This is how I see the development of the Cul de Canard.

Whether you're a flytyer, a car company, a pharmaceutical laboratory or a soap powder manufacturer, design doesn't always make things better. Duck down has its uses: to make a soft, lightweight, semi-translucent dry fly that can be flick-dried. But when ducks' rumps become a commodity – and the circus comes to town – duck.

La Charentonne

The next day we stopped to buy a bottle of cider in Louviers. That done, Vincent and I headed off to one of his friend's beats on the Charentonne, on the outskirts of a small village called Serquigny, about four miles up from Aclou on the Risle, Charles Ritz's beat, which he called his 'jewel valley'.

We arrived to find two cars already parked on the track by the bridge. This was bad news as Vincent only has permission to fish one bank and a hundred yards of both banks below the bridge. The other bank was owned by a butcher from Rouen who, rather than fish the flies which André Ragot (of whom, more later) had proven to be the local WMD, preferred to exercise his right to fish by any method he chose. There he was, belly hanging over a barbed-wire fence, rod in hand, elbow resting on a post, dangling a line lazily in the water.

La Charentonne can be very slow and deep. Vincent told me there were really only four holding spots: the bridge at the top of the beat, an overhanging tree that marked the start of shared banks, a tree further down on our bank and a deep run by the island before the fast shallows. This was more like an orchard than a meadow; we were surrounded by pastoral bliss. A herd of brown and beige speckled cows grazed placidly, making a hissing sound as they idled past us through tissue-paper grass that was dry and filled with seeds, as if they were sponsored by the Normandy tourist board.

We were standing in a postcard.

Very soon I realized that no matter where I decided to fish, it wasn't going to be too long before the butcher and his friend appeared and slung a ledgered worm into the area I was fishing. I had caught two *vandoises* (dace) one after another and as a result they made sure I never left their sight. I couldn't get rid of them. They were like a fart in my chest waders.

I disappeared behind some bushes to try and lose them, crouching about as low as I could so they wouldn't see me. Just when I thought I was out of sight, a wiry-looking fisherman came up behind me with a fly rod stuffed down the back of his trousers, clutching a small spinning rod with a worm hanging from a hook.

'*Bonjour*,' I said in my very best English.

'*Bonjour*,' the fishing gladiator said in reply, ten octaves lower, lobbing the worm out into the pool in front of me. It landed with an authoritative splosh, making sure that even though I might not understand the French language, at least I would understand the French way of marking out one's *territoire*.

I returned to the stretch behind the bridge. But before I'd even cast a fly I heard a '*Plouf!*' under the trees on the far bank. It was a lead weight landing at the end of the short run behind me. The butcher had been waiting for me in the bushes.

By now, I had lost track of whose bank was whose.

That evening, the butcher, who rarely stayed later than five o'clock, was still there at nine, and so were his children. They had discovered the delight of tossing sticks and stones from the bridge. His friend at this point had been whipped into a hot, envious froth at the sight of my unexpected success with the *vandoises*. I had taken ten now, most of them from right under his nose and watchful eye.

I was just beginning to think of packing up when, at ten o'clock, the butcher, his children and his friend were herded into cars by their wives and carted off. At five past ten, Vincent and I had the beat to ourselves.

At half past ten, the river exploded. The water was covered in greengage-bodied Blue-winged olives, and the air filled with the sound of the nibbles and sucks of a thousand *vandoises*, *chevaines*, *gardons* and the occasional small *truite*, all merrily scooping up a soup of ephemerides in the half-light.

By now I was beginning to be able to tell the difference between rises made by a dace, a chub or a roach, even though they all seemed to be the same size. Now I was looking for a rise that was in some way different. Perhaps something larger and heavier, bearing in mind that if a big, old, supercautious trout dared poke its head out from some corner and blister the hot, dusky surface of the stream, the rise would be smaller, lighter and a lot less significant.

The sun dipped behind the trees on the other side of the river, frescoing the meadow behind me with shadows. Blue-winged olive duns were still lifting off the river in profusion. At the head of the deep run by the island a large wake unfurled before being dispersed by the current midstream. A single ring. One that rang alarm bells when I sensed that its tightness and economy had nothing to do with the flow of the river or the water conditions. This rise was a well-calculated event. One calculated to disguise the identity and the whereabouts of its originator.

An old wise trout had stuck its head above the parapet.

If, indeed, this was the trout I thought it might be, it was not going to want to allow too much of its anatomy to leave an element of which it was king. For this reason, I tied on a pattern designed to represent the Blue-winged olive in its semi-hatching form. Its half-in, half-out stage. Just as a sly old trout would like its nose to be when it lifts up to suck in its supper with the maximum ease and minimum commotion. As if through a straw.

I didn't grease the fly. I would only be allowed one, perhaps two, attempts and I preferred the fly to be more in than out of the water.

My first cast was about as accurate as a builder's estimate, landing in some low-hanging branches. I managed to pull it away without the line ruffling the surface. My second was a better effort. The fly fell softly just up from where I imagined the control centre of the circles to be – at the top end of the run where the water was at its blackest. It had landed just ahead of this black spot and was drifting past where I guessed the trout was lying.

Then I saw the single ring again and alarm bells started ringing. Instinctively, I struck.

To begin with, I thought I was back up in those branches, but the branches were making their way downstream. Then there was a fierce rush that stops a fisherman's heart.

By now it was nearly dark, and the first I saw of the fish I had on the end of my line was a flashing upward leap and a splash that lit up the darkness as if a can of brilliant white paint had dropped in front of me from a great height.

Playing a fish in darkness on a river that you don't know is one of the strangest things. You're not fishing, you're fumbling. Padding around in the blackness, making sure you don't disappear down a hole, walk into a tree or collide with a cow. The last thing you think about is whether or not the fish has an escape plan, ready prepared for such a day. A plan it rehearses before it decides that tonight is the night to go out and dine on surface fly.

Luckily, there were no holes, trees or cows and, if the trout had a plan, it had been poorly rehearsed. I pulled it up onto a mud flat I had been fishing from earlier in the day. I could see it was well over two pounds as I rolled it off the mud back into the river and watched it sink back down into the night. I thought how clever it had been to have avoided the ledgers, the spoons, the worms and the lip-hooked minnows. I thought how the French had ruined their fishing yet, in a paradoxical sort of way, they had made it better by making it so much more demanding. Thanks to a butcher (in every sense of the world) from Rouen.

The next day, we were rained off the river in the morning. We sat in the car for an hour listening to raindrops the size of gravel thud down on the roof of the car. I'd noticed that the weed was filled with fistfuls of shrimps with reddish orange front and back legs, so I sat in the car with my little collar box full of essential bits and pieces, tying one up. When the rain stopped and the wind dropped and it slowly began to brighten, I went to the bridge and lowered this leaded, red-legged crustacean down between the planks to a trout I had spotted the day before. One which the butcher hadn't been able to swim a worm down to. My shrimp had hardly hit the surface when it was gone, vanished into the black mouth of what looked like a sizeable trout. The thrashing on the surface brought Vincent to the bridge. When he saw the fish he ran to the car for his camera.

'You've caught the biggest goddam trout I've ever seen here,' he shouted with excitement.

It would have been my second trout from the Charentonne over two pounds, but with my friend suitably convinced and bearing witness to the fact that I had actually caught such a fish, rather than hauling it up through the planks and damaging both the trout and my rod, I let it drop off at the next mid-air thrash. Vincent had wanted to photograph it so he could show the butcher next time he stormed the beat.

I took a couple of *gardons* by the same method before lunch in a local *routier* in Serquigny. The *menu fixe* consisted of a pâté containing large slices of pickled onion and garlic cemented together into a nondescript meat, pork chops, potatoes, carrots and beans, a side salad, cheese and a bowl of cherries, washed down with beer, a bottle of wine, and to finish a coffee and a Calvados. This gave me plenty of time to tell Vincent all about the fly that had done me so well the evening before.

To do this, I took him back in time. Way, way back. To a long-gone time. To the origins of a fly which should never have gone anywhere and should be still around today. Digging deep into the soils of time, what did I find? I unearthed a fly called the Mole Fly.

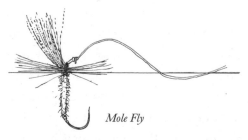

Mole Fly

Born on the River Mole in Surrey a misty century or so ago, the Mole Fly still has a place in my fly box today. It's a fly I cling to on account of its design. Or, rather, its seeming lack of it.

The creator of the Mole Fly (anon.) set out to do more than just develop a pattern that sat on the surface or sank beneath it. The design leaped over all the puffed-up theories of Frederic Halford and the droning minutiae of G. E. M. Skues and his politically correct damp nymphs. The Mole Fly broke the mould. It punched flytying into the modern world. A new world where artificials have to prove themselves. To do this, they need to answer tight and specific briefs. They are artificials *designed* to perform stunts that no fly has ever performed before.

Now long-forgotten, the Mole Fly doesn't imitate the natural upwing fly as it's either making its way to the surface or sitting on top of it, when escape is still a possibility. Rather it imitates the critical time when it is sitting trapped in the surface film and is totally powerless and vulnerable. When, midway in and midway out of its shuck, it is concentrating on escaping from itself – not from the trout hot on its heels.

This makes the Mole Fly one of the very first emerger patterns. In fact, I know of no predecessor. And in the thirty-odd years I have fished it, I have found no better emerger of the smaller upwing duns that satisfies the truly wild trout's pernickety palate, for the following reason.

Journalists say, 'First simplify, then exaggerate.' The creator of the Mole Fly must have been a journalist for its design is, above all, simplicity in extreme. Yet the way it sits in the water doesn't just graphically demonstrate that it is neither nymph nor fully hatched-out adult. It exaggerates it. There's no missing it. This is a fly that is hopelessly and unmistakably easy pickings.

When the Mole Fly hits the water, its lightly dressed, dampened body instantly penetrates the surface. This lightness prevents it dragging down the greased-up hackle and wing resting on the surface, suspending the body of the fly.

To tie the Mole Fly is simplicity itself. Tied with the minimum of materials and the fewest of movements, it is the least likely of all my patterns to put a wild trout down on account of a bulky over-emphasis on design. Like my Funneldun – and the Klinkhåmer – the Mole Fly is, or can be, a template; a design. The colours and the body and wing materials are up to you. The pattern here is for the Large Dark Olive.

The hook is a #14 (but go for a #16). Behind the eye, tie in a length of yellow silk. Tie in a bunch of teal breast feather fibres dyed grey and slope at forty-five degrees over the eye. Tie in a light grey cock hackle. Wind four turns over roots of wing and clip the butt. Now dub a mixture of hare ear fur lightly spangled with pale olive seal fur substitute onto silk and wind to bend. At the bend, whip-finish and varnish.

So, what happened to the Mole Fly?

No point looking under the bed, it split. It headed off to Normandy where the professional French flyfishermen of the day, as we know, are forever on the lookout for killer patterns.

They recognized the Mole Fly's killer qualities and developed their own version, notably the Pont Audemer (on page 87 of Pequegnot's *Répertoire*). As if to say 'hard cheese' to the English flyfishers who allowed their Mole Fly to tunnel under the Channel.

Although a slow-water pattern, the Mole Fly's floating abilities on fast-flowing rain-fed streams outstrip that of our latest, and not so interesting emerger, the Klinkhåmer, on account of the fact that the body hangs vertically, rather than sloping angularly, beneath the surface. A well-greased hackle collar and wing has it bobbing like a trotting float.

Its posture has further merit. Lying as it does on this collar of a hackle, the leader sticks up in the air, holding it clear of the water – and out of sight. But, more interestingly, with no tails – and with the increase in chironomids on our fast-stagnating streams – who's to say the Mole Fly is nothing more than a latter-day midge pattern?

So many great things. More than enough to have you saying to yourself that it was indeed a sad day when the Mole Fly got buried away.

And an even sadder day for that ravaged Charentonne trout, so close to retirement, that I had unearthed it.

L'Andelle

Before the arrival of carbon fibre, there was only one rod material for me. With my unbeaten record of breaking fly rods (if this was an Olympic event, I'd be up on that podium collecting a gold), cane was outside my price bracket. There was really only one material I could afford. This was glass fibre.

At that time, with my strike rate, I got to know every possible glass fibre rod brand and maker. After 'The Carrot' that Hoagy B. Carmichael Jnr fashioned me in glass, the other master at putting together the finest rod that you could lay your hands on (or stamp on – or slam shut in the car door, in my case) made of this marvellously inexpensive material was Serge Pestel, the author of *Héritage d'un Pêcheur à la Mouche* and a high-ranking official in the distinguished French flyfishing club TOS (Truite. Ombre. Saumon.), fly casting instructor (Saturdays at the Bois de Boulogne) and part-time assistant at the Au Coin de Pêche, 50 Avenue de Wagram in the 17th arrondissement, just down from the Arc de Triomphe.

Founded in 1927, Au Coin de Pêche was until recently the oldest fishing store in Paris, famously frequented by Charles Ritz and also Ernest Hemingway during his time in Paris. Sacha Tolstoï, the grandson of the author of *War and Peace*, Leo Tolstoï, was the *maître des lieux*. In its final years, Pierre and Vincent were regulars of this magnificent store, stacked high with tackle. If Aladdin had been a flyfisherman, this would have been his cave. With a life-sized swordfish adorning the facade, it wasn't hard to find. When it finally ceased to trade, the two framed decorative displays of flies, spinners, plugs and lures dating back to the twenties that had fronted the two counters of the shop sold for thousands of pounds each.

Every time I was in Paris, the three of us would all pay a visit. I have a photograph of us standing outside the store. Hooked to the collar of Vincent's sheepskin coat is a two-foot Rapala; Pierre Affre has a rubber squid a foot long stuck between his teeth and I have a glittering two-foot tuna teaser dangling from a pipe sticking out of my mouth. Sacha was an avid big-game fisherman. He '*saura vous conseiller sur le choix d'un leurre à marlin comme sur celui d'une mouche à truite*', so they said.

These were mad days in Paris, spent itching to crash on out to Normandy and fish the Mayfly. Serge was a flyfisherman and shared our flyfishing madness. And it was Serge who first mentioned the name of André Ragot.

André who?

Just after the Second World War, André Ragot and a group of other anglers who fished the Normandy rivers around the city of Rouen were fishing for pleasure – alongside those trout-slayers during the Age of Abominable Fishmongery. As mentioned earlier, this was an extraordinary time in the history of flyfishing. As well as proving that in the right hands a fly rod could be the most effective way of extracting trout, it also demonstrated that you don't have to be a wizard flytyer to knock up the most murderous of flies. Flies of extraordinary simplicity, incorporating no more esoteric materials than what you'd pick on a walk in the French countryside.

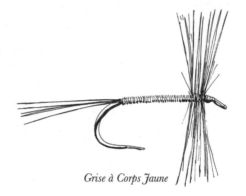

Grise à Corps Jaune

Along with the Cul de Canard, another pattern devised at this time was one called the Grise à Corps Jaune consisting of a hook, a hackle and a bit of thread. This hackle is a grey or reddish brown hackle. Fibres from the same plume are used for the tail. The yellow tying silk should be waxed or tied with soiled fingers – known as 'the touch of the master' by some connoisseurs – so that it takes on a greenish tint.

With a professional fisherman fishing just upstream of you, the point was well made. Fun flyfishermen like Ragot needed flies that were more than just well made. Flies designed to be super-effective were an imperative – and Ragot and his *amis* got to work designing flies that would not just out-think the wariest educated trout, but also outperform the wiliest professional.

But perhaps the most killing pattern to surface (or half surface) during this time that consistently brought home the trout-flavoured bacon was an emerger pattern, like the Mole Fly. This lightly dressed pattern was an imitation of the Mayfly (*Ephemera danica, E. vulgata*) just as it reaches the surface and is about to transform into a sub-imago sitting

half in, half out of the surface. Ragot named his fly the Andelle, after
his favourite stream – France's equivalent of our Wiltshire Wylye.

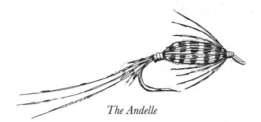

The Andelle

Like the Mole Fly, the Andelle dramatizes the difference between a fly
designed to a brief and a fly whipped up to look like a perfect hand-held
natural. It represents not only the fly but also its behaviour. To ensure
that trout end up in your kitchen – and not in some restaurant – Ragot's
Andelle mimics the most killing stage in the Mayfly's development,
when it's at its juiciest – and most helpless.

The tying of the Andelle is simple enough. The hook is a size 8 or
10. The body was originally ochre wool but I suggest you do what I do
and use a dull-coloured polypropylene. This ensures that your Andelle
stays, if not on the surface, at least in it. An olive-coloured breast feather
is tied in at the head. This large, soft hackle is then folded backwards
and tied off at the bend of the hook with a few turns of yellow thread.

After the war, when only small fish were left in the streams (and not, I
suspect, many of them), a fly's built-in resilience was not of great design
importance, but in these days of stocked waters, I find that after one or
two fish sporting teeth like Dracula with a full set, the thread is very quickly
frayed until the hackle forming the shuck finally (and spookily) gives up the
ghost and opens up. For this reason, I use a thin gold wire to ensure that the
hackle remains in place. This operation I usually complete at the riverside.
I finish off the fly in this way, independently from the dressing in the vice, so
that I can create an imitation of a hatching nymph – by simply folding the
hackle over and binding it down at the hook bend, using the wire.

Impossible to improve? Yes, but I made a refinement.

To turn it into a full-sailed dun pattern, I simply unwind the wire, fold
back the hackle and grease it. Without the weight of the wire pulling the
tail underwater, it floats as proudly as any other Mayfly pattern. Handy

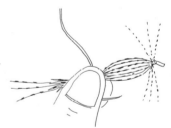

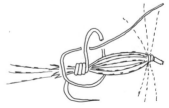

when the trout start scoffing adults on the surface. You simply unwind the wire and fold back the hackle to form the upwing adult.

Say hello to the first artificial fly designed to hatch out of itself.

It was on the Andelle that I caught my first trout on the Andelle. On a *parcours* not too far from the *parcours* where André developed his first prototype, on Charles Ritz's favourite beat. This is the stretch at Radepont named after the small village nearby with a population of seven hundred and fifty at the last count. Fortunately not all flyfishermen, as this beat is no longer a private stretch formerly owned by Ritz's friend, a Norwegian called Monsieur Thranet. It's now open to the public.

On my last day on the Andelle, I had the use of Charles Ritz's very own rods, the ones he had designed and kept for himself. Each with a little Jungle Cock hackle he'd varnished onto the butt, to prove it. Two Pezon et Michel Super Parabolic beauties, lent to me by Pierre, who had joined us for a day and who had been given the rods by Ritz the week before he died, after fishing with Pierre at Radepont.

We started at the bottom of the beat, at the bridge where the road from the Forêt de Bacqueville to Radepont winds down a bendy hill and crosses a narrow bridge. I left Vincent on the bridge casting down at a fish rising just out from someone's garden. A man cutting the lawn was keeping a watchful eye on him. Vincent had to stop fishing to let a coach filled with tourists cross. There wasn't room on the bridge for everybody.

Just up from this bridge, the river slows down, widens, deepens and solemnly parades past the magnificent ruins of the Abbaye Notre-Dame de Fontaine-Guérard, once a monastery affiliated to the Order of Cistercians, dating back to the twelfth century.

It was just after three o'clock. Too early for the Mayfly hatch that begins later in the afternoon, at four, I was flicking a prospecting Andelle into likely spots on the far bank, on the Abbaye side. But nothing was at home, nothing was interested, so I leaned against a tree opposite the top end of the Abbaye garden, waiting, and planning my next move. This was a likely area. I'd seen three trout rising to Mayfly duns on the Abbaye side the evening before. The downside was that in this position you were the centre of attention of tourists on the other side, bored with admiring the gardens, who stood watching you. At least, some of the tourists, but not all.

The people in the coach that nearly pancaked Vincent on the bridge were now walking out of the Abbaye and strolling round the garden opposite me, chatting. Seeing them come my way, I tucked myself away behind some branches. One of the tourists, a tall, attractive blonde, broke away from the party and sneaked behind one of the carefully trimmed, shoulder-high ornamental copper beech hedges out of sight of the rest of the party making their way back to the coach, but in full sight of me, standing concealed right opposite. She didn't even turn to check who might have been across the river.

I knew exactly what she was about to do. Should I cough politely; shake the branches furiously; shout across; wave? But she had her back to me. In the end, it all happened so fleetingly, I did nothing. Down came her jeans, followed by a pair of sky-blue frillies that lay beneath, revealing a pert little backside as snow-white as a cloud. Then up they were all hoisted again and she was off to rejoin her party before I had a chance to wave a warning handkerchief.

I took a small trout that evening on an equally small Andelle slumped, drunk, in the surface film. A beautiful fish, as warm as the river, with soft colouring against her stony grey sides as she lay gasping in the bright green grass.

Vincent was waiting for me at the bridge ready to drive us to dinner at the Auberge de L'Andelle at Point St Pierre. But not before we enjoyed a beer just up the road from the restaurant, where we stood at the bar next to the fattest man we'd ever seen, talking to a man with a croaky voice that sounded like a character out of a Walt Disney cartoon. On the way back across the square we passed a shop displaying lingerie in the window. This reminded me.

'So, what's that beat we just fished called?' I asked Vincent. He told me it didn't have a name. But I had one. The 'Bottom' beat.

I told him what I had witnessed earlier. Vincent couldn't stop laughing.

'Bet you're glad you got that episode behind you!'

La Loue

When Vincent and I are not in Normandy, we set off east to where most of the killer flies, like the Cul de Canard that we used on the chalkstreams, were originated. On the rain-fed rivers of the Jura.

At the same time that the Cul de Canard first made an appearance in the west, an equally effective fly was gaining popularity in the east. A pattern where the hackle was wound along the body, palmer-style, allowing it to float higher – and longer. Back in Normandy, this pattern didn't escape the notice of those professional fly dressers busy supplying the *pêcheurs normands* with ammunition. The most famous being Aimé Devaux. His company still arms French flyfishermen today. Along with the Cul de Canard, Devaux became very interested in this tying style after he'd received some from a mail-order house. At this time, 1943, he was being hunted by the Germans, who were occupying the area. To make money, he joined the professionals and lived by fishing and selling his trout. And it makes sense to pay attention to a fly used by a man to catch fish in order to survive.

This fly was the one mentioned earlier, which Devaux named the Palm-Ailes. *Palm*(er), with *Ailes* (wings). As a general-purpose pattern, on large or small sizes, it is difficult to find a simpler, more effective tie.

News of the Palm-Ailes came to the attention of René Sansonnens in the east, the owner of one of the best beats on the Loue, a river which runs off the Jura mountains on the Swiss/French border. With his jet-black hair and pointy beard, René looks like something out of an El Greco painting. (When I first met him I thought he was Jesus Christ.) It was on his beat that I first fished the Palm-Ailes, hearing that René fished it almost exclusively for his picky zebra trout and gourmet grayling. A tough bunch.

On René's swift stretches, a heavily hackled, high-floating dry 'pounds up' trout appears out of nowhere. But in summer a more imitative fly is required. The dressing needs to be sparse and capable of flicking gently in the riffles, rather than sitting heavily in the flow.

High floaters are not miracle workers. They work when imitating the behaviour of a natural fly. A large dun blown around, a spinner returning to lay its eggs, not yet spent. Or egg-laying sedges. The Palm-Ailes is all of these things.

Palm-Ailes

On our way to the Hotel Gervais-Pape in Chenecey Buillon in the Vallée de la Loue, Vincent and I stopped to peer over the Pont de Châtillon. La Loue was the colour of shoe polish. As we turned to leave, Vincent spotted a large trout cutting a clear khaki slice through the murk taking, not sedge, but stonefly egg-layers crawling all over the bridge.

Back at the car, I spun up a Palm-Ailes from the mess of materials in Vincent's knitting basket and attached it to a stout leader. The hook I used was a #14. Behind the eye, I tied a fiery brown cock hackle, winding it to the bend, making sure the turns of stalk all touched one another – and that the stalk occupied the full length of the hook shank. For the tail, I trimmed the tip of the hackle short. Winding the thread back through the hackle winds, at the eye I tied in two small matching Cree hackle points, sloping back at forty degrees over the body as wings, leaving the two stripped hackle stalks protruding over the eyes, as antennae. Simple.

Everywhere signs said *Privé*. And fishing from bridges in France is not permitted. So every time a car passed we had to lay the rod along the side of the bridge, pretend to enjoy the view, and whistle.

Fifteen feet above the river, I chucked my Palm-Ailes to the side of the fish. It rose and took it as if on tracks, tipping back down into the

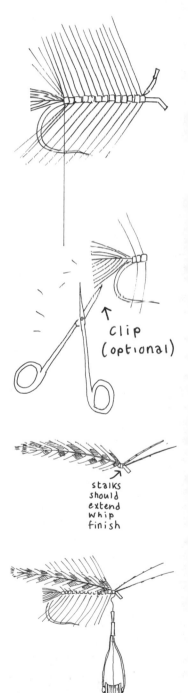

clip
(optional)

stalks
should
extend
whip
finish

soup. Now the fun began, the trout rushing up in front and down below the bridge, while I ran backwards and forwards along it.

'It's enormous,' Vincent screamed, as I flipped the monster onto the concrete foundations of a bridge support.

Then a car came. Suddenly the view became highly interesting again; the whistling, hysterical.

Before the car had cleared the bridge, I was sliding down the bank to land the monster. But the bank was steep, the water deep. I was wearing leather-soled shoes. Vincent wrapped a leather belt round my waist and lowered me down to gill the fish. It weighed a kilo − 2 lb 2 oz of thick, wild fish, its head and tail touching both sides of the fridge at the hotel. But I didn't sell it as a professional would have done.

Instead, back in Paris, I ate it with *beurre persillé*, happy to have been a professional fisherman; for a day.

TEN

South Uist

Ian's Bumble

Hook: No. 16–12
Thread: Black
Tail: Golden Pheasant Tippets
Body: Dark claret seal fur
Rib: Gold wire
Body Hackle: One black and one claret cock hackle
Head Hackle: Black hen hackle, with two turns of
blue jay wing feather in front

Machair Magic: Where Rods, like Wands, are Waved

Tony Bennett left his heart in San Francisco. I left my nose in South Uist.

This is the story of how this happened.

Flying up to the Highlands and Islands from London, I pulled out my little leather collar box – my Portable Flytying Kit (now in a black Muji toilet bag) – pulled down the tray in front of me, clamped a vice onto the side and started whipping up.

On the way to Glasgow, I got half a dozen half-decent Claret Bumbles dressed up if I was in the aisle seat with multi-elbow room; only two if I was stuck in the middle. These days my Portable Flytying Kit looks like a bomb factory in my hand luggage, so now goes in the hold, but my record was fifteen flies between Miami and Cancún, with my left shoulder to the window: Crazy Charlies with milky coffee-coloured wings. There was turbulence. My lunch took flight.

Only grown-up islanders, their friends and relatives from the mainland were on the flight from Glasgow to Benbecula that Saturday morning at the end of June. The rest were stockbrokers on their way to Grimersta, wearing pinky, peachy, plum-coloured cords from the first floor of Farlows – and a handful of hangers-on in Alice bands.

By the sound of it, the islanders were from North Uist. Supposedly one in sixty Scots speaks the Gaelic – or *jockenese*, as one guide on the island refers to it – and more people speak it in North Uist than in South.

My host, Wegg Kimbell, is not an islander. He doesn't speak *jockenese*, but he speaks with great knowledge about the island's history and its people – but, most importantly, its fishing. Although he's only been living there for four and a half years, his love of the island equals that of any old-timer. On the way to his lochside croft, twenty minutes from the airport, where he has been running a bed and breakfast for over four years, we pass a roadside shrine to the Virgin Mary filled with empty 'tinnies'.

'I just love it here,' he says.

Wegg may have only recently set up home on the island, but in between forays to Patagonia and Slovenia, and some very serious jobs in advertising media agencies, he'd spent most of his stray hours fishing the South Uist Estate lochs. These take some knowing – let alone fishing – as I was to find out.

Kinloch, the 'lodge at the head of the loch', sits off the road in a jungle of *rosa rugosa*, escallonias, phormiums, fuchsias, lupins, alders, firs and collared doves – ring-neck doves that collect in a miniature cedar tree and coo-coo the day away. Wegg had to become a gardening expert to convince the lady selling the property that he should be the next owner. He – and his free-range hens. They say that if Wegg's not tracking down browns on the lochs, he's searching for brown eggs in his jungle. I told him his poultry needed taking in hand, but he's as good as married to his twelve chickens.

However, it isn't the cock crowing that gets me up at five on my first morning; he is tucked up in bed. It's me. The sun is pouring through the bathroom Velux and I can see Loch Druidibeg through the jungle – and trout rising.

This dry, sunny weather is something I haven't seen for a while, it being the month of June where, back in dampest, dankest southern England, towns are under water and more salmon are being run over on the M25 than hooked on the Wye. The islands have been free of rain for three weeks. The lochs are low and my first three brownies grab my tiny Silver Invicta hastily before the sun gets too high. The smell of smoky bacon rises out of the jungle, stinging my nose that is starting to peel in the unexpected Mediterranean dryness.

Early settlers in the Outer Hebrides lived by the shore. They were fishermen, not farmers, choosing to settle on the west coast of South Uist. This island is unmistakably shaped like a foetus, and is split into two distinct areas. The east is hilly and peaty while, in the west, sandy dunes protect a string of clear-water lochs with very little peat in them. These are the 'machair' lochs; the most special of special lochs. Lochs haunted by brown trout over four pounds and a place where monster sea trout visit.

These shallow machair lochs are sunk into a landscape of crushed seashells. Rich in alkaline and health-giving properties, this mini ecosystem promotes the prodigious growth of kingcups and orchids, corncrakes and crustaceans – and a population of speckle-backed, white-bellied trout with eyes that sit like pince-nez on the ends of their

The hut at Loch Horisary

noses. Trout that cannot resist the dancing fly. And few anglers I have fished with know how to waltz a fly across a curling wave with greater expertise than my two boat partners, Wegg, and Ian Kennedy, the son of John Kennedy who, as keeper of the keys to the lochs, has taught his son well in the ways of wildness and the wonderful world of the machair.

'You're the only gay in the village,' Wegg enlightens me as I help him wind chicken wire round some stakes, putting an end to his chickens' free-range days. 'The only angler on the island fishing the machair lochs, I mean. Take your pick.'

I was more than just gay to discover this. I was jubilant.

From the top of the islands, the machair lochs on offer are Lochs Bee, Grogarry, Stilligarry, Mid and West Ollay, Kildonan and finally Upper and Lower Bornish. The best of these lochs represent the 'estate fishing', although the Angling Club can provide access to a select few of them.

I chose Stilligarry because walking through a sea of buttercups and orchids on a June day to get to one's fishing is almost as pleasing as the fishing itself. Plus, with sporadic blasts from the Qinetiq missile range, there was no danger of me dropping off and dreaming I was in paradise. I am in paradise.

There is a gentle breeze in our faces as we pull off the gravels, but even though the Gulf Stream washes this coast with a warm sea, making it unusual for it to be cold during the trout-fishing season, I'm layered with every possible layer that Yvon Chouinard, founder of the Patagonia Clothing Company, could supply. My nose sticks out into the sun and salty breeze through a gap.

Wegg takes the oars and whispers instructions to himself from a sub-surface map he has planted deep in his brain. I sit there in the hull watching my ghillie finger every inch of the loch lying under the waves with his knowledge. It's like reading Braille. The exact position of every tiny pebble and mossy rock is relayed back. An oar dips here, or strokes there, positioning the boat where a fly might just be able to lift a fish out of a known lie, when the wind is in a certain direction. Today a bad wind swings from north to north-east. It had been doing this for ten days.

Ian rolls his fly out in front of the boat. It is hard to see what constitutes his team, but I can see they are not the flies I imagined we'd be using. They're tiny. Wegg asks if he can take a look at my fly box and give advice. It explodes in his hand. The lid springs open on contact, bounced asunder by a mass of seriously overdressed, closely packed flies that are so bushy, so springy, you could sit back in my box and watch television.

Ian has a fish in seconds. It crashes through the waves at eye level as a large wall of wave rolls in front of the boat. One scoop of the net and a brownie of two pounds is returned. Now I get the chance to see Ian's flies. Minuscule, scantily dressed Olive and Claret Bumbles tied on 14s. Flies dressed with a delicacy that doesn't match the fingers of the tyer who passes me one to try.

Most of my early boat-drifting days were spent on Orkney lochs, flicking flies on the end of a cast as short as I was tall at that time –

a way my grandfather had taught me. 'Fishing is a relaxation,' this eminent doctor from Montrose told his small grandson, giving me my first lessons in boat fishing and health education.

But it was while sharing a boat with Stan Headley on the South Uist lochs that I learned to develop a retrieve that starts with a long cast, where you fish the attractor patterns on the middle dropper and point while this retrieve is on the move. But then, at the end of the retrieve, you fish the imitation pattern on the bob – an Olive Bumble or Claret Bumble – raising the rod sharply so that it stands perpendicular, surfacing the bob fly and sweeping it over the wave to the boat until it touches the wood. Stan has written about this 'lift and hang' technique in his seminal book on loch fishing.

Stan's initial long cast was a revelation, mainly on account of the fact that its effectiveness was proven almost immediately. The fly at the end of a cast that had delivered two-thirds of my fly line out into the loch had barely touched the water when it was grabbed by one sea trout or other over the two-pound mark. It once caught me the biggest sea trout ever caught on one of the lochs. I believe this sea trout is still the largest on record taken from that loch. But that was a sea trout on Loch Fada late on in the season. (More about this later.)

Today Wegg and Ian are both employing a different drift style to spellbind the fat June browns of Loch Stilligarry. It is back to my grandfather's leisurely ways, for both roll-cast their flies out no further than three rod lengths from the boat, lifting their rod tips up smartly the moment the tail fly pierces the surface. The bob is only ever allowed to sip at the surface, not skinny-dip. From this moment on, the fly appears to have a life of its own, unconnected to angler and rod. The latter follows the fly, rather than leads it as it weaves hypnotically from left to right and back again. It's the wind doing the fishing.

'Why bother with the tail fly?' I ask Wegg.

'All part of the magic?' he replies.

These secret machair lochs are becoming less of a secret. The number of visiting Irish flyfishermen, who no longer have the shallow loch sea trout fishing that they once had, has started to increase. Hardly surprising, for many of the favourite Hebridean loch patterns are of Irish descent.

Suddenly, while that flaky nose of mine is poking around in my cushion box searching for a change of fly, the surface erupts two feet from the boat and Wegg lifts into a brownie nearer three pounds than two.

In the spray and iridescent spume of the image of that moment that I hold in my memory, Tinker Bell tings the tip on Wegg's rod with her wand, a rainbow arches over the island and I realize that no matter how well you attempt to describe any technique, in the end, it's as good as useless. Unless, that is, you learn how to add a tad of magic to your fly.

It was time for me to bandage up my nose and fly home, to come back again next year for another lesson from the island's magicians.

I have been fishing Orkney off and on, but mainly off, for over thirty years. I was sweet little nineteen when my mum sent me up there for the first time, to stay with my cousin Lesley and her husband Sandy, on their farm with fields that run down to Loch Boardhouse.

I had been working hard for a year without a break on a stall in the now-defunct Kensington Market. The stall was called 'Inn Shops' because of the wooden rafters that formed the ceiling of our little corner. We were one of the first to sell velvet trousers, which became the rage back then in the late sixties. We made good money – not that I saw a lot of it, being just a shop assistant.

Selling velvet trousers – and nothing but velvet trousers – the business was dangerously narrowly based. One day I said to the boss, 'Hey, what happens after velvet trousers?'

'Crushed velvet trousers!' was his reply. But I was off to Orkney.

It was here I first discovered the magical effect a Silver Invicta has on trout, tripped through the wave. And how life-threatening it was to hide in the 'stooks' on an evening with Sandy's heavily pitted 12-bore, waiting for the 'dooks' to fly in, and the gun to blow them to pieces.

'I have a deal with the ducks,' Sandy explained. 'I let them eat my barley for three months of the year. They let me have pots at them for one month of the year.'

Then, at the end of it all, there was the Birsay Farmers' Ball. A half-bottle of Grouse ('Tonight the Bird flies') stuck in your back pocket, to complement the creamy cog of home brew handed round the outer skirts of the dance floor. In Orkney, they have two national sports; duck shooting and making home brew.

Soon I was in trouble. Long before I got to the half-bottle, I found myself wandering back across the fields in the half-light, about to present myself to my bed. But first to my cousin who was in charge of my upkeep and welfare. I decided it was best to sleep elsewhere, opting for one of the haystacks in the field behind their farmhouse, with Boardhouse glistening in the thin northernmost early-morning light.

Jock, Sandy's right-hand man, was the one who found me the next morning lying draped over the top of the haystack.

'Auld Tarpaulin won't be fit for the loch this morning,' he told Sandy, who was wondering where I'd spent the night.

And Auld Tarpaulin is what they still call me today when I'm up there fishing the lochs, forty years later. Mainly on Boardhouse loch, where Sandy has fields on the south side of the loch at Birsay, a short walk away from *Bella*, the little blue rowing boat pulled up on the shore.

Loch Harray

But I also fished Loch Harray with Stan Headley, islander, master flyfisherman, author and columnist and member of the Scottish flyfishing team, whom I got to know, I know not how, and we keep something going, in ways both he and I know how to. Mainly taking the piss out of one another.

In those days, when he had a house on the north side of Loch Stenness, there was hardly a sea trout that came up from the sea that didn't get a chance to see one of Stan's flies.

On the loch one day he told me I should go with him and fish the lochs of South Uist.

The end of the season is the time when I look back over the year and sort the oxtail from the soup. The meaty bits of the season from the times just spent by water, tales worth telling at the tail end.

Sitting here in South Uist in September, wrapped up in an armchair belonging to Wegg, laptop on knee, with Loch Druidibeg lapping on the shore outside, has got me thinking of the fly that has treated this 'sometime sea trout tourist', who manages the occasional foray up to the Outer Hebridean salmon, sea trout and brown trout. A fly that casts spells over the huge wild fish that roam this very special biosphere, spangled with lochs.

I refer to Ian 'The Dibbling Diva of the Western Isles' Kennedy's Claret Bumble. A fly with 'Machair Magic', hungrily taken by finny tourists to these shores, that flyfishers in these parts have taken to in a big way, too.

Originally devised by an Irishman, the Claret Bumble was a visitor, too. One that, fortunately, stayed. Educated at Marlborough College on the banks of the River Kennet, Theodore Conyngham Kingsmill Moore introduced the world to the Claret Bumble in his classic, *A Man May Fish*, published in 1960. The interesting design feature of the Claret Bumble is Kingsmill's forensic dissection of the colour 'claret'. He claims claret embraces three colours: a 'raucous and offensive' magenta; a true rich claret, 'the colour of a good burgundy'; and a 'blackish claret'. He claims that, as the season progresses, a wild fish's preferences shift from magenta to claret and then to black-claret. For this reason it is important to get the correct 'claret' shade. Experts do this by increasing or decreasing the turns of palmered black hackle.

Tie in
jay
tip
first

The Bumble that caused the biggest rumble in the machair jungle
was Ian's dressing tied on a #14 hook. Using black thread, Ian ties a
small bunch of golden pheasant tippets and gold wire at the bend and
dubs the body with dark claret seal fur to behind the eye. Here a black
and a claret cock hackle are tied in and wound together back to the
bend and the wire is wound through these hackles to behind the eye
and secured. A small black hen hackle is tied in – two or three turns
only. Finally, two to three turns of a blue jay wing feather are tied in
front. Deadly.

Ian's Bumble

My first sea trout on a Claret Bumble variation has a tale behind it,
too. The tale of a fish I call 'The Fish of Many People's Lifetimes', for
reasons I will reveal.

Ever since I had agreed to join Stan on a South Uist foray, tales of the
huge sea trout to be taken from the island's mysterious machair lochs
kept me awake on the nights leading up to my departure. I knew Stan
would be there to help me when I arrived, but I was keen to have all
the necessary tackle with me before I set out. For this reason I contacted
the salmon and sea trout guru John 'Hotchguru' Hotchkiss, whom I
had fished with just recently on the Stjordal in Norway, about rods and
tackle. It didn't take him long to kit me out, lending me his ten-foot, size
seven, four-piece rod to take with me.

'What about nylon?' I asked him. 'What size tippet?'

John rarely goes totally quiet – at least, not for what seemed like
several minutes, during which I was trapped in a glare of a very serious
nature. Whatever he was to tell me was clearly of great import. In fact,
it was something I will never forget him saying.

'Don't fuck about, Neil,' he said. 'In Uist, you might catch the fish of a lifetime. Don't lose it because your leader snapped.'

Fifteen pounds tippet it had to be.

Now I was so hyped up about these stories of sea trout over ten pounds being quite the run of the norm on Uist that, when our ghillie rowed Stan and myself out onto Loch Fada on my first day, I was breathing heavily with anticipation. A salty fresh sea trout of huge proportions was the order of the day. But when nothing had moved to either my fly or to the Scottish team member, I turned to the ghillie and squinted at him.

Feeling he had to do something, he took my fly off and whipped on a Claret Bumble variation tied by a friend of his who had been fishing the week before with great success.

'I saw something turn about fifty yards straight ahead of you, Neil,' Stan growled between bantering with the ghillie.

I remember Stan telling me that when he's drifting, his eyes aren't on his flies; they're well ahead of the drift, looking for signs of fish.

The wind had picked up and it was only two casts away that I realized I was approaching the spot where Stan had seen his fish turn. I finished my dibble, bringing my top dropper straight to the wood, and shot out a long, straight cast right to where I thought Stan had directed me.

On impact, the exact second the fly hit the water, it was engulfed by a huge swirl and I knew immediately I had one of those average double-figure sea trout attached. Hugh Falkus calls this the 'crunch take', when a fly lands on a fish's shoulder and it turns on it with an instinctive aggression.

'It's a salmon,' Stan announced with the confidence of the champion.

'It's a sea trout,' the ghillie whispered on a breath that was lost in the waves.

'That's no sea trout. Not that size,' Stan insisted. 'I've been fishing this loch for years and never taken a sea trout that size.'

Whatever it was, it was down deep for a good few minutes. I was in no hurry to bring it up. And the mystery fish was in no hurry to show itself. When it did, it surfaced horizontally, bobbing up like a submarine, its spade of a tail slicing waves.

'Fuck me. It's a sea trout,' said Stan in a rare moment of submission. Now hell broke out on the boat. Who was going to land it?

In the end, Stan lifted the fish aboard. Sea-run, and now totally run out of breath.

'Let's put him back,' I said to the ghillie, who had the fish cradled in his arms, priest about to do the tapping.

'You must be joking, Neil,' he said, tap-tapping away.

I turned to Stan for his opinion. He was wearing a 'You must be joking' expression on his face, too.

'This . . . Is . . . A . . . Fish . . .', the ghillie was punctuating the sentence with taps on the fish's head with his priest, '. . . Of . . . A . . . Life . . . Time.'

On the word 'Life' the fish was dead and I had a fish of a lifetime that had to be stuffed.

On the scales back at the Lochboisdale Hotel, my fish weighed in at half an ounce over ten pounds.

At the bar, I looked at all the other trout taken from the island. So many over ten pounds.

But the records were checked and the fish was certainly the largest taken from Loch Fada since records began in the mid-1850s. Although John Kennedy, who joined me at the bar for a drink, was quick to tell me that a sea trout he took at thirteen pounds from just below the outlet to the loch would have been the record, had it been taken a few more feet up into the loch. I felt his pain.

I had the fish stuffed by the same taxidermist who stuffed and mounted all the other record fish in the hotel. And I still enjoy telling the story of its capture to whoever happens to be standing there admiring it.

And what a story it is. Although in telling it I forget to mention minor details, such as the fact that I didn't actually spot the fish to start with; neither did I actually land it. And it wasn't caught on my rod, or on one of my flies. I didn't even carry it home or put it on the scales. In truth, it was the fish of many people's lifetimes. One of them, thankfully, was mine.

∼

There's a reason why South Uist is called South Uist – and not just Uist. It's because there's a North Uist, just north of it. I've fished the lochs there and hooked sea trout almost as big as on the South Uist lochs. Fish you never forget; fish I've never been able to land. To catch these monsters, the flies you use and the way you fish them are practically the same. But when it comes to the practical jokes on the island, it's not the same. Not at all the same.

The Langass Hotel in North Uist sounds like nowhere on earth. In fact, it's the centre of the earth if you want to eat, fish and relax. In that order. 'Eat' is way up there.

Attempts by some of the top restaurants in London to try and poach (you would have thought they'd know how to do that) The Chef, John, have been made many times, but failed. He's happy there. And we're happy he's there. All the guests are happy he's there. Let's talk about his lobster, freshly caught that day from the sea.

Now, I think lobster is the most overrated food form there is. When it comes to taste, it's nothing. But when The Chef puts them on the menu, they sing. A chorus of taste. It's opera in a shell. And I don't like opera. But when lobsters start those arias, I listen – and delight.

So, if you want one of the best meals you'll ever have in a hotel, if you haven't already done so, take up sea trout fishing and get up there

and eat. Then fish. In that order.

But I did have one spot of bother with my total enjoyment there. I ran out of pipe tobacco. It was on the Wednesday night. I remember this because when I went searching for some the next day, on the Thursday, I discovered a weird thing.

It's all aboard a bus to take you to your fishing. It leaves after breakfast. The Chef joined us that Thursday morning; he needed something from town. We stopped at a wee shoppie on the way and I hopped out to get tobacco.

When I walked in, the woman behind the counter was on the phone. This gave me time to check if they had baccy. They did, but a limited selection. When she got off the phone, I asked her if she stocked Condor.

'Aye, we have Condor,' she confirmed. 'But I cannae sell it tae ye.'

I laughed. She didn't. She was serious.

Now, up the Hebrides, it's the land of what they call the 'Wee Frees'. The Free Church, where it's forbidden to work on a Sunday, and fishing is considered work up there. But, more importantly, you can't buy alcohol on a Sunday, either.

'But it isn't a Sunday,' I said, thinking that the sale of tobacco was banned on Sundays too.

'Sunday, no alcohol. Thursday, no tobacco.'

I studied my shoes for a moment, looked up and said, 'Look, I have the greatest respect for the traditions and religions on the island, but I'm a tourist. Can you not let me have a wee packet of Condor?'

'Sorry, no.'

I was starting to lose it, trying to find some way of reconciling the need for a smoke, yet showing respect for those on the island who had bought their baccy the day before. Or who could hold out for the day after. Those islanders who can handle the situation, because they're in the know. And have trained to be within the rules – and be without.

'I know about the Sunday ban, but not the Thursday. Can you not make a special case? I'll know next time,' I pleaded. It must have been painful to listen to.

'Sorry, no,' she said, tidying the chocolate display.

I was looking around for help when my eyes drifted out of the window to the bus. It was rocking. Through the window I could see people falling about. With laughter.

Then it clicked.

Back in the rock 'n' roll bus, I discovered The Chef had phoned the shop from his mobile and told the woman, who just happened to be a member of the island amateur dramatic society, the scam.

Someone said to The Chef, 'It's not a good idea to do that to Neil.' And, you know something? He was right.

When I got back to London, I rang up the local rag, and placed an eight-by-four-inch classified ad in their October issue putting just about everything The Chef owned up for sale. From his treasured Rhode Island Red hens that laid the most delicious eggs that we had enjoyed for breakfast (and ideal for smoking), to the brand new nine-foot, three-piece Sage trout rod he had barely had time to leave the kitchen to flick about. And his turkey.

At the bottom of the advertisement I put The Chef's address and phone number, informing the reader to contact him any time, but not Thursdays.

It got a lot of replies, I can tell you. Mostly distraught calls on hearing

the island's treasure might be leaving, I would imagine. But I know The Chef has something up his sleeve for the next time I go up to North Uist and stay at the Langass. So far though, I haven't been back. Yet.

It's not the food (I say to myself) and it's certainly not the fishing (I lost a fish close on ten pounds during my stay).

I don't know what it is, but I think what The Chef's got cooking up could be very, very nasty indeed.

A super-spiny lesser weever fish in the *bouillabaisse* springs to mind.

ELEVEN

Cuba: Cayo Largo
The Hamster

Hook: No. 2/0 circle hook
Thread: Brown
Eyes: Dumb-bells, to desired weight
Flash: Flashabou strands
Wing: Orange and Tan marabou
Body: Tufts of khaki yarn or Widow's Web, trimmed

It Takes Two To Tarpon

WHEN I GET BACK FROM A good fishing trip abroad, or simply a couple of hours on the chalkstream at the bottom of my garden – I always catalogue it in a letter to my good friend in New York (or Woodstock, these days), Nick Lyons, who doesn't get out as much as me; if at all.

As he is a man of letters himself, I know he won't mind me sharing a little bit of one of these letters with you. At least to tell you the tale of 'The Tango Tarpon'.

'As you know,' I wrote, 'I've been writing the scripts for a TV series that appears on the Sky Sports Channel called *The Take*. A gentle programme about anglers enjoying fishing; and all the other things apart from just catching fish. One thing I've had a lot of practice in! So I'm a natural! They planned to do a programme on saltwater flyfishing in Cuba. I volunteered to go along. What a difficult decision . . .'

We stayed at 'the Beaten-up House' – La Casa Batida – a forty-minute flight due south of Havana, on Cayo Largo, one of three hundred pearl islands that form the Archipelago de los Canarreos, a shell necklace that hangs round Cuba's south-eastern coast. Cayo Largo is Cuba's fun resort. Because it's fun, at that time no Cubans were allowed there; only Spaniards and Canadians, and the occasional European.

It's a flat, sandy island with dizzy palms, bleached white beaches and a sea so blue it hurts your eyes to look at it. We stayed at the Sol Club, a Spanish-owned hotel, laid-back, shipwrecked-shanty-town-style. Rows of single-storey wooden shacks, distress-painted sky-blue and pink, nestled around the concrete shores of a long, trailing swimming pool that formed the backbone of the complex, with the sea on one side; scrub on the other. The rooms themselves looked as if they had brought back the Incas to do the decoration, but the whole place was only five months old.

Every evening there was Cuban cabaret, with dancing girls and people jumping up and down, all of which you could keep an eye on from the bar, which was the safest place if you wanted to avoid being picked out of the crowd by one of the rubber-limbed girls – to salsa, they say. The service has the same snap to it. If you hand in your laundry two minutes late in the morning, the shrieks aren't from the parrots, they have the cat-o'-nine-tails out.

As I sat on my balcony overlooking bronzed blondes volleyballing the afternoon away on the beach below, beside me a long, long Ron Matusalem served in a scraped-out coconut shell with a straw, I said to myself, 'Only a fool would have volunteered to put up with this.' I was suffering the same sort of hell that had inspired the phrase 'a rum deal'.

The fishing lodge was down a track – an ABBA track, on the taxi driver's tape deck. If you know the words to 'Chiquitita', you can while away the three-minute journey time as you head for the marina where Italian Fabrizio Barbazza (all the fishing lodges seem to be run by Italians), an ex-Indianapolis racing driver, has his house, which is also 'the lodge'. This means he has a bathroom and a hairbrush you can use. You put your rods up in his dining-room.

SABALO

He has four boats and, at the last count, three guides. We had the top guide, Marcos, a quiet Cuban, who doesn't shout. This took some getting used to. He was on the main boat, along with a cameraman, a sound man, and a flyfisherman. There was another boat, captained by Fabrizio, which transported the two producers and the other flyfisherman waiting his turn to fish.

Fabrizio told me that we wouldn't see a bonefish under four pounds. I told him that he was not only a great host and an accommodating lodge owner, he was also a great bullshitter! But when we shipped out at the end of the week, it was true. We hadn't seen or caught a bonefish under four. But then we didn't see as many bonefish as we had seen further east, at the Jardines de la Reina. Those we saw were all loners – and huge. We had them up to ten pounds. Espen Myhre, my twenty-five-year-old Norwegian fishing co-star, who was doing most of the bonefishing, had bones of six, seven and eight pounds under his belt, making casting very difficult for him.

My Fish Number One was a ten-pound jack on a popper, from a deep channel between two flats. It came for it, dived on it, but I forgot to strike and off it shot. In a peak of rage, I slammed the popper back on the water and the jack turned and hit it like a cruise missile as it lay static, doggo on the surface. It took half an hour to bring to heel. In fact, I had to drag it into shallows six inches deep, turn it on its side and beach it to tire it out. And I had a barracuda. Then the sun went down.

It was the tarpon I was after. That was to be the next day. Needless to say, I was first down on the mooring quay that morning.

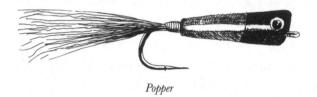

Popper

When the entire ship's company – Espen and Marco – was assembled, curious, apprehensive faces eyed me, for my expression must have resembled the horizon when a storm is coming. Rapidly glancing over the side of the Hewes skiff, and then darting my eyes in the direction of Marco standing high above us on the platform, I paused dramatically, and cried out to him:

'What do ye do when you see a tarpon, man?'

Poling his way from the dock, Marco shrugged.

'Not just any tarpon, I say! A white tarpon!' Espen started giggling. He was on to the wind-up. 'It's a white-headed tarpon, mind! With a wrinkled brow and a crooked jaw.'

The day before, when I had been sitting silently behind Espen, standing up front of the skiff, he had turned to see what I was busy reading as I waited my turn.

'Marco! Have you not read *Moby Dick*?'

It was time to wind down the wind-up. But Marco was in no mood for anything other than getting us out of the dock area and across the bay to a flat where he hoped the tarpon would be crossing, just as the tide turned.

'Whose dick?' Marco asked, his full concentration set on powering through the winding channel towards the sea, past islands little and big, some rocky and wooded, grassy and green; others, cities of cranes, scattered with oilcans and scrap iron. Shaving the skiff clear of the last no wake sign, Marco got us out and away.

At sea, we still had not yet lost sight of land. If mangroves are land. 'Ronald Reagan said ketchup was a vegetable,' I thought.

Espen and I knew it would be at least another half-hour before we reached the chosen flat. It could be many hours before we found the tarpon we were after. But we had unhooked a large barracuda without losing any fingers and thrown a convincing number of flies at the half-dozen permit that had pounced on us, so we felt lucky. Anyway, we had time. We had more hours in the day because we didn't have to travel to the fishing. Or have to leave late afternoon to get back before sunset. In fact, we didn't have to leave anything. Creature comforts are never far away at the Sol Club.

Here and there we saw mangroves the size of rugs, others as large as a country estate. Mangroves on all sides. Some were fronted by pure white flats, spread out like newly laundered aprons. Then the water turned yellow, and deepened. Three feet is deep on these flats. Without any indication of the plan, Marco cut the motor and shinned up to his platform and began poling.

Flocks of white black-headed terns were flying above a school of working fish that ruffled the water. It was my turn up front. The target, tarpon.

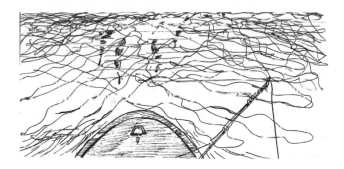

The flat was sand, with dark ochre beds of seaweed. Not my favourite combination for spotting low-lying fish, but tarpon would be travelling midwater and would be black against yellow. I rolled back on the balls of my bare feet, flexed my shoulders and prepared for action. I stripped out twenty yards of line, the maximum I set to cast to any approaching tarpon.

I allow myself one clean double haul. One only, unless the wind is up, then, with the water ruffled and a higher likelihood of the evidence of a dud cast being concealed, I cast as many times as it takes to get my fly to the tarpon. Two lengths in front of it, giving the fly time to sink to cruising depth; preferably below this line so that I can lift the fly in front of the tarpon's flat, bony snout.

This gives the fly the appearance of a food item escaping in the same element as the tarpon, not parachuting in out of another element, from the sky above. In nature, baitfish don't arrive in front of tarpon in this way. Even the hungriest rogue tarpon knows this. This isn't so much the case with competitive 'schoolie' tarpon in a pod. They rush any likely-looking food item in an attempt to get to it before their neighbour.

But it was not these tarpon we were after. We were after school-leavers; grown-ups. The ones that prowled the ocean and the flats in fewer numbers, but greater weights.

The little white terns, in their thousands, continued to scream and screech their own protests as we poled across their hunting ground. They, too, had to eat and their meals depended on the tiny minnows on the surface, now concerned with the matter of self-preservation.

Further away across the flat, two pelicans were hard at work on a shoal of sardines, gliding high above the flat, suddenly collapsing their wings and tumbling head first out of the sky and into the sea, bobbing back up like plastic ducks in a bath. Throwing their floppy beak-bags over their shoulders, they let their contents slip down their throats.

After one, two, three hours poling and waiting without seeing anything, standing like a coiled spring ready to pounce at the first sight of a tarpon, the mind begins to drift and notice such things. Then it was Espen's turn up front; then mine again; then Espen's. As the gentle sea breeze lifted the pages of my book and chapter flicked after chapter, *Moby Dick* slipped further and further away… And a day had gone, without a sighting.

Marco was frustrated. But we had been – and still were – tough, single-minded customers. We only wanted one tarpon; but not any tarpon. One of appalling size. White. Black. Any colour!

Marco could have given us a boatload of fish. This he had done when we were after bonefish. But we wanted that one fish; one whole boatload of it.

When you have fished Cuba for twelve years running, you notice trends. Unlike bonefish, tarpon are either there, or they aren't. Most saltwater flyfishermen with only a week of fishing ahead of them – perhaps their only trip that year – don't have the time for such specialist behaviour. But this was my third week in Cuba that year. I had this luxury. On the previous two weeks in the Jardines de la Reina, on the houseboat *Halcon*, the tides were right and we had intercepted tarpon at the best time: at five in the morning, as a purple sun tipped over the mangroves, after an hour's boat ride through darkness. We fished to tarpon rolling in the low light, like drunks thrown out of a late-night bar after closing.

My partner Philip and I had had a tarpon apiece on at the same time. A thirty- and a fifty-pounder. A fifty-pound tarpon to celebrate my fiftieth birthday.

The following week, on the Tortuga, the tides had changed, but we still encountered the occasional rogue tarpon, although we had to chase after them into the high seas. Tarpon of over a hundred pounds. My one chance at a throw at one resulted in nothing. Trailing behind the skiff, my line wrapped around a rock way down deep. Vincent, who was sharing the skiff with me that week, dived in to release it, fully clothed. There were sharks following, but one whiff of his sneakers ruined their appetite.

At Cayo Largo, the tarpon, like the bones, take some finding. To be fair though the weather had been overcast all week. I had two textbook shots; but before I tell you the story of 'The Tango Tarpon', let me tell you about the tackle.

I fish a nine-foot, seven-weight for bonefish; a ten-weight for permit and tarpon. But I had a twelve-weight up for 'that tarpon'. On my first tarpon, no bigger than twenty-five pounds, the reel-line broke. Not the mono, the reel-line. There was to be more to come.

The next day we spent all day looking for a shot at a tarpon. There was a lot of sitting around with the film crew from the spare boat, watching one another hunt fish. I had my copy of *Moby Dick* to read as I sat there, bobbing on the high seas, waiting for a giant tarpon to head my way across the flat.

With not much doing, the director decided to cancel the whole scene. He got Espen and me up in the front of one boat and had us talking about what beautiful weather we were having and how great this and that were . . . then suddenly Marco whispered that there was a big fish heading our way. His warm, soft voice chilled the back of my neck like a hard frost.

The tarpon didn't take much finding. We could see this U-boat a hundred yards away.

'It's a shark,' I said.

'It's a tarpon,' Marco said. 'The biggest I've seen in ten years.'

Eyeing the imaginary sixteen-dollar gold piece I, like Captain Ahab, had nailed to the mast, I jumped up front; keeping the cool Marco had breathed all over me. Fifty yards away, the tarpon slid out of a blue channel, disappeared over a dark hole and shimmered into casting distance over a light sea bottom. I held back. I held back, despite Marco's urgings to cast. I held back . . . I held back until the black log of a tarpon was alongside the boat, a roll-cast away. My tiny five-inch, long-nosed streamer – in comparison with this five-foot fish – looked ridiculous. I chucked it anyway, six feet in front of the sub, and let it sink, lifting it up in front of his nose as he passed.

He turned to look. His head and the whole of his body turned. I was pumping at the fly with a piston arm. It followed. Seeing that the Zeppelin was only seconds away from boarding the skiff, I stopped and let the fly dive. Then I stripped again.

The tarpon lifted up out of the water six feet from the boat, and sucked my #2/0 streamer off the surface, his vision opening up in our direction. In a huge eye the size of the glass on the front of a washing machine door, I saw the reflection of what he was looking at: me. I, the skiff and everyone on board were tumbling around and around, awash with sea, sky and foam in the roll of his wake.

#2/0 Streamer

The second he slammed down those prehistoric, silver-plated, toothless jaws on my streamer, like a huge Mississippi steamer attempting to back-pedal yards from the thundering falls, he tried to put the entire movement into reverse. But the game was up. Furthermore, he knew it.

Seeing us and, as he made his escape, feeling us – realizing he was now a *part* of us – he leapt in the air, drenching us poor boat people before heading off back to Islamorada.

To make sure the hook was set, I leaned into my rod. One, two . . . but I didn't manage to set the hook a third time. The rod snapped at the butt. But this didn't stop the tarpon. It jumped again in a chandelier of crystals.

It didn't stop me, either. Handing the part of the rod with the reel hanging off it to Espen, I hung onto the shattered top section, the tarpon flip-flopping its way westwards, now just as much a part of the horizon as he was a far-distant part of us.

With two hundred and fifty yards of backing out, and only twenty-five to go, something had to give. Marco had the motors started and was heading off to Florida after the fish, but the weight of the line, the boat, two anglers, a film crew and everything else was too much and the twenty-pound line bust at the Albright connection to the eighty-pound shock tippet. The only place it could go.

Marco put the fish at a hundred and fifty pounds. It could have been a record-breaker for the lodge. It was a rod-breaker, for me. And a heartbreaker, for everyone.

Why 'The Tango Tarpon'?

Well, sometimes it takes two.

The 100 tarpon takes out to sea

Brad was my boat partner that day.

A hairdresser and crazy-keen, New York State trout fisherman, Brad had never fished the salt before, let alone seen a tarpon. So when Austin picked us up at 7 a.m. from the Sol Melia in Cayo Santa Maria, a fifty-minute flight from Havana, to drive us to the dock, twenty minutes away, I knew I might have to give Brad some advice. Me and Eulises, our guide, who was there waiting for us at the beach bar.

Cayo Santa Maria is a tarpon-only lodge set on the Cuban north coast. No bonefish. They'd all been netted and eaten a long time ago by the local fishermen and the workers at the surrounding sugar plantations.

The Sol Melia Cayo Santa Maria is the sister hotel to the Sol Melia Cayo Largo on the south coast. On arrival at the airport, you are herded onto a coach and taken to the hotel. When you arrive, you're directed to the check-in desk, then rounded up and taken into a large room with seats and desks set out like a schoolroom. Here you are briefed about where everything is, the facilities available to you, what you can and can't do and how you can do what you want to do if they haven't already mentioned it. You're given a wristband that you are told to wear all the time, as this will be your passport to doing all those things they've just told you that you can do.

It was like being at school again and when Vincent and I first went there, Vincent couldn't resist it. At the end of the presentation, we were asked if we had any questions. Vincent stuck up his hand.

'Please, sir. Can I go for a pee-pee?'

Although Brad was still very much a beginner at saltwater fishing, he was keen to learn – about everything. When I handed him the fly that had never once failed to interest every tarpon I had thrown it to, he was anxious to learn how he could use his hairdressing skills to manipulate fur, feather and hair round hooks.

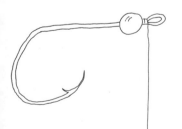

'How did you tie that? How did you tie that?' he shrieked in wonderment.

'It's simple,' I told him.

'Tell me. Tell me!' Brad insisted.' So I told him.

'You tie a set of these weighted dumb-bell eyes on top of the shank behind the eye with figure-of-eight wraps and maybe add a dot of superglue, epoxy, or cement.'

'Got it. Got it!' Brad said, bending down and squinting at it at super-close range.

'Next, work the thread back to the beginning of the bend of the hook and tie in a few strands of Flashabou. On top of this, tie in a bunch of orange marabou. Then, on top of this, tie in another bunch of tan marabou.'

I was really getting down to it. And so was Brad.

'Fantastic. Fantastic!' he said.

'Now adjust the hook in the vice so that the point is up and you are tying onto the underside of the shank. Tie in a strand of khaki yarn or Widow's Web across the shank, perpendicular to it, like the eyes, but on the underside of the shank. Then, in front of this strand, tie in another strand of the same stuff, then another and so on, pushing each strand up against the last one.'

'Great! Great!'

I had a very receptive audience. So much so, it was beginning to drive me nuts.

'Now continue to tie the yarn strands until you reach the eyes. Knot the thread in front of the eyes, cut, and cement the thread where it was tied off.'

'Will do. Will do.'

'Now trim the yarn so the body is an oval, helmet shape. And there you have it.'

I was finished. And happy to be.

'That's great! That's great!'

I gave him one of my flies to look at.

keep yarn tufts same size

Repeat, pushing each strand against the last one

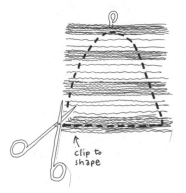

clip to shape

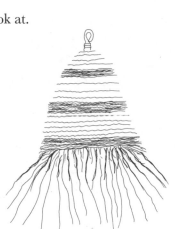

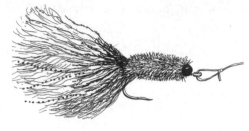

The Hamster

'Hey, it looks just like a hamster.'

'That's good, because that's just what it's called, Brad. At least, that's what I call it.'

'You're right. You're right!'

'One thing.' In actual fact, I hadn't quite finished. 'This is a 2/0 circle hook. Never, ever fish for tarpon with a fly that isn't tied on a circle hook. They'll jump off.'

'No, never. Never, never!'

All morning I found myself giving Brad tarpon tips.

'Brad, tarpon fishing is very different from fishing for trout. For a start, the strike. You don't raise your rod like you do in fresh water, you 'strip-strike'. You pull the hook into the tarpon's jaw.'

'I won't. I won't!'

'You don't move the rod. And always 'strip-strike' with fingers holding the line against the cork. Not flying free.'

'Don't worry. Don't worry!'

'When you tie the fly onto this hundred-pound shock tippet, tie it on a loop so it can swing around free. I use a loop knot called the "Clifford".'

'Will do. Will do!'

'And when you tighten the loop, don't clip the excess off too close to the knot. Leave a tuck so the knot can tighten and doesn't unravel.'

'Sure. Sure!'

And so it went on. At least, so I went on until eventually Brad hooked into a tarpon. Forty minutes later we had it on the boat.

'I got him. I got him!' Brad was ecstatic.

'Well done, Brad. That's brilliant.'

'Brilliant! Brilliant!'

Eulises clamped his Boga grip to the jaw of the tarpon and lifted it up off the deck, high in the sky. It was longer than Eulises. He had to stand up on the platform so the tail didn't trail on the deck.

'*Sesenta*!' he announced.

'Sixty pounds, Brad.'

'That's great! That's great!'

'It must be at least thirty years old.'

'Amazing. Amazing.'

'Yes,' I said, taking a closer look at the monster as Eulises held it in the water next to the boat to revive it. Now it was my turn to be unable to resist it.

'Born some time in December. The fifteenth, I'd say.'

Brad looked at me as if I'd just told him he'd won the lottery.

'Mmm. A Sagittarian,' I told him.

Brad went crazy.'But so am I. So am I!'

Now Brad had tattoos. Lots of them. When I first met him, I had to remark on them. You have to say something about them, if only to get that thing out of the way so you can get on and talk about something else

'Great tattoos, Brad.'

'Thanks, Neil.'

'Now tell me . . .' and off you'd go on another subject. Job done.

Looking back, it was Brad who got me thinking about tattoos. He gave me the idea I should have tattoos, too. But not lots of them, like Brad. Perhaps just the one. I had an earring in my late teens, so why not a tattoo in my late fifties? Out tarpon fishing, you should have a tattoo. All seafaring people have tattoos. It's what you do out there on the burning deck, skinning muscles. But not an anchor. Something more original. Nothing like Brad's tattoos, with wet trout flies up one arm and dry flies on the other, a rod and a reel tattooed up one leg and a landing net up the other, a leaping trout on his belly. No, nothing quite as subtle as that. This was okay for Brad, in New York in the winter when you had several layers of clothes to cover the art gallery up. Out on the flats in his flats gear, he looked like an ad for a tackle shop.

I got thinking about what I'd have tattooed, and where, one day when I was sitting behind him on the skiff, looking up at him standing there on the platform with his back to me.

When I'm up there on the platform, I like to fish with no shoes on, gripping the deck with my toes. I don't wear a shirt, either. Just shorts. Of course, I have to slap more sun oil on my body than BP can legally dump in the Gulf, but I never burn. So I decided the best place for a tattoo was in the small of my back, just above my shorts. Nice and discreet. And what I'd have tattooed is a wavy water line, parallel to the top of my shorts, with the tail of a bonefish, tailing. A tailing bonefish. I did a sketch of it when I got back to my room.

I talked to Brad about it.

''Must hurt, all those tattoos, Brad?' I asked him.

'Nah, not really. But there are places that hurt more than others.'

'Oh, yes? Like where?'

'Places where the skin is very thin. Under the arm, behind the knee . . . in the small of the back.'

It's probably for this reason that I still have that sketch here in front of me on my desk, not behind me, in the small of my back.

Later I discovered Brad's real name wasn't Brad at all. It was Michael. Everyone called him Brad, so I just called him Brad, too.

'Why Brad?' I asked one of his friends in the fishing party he came with.

Apparently, before he changed career directions and became a hairdresser, Brad was a ballet dancer, and a very promising one, too, by all accounts, but he gave it up. I was curious to know why.

'One performance, he pirouetted backwards off the stage and fell into the orchestra. From then on, everyone called him "Pit". Brad Pit.'

I had to think for a moment, but I got it.

'I got it! I got it!'

TWELVE

West Florida

The Gurgler

Hook: No. #2/0 sea hook
Thread: White monocord
Tail: Khaki bucktail topped with twelve strands of Flashabou
First Body Hackle: Two white saddle hackles, palmered
Second Body Hackle: Two orange saddle hackles, palmered
Body and Head: Two half-inch strips of cell foam

Snooping on Snook

HE CAME RUNNING OUT OF THE sea at me.

'What the hell d'ya think you're doing?'

I could see he wasn't a happy item long before he got to me. As brown as a nut, a head like a shrivelled raisin, psychedelic flowers bursting out all over his Tommy Bahama Bali Bloom swim shorts, stock number TR9622, he looked the sort of guy who flattens sandcastles and puts stones in snowballs.

'Fishing,' I screamed back at him.

'There's no fish here. Just kids swimming. Beat it, buddy!'

He was wrong. There were more fish than families out there. He just couldn't see the shoals foraging around in the clouds of sand, shrimp, clam and crab his family were puffing up as they jumped around in the drifting tide.

This wasn't the first time I'd caused excitement on Venetian Beach. The day before I'd had a family re-enact scenes from *Jaws* when a six-pound snook took my fly. I had been watching the dark shapes of this snook and his friends zipping in and out between the legs of a family playing ball in three feet of water, oblivious to the fact they had as good as opened up a restaurant, their clientele queuing up around their ankles waiting to be served.

When my snook took off through the middle of them, then they got the idea all right. But for them the fish wasn't a snook. It was a barracuda! . . . A piranha! . . . A shark! So there was panic. The screams from my reel didn't help.

When I held up the snook after a ten-minute struggle, they laughed it off. But no one saw the funny side today. Today the only thing I caught was the ever-watching eye of a protective dad in his holiday shorts who didn't like me whipping the sea to foam near to where his children were playing.

'Sorry!' I said, heading off down the beach towards the third rock outcrop from the entrance to Venetian Village, the only feature that might attract a passing snook.

I was in luck. Nobody was there. No families, no swimmers, just a couple of dozen snook patrolling off the point of the groyne. Close in, despite a low tide.

I prefer to fish where there are families. Snook might not like a lot of things, but beaches, moorings, bridges, gardens, restaurants, they love. Anything that keeps them close to people, as I was to discover the next day.

VENETIAN BAY BEACH

I was up and out at 2 a.m., leaving Wiggins Pass ten minutes later.

As I sped off downtown to meet Roan, the Plymouth Neon and I had the US41 Tamiami highway to ourselves. We slowed down only to pass a pod of police cars standing stationary across the fast lane at the lights at Pelican Bay, their own lights flashing.

At this hour, Naples is a morgue.

Thelonious Monk's 'Round Midnight' came on the radio as I passed the airport Pulling Road junction, then a mile on to the Joe Cool Fly Shop sign, down a private street and through showers from garden sprinklers switched on early before temperatures reached 90°F.

Roan was outside The Mangrove Angler on the East Tamiami Trail with his pick-up and Pathfinder skiff waiting for me.

Roan B. Zumfelde had been an international banker working in the UK and Switzerland until five years ago when he had packed it all in to be a guide. With no wife or family to support, he spent every cent he had on his pick-up, trailer and skiff. He had got his first job with some billionaire he had befriended who hired him to guide guests and business acquaintances.

'I'd spy out for fish for my clients – and spy into their conversations for my boss.'

Roan had hooked a bonefish of over twelve pounds at Dead Man's Key in the Bahamas and had his mind set on moving there for good one day, but right now he guided out of Naples for snook, redfish, jacks and tarpon.

Launching the skiff in the pick-up's headlights, we set off into the night, powering along the Gulf Shore beaches through warm night air. The bow heaved up and down on a gentle, solid swell, lowering slowly as Roan cut the speed to creep through Doctor's Pass into downtown Naples.

If boats had bedroom slippers, Roan's boat would be wearing them.

Tippy-toeing along the bottom of people's gardens, snooping around in the spooky lights, we were midnight burglars.

Now this area isn't the sort of place you can afford to rest your head unless you've made a dollar or two. The waterfront properties are either second homes for well-heeled folk who come to Florida to escape the New York winter, or permanent homes for those who've shipped out completely and retired there.

No bungalows here. The houses are mansions three or four storeys high with Greek columns, balconies and roof gardens set in landscaped grounds with terraces, patios, swimming pools and fountains. Each one with a mooring sticking handsomely out into the bay with a gin palace tied up there.

These vessels are places where you and I would be quite happy to set up home and spend the rest of our days cruising round the world. Let's just say they make your eyes pop.

But our real interest wasn't the bling, it was the blind. The blinding light from the illuminations at the bottom of the moorings out there, in place to stop the likes of Roan and me creeping around in the darkness, smashing into something.

Roan poled us close to a light hanging six feet above the smooth-surfaced water, wrapped in a cloud of bugs. There were still lights on in one of the downstairs rooms: a chandelier, but nobody was walking around inside.

'There's probably no one at home,' Roan whispered. 'These houses are only used two or three months of the year. Maybe there's a maid, so keep the noise down.'

There was no noise. The area around the light was like rice in a soup, thick with baitfish. You could see tarpon nosing around, patrolling on muffled fins. Roan told me to cast into the bubbles of feeding tarpon that were silently rolling into the baitfish, sucking them in soundlessly, turning the surface of the water like the pages of a book. Snook followed behind them, mopping up any half-chewed baitfish that had escaped inhalation.

Try as I could, and I did, I couldn't interest a single take. They'd seen a fly or two, or ten. I was certainly not as successful as the Professor of Sociology and angling writer Nick Curcione, who had been there the week before when Roan had guided him. He didn't land any snook, but he jumped a few tarpon, tucking his rod under his armpit, hand-winding the line in, to Roan's disapproval.

'This ain't no spin boat. No spinning allowed on this boat!'

We moved on.

Bayside Seafood Grill and Bar is one of Naples' most beloved waterfront restaurants, renowned for its exhilarating views of Venetian Village and Bay, and cuisine that is an art form unto itself.'

When you read the website of the exquisite, squeaky-clean Bayside restaurant, the last thing you think about is flies, let alone throwing flies at it, but at four in the morning that's all you want to do. The lights inside – and the ones hanging outside over the Bay – attract diners in the evening. But when everyone's tucked up in bed, it's the prime feeding location for the other hungry inhabitants. This is the time snook come snooping.

'Cast at that light. Try and hit it.'

venetian BAY at mid-day

Roan told me this was the way to ensure your fly landed right on the button. His instructions were whispers. There was nobody around, but it seemed like everyone was in earshot, listening.

My fly hit the wall underneath the overhanging light fitting and fell into a pool of yellow. Two, three, four, five pulls . . . and my rod was bending over, the reel a-spin. Fortunately my Penn sounds different from my Hardy Princess. It doesn't do sound, just whirrs. A killing machine fully equipped with a silencer – like my guide. For the first time ever, Roan didn't start whooping and hollering with excitement when the snook took off into the blackness.

Roan leaned forward and breathed something at me. 'A six-pounder.'

No photographs. It was on to the next one, but only after I'd nursed a bleeding hand trying to pick up the snook to flick out the hook.

'Mind those gills, boy. You can shave with them.'

Too late. I was now fishing with a handkerchief wrapped round my hand. I'd lacerated a foot the day before on the beach, when I'd kicked a snook I'd returned to revive it.

'Bet you didn't think you'd bump into a snook that size in a shopping centre!' Roan whispered.

'Quite a fish restaurant they got there,' I said.

On the way back to Doctor's Pass, we tried another set of 'spooky lights', just before sunrise. Lifted up on the crest of a hushed wave that rolled our way from a passing early-bird blue water fishing skiff heading out into the Gulf, we inched close to the mooring belonging to a mansion where it became clear why the Bay was called the Venetian Bay. No prizes for guessing where the architect got his idea.

With its balconies, pillars and cornices, it made me feel I was on the Grand Canal in Venice, casting from a gondola just down from Ponte di Rialto, in front of Baldassarre Longhena's elegant white marble-fronted Ca' Rezzonico.

Tarpon were rolling all over the place.

Roan suggested I fish a popper he had tied called a 'Gurgler'. With a foam upper and lower lip, it bubbled, burbled, glugged and gurgled its way across the surface, side-spitting any water that impeded its progress, from both sides. It made quite a commotion; that was its purpose.

Roan's voice was now way down in the carpet.

The Gurgler

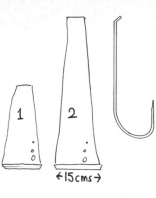

To tie a Gurgler, Roan says a #2/0 should do it. Place it in the vice, point up, and bend it down. Now tie in a short strip of foam, 15 cm wide, behind the eye. Secure. Wind the thread to the bend and tie in a bunch of khaki bucktail. Overlay with a dozen strands of Flashabou. Now you're all set.

Next, tie in a second strip of foam followed by two white saddle hackles and palmer forward three-quarters of the way up the hook. Now tie in two orange saddle hackles and palmer to behind the eye. Pull the foam at the bend over the body to form the all-impressive 'gurgly' Mick Jagger lips. Secure at the eye with several full-strength half hitches (no halfways with those half hitches!) and varnish. Clip foam ends, so hook eye just peeps out.

Two black beads superglu'd to 15lb mono

Add to Whipfinish (optional)

You have an option: superglue two black beads to a 1.5 cm length of mono, allowing 1 cm gap. Whip on, on top of whipping.

'Draw it through the water easy,' Roan whispered. 'Raise the rod tip with your right hand . . . drop it again and collect the line with the left hand in one easy, effortless, continuous movement . . . You got it.'

As we cast through a cobweb of ropes woven by the owners of the *Palazzo* to confuse anglers, a tarpon appeared on cue, from nowhere. Grabbing 'the commotion', it lifted out of the water into the darkness on the edge of the pool of chrome. Transforming into twisted silver as the light shocked it with a flash of electricity, it crashed back into the water, shattering the silence.

A light went on in the Palace.

After two more jumps, the tarpon threw the hook as only a fish with sandpaper tonsils can.

'I'd say a fifteen-pounder. A baby,' Roan breathed.

I quickly stripped back the line, scanning the water for telltale bubbles, poised to cast again.

'I think they know we're here,' Roan whispered.

'Yeah. No bubbles,' I said.

'No, I see people in the house.'

At 7.50, the sun rose. Like someone had flicked a switch.

At Gordon's Pass, the tide was running out. All along the rocks tarpon were busting. On the elbow of the rip, we swung into the powerful tidal race, letting it rush us out of the Bay and down the sea wall.

I shot flies like out of a machine gun on fast casts, as close to the rocks as I could get, landing them between the legs of snowy-white egrets picking up the dazed bits of baitfish smashed by the snook and tarpon.

I thought it was an old man blowing his nose behind us, but it was a dolphin, puffing like a horse. A leopard ray leaped out of the sea almost landing at my feet.

The sun was warming things up. It was all happening.

A snook appeared out of the rocks, snatched my fly and tore back into the rocks again.

I took three snook up to eight pounds before my arm finally dropped off and we shot off the end of the sea wall into the Gulf.

At 9.30 we headed back down the beach for the dock. We passed a block of apartments each with their own little balcony and regulation yucca plant. Round the back, so Roan told me, they had dug out a lake

between this apartment and another one, leaving enough room for a car park overlooking the lake.

'But you don't see many of them stoo-pid Smart cars parked there any more,' Roan said, a big grin slicing his face in two. 'At least, not for long.'

'Too small a car for you Americans?'

'No, alligators come out the lake and eat 'em whole. One gulp.'

On the way back, Roan stopped the skiff in a narrow canal lined with pretty houses that would have been a suburban street, had it not been filled with seawater.

'Chuck a fly into that garage,' Roan said, pointing at a boathouse tucked right next to someone's back door. A snook had busted right up against a wall inside.

It was a tricky cast. I had to get my fly through the space where half the door was swung open to the canal, past a rowing boat moored inside, avoiding some ropes and bits and pieces stacked up all over the place. Third cast, I managed it. The snook rushed to greet my fly.

Putting on full pressure, I yanked the five-pound snook out of the boatshed, off someone else's property onto ours.

'Are you allowed to do this?' I asked Roan. 'What's to stop me casting through that kitchen window, hooking up to a handbag on the table and running off with it?'

Roan laughed. 'Nothing. That's my sister's house. She operates catch and release in there!'

The next day I slept late. Mid-morning, Roan and I headed to the top of the backcountry; mangroves out in the ocean. It was a long journey in blistering temperatures. Roan wanted to find me a redfish.

I was up front scanning every half-litre of water as we approached the mangroves, my eyes sizzling like fried eggs in the sun. Then I spotted it. Someone's mobile phone bobbing in the waves. Someone's big red phone, aerial and all, circling the boat with the ghostly shape of its owner directly underneath.

It was a tracker attached to a manatee, the 'sea cows' that cruise serenely round these parts with their paddle-like flippers grazing in the shallower waters. It had a deep scar across its back. An old wound where it had been run over by a Sunday speedboat out of Naples when it surfaced for air, which they have to do every twenty minutes. 'Idle past. No wake', say the signs sticking out of the sea, marking out their territories.

It was hard to tell how old it was, but the Florida manatees can live up to sixty years. This was a small one, about the same size as Roan, who told me that they grow to five thousand pounds. Ancient mariners used to mistake them for mermaids.

'When you're out at sea for a long time, you make your own fun,' Roan sniggered.

As we left, it stuck its nose out of the water and snorted.

With the remote control electric motor on, which Roan operated with his foot, we purred parallel to the mangroves. Some baitfish fizzed. The only redfish we saw grabbed my fly and wound my line round a mangrove shoot. We managed to unfix it, but the knot I'd used to tie on the fly unravelled and the red escaped, inches from the boat.

I took two more snook before we got back to the mooring. One snaffling around in some rubbish at the bottom of someone's garden, another that had parked itself in the shadow of a large red Yard King Ride-On Lawn Mower. This one I missed. I trout-struck – vertical move – instead of strip-struck – horizontal move – and that was the end of that.

'What you up to tonight?' Roan asked as he secured the skiff to a mooring behind the Mangrove Angler.

'Thought we'd try out that fancy Bayside Seafood Grill. But I don't know if I have enough money.'

Roan nodded as he walked down the pier.

'Yep. You should have gone for that shot through the kitchen window.'

snook - at arm's length . mind those gills!

I don't hire guides out of Naples any more. I still go back there. I still fish. I still catch snook. In fact, I caught my biggest snook there just the other day. But not from a guided skiff at $450 for a morning bash. From the beach, for free. And not staying in some fancy hotel. No, shacking up at the 'Buzz' Lighthouse Inn, family-owned since 1978 and comfort-controlled by Mrs Judy Dugan, right across the road from the luxury Vanderbilt Beach Resort; a block down from the Ritz-Carlton. Here I have my own bedroom, sitting room, bathroom, kitchen and two verandas. One facing east, the other south, so your towels and swimming gear dry quicker than in a tumble dryer. And you've got all the seaside paraphernalia you could ask for: shell wallpaper, pictures of sailing boats, miniature plastic anchors, china mermaids, model tropical fish struggling to get out of loosely hung netting, and buckets of sand left by the family who had the room before you. All for the price of a Mojito, a Margarita and a Trouble in Paradise cocktail at the beach bar at the Vanderbilt, the best place in the world to watch the sun go down. And I don't even have to put shoes on to get there. I just hotfoot through the shadows (at midday the tarmac's a griddle) across a strip of grass, over a road, down a side entrance and forty seconds later, I'm there, on the beach.

So, this big snook I was talking about. You have to get up early to go strolling with a fly rod along the beach. First, because the sun coming up is a sight to behold, even though it rises behind the beach-facing hotels, casting big long shadows way out over the ocean at 6.30 a.m., when you first get sight of it. Second, because this isn't a fisherman's beach, it's a sunbathers' beach, so you don't want to take anybody's eye out.

I'm usually walking down the beach, flicking a fly into the surf, getting into the swing of it, in semi-lightness, at around 6 a.m. The first beach power-walkers and joggers aren't on the sand at this time so you don't have to check right and left every time you cast a fly. Later in the morning, it isn't casting that's the problem; the beach is so crowded that finding a square foot in the sea to land a fly is the challenge.

But that's a lot later. So I'm there early. Whatever the tide.

I like a bit of a wave and a high tide, with no dolphins or groups of lovesick manatees roaming the drop-off; and with the sun behind you, so there's no early-morning glare like you have on other early-morning forays on rivers and lakes. But I'm not fussy. The people who pass by say 'Good morning' and you don't feel too bad if you've never caught anything, because they never ask. But I usually catch something. And it's often one after another, like someone pulled a switch, with big long breaks of nothing.

A ladyfish or two usually do me the honour. The silver, shiny, googly-eyed ladyfish, with a forked tail splayed out like two fingers. They call them 'the poor man's tarpon' because hook 'em and they leap way up high up in the air.

A strange fish, but I'm a great fan. Mainly because when one hits your fly, it usually does so just when you're starting to think it's time to walk back for a shower. Then, when you least expect it, bang. It makes your day, even though the day hasn't started!

I have a favourite place. Historically, it's where those ladyfish seem to hit most regularly. Turn left up the beach from the Resort and you pass three large hotels throwing long shadows across the beach, out to sea. In between, there are golden highways of sunlight reaching out to eternity.

It's in that dark band, at hotel-width, in between hotel three and hotel four (called the Brighton, funnily enough) where ladyfish seem to cluster. Always in the Dark, never in the Golden Path. That day there were clouds of tiny baitfish hanging in the wave, sparkling like copper tapioca.

Every morning, I fish the same fly. A white shrimp pattern, with white legs spangled with bright bits, a long white calf-hair moustache with Krystal Flash rolled up in it and two large black beady eyes, all whipped up with pink tying silk. It does the trick.

But you do get the occasional person out for a stroll on the beach who isn't doing it for the exercise. They do it because they're up. You can recognize them. They're showered and ready to face the day, their deodorant freshly applied, powerful and unfaded. You very quickly become an expert on which deodorant smells of what.

One of these get-up-and-goers, a grandmother with a wide-brimmed hat, stopped to ask me if I'd caught anything. Yes, I had. I'd taken six ladyfish up to a pound and a half. An early-rising family had been swimming there and jigging up and down. A good place to start fishing, but I didn't go into this sort of detail.

'Six! Hey, we should open a restaurant out there,' she said, suitably impressed. She walks the beach at the same time every day, so I took her as an authority on fish catches and felt good.

She'd barely walked fifty yards when a seventh ladyfish grabbed my fly just as it hit the waves, on the border between the Dark and the Golden Path. It flicked up into the morning with a flash, burrowed back down into the darkness and made a run for it, finally giving up.

It was when I was unhooking and returning it to the foam that I noticed the handle on my reel was coming loose. As I was tucking my rod under my arm to fix it I felt my line pull away. I thought a wave on the incoming tide rolling back had grabbed it, but I saw a large yellow fish, its back half out of the water, shake its head and head out into the Dark with my line.

At first I was confused. It must have foul-hooked itself. I thought it was a small shark because it didn't steam off like a bonefish, it acted like sharks do. It eased itself away as if to tell me, no sweat, everything's just fine; I wasn't going to fool him. But I had fooled him, all right.

He was well hooked, and the deeper into the Dark he got, the further back to the shore I was able to pull him. I guess he was confused, too.

More than landing this fish, I wanted to see what the hell I was attached to, so I was anxious to get him in close. But he would sidle off slowly, no panic, no rush, as if nothing had happened. As if this sort of thing happened to him every day. The fish was so nonchalant, maybe this sort of thing does happen to him every day.

Holding him in an incoming wave, I eventually managed to walk back and slide him onto the beach, allowing the last wave to roll him ashore, high and dry. He arrived at my feet like a landing craft, belly down.

When the second wave rolled in, it turned my fish on its side and I could see just how big it was. A snook of seven pounds.

With my Abel pliers, I flicked the hook loose as he lay there rolling me in his deep-sea eye, not a bit put out. I wished I'd brought my camera. My grandma wasn't even in sight to witness my catch. But I met her on my way back along the beach to the Lighthouse.

'Caught any more?' she asked me as we passed.

'Yes, two,' I said, saving her the details.

'There's a few more people fishing back there,' she told me. 'But they haven't caught anything. I asked 'em.'

This must have been the handful of bait fishermen that tend to hang out where a creek runs into the sea.

'You see, if we're going to open that restaurant, I wanna know who we got as competition,' grandma said, with a wink.

You betcha.

THIRTEEN

Wales

Jambo

Thread: Black monochord, throughout
Hook 1: No. 10 treble lopped on 15 lb monofilament,
the shank covered with silver tinsel
Hook 2: (and body): No. 2 black salmon hook,
with black floss ribbed with wide silver tinsel
Wing: Black bucktail topped with six strands
of silver Krystal Flash or Flashabou
Head: Black deer hair wound 'Muddler-style',
trimmed to bullet shape

The Princess, the Castle and the Dragon

To WALK ALONE IN A WOOD IS like trespassing in a fairytale.
To walk alone along a river at night is like taking the wrong path in a nightmare. The whirr of hidden wings; the strange rustlings that may or may not be the work of the wind; being looked at from every angle by a multitude of eyes. Then there's the plodding splashes somewhere out in the blue/black inky darkness.

Something's coming at you from across the river.

We all get depressed at times. But double depression? The DDs? Want to know what this is? Just in case you should ever get it? Well, it's this:

It's watching the value of your investments get smaller and smaller (as we all have over the past few years) as reports come flooding in that the sea trout being caught on Golden Grove are getting bigger and bigger. And you're not there. Well, you were. But now you aren't. Double depression. See what I mean? You don't? Well, walk with me into the darkness . . .

Golden Grove is where I was invited to fish a couple of years ago. This is Sir Edward Dashwood and his partner's fourteen miles of double-bank fishing on the middle Towy, stretching from Llandeilo Bridge to Llanarthne. A golden investment if ever there was one, now he's had the nets lifted.

Downstream, Sir Edward has a share in the renowned three-mile Abercothi beat, with a mile of the River Cothi that licks the sea trout out of the tide at Carmarthen up to his guests awaiting their silvery arrival above Nantgaredig Bridge.

Tended by Sir Edward's omnipresent ghillie, Cyril Fox, if you're a fisherman at Abercothi – and resident at the recently converted farmhouse on the riverbank – quite simply, you never want to move anywhere else. Unless, that is, you are invited to sleepwalk upriver, through a choir of bats calling up ghosts from the past, to Golden Grove; an invitation kindly extended to me, and gladly accepted.

Jamie Harries arrives in a Range Rover and hops out with the air of a businessman. Resident ghillie on Golden Grove, until recently he ran his own highly successful bakery for ten years, so he knows what a customer is and understands what his clients expect.

But his reassuring confidence is more deeply rooted, for with a CV like his, Jamie could have arrived in a chariot. His fishing skills are legion. He has fished the Towy regularly for twenty-five years; been a member of the Welsh flyfishing team; and dabbled flies in faraway places such as New Zealand, Canada and Scotland.

In his time, he has befriended all the resident experts on the river, such as John Graham. Sea trout sorcerer and flytyer, Graham is the inventor of the Jambo, a surface lure that has fast become the shining light in the midnight fly boxes of every Towy flyfisherman – and far beyond.

'Knowledge is king,' Jamie tells me as we walk the beat that I will be fishing later that night. Beat 1: A good place to start. 'And putting the time in,' Jamie adds with a look of intent.

For him, sea trout fishing is the hardest of all fishing. 'You are up against so much. But when things go well, you must get out and make the best of it. In the dark. Stripped of all your senses.'

Jamie is weary of reading articles glorifying sea trout fishing. Stories of large bags that make it sound easy. I reassured him that if I were to write anything, I'd avoid such descriptions. However, although he may not have wanted such things written, deep down, I was praying for just such a night to write about.

Towering over treetops on the other side of the river, standing on a hill halfway down the beat, is Dynevor Castle, now in ruins on the skyline. Jamie points at the black shape of a log arching out of the water on the far side of the river.

'That's the Dragon's Head. That's where I'd put myself tonight.'

I promise him that if I can find the spot in the blackness, I'll be there. By the castle, with the dragon, and my Princess. My Hardy Princess reel stoked with hundreds of yards of stout backing.

I ask if he has any other snippets of advice to give me.

'I do,' he says, as if he's been saving this for the very last on account of its surprising imperative. 'Expect the unexpected. One night I was sitting in a hollow and a badger came and sat on my head.'

Earlier that day, hanging over the Nantgaredig Bridge waiting for Jamie, I watched the shapes of many sea trout materializing out of the semi-stained water below. Conditions looked good. I had all the hopes in the world.

The die is set, I tell myself. Nothing can change this now.

But Jamie had barely gone when the skies darkened, the heavens cracked open and an electric storm came hurtling down the valley, heaping river water up like a clash of tides. Leaves spun noisily round my ears. Afternoon became night. I ran for cover.

The unexpected had arrived, unexpectedly.

It is two o'clock the next morning when I judge it safe to stick a nose outside. The rain and wind have dropped. The roads are strewn with branches as I pick my way through the darkness to the beat. With rod up and torch off, I fumble my way down an angry river I can hear, but can't see. When Malcolm Muggeridge said, 'There is no such thing as darkness; only a failure to see', he hadn't set out for a night's sea trout fishing.

Tonight, he might have done.

The wind whistles over an empty field that I remember sits behind where the Dragon Head lies cloaked by a thicket of trees. I wade out. Like a blind man I shuffle across a gravelly riverbed knowing I'm shuffling in safety. You have a better chance of stumbling across a rock in your own bed than on the bed of the River Towy. The water feels thick. Like soup.

My eyes try to part the darkness. At night, you think that by straining them you might just be able to squeeze out images, like juice out of a lemon. But you can't. My eyes sting.

Not knowing the depth of the river in front of me, I fish a floating line and one of John Graham's Jambos. He believes 'in' and not 'on' the surface is the best solution for surface lures, so he has designed it to do just that. Here's how I tie it. The tricky part is preparing the hooks. I put a #10 treble in the vice and run black monochord down the shank. I thread fifteen pounds of monofilament through the eye of the hook and bring both ends around the back of the hook and back through the eye. I pull both ends of mono tight and bind them down on the hook with the thread and cover with silver tinsel, to eye; whip-finish, varnish.

While this is drying, I insert a #2 hook in the vice. I use a black salmon hook. I catch the two ends of mono on the treble with a few turns of thread. Then I bring one end through the eye and back down the shank, wrapping the thread back to the eye, trapping in both ends. Now I whip-finish and varnish this and leave it to dry. That's the hook done – for now.

Now tie in a length of black floss and wide silver tinsel at the bend and wind three-quarters up the hook shank. In front of this, tie in a mixture of bucktail and flash material. This can be black, blue, or yellow. Black,

Black
cellire
varnish

Twist mono before
securing

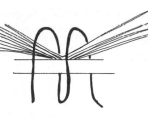

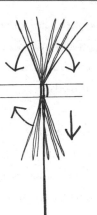

Pack each turn

for me – and silver Krystal Flash. No need for body material as this just adds to the weight of the fly. Behind the eye start the deer hair spinning and packing, as you would do if you were tying a large head on a Muddler Minnow. With this complete, trim the bottom flat. Finally, trim the head to a bullet shape tapering out from the eye.

Now back to that hook again. Take it out of the vice and carefully snip the hook off at the bend with the scissor part of a pair of pliers, leaving the flying treble hanging dangerously below the body. Mind your fingers!

My Jambo spends the night swishing back and forth across the dance floor of a bat disco, unable to pick up anything. The first cool light of a dewy new day catches the razor-sharp edges of the 'V' my Jambo is still carving out of the river as I figure-of-eight it back from the spot I have been casting to all night. A position just below where I believed the Dragon's Head would rear up at any moment, out of a thin tissue of early-morning mist.

At four o'clock, there is enough light to see what I hadn't been able to see. The Dragon's Head isn't there.

At 4.02, I can see that the Dragon's Head can't see me, either. It is underwater. Water the colour of Welsh earth.

The river had been unfishable all night, and remained so for the rest of the week. Then, when it cleared and I had cleared off, my double depression set in. In the shape of two double-figure sea trout.

The first, at fifteen pounds six ounces, taken three days later by Mr Udale – from the Dragon's Head. The very spot where I had shuffled around with so much hope. Then, a week later, a second monster at an astonishing twenty-one pounds.

Now I'm back home gazing over the chalkstream down the track from my house. Here, no matter how hard the rain (never enough), it takes at least three months before it even starts to consider trickling through the barrage of ancient chalk filters on the Berkshire Downs, to my River Kennet below.

I'm still recovering from that symphony of darkness – and the DDs. My therapy: DD-ing. Dibbling in daylight. For trout . . . I can see.

My see-trout, I call them.

FOURTEEN

Wales

Blockhead Spinner

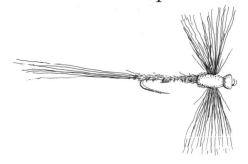

Thread: Brown thread
Hook 1: No. 12 barbless
Thorax: Thin, brown cell foam
Tails: Grey hackle fibres
Body: Golden/reddish brown seal fur
Wing: Cream Antron yarn

The Doctor's Cabin

AT AN AUTUMN SPORTING AUCTION, Steve and I had decided to bid
for Lot Number 14. A day's ratting in Norfolk. Never done it
before. Sounded fun.

Since the room was filled with flyfishermen on the lookout for
a bargain week on the Varzuga, or a couple of days on some fancy
beat of the Tweed, a day standing outside a barn watching dogs shake
the living daylights out of rats didn't really seem a lot that would be
oversubscribed. Not the assembled crowd's bag somehow. But our sort
of bag it certainly was and we were sure we were in for a bargain.

Bidding started at £200. (Proceeds going to the Salmon & Trout
Association.) Steve and I were willing to bid up to £400. But a wagging
finger at the back of the hall had the same idea and when the bidding

streaked past our top price and the hammer went down at £420, we were mighty disappointed.

'You dirty rat!' we screamed.

The bid went to an American who had moved to London and taken possession of a small dog. At this point, rather than feeling sorry for ourselves for losing the bid, we began to feel sorry for the poor pup when that barn door opened up and it found itself faced with a score of vicious rodents, teeth flashing menacingly in the afternoon sun, growling like tigers.

But we got our second choice. A day on a small private beat of the River Usk, just north of Abergavenny. We were to meet our host at 9.30 a.m., so we stayed over at the Gliffaes Hotel near Crickhowell with grounds overlooking and leading down to the river.

Our host wasn't expecting what he saw when we arrived. Steve was dressed for the kill. Tweed suit with velvet collar. Highly polished Lock Brothers knee-high boots, his blond Warhol tresses hanging like a lampshade around his head. We were walked from our car, parked in a field, to a small wooden cabin overlooking the river. Set on one floor, it had four small rooms. A living area with kitchen, two large bedrooms with several double bunks, a shower and toilet. This was our host's holiday home where he and his partner spend a month or so every summer with their children. It had been in the family for three generations.

It was suggested we start fishing straight away, so we were escorted to the top of the beat with the plan to fish our way back down for lunch.

'But mind that barbed wire when you're crossing this fence,' our host warned, whereupon I walked straight into it.

I thought the tiny newly sprung leak in my chest waders might just be all right, but when the icy cold hand of the Usk started creeping up the side of my leg, I decided I'd better dry off so I headed back to the cabin where our host was making tea. Pulling off my chesties, I stripped to my long johns and socks and hung them over the terrace railings to dry. Then I sat down next to them, my bare feet up on some cranky old piece of garden furniture.

'There's something very relaxing about a cabin,' I said to the owner at the same time as realizing that I was probably sitting on his favourite seat, in my underpants, feet up on some precious heirloom, pipe ablaze.

'There is, isn't there,' the host agreed, taking in a long breath and sitting down opposite me, facing upriver.

Suddenly his eyes shifted from me to something happening directly behind me, over my shoulder. The expression on his face changed. When he started leaning forward to make sure what he was looking at wasn't an illusion, I turned to see what this might be.

Just up the river, what appeared to be a Victorian bust was floating down the river. It was Steve. Halfway across the river. His head and shoulders 'sitting' on the surface, water about to lap over the top of his chest waders. Arms, elbows, hands, rod, reel and line were all held way above his head as he cast a long line to a fish he'd spotted rising under a tree on the far bank. I turned back to my host.

'I've never seen that before,' he said, letting out the breath he'd taken in moments before in disbelief.

About seven o'clock, we were beginning to think it was time to go, but our host wouldn't let us. He unroped a small rowing boat pulled up in front of the cabin where the bank wasn't set at too steep an angle. He wanted to take us to the top of the beat and float us back down again to fish the evening rise on the way, which is what we did with great success. The more the daylight disappeared, the more the trout seemed to appear, rising all round the boat.

At that supernatural batty dusk moment, just as darkness falls and the sky looks like one great bruise, we arrived back at the mooring where the bank was at its gentlest angle.

I was perched at the back of the boat, hands behind my back, gripping the place where you'd mount the motor engine if we'd had one. Steve was up front. Without instruction, he took the initiative and vaulted out of the boat up the bank to secure the boat. What he also did was redistribute all the weight from the front of the boat to the back, flipping it down at a forty-degree angle. Over I went, backwards, in slo-mo, like a well-rehearsed circus act.

Now Nick Lyons once told me when he slipped into (and under) my chalkstream one evening that it's a magical experience.

'One moment I was watching the hatch from my point of view,' he said, 'the next I was watching it from the trout's.'

After some elegant subsurface somersaulting, I emerged thoroughly dampened, but undamaged. My pipe may have gone out, but it was still securely clamped between my teeth.

As charitable as he most certainly is, I often wonder if our host was quite so enthusiastic about offering a day's fishing at his holiday retreat at the auction the following year.

Back in those days, the hatches of a fly called the March Brown, or *Rhithrogena germanica/haarupi* for those of you who went to Oxford, on the Usk were like the Mayfly on the Test, such was their profusion. That was before some hill farmer with the IQ of a haystack decided to tip a few gallons of sheep dip into the river and hey presto! We haven't seen a bottom-hugging March Brown nymph since. At the time of writing, the transplanting and restocking of the river with March Browns from other rivers is up against huge opposition. No one other than the opposition can see why.

It was on the Usk during a heavy fall of March Brown spinners when I first started to get my head around a design for spinners of the larger upwing flies. A spinner pattern with a head that sits on the eye.

It was late afternoon, and I was tucked tight into the bank under a pine where the river twisted and turned off a shallow riffle into a deep run. The trout were lined up on the drop-off. I couldn't see them in the high water, but I knew they would be there. Suddenly, another angler appeared, jumping out at me from behind the tree, with a raccoon on his head. He said it wasn't the weather for his usual trilby. The wind was cool, sure enough. And he'd had enough, for sure.

There had been a hatch of March Browns earlier. He'd taken sufficient fish to warm his net, but now it was time to go. But not before I told him that the hatch may be over, but not for the trout.

If rivers truly run in your veins, you can really never have enough of those days spent on a prime rain-fed stream like the Usk. I'm busting blood vessels to get out. I'm fishing the bath. I'll fish any stream. Whatever the weather. Come hell – or high water.

But that week on the Usk, the Almighty had made water levels drop as fast as they'd risen. He'd laid on a feast of March Browns – and he didn't just give us one bite of the cherry, he gave several: the nymph, the emerger, the upwing dun – and now, in the evening, just when my friend and his raccoon were off home, He gave us the spinner.

If March Browns are my favourite fly, the spinner is my favourite stage in the life-cycle. They are the most handsome of insects. Their fragility and their translucent colours glinting in the sunlight like small stars make them more beautiful than butterflies. But unlike butterflies, when lying on the trout's dinner table fully spent after egg-laying, they can be hard to detect. If, that is, they're sitting on the river surface correctly. And they can be even harder to spot when carpeting the fizzing riffles just below where they had started dancing, at the tail of the pool the local in his loco headgear was leaving.

I have thought long and hard about spinner imitations. Over the years I have come to the conclusion it isn't the pattern that needs examination (I'll come to this again in a moment). It's not even the design (I'll come to this in a moment also).

At first, I concluded the design feature that needed imitating to create the perfect spinner design wasn't the colour. The top two features were shape and size – the outline. With this decided, I developed many patterns. But no matter how good they were, I found myself coming up against the same problem that had faced me when designing hatching nymphs and midge pupae. The problem that had led me into originating the Suspender nymph so many years ago.

So what was this?

It was knowing for sure that my imitation was behaving exactly like the natural. That my hatchers were sitting, not in the film, but suspended directly underneath it. Now I was faced with a similar problem once again. How to make sure my spinner pattern was sitting flush with the surface film. Not on top or underneath, but horizontally *in* it. Now here comes the physics lesson.

At school they taught me that there are two ways things float. To demonstrate the first way, my physics teacher chucked a match in a glass of water. It floated – and bounced back to the surface when submerged. This was called buoyancy. Wood and cork (and deer hair) are buoyant. For the second way, teacher carefully placed a pin on the surface. Now this pin was heavier than water. So how come it didn't sink? Tension mounted in the classroom – and we learned about surface tension. Prick this and the pin sinks. So, whereas my Suspender nymph depended on a buoyant material (Ethafoam) wrapped up in a nylon stocking material,

my spinner patterns depended on the totally undependable surface tension to prevent them sinking off the scene.

But, unlike a pin, my spinner imitations did have lifejackets, of sorts. One at the tail – and a set of hackle fibres sticking out, at the head. So the thing was a trifle *Titanic*-proof. But trifle wasn't sweet enough for me.

So, I hear you say, why don't you just tie those tails and wings with a chunk of buoyant material, like deer hair, and Bob's your auntie?

Well, I could. But I didn't. Remember, we're imitating something slender and fragile here. And shiny. To avoid the Incredible Bulk, and the need for two big lads and a wheelbarrow to carry it around, better to use a slender and elegant synthetic yarn – like polypropylene, or Antron – shaped to size and outline. Buoyant materials, as I learned when I was developing the Suspender nymph, work best hanging in the gluey film, the surface tension that cradles the spent-out spinner.

But rather than stuffing a stocking with this material, I simply formed a 'wing pad' of foam at the thorax, leaving a little bit sticking out over the hook eye to imitate the natural's head and to support the weight of the eye so the fly doesn't nosedive. So how do I tie this thing?

To tie my Blockhead Spinner, first I tie brown silk behind the eye of a #12 barbless hook. Then I whip in a small length of thin brown cell foam at the thorax, two-thirds of the way down the hook. I now wind the silk to the bend, tying in a bunch of grey hackle fibres on the way, as tails. I dub the silk with a golden/reddish brown seal fur and wind this three-quarters of the way up to the eye.

To form spent wings, I figure-of-eight a length of cream Antron yarn, lightly dub over the roots and clip the wings to length and shape. Finally, I pull the foam over the wings and thorax, clip the thread, whip-finish and trim the foam so that it sticks over the eye.

So, what do we end up with? An easy-to-tie spinner that stays put exactly where naturals put themselves. And an imitation with an uncanny resemblance to the natural, made from materials that don't fall apart.

As I keep saying, life's too short to fish the wrong fly.

But March Browns in spinner form aren't the only insects that like to make an appearance as the sun sets behind the hills. Or the woods, when I'm at home. Living by the river that you fish has many advantages. Not having to travel to get there is one of the more obvious delights. Being able to stick your nose out of the window and see if you can smell if the hatch has started is another. And you have your very own on-site Fly Lab.

You don't need any qualifications to become a self-proclaimed nature detective on my river. All you need is an open mind and a bit of enthusiasm. Having moaned the roof off about the dire state of the fly life on rivers both rain- and chalk-fed — filling in forms for the Environment Agency, applauding the Salmon & Trout Association's action on the issue, writing to my MP (Minister for Pollution) – guess what? Recently, there have been times when it's been hard to breathe in on our beat.

Where have all the Yellow May Duns suddenly appeared from? After a desperately poor showing of Large Dark Olives, this year they were winging their furious way right into the middle of May. And the small fly? Big time.

With such poor showings in the past – and then suddenly some outstanding performances – I think the lifespan of the *baetis* nymph isn't restricted to just the one year. I think they can hold back to two, even three. Why else should the amount of fly double from one year to the next? Or maybe conditions have been more favourable for egg incubation

Whatever it is, something very strange is going on. But then, with fly life, strange things do go on. Especially after dark.

A few years ago, we had a real mystery. Blue-winged olives were plentiful enough; at least the duns were in the evening. And male spinners; clouds of them. But there were no female spinners, evening after evening. And when the hatch started to slow down and female spinners kept not appearing, I'd wait and I'd wait . . . and find myself strolling further and further away from one of the blue-winged olive's favourite egg-laying sites at the top end of the beat . . . across the water meadow . . . over a gate . . . down the road . . . over the railway line . . . across the canal bridge . . . to one of the two public houses that bookend my beat.

Later, one particular night, bat-eyed in the half-light, I thought it better to fumble my way back the long way round, on a footpath that takes me past the keeper's cottage. It was the dead of night when I got to the stews beside the river keeper, and all I could hear was the familiar slosh-splash of hungry fish. I thought the Boss had been midnight-feasting his fingerlings just before I arrived. In fact, they were after Blue-winged olive spinners.

To the pub...

That warm July night, I took my largest fish of the month. Using my very best, mothy eyes – and my trusty Hockey Mom, my favourite B-WO spinner pattern. The fact is, in late July and August, often the best Blue-Winged Olive spinner fishing is after dark, when the females hit the warm airwaves. On my chalkstream. And on rain-fed streams, like the Usk.

Now, if I'd gone straight back home that evening, and not embarked on a drinks detour, I would have been in front of the telly, believing the fishing had finished for the day – and not out discovering that the fishing was actually just starting for the night.

Consider the Pale Evening Dun. When did you last see one of those? Forget Polaroids to spot this pretty little fly. You need ultraviolet glasses. The Pale Evening Dun leaves it to the very last knockings before poking its head out from under the sheets. More often than not, mating and egg-laying happen after dark.

... and back

Again, this is something I witnessed on the way back from the pub. Sucking the last drops of moonlight out of the sky to tie my small cream-coloured pattern on my line, I set to work casting to the many steel-rimmed, moonlight rings expanding out in the river. But let me tell you a bit more about that Hockey Mom of mine.

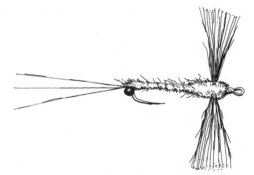

Hockey Mom

When did someone last tell you the facts of life? Well, here it comes again. Mom hits that great dance floor in the sky. Pa jumps on her, mid-air. Mom heads off home, spreads herself out on her waterbed and drifts off to sleep. Meantime, Pa goes down the pub and falls in the river on the way home. The sex life of summer's high-flier, the Blue-Winged Olive, is fascinating. At best, it's guaranteed to have you guessing. You and the trout, both – and the male of the B-WO species. At worse, it can drive you shouty crackers.

After a hatch of B-WO duns, you might expect to see spinners dipping and diving around the bushes the next evening. And when you do, a spinner fall at sunset. Don't you believe it. You may see spinners, but look closely. Chances are they will be males. Just males. Males asking the same thing as you. Where are the girls?

If you want to identify the sex of fly buzzing round your ears, and therefore whether or not you'll see female spinners on the water that evening, swipe one out of the sky, perch it on your finger and you'll notice males have two hooks at the tail end. A pair of claspers they use to grab their girl when she can be bothered to show up to the party. They don't want her disappearing again. Then look to the other end where you'll find what you'd expect a guy to have after he'd had one long-distance flight after another, night after night: red eyes.

When females do turn up to this airborne orgy, it's easy to identify the Moms. They're the ones with bodies shaped like hockey sticks, their tail ends wrapped round little green egg sacs – the ones being pounced on by sex-starved males. When you see this, it's time to get to the river.

There you will have already marked out where you think the best fish will be lying, waiting to be served up soup plates of spinner to spoon in. Again, don't you believe it.

To ensure the survival of their species, olive spinners crawl beneath the surface to lay their eggs. Tricky, but essential, stuff. For, if they didn't, those eggs would very quickly be washed down to the sea – and bye-bye, Mr River Fly.

The female B-WO has other ideas. After the party, when she returns to the river, she doesn't take a bath. But she doesn't just plonk her eggs in any old place, either. Instead, she grabs her green shopping bag of eggs, gets her friends together and heads upriver to a shop 'n' drop spot they all know well. And you and I? Well, we should follow their instinct, for that's where the trout will be waiting. I know one thing. The B-WO females like fizzy water to lay their eggs in, with a good flow to snatch away that load of eggs and deliver them safely to clean, well-aerated gravels. Just downstream, in the slacker water, will be the wild trout, keeping their heads down, sucking in

the lowest-lying spinners. To address these low-profile patrollers, I have a low-profile spinner pattern.

If you wade into the water and scoop up a 'spent' female, you'll note that not all of them are in such a hurry to let go of their shopping bags. Many lie in the surface film, their hockey stick shaped bodies curled beneath the surface, pulled down under the weight of that hefty green egg sac. I say hefty, because if that bag wasn't heavy, it would be no use at all. Instead of sinking, it would float (down to that sea again).

And it's this weight that allows us to design a pattern that exaggerates the helplessness of the fly we are imitating – and therefore its greatest attraction to the trout. Just like we do with the hatching dun, the emerger, only this time it's a submerger.

Originally, I used a small tuft of green DFM wool to imitate the egg sac under the curled tails, but these days I use something a little heavier: the smallest of green beads. To have your fly sitting perfectly half in, half out of the surface film, just grease the wings and let the tail end sink.

So, to tie the Hockey Mom, wind some rusty brown thread two-thirds of the way down a #16 hook. Not a #14. Harder to see in the half-light or near-dark, but we use too big a hook these days. If you want to fool pernickety wild trout, give them less to argue about.

Tie in a 'post' of white Antron and split with figure-of-eight to separate wings so that they lie 'spent'. Thread a small, light-green mixed-chalk embroidery bead (fifteen grams) onto two-pound fluorocarbon nylon and trap in loop. Tie in loop so bead hangs round hook bend. Now tie in three Microfibetts so they lie over the bead. Dub silk with three parts hare poll, two parts ginger and one part hot orange substitute seal fur. Wind to a wing of white Antron. Figure-of-eight round each wing. Wind in two turns to behind eye, whip-finish and varnish. Job done.

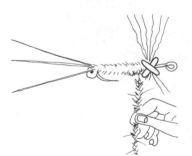

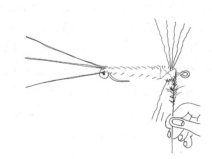

LEFT VICE BEHIND.
NO PROBLEM

Late-evening fishing on any stream can be highly rewarding. If you can stay on. But not so if you don't have the right fly on the end of your line, at the end of the day when the light starts to fade and it's too late to tie something else on.

When I'm fishing the Usk – or somewhere else more than a mile (or many hundreds of miles) away from my flytying bench, I have my collar box. It's my mobile flytying kit. A small case stuffed with a ragbag of snippets from my base-camp kit, just in case I meet up with fussy trout fussing over something I haven't got in my fly box and which I might be able to tie up from a handful of the carefully selected minimal number of materials I keep stored away there. This collar box has enough bits and bobs to whip up flies on the spot; on the riverbank. Flies that don't have trout twisting their heads from side to side appreciatively, like people do at art exhibitions. No, these are flies trout are gagging for. Flies designed to be pounced on and wolfed down wantonly, like they were Pot Noodles.

Contained in this little leather box is my whole approach to flytying. And a chunk of one of my favourite flytying materials which best represents how this minimalist style can work – anywhere. But more especially on the riverbank. A very special material that didn't come from an overpriced tackle shop. It came from a bargain basement junk shop. A mink stole. Holding it up in the cellar light, I didn't see it wrapped round the shoulders of a lipsticked beauty. I saw it sticking in the lip of a trout out at some society sedge hatch.

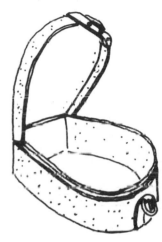

Sitting backside on bankside, my last sedge up a tree or stuck in the lip of a long-gone trout, it's got everything I need to whip up a replacement.

The design of my Mini Minx is deliciously ingenious. Great for tying mini-size sedge of any shape, size or species. Like Michelangelo carving that horse out of marble, I just take my stole and steal away everything that isn't body, wing or sedge leg material.

The fluff at the base of the hairs I keep for the body. Rich and creamy, it's the perfect match for the bodies of every succulent sedge ever likely to bump into you. For wing and legs, I keep the hairs.

Here's how it comes together.

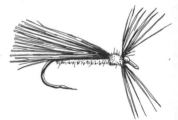

When I've stacked a bunch of hairs (in a used 12-bore cartridge I found in the field on my way to the river), I tie them in behind the eye, butt ends pointing towards the bend forming a wing sloping over the body. Before I secure this wing, when pulled back, I make sure the points protruding over the eye are the same length as if I had wound on a hackle. Next, I dub on a bit of fluff to cover the silk turns between wing and protruding hairs. Then I pull back the points with thumb and forefinger forming a 'hair hackle', spinning hairs underneath the hook so they stick out above *and* below.

I was tempted to say something more than just a polite 'Good evening' to a fisherman with a pheasant as a hat, with no hope of catching anything, whom I met on the banks of the River Usk while waiting for the evening rise. Watching him as he talked to me, I was sure I spotted that he only had one tooth in his head.

'August,' he said. 'Nothing moves until dark.'

Hat Man turned out to be a philosopher.

'Hope springs eternal,' he huffed after everything I said, regardless of how hopeful I sounded. Then he said something that had me thinking. Hearing that this was my first visit to this beat, he said, 'You can't understand a river in an afternoon.'

I thought, how true.

Then he spoiled everything: 'I haven't seen a sedge all month' – and off he went. Home to brush his tooth, I thought.

I almost packed up, too. But I didn't. I stayed late, just as Hat Man had suggested. There was no sedge hatch, just as he had warned. But I fished my Mini Minx anyway, just as I had planned. And I caught two speckled trout, just as I had hoped. Just as I knew my Mini Minx would do.

On my pitch-black fumble back across the field that night, I thought over the two lessons I had learned. First, when I tie a fly on the bankside – as opposed to at my bench at home – I always seem to tie in something that's in neither of my flytying kits. A thing called confidence. Second, if there are no flies on the water, you won't catch anything if your fly isn't on the water, either.

Sometimes flyfishing can be just as uncomplicated as flytying.

∼

When I heard that George Melly, jazz and blues singer, critic, writer and lecturer, was also a flyfisherman, I thought, 'Great.' When I heard he had a house and some fishing on the Usk, just up from the Gliffaes, my favourite fishing hotel, I thought, 'Great; he likes the same sort of river as me.'

One evening, when I saw a fisherman on my river that I didn't recognize as one of the syndicate, I said, 'Great gadzooks! That's George Melly fishing there!' Watching him fiddle around tying on a fly, I thought, 'You've got to go and say hello.'

'Hello,' I said.

'Hello,' George said, fiddling with his fly.

'Nice fish there,' I said, nodding in the direction of a trout rising to every fly that came down, as if on tracks.

'That's the one I'm after. He looks a right bugger.'

It was late. Sedge and B-WO spinner were everywhere, so there was lots of action – and lots of other fish. But George's mind was set on this one. And 'Good-time George' looked like he was having a good time.

'Is this the first time you've fished here?' I asked.

'No, I fished here this time last year. The owner invites me.'

Normally, I would have wished him good luck and let him get on with it. But I wanted to tell him – or not tell him (I couldn't make up my mind which) – that the fish he was after had been on that same spot all season and no one had got anywhere near interesting it, with anything. Dun, spinner, nymph, anything.

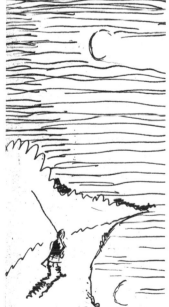

'Fished here long?' George said, fly now suitably attached.

'This is my thirty-ninth year,' I said.

'Lucky you.'

I noticed he was wearing what looked like a Salvador Dalí watch.

'Good luck. And nice to meet you,' I said, letting him get on with it.

'Are you the chap that lives just up the track?'

I was off. But now I was back again.

'Yes. Lucky me.'

'Right,' George said, stripping line from his reel and preparing to cast. I stood back.

Whisk-whisk-whisk-whisk. His line shot one way on the back cast, another on the forward cast, then sideways, every which way. Finally, it shot out an ugly clump of floating tangled stuff that landed several feet in front of the trout, even more feet to the side of it. The fly was nowhere to be seen. It eventually popped up, surfacing several feet away from the pile of line.

I stood there biting my lip. Things didn't look good. I wished I hadn't been there. But I was, and because I was there, I saw what happened next.

Rather than rush under the bridge, which is what this particular trout had done when all of the rods, including myself, had made any attempt to get a fly to it, the trout curved majestically round like a Spitfire, and headed straight for the knitting.

At this point I'd have been furiously trying to gather in line in an attempt to straighten things up. But George was quite content with the arrangement. Likewise the trout.

On seeing George's fly, it opened up its mouth, sucked it in, turned and headed back to his midstream position with it, doing all the straightening that was required. All George needed to do now was hold on, which he did, and land the trout, which he also did, thanking me for offering to help him do so.

'That was a near thing,' 'Good-time George' said.

'Lucky you,' I said.

FIFTEEN

Argentina: Corrientes

Neil's Eel

Hook: No. 2/0
Thread: Black
Under wing: White Arctic Fox Hair topped with
Copper Krystal Flash
Upper Wing: Black Icelandic Sheep Hair topped with
four strands of Holo 'G' tinsel, topped with Black Ultra Hair
Cheeks: One Black Schlappen feather, either side
Head: Black deer hair, tied 'Muddler' style
Eyes: Self-adhesive eyes covered with a dab of epoxy

Restaurant in Birdland

'FIRST YOU STEP, THEN YOU CHANGE directions. Don't try to do both at the same time,' implores the instructor at La Marshall, a tango school in a sparsely decorated apartment in El Centro de Buenos Aires.

When you head north to Santa Fe, the first step you take is to get to know the wildlife and to find out exactly what fish you want dangling at the end of your line, for there are many. And when I read the list, I ended up in a tangle.

Monjita Dominica, Chinchero Chico, Martin Pescador Mediano, Carpintero Bataraz, Coca Corona Rojiza, Juan Chiviro . . . it went on and on. One hundred and twenty-six names in all.

Surely they couldn't *all* be fish? Perhaps they were members of the Zabala family – our *correntino* Indian hosts, with whom we were to spend a week fishing in and around their river island? Nice people all, I'm sure. But a tribe of them? And me? Squeezed into a measly five hundred acres of forest where plants and multicoloured creepers, packed together like wires inside a cable, were fighting for their life to reach the light?

Daniel Arballo, the Argentine manager of the outfit that set up the trip, put me right.

'These aren't the fish, or the familia Zabala. It's a list of some of the birds you'll be sharing the island with. Do you want a list of reptiles?'

I'd met crocodiles – *yacarés* – on previous trips to the area. And a large aquatic boa constrictor, the *curiyú*.

'No, thank you. Just talk to me about how fang-tastically tooth-proof the tents we'll be sleeping in are.'

the hopping hornero

I had always been intrigued by the early-twentieth-century gadabout MP and angler/writer John Waller Hills, author of *A Summer on the Test, River Keeper* and *A History of Fly Fishing for Trout*. In particular, why he should ever have wanted to stray from his southern England chalkstream beats. Even to go to the toilet.

Talk about dreams come true. He fished the Houghton Water on the River Test after Halford and his Dry Fly Revolution had blown over – and while the legendary William Lunn was Head River Keeper. He also had fishings on the Upper Kennet, at Ramsbury, once again where Halford devoted some of the best years of his life in an attempt to improve it.

What on earth – where on earth – could have tempted him away?

Back in Halford's day, contrary to today's perception, fishing on the Test and the like wasn't up to much. At least, not up to the stocking policies they have today. In 1889, fifty days' fishing only landed Halford twenty-five fish. Which might explain why Hills, a member of the Houghton Club at the turn of the last century, took serious time off in search of new waters – not just up- and downriver or in neighbouring counties.

Hills was a little more expansive. He sailed over ten thousand miles south – to Paraguay, Uruguay and northern Argentina. And when he came back he wrote two books about his fishing adventures. *The Golden River* and *Dorado* may not be as well known as other titles of his, but for me, they are the most remarkable. Especially one of the photographs in *Golden River* of Hills and a companion standing on a muddy riverbank holding a golden dorado each. One at forty-five pounds, the other thirty-five pounds. The caption reads: 'Before Breakfast'.

As a dyed-in-the-wool chalkstream angler with a lust for adventure myself, I decided to follow in Hills' footsteps to find out what attracted him to this little-known area tucked under Brazil. Places like the Iberá Marshes. Ten thousand square miles of river, streams and ponds with slow currents and sand bottoms. A floating field of flowering rushes, water lilies and hyacinths. The region may no longer be crawling with Indians brandishing poisoned darts, but it is certainly still snapping with fish sporting teeth that rip the hair off your streamers faster than the best Brazilian body wax.

Goya

And here I was at last – in the *Esteros del Iberá*, in search of Hills' beloved, toothsome *el dorado*. Following the same route taken by Sebastian Cabot in the early sixteenth century, in search of the mystical Eldorado. On a river; just like the picture in Hill's book. By the jungle; just like another picture in his book. Swanning up a braid of the second-largest river in the world, the Paraná; just like yet another picture in his book. In a high-speed, jet-propelled motorboat; just like the picture in the latest Yamaha Marine catalogue.

In *guaraní*, the local Indian dialect, Iberá means 'shiny water'. With this in mind, I leaned over the side of the boat and pinched my reflection in the water to check I wasn't dreaming.

The Guarapo Abierto Lodge, named after the island in the Paraná River, is situated thirty kilometres south of Goya in the province of Corrientes, in north-eastern Argentina. Regular forty-minute flights run from Buenos Aires to Resistencia, with a three-hour drive to the Puerto Goya dock.

Accommodation at Guarapo is under canvas – but this is not to be underrated. Some might say it's swanky in camping terms: eight individual structured safari tents affording enough room for a single bed (no four-poster sleeping bags, please), a table for your bag – and a bedside lamp. They're small (even the mosquitoes have round shoulders) but cosy.

The kitchens and separate shower rooms are wooden affairs. The dining and tackle area is another spacious tent. Under normal weather conditions, you meet and eat outside in the shade of a large tree. Or under the stars.

Six guides born on the island, all brothers, sons, husbands, take fishermen to places where other local anglers and guides don't go,

after fish Englishmen are just beginning to hear about – and ones they haven't.

There are sixteen different species; the surubi, a man-sized catfish; the palometa, the piranhas' ugly big brothers; the tararira, straight out of central casting for *Jurassic Park*; the cabeza amarga, a cousin of the peacock bass; the dentudo, with teeth like a maco shark; the sábalo, a South American carp; the boga; the bagre; the armado – and the pezpero ('chafalote', or 'dog fish'). But I have another name for it. Of this, more later. For I was after just the one: the golden dorado.

Camp owner Juan Manuel Morsella, who celebrated his thirty-eighth birthday with us on our second night, wanted 'somewhere he could fish round the clock'. He approached the Zabala family with the idea of setting up a fishing camp by their river. They agreed and he left his job as the manager of a hazardous waste disposal facility in Buenos Aires and began inviting other adventurous flyfishermen to join him at Guarapo; to fish, but also to get first-hand experience of authentic *correntino* culture and customs. His CV makes him amply qualified to ensure that no time is wasted doing this.

With two boats packed high with provisions, our powerful 175 V6 outboard gave us wings. We lifted up and flew the thirty minutes to Juan Manuel's riverside camp, past strange trees and gleams of wild oranges in the tangle of an ever-changing green wall of forest. At the small trestle dock, the thirty-strong Zabala family, incorporating three generations, had decided to downplay our arrival. Only two of Señor Zabala's five children were there, waiting to greet us: Juan and Javier.

There were six of us in all: Juan Manuel and his friend, Daniel; Sean Clarke who, since I just happened to be in the area at the time, had invited me to join the small party he was guiding, on their return from Tierra del Fuego; Chris, a neighbour of Sean's; Lord Guanaco, who bounds deerlike wherever there is fish or bird life, to the musical strains of 'Maria' from *West Side Story*; and me.

By the time we had unpacked, it was dark. Under the moon we talked about our next day – and the dorado, *Salminus maxillosus*, which has nothing to do with the salmon family. It is a close relative of the Characidae carp of old, but that's where any similarity ends. All you really need to know is that the golden dorado is especially aggressive. It feeds exclusively on other fish, which it attacks head-on, killing them with its crushing, pit-bull terrier jaws. It then gulps its food down from the front end to avoid getting stabbed by spiky fins. Perfect after-dinner talk.

But it wasn't the dorado we feared that night. It was the teeth of an approaching storm that had the fields floating with cattle, the water hip high, horse height.

The next morning, a peek through the crack in the tent revealed an emerald-green forest standing against a sky scurrying with galleons of wispy clouds. It looked as if the storm had passed us by. But there had been torrential rain upstream. The river slid past our breakfast table like carrot soup. In the kitchen, la Señora Gladys Zabala, Beatrice and Andrea made sure the bacon wasn't too crispy. Joanna, our 13-year-old fix-it girl, served us fruit and coffee. Tuti, her 19-year-old husband, was to be our guide. With high cheekbones, wide brows and sad, firm mouths, the Zabalas are a handsome family – both gracious and dignified.

A frog the size of a small dog sat in the shade watching Sean and me board Tuti's jet-propelled dugout. Sean was a solid, safe caster – whichever arm was doing the casting – which made him the very best of boat partners.

We started by fishing small side streams, fifteen metres wide, waist-high in hyacinths that squeaked as we slipped past their rubbery stems. Tuti poled us downriver, leaning heavily on a branch that his hard-working hands had sanded down over time. It looked like a dried bone.

The Paraná delta is a cobweb of thousands of these streams and rivulets. Narrow alleys patrolled by gangs of marauding dorado, one on every street corner, waiting to mug your fly. Turning the river into a street map isn't too bad an idea when you're trying to figure out where to cast your streamer as you float on down. I think of the currents as a flow of traffic and work out where the intersections might be. Here is where the dorado lie, ready to ambush.

I look for areas where traffic is congested; where a lively current is compressed between two logs or rocks; where rush-hour office workers are funnelled into a subway; submerged reefs; a flyover where a fast, smooth racing glide flows over a sandy bed.

I make short casts: fast and furious. Plenty of them. I cover lots of water. I don't worry about slapping the fly down. With the boat chasing after the line I shoot, I can never retrieve fast enough. My right hand pumps the line back like a piston, but the fly never moves as fast as I want it to – even though my elbow is whisking the heavy tropical air laden with smells of fruit to a yoghurty froth.

Just before lunch, a murderous dorado slipped out of the carrot juice current and slit the throat of my streamer. He had been holed up in a dark eddy where the water turned sharply from the bank, throwing any food item on a tilt.

When a dorado takes your fly, you know about it – instantly. And the jaws are even harder than its teeth. As with a tarpon, hooks need to be well sharpened.

Typically, my dorado's first instinct was to leave the planet. It leaped four feet in the air, twisting, shaking – its head knocking its tail in a flash of golden sunburst. Then it bored deep, my line humming like a harp string as it dragged the dugout downriver. The first rush of a dorado is like nothing on earth. However hard you hold, you'll be lucky to stop him in under a hundred yards.

Then there was a twist, and a downward acceleration. Ten minutes later, it surfaced to lash the water into ivory cream. It was beat, and I soon had it snapping at the business end of a Boga grip. Eight kilos; a baby. I wouldn't have liked to be its dummy.

Guarapo is a catch-and-release lodge, so back it went. After a scrap with Mr Dorado, it's wise to check over your tackle and make sure it doesn't need hospital treatment. I fish a four-piece Sage travel rod, a nine-foot, eight-weight, with a leader just short of the length of the rod, an eight-pound tippet with a six-inch wire trace at fifteen pounds, attached to the line by a small swivel.

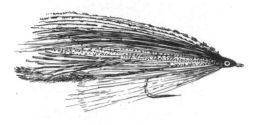

The Andino Deceiver

I was fishing an Andino Deceiver. A streamer tied up for me by one of Argentina's finest dorado flytyers, Mario D'Andrea. A top dorado guide, if he's not out on the marshes, he manages the Orvis Fly Shop in Santa Fe.

The Andino Deceiver is a fly developed by another Argentine flyfishing guide, Carlos Ingrassia. Here's how I tie my version. (Turn away, Carlos!)

With the hook bend up in the vice, I tie in a bunch of white bucktail as an underwing. I now turn the hook back up the other way. An eighth of the way up the shank, I tie in two orange Schlappen hackles, one either side of the hook. These should extend three times the length of the hook. I top this with a bunch of yellow bucktail not quite the same length as the hackles. Topping on, I top this with a bunch of silver Flashabou. This should extend the entire length of the hackles and shimmer at the tail. Next, I top the lot with a bunch of orange bucktail and a wodge of crimson bucktail to form a 'shoulder'. Enough?

Not quite. Next I crown the whole caboodle with eight peacock herls. These should swoop over the back of the fly, touching the tips of the hackles. As cheeks, I tie in two small bunches of Krystal Flash.

Finally, I form a small head with my whip finish. With enamel paints (the same sort I once used to glorify my Airfix model aeroplanes), I paint a white eye and then, when it's dry, over it a black eye with a white pupil. Done. If you've tied it well, it'll wink at you.

This caught us many dorados. But then there isn't a bar, a restaurant or a club that Mr Dorado frequents in northern Argentina that Mario doesn't know.

Varnish
black
thread

White
enamel
paint

Black
enamel
paint

Back at Guarapo, Chris and Lord Guanaco had survived several serious dorado hits, but not serious enough for the dorado. They had taken many palometas, larger member of the piranha family, that razored each and every one of their streamers. They had set out that morning well stocked in the fly department. They returned that evening with their flies in the Accident and Emergency department. If palometas aren't chewing the hair off your hooks, they're snapping at the tails of all the other fish in the stream. You're a lucky man if you catch any fish with perfect fins. Even dorado. If a palometa can't fit you in its mouth, it nibbles bits off you here and there when you're not looking.

It hadn't been a good day. Everything had been against us. The river never cleared and the tropical storm was still rumbling around. The frog joined us for dinner in the tent, crunching through Malteser-sized beetles we threw at him that were trying to headbutt their way into the tent, sounding like heavy rain outside.

That night we discovered what heavy rain really sounds like.

Lightning flashed with such vehemence and frequency, it lit up the tent. I could have read a book, but fear had my pupils popping with burst blood veins.

The next day, on our trip downriver, burned-out trees hit by lightning smouldered just yards from the camp. Floodwater had torn all manner of things from the banks. Branches of strange trees, bundles of plants, blue-flowered with myriad leaves, fruits, nuts, and any hope of us catching anything were now sailing downstream. But despondent as we were – and as wet as we had been that night – we were still laughing.

We hadn't lost our sense of humid.

Tuti cut his way through some water lilies with a machete to get to where a stream had burst its banks and flooded a large area, forming a lake that to all intents and purposes looked not unlike Blagdon. As we drifted across it, I felt I'd done all this many times before. (I probably had done at Blagdon.) It was here where Sean caught his first dorado, casting a long line into the deep hole at the end of a row of reeds. It had him letting out the screams I had tried to articulate the night before. It took an Andino Deceiver tied with yellow saddle hackles, on a 3/0 hook, about five inches long. Not a standard Blagdon pattern.

At the end of the lake, my rod bent over and I thought for a minute I had another dorado. No, I had caught an IKEA bathroom mirror. A see-through herring of about four pounds. A pezpero. A Perspex pezpero, even. Holding it up to the light you could see its little heart ticking. And its breakfast. I put it back quickly, keeping my fingers clear of its fins that resembled Swiss Army knife saw blades. Out of the water, it looked like something you might expect to dredge off a weed-rack. In the water, it waltzed in time with the flow, like Cinderella's ballroom gown. It had taken another Andino Deceiver, in green.

On our way back, we stopped at a Y-Junction where Tuti told us five dorado had been caught the previous week before the storm. All on the same black fly with tinsel tendrils, all three to five kilos. And one at twelve kilos that almost jumped into the boat and got stuck into Tuti's client.

That night as we walked along an avenue of candles in poles towards the dining tent, Juan and Daniel were downhearted. The river hadn't delivered the fish it is capable of producing. Normally, they could guarantee a minimum of ten dorado a boat per day – with lunch in between.

In the tent, the air blue with mosquito coils, we attacked the barbecue with the voracity of a dorado released from a wholegrain diet: an *asado de tira*, a cut peculiar to Argentina, consisting of a chunk of meat sandwiched between a two-inch-wide rib and fat the colour of butter, three inches deep. This I carefully sprinkled with industrial-strength

The Dining Tent, GUARAPO RIVER

chimichurri sauce – uranium with just a splash of plutonium. Just enough to blister your taste buds. Figs and flan followed.

Juan Manuel also talked about the week before the storm – and about the savage ten-kilo surubi that snaffled a fly and gave its captor an hour and a half of unofficial tango lessons midstream. She was a businesswoman from Rosario. Luckily she wasn't a striptease artist, otherwise most of her show would have consisted of her peeling off sticking plasters.

He also told us that the Zabala family never forget any of the visitors to their island. They don't remember names though; they link faces with anecdotal incidents.

'And how will I be remembered?'

Juan didn't stop to think.

'The Englishman and the rain.'

In the twenties, Hills had written: 'Had it been possible to quench our spirit of adventure, surely the rain would have done it.' It hadn't for him, and it didn't for us.

Mercedes

'Looks pretty dead to me,' I said, turning to Michael for comment.

'Looks like one huge, dangerous handbag to me. Like Maggie Thatcher's.'

'Hers wasn't alligator skin. It was made from the skin off the backside of some backbencher!'

With that, the alligator winked in an agreeing sort of way, lifted its jaw in a half-yawn and snapped it shut again leaving a tooth the size of a mobile phone strategically jutting out over its lips, just to remind us it was alive and even more formidable than any English prime minister, male or female.

This Corrientes croc, or *caiman*, was eight feet long.

'I feel I could just climb aboard that four-legged tree trunk and fish that mother downriver.'

Carlos had punted the skiff a rod's length from the grassy bank where the giant *caiman* was sunbathing so that I could take a picture. With my focus full out, it filled the lens with its scaly nastiness, and my nostrils with the smell of super-bad reptile repulsiveness. This halitosis horror was telling me that it was having similar ideas as our guide – but thoughts of us *inside* of him, rather than floating down on *top* of him.

'Shall we go?' I suggested politely, in a prim, girly way. Carlos lifted the anchor. The outboard snarled. The croc lifted an eyebrow – and let it drop again, unimpressed.

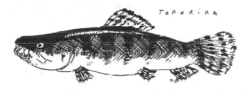

We left the main river, cut across a lake the size and colour of the sky and continued our way towards the horizon via a thin, crystal-clear braid. Fish showered out in front of us like water from a hose. So many fish. Mainly sábalos, bocas and palometas, the big brother of the Amazon piranha, with more sets of dentures than a National Health dental surgery. But also a shoal, or rather a gang, of juvenile golden dorado that had been hanging around the corners of a deep hole, vibrating violence, waiting with stiletto teeth for some fish to pass by – and to attack.

'That's what we're after!' Michael whispered over the motor, following a passing dorado with his rod tip.

'*Déjarlos!*' Carlos screeched, telling us to leave them. These dorado were too small; too spooked.

Carlos had taken us out for an hour before lunch, to show us round. Three hours earlier Michael and I had climbed off the overnight bus at Mercedes, four hundred miles north of Buenos Aires. A nine-hour drive in a Flecha Super Coche Cama, Generation 2000, Marco Polo, Paridisio 1800DD. The business. First-class, upper-deck comfort, with seats that fold into beds. With a movie (we had *Seabiscuit*), or some of the best views imaginable out of the window. All for the price of a single, standing room only, from Reading to Paddington. But I was tucked up asleep all the way.

Mercedes, a Spanish colonial crumbling cake of a town dating back to the mid-1800s, is on the south of the *Esteros del Iberá*, the Iberá Marshes, a 13,000-square-kilometre water filter. Here the headland reaches of Rio Corrientes offer something the mighty and muddy Paraná River, its neighbour and the second-largest river in the world, doesn't offer. Sight-fishing – in *Evian*. The chance to see not only the fish you want to catch, but also those you don't really want to.

'Have a throw,' I said to Michael, nodding in the direction of a deep-down, thirty-pound *surubi*, a primeval fish with more whiskers than a shaving brush, busy vacuuming the riverbed in front of us.

'I don't do catfish on fly,' Michael Beale, my boat partner, who had organized the trip, replied.

The braid carried on for another ten minutes. A side stream in a tangle of side streams and lakes formed over centuries by a concentration of *embalsados*, islands of floating plants that collect together and form dams. A waterway in a state of constant change.

We popped out of the steamy jungle of knee-high water hyacinths and waist-high reeds fizzing with small bugs like a cork out of a bottle, into an airy marshland plain. A solitary white estancia stood in the distance. A single clump of trees in an empty skyline as broad as a continent. A hundred thousand wading birds turning their heads to watch us pass. We were in Birdland.

Binoculars in hand – and *Collins Birds of Southern South America and Antarctica* open on my knee – we made our way back up a canal six hundred yards long that Carlos had dug so that he could take the skiff up to the front door of his estancia. I watched a Persil-white-bodied, blacked-headed jabiru wearing a scarlet bow tie stab a fish over a foot long, lift it up in the air and swallow it whole. A nasty jab it was, too. I could see how it got its name. These heavyweight storks stand four feet tall.

'How come you never get lost here?' I yelled to Carlos over the roar of the outboard. He couldn't hear.

'Romney Marsh!' he screamed back. Not an answer I was expecting.

Was Romney Marsh as impossible to navigate? I tried to picture what it looked like. Did it really look like *this*? Could somewhere in Kent put on a display of so many birds?

'He didn't hear you!' Michael shouted, pointing at the sheep nibbling by the canal. 'That's what he's talking about. His Romney Marsh *sheep*. A breed.'

Michael had been a sheep farmer in Patagonia before he opened his homely El Encuentro Lodge on the Rio Grande, on the Chilean border. This trip to northern Argentina was our first fishing as buddies, rather than as guest and guide.

We crossed the field towards the farmhouse. I stopped to stare into the faces of the monster sheep standing in temperatures of thirty degrees with more wool on each of them than on the chunkiest Marks & Spencer jumper.

'You're looking at lunch.'

Carlos Sanchez's Estancia El Dorado near the non-town of Boquerón – the dot on the map is bigger – is forty miles north of Mercedes, an hour and a half's four-by-four hike across flood-damaged tracks held together by blocks of cement and white mud. To experience rock 'n' roll there was no need to switch on the car radio. The Estancia has been in la Familia Sanchez for two generations, but it has only been a fishing lodge for a few years. As a cattle ranch it is one of the most traditional in the Province of Corrientes. Dressed in striped *polainas* (leggings), linen spats, wide leather belt with a *facon* (dagger) stuck down it in the small of the back, *espuelas* (spurs) and the token *revenque* (horse whip), necktie and hat (worn brim back when riding), gauchos prance proudly around the fields on horseback like medieval troubadours – armed with syringes. It was foot-and-mouth prevention week.

The Estancia is situated in the middle of a protected Federal Reserve

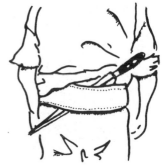

and don't the birds know it. And the dorado. With a strict catch-and-release policy, this fearsome fly-taker sits at the top of its food chain.

This was my sixth trip to Argentina after the golden dorado. I had made some interesting observations.

Although the method is a top tactic for dorado in big water and swirling pools, fishing a four-inch streamer blind on a Teeny line can be a mindless affair after the first day or two. So, in the past, I had changed to a popper made of strips of Plastazote, cell foam, mounted on #4/0 hooks, tied for me by Roan Zumfelde of West Florida. I started fishing these Gurglers to tarpon rolling in the mooring lights at the bottom of people's gardens in downtown Naples.

As my Gurgler spluttered across the surface of a pool the size of a football pitch (and twice as muddy), spurting six-inch streams of water up behind it, at least I could *see* some action. And action I got. Dorado had come snapping from great depths to dine out on the commotion. Often when I hooked a dorado his partners in grime would break into a feeding frenzy and try and pull the Gurgler from the hooked dorado's mouth. One time, a deranged dorado managed to rip the pop-pop-popper off the end of the nose of a dorado I was playing and got hooked up itself. Do dorado laugh? The one that escaped as a consequence must have. So I was full of hope for my gurgling Gurgler.

'That no work.' Carlos wasn't as enthusiastic about my fly box as the popper-pickin' Paraná *peces* had been in the other places I had fished in the *Esteros*.

'Try it. But it no work.' And so I did – and he was right, it didn't.

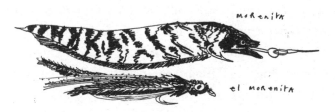

Fortunately I had a box of streamers that looked so like the morena marsh eels that drive dorado delirious, I was worried Greenpeace would appear in an inflatable, buzz me – and ban me from using them.

'Those no work,' Carlos repeated, turning his nose up at my slimline beauties. They needed to be white, or lime. Or, even better, black with some red or orange in them.

'Try them. But they no work.' So I did – and he was right, they didn't, either. So, that night, I fiddled around and came up with a pattern that did work. Hello, Neil's Eel. In black.

Just down from the eye of a #2/0 circle hook, viced bend up, I tie in a bunch of copper Krystal Flash and a three-inch-long pile of white arctic fox hair. Turning the hook back, bend down in the vice, I wind in a five-inch bunch of black Icelandic sheep hair topped with four strands of silver Holo 'G' tinsel followed by a heap of any synthetic pulse wing material – Super or Ultra Hair – of the same length as the other materials. Then, either side of the fly, I strap on two black Schlappen feathers, for vibrancy and to give the fly a wiggle. For the head, I tie this as I would a Minnow Muddler, with deer hair dyed black. To finish off, using a dab of epoxy I attach a googly epoxy eye either side of the head. To make a white version, I just use the same materials, but in white. Keep it simple.

'That's not simple, it's simply ugly,' Carlos said to me, congratulating me on my invention. And that was my first few hours at Estancia El Dorado. That day I learned that clear water requires clearer thinking. And timing. Early morning and evening were the taking times. With March temperatures well above 90° F, the afternoon was for sleeping.

That day, I also learned another thing. Dorado fishing isn't done exclusively from a skiff. Carlos encourages bank fishing. He'd power us to a point where a stream trickled off the marshes into the main flow and have us shoot our flies into the race and run them back through the smooth, in a jerking motion. Then, take two steps down, and repeat the action.

sink eye
in a bed
of epoxy
and
cover with
thin coat

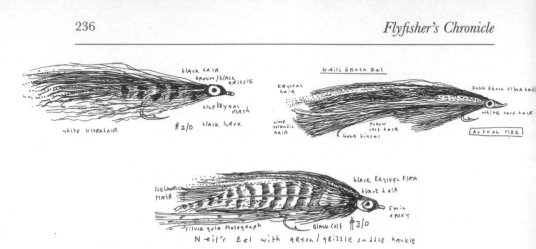

N-eil's Eel with green/grizzle saddle hackle

I was now fully equipped with a box of boss-eyed, black-and-white streamers resembling an artist's impression of either a Scottish widow or the abominable snowman wearing jewellery. And it was on the former that I had my first two dorados, as swiftly as the current that I plucked them from.

The dorado doesn't mouth your fly; it mugs it, ripping line off your reel in a way only a bonefish knows how but, unlike the toothless bony, the dorado keeps on ripping. With dentures that inspired the design of a diamond-cutting drill bit, the dorado takes no prisoners when he gets his mouth around your fanciest flytying materials. The dorado also shares another flats-fish characteristic. Like a tarpon, it loves a leap. And just as a tarpon turning in the sunlight blasts silver against the ocean, the dorado does the same against a cobalt sky – but in gold. These days, although bigger dorados are caught on fly and bait, a serious dorado is anything over fifteen pounds.

One afternoon, we visited the Italian Corner, named after an Italian who caught a dorado over twenty pounds from there. The technique used to fish it is simple enough: you stand at the front of the skiff as

Carlos drifts the boat down the centre of the river, which is thirty yards at its widest. He then slows the boat as you approach a known hole that can be as deep as an office block.

Even so, you fish a floating line; my preference, no matter what fishing I do. A #8 weight-forward on a nine-foot Sage 4 pc. My leader is eight foot, with a thirty-pound butt, then twenty pounds looped to fifteen pounds and a six-inch thirty-pound wire trace. Piano wire, for me. It may not have the flexibility that might be preferred, but it can stand the torrents of terrifying tooth-power that are likely to descend on it. And a floater, because dorado rise. Not to fly, but to the *bouillabaisse* of yellow fry that parade the surface like liquid seduction. Believe me, there can sometimes be more fish flesh than water in some parts of these rivers. One thing a dorado can never do is die of starvation.

A rising dorado doesn't always mean it's a dining dorado. A head and tail rise is a dorado playing; or whatever he does when not feeding. A 'busting' dorado is one you steer the boat towards.

With the position marked, you stand at a right angle to the boat, which is pointing downstream, and cast as close to the far bank as you are able. Then you mend your line, upstream. As soon as you feel it straighten out in front of the boat, you start the retrieve. This 'swing' is the killing point, in a textbook sort of way, and it was at this exact point where my biggest dorado took my fly. Fishing dorado is a series of calms before storms, when a dorado suddenly storms your streamer.

Drifting gently down, a thousand miles from anywhere, the sounds of the *Esteros* intoxicate. The chublike *sábalos*, vegetarians in a land of flesh eaters, graze in the shallows, slurping continuously at soupy grasses. For vegetarians, they are very noisy eaters. Frogs 'chime' like a thousand tiny cowbells. The float in the petrol tank ticks away like the pendulum of an old grandfather clock as the boat rocks gently. Your thoughts, and time, like the skiff, drift away down the river.

I was just thinking that my black, blue and purple toe, which I had broken leaping barefoot up onto the front of the skiff on my first day, resembled one of my snaky black beauties, when suddenly everything came to a dramatic thudding end. My thoughts – and very nearly my rod – were snatched from me out into the swirling depths. The dorado hit me on that turn and instead of making its escape downwards, it was three feet in the air, all three feet of him. After four or five further leaps, he headed downriver while Carlos headed upriver to the shore, steering the boat to a place where we could beach the monster; although I rather suspect the real reason was to get me off the boat lest I slip and disappear into the swirling waters. I was Scottish country dancing with excitement.

On my last day, on my final drift downriver, I spotted a dorado swing out of a fast run near the bank and glide over a strip of yellow sand in the shallows. I had an idea – and I asked Carlos to run the boat ashore. He was surprised to hear this request because on my last trip ashore, while wading barefoot through some marsh, I had very nearly stepped on a *raya*, a freshwater stingray that lies hidden in inches of water, with a killer tooth – on its tail. If this whips round your ankle you've got two hours to get to a doctor. Some of these freshwater river mines are three feet across, the size of a hospital blanket.

Safely ashore, I crept up behind a sand dune and pointed to a dorado repeating a swinging motion out of the swirl onto the sand. Carlos insisted I chuck to it, but the splash of the streamer would have scared it. Instead, when it had returned to the blue deeps, I cast my fly and let it lie motionless on the sand, waiting for the dorado to return.

It wasn't long before another dorado fanned out of the fast water onto the shallows and headed to where the trap was set. I had hardly lifted my fly two inches before the dorado pounced.

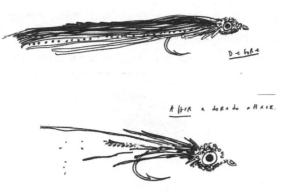

As the minor dentistry was taking place to remove the remains of my shredded snowman from the jaws of this eight-pound dorado, Carlos congratulated me on my tactic, saying that it had triggered something more than a need to feed inside the armoured skull of this set of golden gnashers. It had touched an instinct much deeper down in its prehistoric psyche. Violence. We'd played mind games with it.

On our return, Michael, who had spent the day birdwatching on horseback, was waiting for us with a freezing, fingertip-stinging can of *Quilmes* in each hand.

'Mind over matter,' Carlos told Michael, explaining the incident later that evening.

'Mind over maulers, more like it,' Michael replied. 'Shall we eat?'

After dinner, Michael sat me down outside on the verandah to watch the live show. High up in the tree next to the terrace, a spotlight spreads a large pool of light on the lawn. When the sun goes down, this area quickly becomes heavily populated with *sapos* (not to be confused with *sopas*, the word for 'soup'). These are large green toads that inch closer and closer to the tree as if under the influence of hallucinogenic drugs, gazing upwards at the light as if Toad Almighty had just descended to earth.

The first time I saw the event described next it made me jump. Gate-mouthed I watched it happen. Out of the ink-black night this huge *búho*, a great horned owl, swooped silently into the light, surgically extracting one toad after another, with ten-minute breaks, lifting them out into the darkness in its silvery talons.

A friend of mine who had returned to London after visiting Corrientes found one of these *sapos* sitting on his bed in Kensington. It had crawled

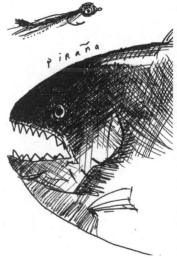

out of a shoe that had been left outside one night. The *guia* I told this story to couldn't understand how soup had found its way into someone's shoe. It's easy to get these words mixed up in Spanish.

Michael was anxious to hear all the latest news from England. He'd heard that John Goddard had died. When John had visited El Encuentro Lodge, Michael had guided him.

'I fished with him many times in his last years,' I told Michael. 'On one of the lakes where he was a syndicate member. The fishing was good. And it was always fun.'

On the larger of the two lakes, the one without the boat, John would unfold his camp seat and plonk himself right at the end of the little peninsula that juts out into the lake. I'd fish behind him, casting on one side or the other, depending on the wind direction. In this rearward position, I'd wear my Taliban hat. It had the rare ability of being able to catch every stray, low-flying, wind-driven trout fly heading my way – before it caught me. It was the perfect flyfisher's crash helmet. Originally designed to protect the wearer's head from the cold Pakistani winters, when fishing behind John (or sharing a boat with him), it protected the head from a different kind of cold. Cold steel.

I could have wandered round the lake, I suppose. But I liked to keep close so we could natter. John was really not into straying too far from his base camp seat.

'Got any ideas for another book, John?' I once asked, knowing that he'd just had two books of his fly patterns published relatively recently. 'You must have written everything you want to write?'

There was a long pause.

'Funnily enough, a publisher approached me the other day,' John replied. 'He said I should write an autobiography. A book about all my fishing experiences.'

'That's a great idea, John! So, what are you doing here with me? You should be back at that desk writing it!'

'Oh, I've written it,' John said, never taking his eye off the damsel nymph he was retrieving.

'So, when's it being published?'

'The publishers want me to write a bit more.'

'So, what are you doing here?'

'Oh, I've written three more chapters,' John revealed after a short pause. 'I sent them off a couple of weeks ago.'

'So, what did they say?'

'Oh, I haven't heard anything from them so I suppose they're happy with it.'

A month later, John rang me to ask me to fish with him on his beat on the Itchen. Could I pick him up from his house at eight o'clock?

It's a good hour and a half drive to the river. We had to make a detour to pick up a 'double-figure' trout John had put into a Hampshire trout smokers. With that and fishing, it was a long day. On the way back, we were both a little quiet and there must have been a good half an hour on the M5 when we didn't say a word to one another. Here I was, sitting next to John Goddard, in silence. What a wasted opportunity!

'John you were around during the stillwater revolution back in the sixties,' I said. 'It must have been exciting times.'

'It was, Neil. New stillwater patterns were being tied up by the hour. New fisheries, new techniques. The flyfishing world changed.'

'And you must have fished with many of the greats of that era. Bob Church, Alan Pearson . . . Richard Walker? What was Richard Walker like?'

'Dick and I were good friends. But we did more coarse fishing together than flyfishing. He was so influential.'

'And you're a very good friend of Lefty Kreh and so many other famous anglers around the world.'

'Yes, but I haven't seen Lefty for a good few years now.'

'I tend to forget that you're also a bit of an icon in sea fishing circles.'

'Oh, yes. I've travelled all round the world after record game fish. Did you know that I caught the world record barracuda . . . on fly?'

'That's amazing, John. Tell me, you used to go a lot to New Zealand . . . and I remember you once took a party floating and camping down a river in Alaska . . .'

This time, there was a very long pause.

'Neil . . . you should read my autobiography.'

Two months later, *The Passionate Angler* hit the shelves.

SIXTEEN

Argentina: Patagonia

Rolling Ricky

Hook: No. 20
Thread: Clear nylon, or 8X Fluorocarbon
Bead head: Extra small black/lead
Body: Flat strip of green Super Hair
Rib: Clear nylon, or 8X Fluorocarbon
Thorax: Peacock herl

Fight Club

IT WAS IMPOSSIBLE TO CALCULATE the risks of driving without a licence in the early hours of the morning with no other cars about. It was unlikely that the heavily armed *policia caminera* would have a road check on the dust track from the *hosteria* to the metalled road. But on my return trip along this *camina pavimentado* – the only road that wasn't a dust track in a five-kilometre radius – the chances were quite high. If you're stopped, you're questioned, your papers are checked, and you're searched, hands on the bonnet, legs astride. One *policia caminera* frisks you while another stands guard with a sub-machine gun.

I'd snaked past three patrols, one on the trip from San Carlos Bariloche to Villa La Angostura, one on the road to the airport, the other where the road tapered into a sandy track that looked like egg

yolk sliding down the Andes. Fifty kilometres on, at the end of this osteopath's nightmare, snuggled Angostura.

Patrols or not, they couldn't stop me for speeding. It took me four hours to travel the thirty miles. Not taking into account two stops to change punctured tyres. Thanks to potholes, I arrived at La Granja in urgent need of traction.

I later discovered that the little old German lady who owned the replica of a Swiss chalet where I was to stay not only made her own bread, jam, salami and sausages, but she also filled and hand-sewed her own mattresses, using the feathers from the ducks she reared to make pâté. If I'd known this on arrival, I'd have skipped tea and headed straight upstairs to rest my back. Instead, I went back into town.

There was nothing I could do about not having an international driving licence, but I could get a local fishing permit. The heat hummed off the hundred yards of concrete that made up the centre of Angostura; fishing was out of the question. Even so, I was anxious to get to the Correntoso.

The Correntoso

I'd come a long way and planned this moment carefully. I'd travelled across the world to get to a country that has summer when we have winter; where people have farms the size of Wales; where the total population is only marginally larger than London's, yet the land mass is four times the size of Britain; where inflation rose to 20 per cent in the three weeks I was there; where a million pesos bought a box of matches with three boiled sweets as change; a country we were still technically at war with.

I crept down the wooden staircase in the dark the next morning to get to the car. The boards creaked like a Spanish galleon tossing on a high sea.

I had brought only one rod, one reel, a floating and a sinking line on spare spools, a box of small flies, a wallet of lures and some local flies I'd bought in a fishing store in Bariloche: it was tough getting them, my Spanish rivalling only my Hindi in fluency.

As I cartwheeled my way round the shop trying to convert what I wanted to say into body language, I stumbled upon something I thought might spark off a meeting of minds. On the counter was a copy of the American *Fly Fisherman* magazine in which Nick Lyons had written in his 'Seasonable Angler' column about a day spent fishing with me. Pointing at my name, I pleaded, 'Hey, that's me! That's me!'

I was hoping this might get him to open up the drawers behind the desk, where I was convinced he was hiding the killing selection he sold only to his local friends. He was not impressed. Why should he be? I left with a bag of tourist bugs the size of small cars, with rubber legs and googly eyes.

I arrived at the Correntoso without international incident. But just down the track from La Granja, a set of teeth came at me out of the darkness. They belonged to a gigantic woolly dog whose honking bark neutralized the sound of the car horn as I sounded it in an attempt to make him release his jaws clamped round my front wheel. In the end, I slammed my foot on the accelerator and ricocheted from rock to pothole, the canine optional-extra spinning round like a sword on the wheel of Boudicca's chariot. He flew off into the woods somewhere before I joined the main road.

The Correntoso beat is a five-hundred-yard length up from Lake Nahuel Huapi, the largest *lago* in northern Patagonia. The lake should look like a sea, but it doesn't, for behind it tower the Andean peaks that shrink the Swiss Alps to the size of starter slopes in comparison.

The clinically clear, steely-blue Nahuel Huapi licks the feet of the Andes with a warm tongue. Temperatures invite swimming, if only to escape the midday swarms of *tábanos*, needle-nosed horseflies that steam out of the 90° high and suck blood 8.3° higher. I parked at the inlet and stood on the bridge that took the road on up into the hills. The bridge consisted of two rusting RSJs set apart at vehicle wheel distance from one another. I was alone. Looking down, I found it hard to judge the depth of the water. If it hadn't been for the occasional glint on the surface, I wouldn't have known that water was there at all.

My information had been correct. The water was in prime condition; I'd done my research well. All those phone calls to Mel Krieger in San

Francisco had been worth the expense. The hours sent stalking Laddie Buchanan in Buenos Aires had been worth the shoe leather. Buchanan, a man who knows the fishing spots in Argentina as an ophthalmic surgeon knows his way round the retina, had told me that where I was standing was the only place that hadn't been mugged by heavy rain clouds on a recent rain-raid from Chile, making fishing impossible in many of the more popular areas.

I looked back down into the crystal-clear water, watching the trout keeping themselves steady in the current with flickering fins. I wondered what fly would entice them to change positions and lift to my hook and allow me to inspect one of them at close quarters. At that time I had never seen a truly wild, stream-born rainbow before. I watched them holding their noses to the current, many of them in deep, fast water, slightly distorted as I looked through the glassy, convex surface of the pool, the surface pushing and swelling smooth against the resistance of the log piles of the bridge.

I didn't spot the big trout at first. He was, well, too big – ten pounds or more – holding himself on the stony bottom in a varying mist of gravel and sand raised in spurts by the currents. But, apart from winching an iron-filled nymph from my position on the bridge, there was no way of reaching him. Anyway, this wasn't my style.

Downstream at the outlet, where the stream broadened out into a lake, a fisherman had taken up position on the point. I walked back down on the other side of the tiny inland estuary. He waded out into the lake with great purpose until the water lapped across his chest and round his elbows, held high up at shoulder level. He knew exactly where he was and what he was doing. His tackle was heavy, Big Game. A powerful carbon rod exoceted a long, heavy line out into the deep blue water where the stream churned at the cobalt Nahuel Huapi. His line was a weight-forward, with a dark green Hi-speed Hi-D tip. You could hear the *zing* of lead. A fluorescent-red running line came off his rod tip like a spurt of blood. He had cast a couple of yards short of a whole fly-line.

'*Buenos dias*,' I hushed across the water. This man knew exactly what he was doing.

I realized I was hopelessly underpowered and decided to flick my rubber-legged bug around the rocks. The location, the conditions were perfect, but Buchanan was right: I'd arrived three weeks too late to catch one of the Correntoso trophy rainbows. The areas within casting and wading range – I had only a five-weight line and thigh boots – had been awash with rainbows up to twelve to fifteen pounds in November when the season opened. Now it was the first week in January, high summer. The big trout had returned to the deeper, cooler holes in the lake.

The man-on-the-point's rod bent over. I turned and walked back up to the bridge, the sun just beginning to set fires to the tips of the pines. A bus was crossing the bridge. The driver was leaning out of the window, guiding his wheels along the two iron channels, never once letting his eyes catch the twenty-foot drop to the river below. If I lived in these parts, I thought to myself, I'd walk to work.

I made my way back down the other bank, to the point. The man's rod was still bent double. He was holding it high above his head, the fish still pulling line; his reel shrieked like a wounded rabbit. Standing in the water, he was a pinhead against the expanse of water in front of him with the mountains behind that. A gauzy veil of golden light inched its way down the Andes.

He beached the trout at my feet and held it up to me, his thumb beneath its gills. It was the length of his arm and even broader than his smile. It had taken him an honest thirty minutes to land it. His reel was the size of a hand, fingers splayed out. He told me that the most important piece of tackle was his reel.

'A fish like this would melt a reel like that on its first run,' he told me, pointing at my Hardy Princess.

'I'd need to catch one first,' was my reply.

'I have four hundred yards of backing on this spool and I still get worried.' He didn't look like a man who worried easily. His rod, a nine-foot Orvis, could land tarpon. His hand swept the area of the point and he offered it to me, adding that I'd be wasting my time unless I could reach the deep channel. He pointed into the distance with his black rod.

The sun was up now, the heat pouring down, making a sound like overhead power cables. Before he left, he pulled at my sheepskin patch safety-pinned to my shirt.

'Take these little flies to the inlet above the bridge this evening.' I nodded.

'*Y muy bien!* A Leoni's Barbarous, tied by Boyadel,' he added, spotting my leggy lure. 'It's a secret weapon in these parts!'

No police check for weapons on my way back to La Granja. When the sun started to drop, I returned to the inlet, as instructed. I tied on a small sedge pupa, casting it into the centre of rises until there were so many centres that I fished blind into the froth. The largest trout I hooked into was three pounds, but I think I had one on that was bigger. He headed off across the lake with such power that I would have had to have crossed the Chilean border to land him. For this reason, I was happy that my line pinged back at me unaccompanied, a dozen turns from my backing.

My passport was back at La Granja – and I still didn't have a driving licence.

Sedge pupa

Rio Rivadavia

Argentina has changed much since I first went fishing in central Patagonia in the summer of 1982, months after the Falklands War. There weren't many English flyfishermen there, for obvious reasons. This has changed, too.

There's a story put around the British flyfishing fraternity that has now infiltrated the ranks of the general public at large. It's the following: that there's really only one place to go in Argentina and this is TDF. Or Tierra del Fuego, as it's referred to in my *Reader's Digest World Atlas.*

It's been put about by the flyfishing outfitters in a message aimed largely at salmon fishermen, who have a passion for large sea-run fish. But, more importantly, they have the money. The ready dosh to fly the thirteen hours down there, and a further three hours after an overnight in BA. Or Buenos Aires, as it says here on the map.

Off they all go to spend a week in a most inhospitable wasteland. Where the wind has blown away the very last remnants of vegetation and culture – and your socks, too, if they weren't stuck to your feet. Where, throughout Argentina's young history, even the keenest of the early European ground-grabbers chose to trek around and avoid it. Where they share accommodation with fellow trophy-trout-seeking Englishmen wearing identical foul-weather gear, armed with all the bad news, political moans and the same after-dinner jokes you would think they'd have wanted to get away from.

And when they come back and people ask how they managed to get the top layer of skin blown off their faces, they smile and say that they've been to Argentina. In fact they haven't been to Argentina at all – they've been to the moon. They've been to the moon, not in a spacesuit but in regulation Simms breathables.

For some time now I've been urging flyfishers to broaden their horizons, if on the horizon they see Argentina as an interesting place to let their fishing take them. I've advised they head north, to Corrientes, after dorado. All of which can be arranged through the same outfitters that plug down south.

But I'm fighting a losing battle. So I've been trying a different tack. Go south, yes. But not way down south. Go central south. South of San Carlos de Bariloche in central Patagonia. To the Fight Club, because nowhere in the world do rainbows fight grimmer than in the Province of Chubut, on the Rio Rivadavia. Where you can have a good fight – with fearsome fish, not ferocious winds.

I had first heard about this magical river from my good friend Michael Beale, the Indiana Jones of the region. Michael, his son Benjamin and his family are the pioeneers in the area. Between them they run the El Encuentro Lodge further south on the Rio Futaleufú, also known as the Rio Grande, near Esquel. But the first place I laid down my head to fish the Rivadavia was at a fly lodge called the Arroyo Claro, the 'Clear Stream', situated a few kilometres south of Cholila, just outside El Parque Nacional Los Alerces where the Rio Rivadavia begins and ends.

With not a single picture of a fish anywhere to be seen in the lodge – saddles, bridles and reins hanging from every peg and a stable door in my bedroom leading out into a paddock filled with fillies – I was beginning to wonder if we'd arrived at a riding school rather than a fishing lodge. The owner in those days – and the guide who was going to join Michael and me on the days we had planned – was Jorge Graziosi. A bit Italian, a bit Dutch, a bit French, Jorge had cut his teeth as a farmer and a guide in the area. Born in Buenos Aires, and a perfect English speaker, he had once been a member of the Argentinean ski team. Snow or water, I never asked. But judging by the way he slalomed Michael and me across rapids and round rocks in his inflatable, I would wager a bit of both.

This being my first visit to the area, I had done some research before I left England. I'd been intrigued to read in an article in *The Angling Report* that the best fly to have in your box for the region was an ant pattern. A pattern the writer called the Chernobyl Ant; a relatively  unknown pattern at that time. Always preferring to fish small flies, this news was most pleasing. But not being acquainted with this fly I visited Brian Fratel at Farlows Fishing Emporium, Pall Mall, just down from Piccadilly Circus, to see if he had one in stock. Sliding open the drawer of the display cabinet, my fingers made straight to the corner where the smuts were cowering. But Brian went off in a different direction.

He was launching a huge crane-shaped fist into another corner where flies resembling inland shipping were docked. Four inches long, built of layers of foam a quarter of an inch deep, with what looked like a row of rubber oars sticking out on either side, the fly he lifted out from the compartment looked more like an ancient Greek warship than anything hymenopterous. I turned to Brian in amazement.

'Do I need to smash a bottle of champagne against the side of this before I cast it?'

'Your ant ain't an ant,' Brian informed me. 'It's a "hopper".'

On our first morning, Jorge's pick-up was saddled up outside the Arroyo Claro, his black, bubbly, twenty-foot inflatable all ready to head Michael and me off to the boca of the Rivadavia, twelve miles away. To the strains of the Auld Reekie Scottish Dance Band's chart-busting tape *Capital Reels* we reeled our way through the Parque, tipping our caps in respect as we passed the ancient *Fitzroya alerces* conifers that took seed over two thousand years ago in Roman times, before the birth of Christ, and which gave their name to the Parque. Clouds of small game birds burst out in front of us.

'Californian quail,' Jorge told us. 'They never used to be here. I introduced them about ten years ago. Now they're everywhere.' I was hoping he had also introduced trout into the Rio Rivadavia I was to fish for the first time.

Running between Lago Verde and Lago Rivadavia, Rio Rivadavia is eight kilometres long and fly only. You are dropped off at the boca in the morning and just when it's time to go home, you pop out of the end of the Rio into the lago below where Jorge's pick-up is waiting to take you home. As Jorge rowed us along the shoreline of the lago towards the boca, I showed him my 'ant'.

'That's no ant. It's a Fat Albert.' Well, I thought, that's another name for it.

'Same thing,' he said. 'Stick it on.'

At the inlet, we were sucked into a blue, fast-moving, twelve-foot run that cut deep into the bank. The cut was twelve feet deep.

'Now stick your head over the side of the boat,' Jorge said.

There, rising and falling, swinging from left to right, were rainbows up to six pounds, not one under two pounds, hanging there in the current.

'Keep that Albert ant on,' urged Jorge. 'You're going to need it.'

The banks of the Rivadavia are overgrown with willow, southern beech, arrayanes and bamboo and the water is too deep to get into and wade it down. It's only possible to fish it seriously in a boat. The system is that you float down and stop at likely spots inaccessible from the bank – a gravel run, a logjam, a fallen tree, a deep cut – and fish it through.

Our first stop was the Colehual, a long, shallow, gravel shelf sloping into a deep, fast-flowing run. It's here where the Colehual stream meets the main river and where you meet some of the fussiest and feistiest rainbow trout you are ever likely to meet on any wild stream in the world.

Jorge beached the inflatable at the end of the gravel bank and we climbed out to wade and fish it up. I quickly realized that whereas my sitting room at home has wall-to-wall carpet, the Rivadavia is carpeted with trout. Without moving, we could see twenty or thirty rainbows lying in scoops, their heads on a pillow of crystal-clear water. Grey shapes on sparkling stones.

No gravel flat is more famous – indeed more notorious – than the flat we were creeping up with caution so as not to step on its finny contents. Fish were everywhere. Stop to cast to one a few yards in front of you, and look back; behind you there will be a dozen or more fish licking your boots and the grubs off the gravels you've disturbed.

A rainbow lifted to something coming down in large numbers. Here was my chance to hit it with my nuclear insect.

'Give me a foot of two-pound,' Jorge asked.

'Sure,' I said hesitantly, fearing that the weight of my ant would break such a lightweight tippet.

I handed him the line. Stripping off a length, he tied it onto the bend of the #6 long-shank hook of my ant. Pulling a nymph pattern on a #22 from his sheepskin patch, he tied it on and threw it back at me.

'Fish that lot down. And keep an eye on that ant. When it dips under, strike. It makes a great float.'

Getting the fish to your heels might be easy. But not getting them to take your little nymph. The current is so powerful that even in chest waders you can't wade any higher than just above the knee for fear of being swept away. The water piles up in front of your thighs in water only two feet deep. Jorge had told me small bead-head nymphs are a handy weapon here – but with a tungsten head. Anything lighter and nymph fishing is no better than dry flyfishing. The current is so strong everything is swept to the surface, giving the few fish I caught a formidable fighting strength. You're not playing a trout, you're playing the river for, turning on the current, the fish know just how to fix the flow to their advantage. Muscular, with sinews like whipcord, Rivadavia rainbows leap like tarpon, head over heels – always heading downriver and round bends. By the time you have caught up with them, often after having to climb back into the inflatable and take up chase, you're lucky if you end up in the same river. A bonefish you can move on a flat. A Rivadavia trout, you can't. In white water a foot deep, I couldn't move a fish of two and a half pounds. It clung to the pebbles as if it had a sucker strapped to its belly.

Since that first visit, I have fished the Rivadavia and the gravel shallows at Colehual many, many times – with many different guides. It was while fishing with guides that Michael Beale introduced me to that I developed two approaches; tactics I now adopt when fishing any gravel run on the Rivadavia in the Argentine midsummer, when the trout are as tight-lipped and as tricky and troublesome as they come (and they don't come to your fly that often). Two approaches, and two patterns that I devised to imitate the most prolific food items on the

Rivadavia trout's summer menu: midge and caddis larvae. Patterns that over the years have been tested by the piscatorial equivalent of the National Institute for Health and Care Excellence, the body that decides whether or not a new drug can be released. These clinical tests don't come cheap. The average pre-tax cost to bring a new drug to market is approximately £700 million. Air fares aside, the research needed in order to manufacture the first of these proven patterns cost me pennies: no more than the price of a pack of micro tubing called Ultra Lace.

With most flies that find themselves taken into the maws of monstrously fussy trout – their artificiality unheeded – size is everything. For this reason, when talking about my larva patterns, we dispense with the word 'big' because we're not talking about flies that can be seen from outer space here; rather, the opposite. Both patterns are minute, but only take a minute to tie.

When it comes to midge patterns, we still live in a Stillwater World. We've only just started fishing midge pupae on rivers. Similarly, when it comes to midge imitations, we are still living in a Pupa World. Midge patterns still have that fat stuff up behind the hook imitating legs, wings and bits and pieces about to explode into the adult. Pupae, yes; but you don't hear a lot about midge larvae. Maybe because they hide themselves away in the mud and marl. In stillwaters, that is. But not on rain-fed streams where changing water levels shift things around in a flash, including tasty goodies that thought they were safe. And here was my breakthrough.

For weeks I had been confronted by one of those large, glum-faced Colehual rainbows hogging a shallow dip in a fast run. I'd put every imaginable delicacy on its plate. I'd even stood behind it, scooping up everything tumbling down its food lane. This miserable monster wouldn't have moved had I walked up and kicked it, which I very possibly might have done.

If, that is, Gonzalo hadn't put me right.

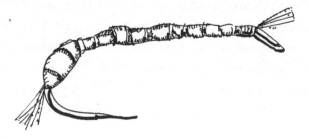

Gonzalo was once a chef in a five-star restaurant on the Paris Rive Gauche before he packed up his pots and pans and became a fishing guide. Who better to know what's on the menu? He'd taken trout from this gravelly run and noticed tiny midge larvae spew out when he removed hooks.

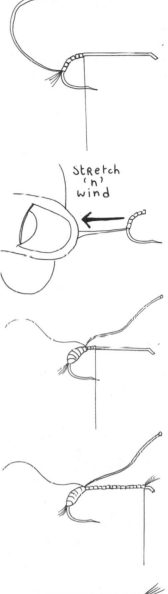

Gonzalo's larva pattern is tied with rayon thread. But I use Ultra Lace. This thin soft tubing is perfect for shiny, slimy, translucent bodies. Midge larvae can be black, brown, tan, cream, red, green and translucent. I match the hatch by threading floss materials of the required shade through the Ultra Lace. The hook is a #22. Simply tie in a sparse bunch of white DFM wool and a length of Ultra Lace to match, halfway round the hook bend. At the bend, form a head slightly larger than the body. Tie in thin gold wire. Wind thread to the head, tying in another small bunch of white DFM wool to behind the eye. Now stretch the Ultra Lace tight, wind to behind the eye. Secure and clip. Wind wire to the eye, forming narrow segments. Secure and clip. Whip-finish in front of DFM wool. Varnish. Clip wool 'breathers'.

But this wasn't the solution for every occasion. A second pattern was required. This became apparent when I was fishing a gravel run a hundred yards below the Colehual. My guide this time was Alun Lloyd from Esquel. Once again, we were watching fins bristling, trout swerving right to left, mouths opening and shutting and my nymphs trundling down the gravels, in inches of water, feet from my feet, rolling past rainbows and browns that were ignoring them comprehensively. They didn't even bother getting out of the way as my flies sleepwalked past them.

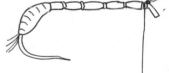

On these shallows, to take a closer look, all you need to do is just step across the backs of trout lying there like rocks, and take a peek. The river is tiled with them. Some the size of boulders. In water as crystal clear as ice off the snow-topped Andean *cordilleras*, you can see exactly what they're feeding on, in great detail, as if you were looking at it under a microscope. This time, it wasn't midge larvae they were hoovering up, it was tiny green caddis larvae. The dressing for these had to be small and minimal in the extreme – and the physical size of your fly has everything to do with the number of materials you incorporate into your dressing.

To slim down to smaller sizes – and here I'm talking about nothing larger than #20s – the fewer the materials and procedures the better. A lot fewer than the number of materials it takes to tie up an exact imitation with those legs, wings, tails, thoraces, eyes, bodies, thread windings. Good grief; the guys who dream up these patterns sure like their whippings – and deserve a damn good one for their efforts.

Like Gonzalo, Alun is a minimalist flytyer, using few procedures and materials wound on firmly, but lightly. He doesn't tie flies; rather he breathes them onto hooks. He believes, as I do, the smaller the natural, the more invisible become the things that need to be imitated. Which is why Alun's imitation of those tiny green *Rhyacophila* caddis larvae pleased me so much. It was my own flytying philosophy wrapped round a hook: the less you give a trout to argue about, the more likely it is to take it into its mouth. My argument against imitating any natural too exactly.

Rolling Ricky

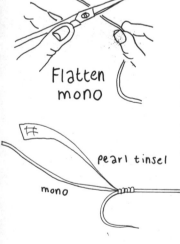

The Rolling Ricky, the name I gave my caddis larvae imitation, is simple to tie. It has a small black or lead-coloured tungsten bead head up front, a couple of turns of peacock herl behind this and a slender pearl tinsel body covered with clear monofilament behind that. The hook is a #20.

On some days in the early season, midge larvae come rolling down over the gravels like scarlet tapioca. Likewise, greengage-coloured *Rhyacophila* larvae, which are prevalent in the stream in summer months. Both midge and caddis larvae present the same challenge to the progressive flyfisherman – beyond devising the perfect imitation. The challenge is finding a way of making this perfect imitation imitate the correct behaviour of a freshly released natural that has lost its grip in the powerful flow of a rain-fed stream and finds itself skydiving down a stream where there's no sky, only water.

To fool heartless trout, your pattern must size up to the natural – and here's where the problems start. Your perfect imitation needs to be tied a hook size too small to cradle a bead head that is capable of supplying the necessary weight to enable it to plunge down and find the level in a fast-flowing stream where the trout expect to see their next meal tumbling down the gravels towards them.

This is sight-fishing at its most accurate. But even if your pattern gets down to a decent depth, without sufficient weight it is incapable of being 'controlled', or rather 'directed', by the flyfisherman to a trout Blu-tacked to the gravels with an insane intensity. Trout always in the same position; day after day. Always unwilling to make the tiniest move towards anything that doesn't appear right there, slap-bang on their dining table – at plate level. A knife and fork distance from their mouths. For this reason, you need to have total control of your imitation and not let the current have too much of a say on where it is positioned in the stream, or the direction you want it to head.

On top of this, these are some of the smartest trout you could ever be unfortunate enough to find yourself up against. With the appetite of a piranha, the pickiness of a sparrow, they are as spooky as they come – and go. If anything unfamiliar appears, above or below the surface, they spin around like demented ballerinas. When they settle down, they go on to sulk like schoolgirls for an hour. They even scare themselves.

So, how do you get the depth – and take control? How did I manage to take this weight off my mind?

I deduced that even if bead heads are the answer, I'm not a great fan of them. Shiny gold or silver beads can be a big giveaway of a fly's fakery on any wild trout catch-and-release stream, like the Rivadavia.

However, because the Rolling Ricky and Gonzalo's worm are dressed on the teeniest of sizes, I will give the dull, black, lead-coloured tungsten bead the benefit of the doubt. Tired of watching the prize trout I was after taking up position somewhere in the next county when my weights bounced by, in a state of total neurosis I came up with an idea that allows me to fish a ledger without these trout clanging alarm bells.

In New Zealand, as in Argentina, to get depth they fish 'nymphs in tandem'. Here a length of tippet is tied to the hook of a heavy nymph. To this a smaller nymph is tied so that it trails behind the bigger fly, at a depth it couldn't sink to on its own. Like beads, this system can be highly effective, and I considered it to be a solution. But, like beads, it's not the solution on all streams, at all times. In the clear Andean snowmelt, you can watch trouts' eyes glaze over as the contraption passes them by. Worse still, you can see them head for the hills. I headed back to the drawing board. There had to be something better.

My approach, Tactic No. 1, which I finally arrived at when deciding on a top-grade sink system, incorporates the last nine inches of the leader. Before I tie on my tippet, I tie on a short length of four-pound 4X mono, then an equally short tippet of two-pound 8X fluorocarbon. This length of mono is my shot trolley. It's where I clip on BB shot between the knots so that they won't slip on down to the fly, wrecking any chance of me ever extracting anything off the gravels. But, if the trout are really picky, this system can look suspicious, and you need to get shot of the shot. For this reason, I went on to develop a further sink system: Tactic No. 2, The Patterson Plunging Pellet. And here's the thinking behind this.

When river junk heads their way in the current – weed, bark, riverside rubbish – trout either ignore or investigate it, but they never skedaddle. So I take a length of eight-pound monofilament and loop it at both ends leaving a 1 in. (2.5 cm) gap in between where I wind close turns of lead wire. To prevent it unwinding, I smother these winds with epoxy. Now the rubbish part: to camouflage the scary lead, before the epoxy dries, I roll it in countryside junk. Crushed leaves, bark, dried seeds – anything that makes it look like forest debris rolling down the stream, not something that might alert a trout on the lookout for funny goings-on. Then, 9 in. (23 cm) behind this, on a 6–8X tippet, I put my larva.

The result: I get depth and control – and the trout don't get freaked. In fact, the system is ignored. But on a couple of occasions a trout not only investigated but actually grabbed my ponced-up Patterson Pellet wrapped around in bark and bankside debris. I can only guess it was mistaken for a caddis case. Or maybe the trout just wanted to put on weight.

Either way, I have a whole range of Patterson Plunging Pellets of different sizes and weights. All junked up with different trash outfits, in the characters of various streams.

Now, here are a few things worth considering. First, epoxy is a 'liquid weight', so add this to the calculation when working out how much lead wire you will need for your Pellet weight. Also, use organic vegetable matter as roll-on rubbish. Stones and gravel don't tumble down like grass, or sodden bark. That's unnatural.

When it comes to tying the Pellet onto your cast, you can either loop-to-loop it, or Surgeon Knot it. Likewise, with the tippet. This should only be about 6 in. (15 cm) to 9 in. (23 cm) from the Pellet – using the lightest tippet material you dare. I've had fish up to four pounds on 8X – 2.4 lb Grand Max Riverge, in fast water. (It kills the guides to see you do it!)

A good deal of my small larvae tied on #20+ hooks have such small eyes I find it easier to tie them onto the tippet material at the bench when I have the light – and the patience. I wrap these casts round a piece of card so, if I want to change pattern, I just loop the old one off the Pellet and loop the new one on.

Now, because larvae patterns are small and trout less willing to move to feed, I sometimes add a dropper and fish two larvae. Usually in deeper water where I know trout are moving around, or hard to see. Or to test colours. Because I have control of their destination, multiple flies allow you to fish two current lanes, two water depths and even two insect stages at once if you think the trout might just fancy a larva and, let's say, a pupa.

All told, it's a rubbish idea, but it sure does the job.

The Spring Creek

The sprinklers were sprinkling. Temperatures had been in the tolerable high twenties all week; stinging when they stroked the mid-thirties. About normal for February.

But I like my surroundings to be green, not yellow; damp, not dry. For this reason, I'm perfectly content to sit on the deck gazing across the Rio Carrileufu to the *cordilleras* beyond, sharing liquid refreshment with the grass, listening to the hoses hissing like a thousand snakes.

Snakes of any shape or size have never been a problem in Chubut, or anywhere else in Central Patagonia. In all the thirty years I've fished these parts I've never seen nor even heard of one being seen.

But the danger right now isn't long, scaly and slithery. It's small, short and furry. Small, but big enough of a threat to terrorize the locals, put off potential visitors, postpone the opening of a school at Villa Futalaufquen, close campsites, lodges and *hosterias*. And, last week, El Parque Nacional Los Alerces a mile down the dusty track. A strange phenomenon is happening here. A bush of the bamboo family is blooming.

Up to six metres tall, with a prickly Hendrix hairstyle, the *colihue caña* – which the Mapuche people in the area still use to make a musical instrument known as *trutruca* – is flowering, seeding and dying, never to bloom again for another sixty – some say seventy – years. No one knows what triggers this curious natural event.

These dead, dried-out bushes can pose a serious risk of forest fires at this hot, rainless time of year. But there's more. The sudden release of a vast amount of cane seeds results in an explosion in the population of mice that come down from the mountains, bringing with them hantavirus, a disease that is potentially fatal if humans become infected through contact with rodent urine, saliva or faeces.

Any other problems? Yes, my favourite spring creek that runs into the Rivadavia is slap-bang in the middle of El Parque.

Away from El Parque, at this time of year there's no problem working out where the landlocked salmon will be gathering. I had one at the beginning of the week at the boca, where the Carrileufú leaves Lago Cholila and shallows off for five hundred yards at the start of its twenty-mile journey through Butch Cassidy country to Lago Rivadavia. It took a Czech nymph. It must have wondered what the hell that was doing there.

To fish the creek in El Parque poses considerable problems. But, right now, arriving to find the place crawling with other flyfishermen isn't one of them. No one dares go there. They haven't for weeks.

The problem is waiting for the perfect set of circumstances to go there. It needs to be what Diego Viganó, my friend and neighbour, and I called a 'burn and blow day'. Hot, to sterilize the ground. Windy, to clear the air. Never have conditions been so critical. Not for catching fish – as is normally the case – but for not catching what could be there, creepy-crawling round the creek in the *caña colihues*.

Time of day is also critical, for sight-fishing is the only way to fish in this steamy forest of *ñires* with their crisp, flaky bark, thorny *rosa mosqueta*, *maitens* and pin-sharp rushes sticking out of the creek like javelins. Not forgetting the prickly *calafate* bushes. End up in one of those and you end up in hospital.

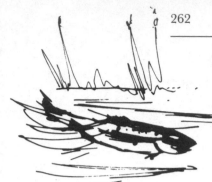

The best time to head out is late morning, when the sun is at its highest, lighting up the deep, aquamarine pools so you can spot the rainbows and brookies that have moved up out of the Rio Rivadavia to spawn and decided to stay. They average three to six pounds.

Anything smaller in the creek gets eaten.

It's a twenty-minute drive through El Parque along a powdery road where the smooth tops of immoveable rocks lie as low as landmines in the dust, only revealing their real size when it's too late to swerve or slam on the brakes. There's a small clearing just off the road. No signs, no directions, you have to consult your AA Book of Instincts to locate it. It's here where you park in the shade of the *lengas* and the tallest *maitens* I have ever seen to get set up.

Getting to the creek is an adventure in itself. Imagine the first day of the Christmas sales in Oxford Circus. But instead of people, you have trees. This is the path through the woods you have to take. After this, you have a squishy-squashy marsh to negotiate.

Herefords are your guides here. Cows are the only creatures that can pick their way through this maze of swampland. Many never make it. But only horses are here today.

Tiptoeing between the cow prints, skipping from one grass-topped sod to another, is pure ballet. But you get there in the end. The mud sticks to your boots for the rest of the day because when you get to the creek you can't get into it to clean it off. The water level is a constant four to five feet from one side of the bank to another. There are one or two places where it does shallow off. But dare wade in and you sink and disappear into a thousand years of soft silt.

In between water plants from outer space and storm-blasted trees that have fallen into or across the creek, the water is so clear you feel you have to touch it to make sure it's actually there. But you don't; for to do this would mean lying face-down on the ground, or perhaps across one of the many rodent roads that criss-cross the forest floor. You take it on trust.

As we poke our heads over a clump of dried *colihue* canes hugging the bank, a six-pound rainbow glides past – right under our feet. It looks as if it's suspended in air. The breeze ruffles the surface momentarily. It disappears.

There is no flow in the creek; or, if there is, it's hardly detectable. If your nymph moves in the water, it will be a lick of Patagonian wind that has pushed your floating line on the surface, in whichever way it is blowing.

The surface clears and our rainbow reappears out of the shade on the far bank and rushes towards us in the direction of something highlighted by the sun. Something white lying on the mud behind a patch of the sort of weed you buy in pet shops to put in the tank with your goldfish. But this rainbow is no goldfish. It head-butts the object in a cloud of silt and cruises back to the far bank, chomping; dissolving into the darkness.

We wait.

Fishing the creek is a waiting game. You spot your fish. You lay your fly on the mud where you first saw the fish and leave it there. You become a tree, a bush, or a bunch of cane – anything static and looking permanent, for as long as it takes. If there was ever proof that trout are home-loving creatures, this is it. They might patrol round their backyard – a secure surrounding area – but they'll be back, five, ten, fifteen minutes later. Especially if a trout knows there's something of culinary interest on the dining-room table.

Our fish is back again almost immediately. It lifts the mysterious morsel off the mud and tears off a chunk. Now we can see what it is. A dead mouse.

In safer times, I have spent hours wondering what these creepy creek cruisers feed on. They float about motionlessly, hardly a fin moving. Then they tip downwards and shake their head backwards and forwards, puffing out silt like they were lighting a cigar.

Occasionally a trout will suddenly break the silence in the forest and take something from the surface. A sedge – for there are caddis cases to be found in amongst all those rotting logs – or a terrestrial bug of some sort. I have never seen any hatches though, so Mayfly nymphs aren't the objects of their desire. But in water as still and as placid as a water butt, there must be midge.

For this reason, I suspect their main diet is midge larvae. However, I have yet to design a pattern that they are confident or curious enough to put into their mouths and just perhaps dine on. Nevertheless, imitating a food form that moves under the silt, not on top of it, is the ultimate flyfishing challenge – perhaps the most impossible. Sure beats me.

There are scuds, though. Shrimpy things. Small, dark and to be tied on tiny snack-size hooks. Anything larger is too much of a banquet for these supercilious specimens.

My Mud Scud is tied on a #20 emerger hook, but there's really nothing to it. Nothing, I say, is good. For nothing is something a trout can't find fault with. On small sizes you use fewer materials, in smaller qualities, with fewer movements. And no fancy additions a wise old trout would spot as a fraud. I slip a small tungsten bead on the barbless hook, tie in a few strands of dark olive mohair at the bend as legs, dub a body with the same mohair, rib it, whip-finish and varnish. Done.

This, for me, is all that is needed to excite just the right amount of tummy-rumbling curiosity from a passing trout. It doesn't mean every trout will take it in its mouth. What pattern can ever guarantee that? But, armed with my scud, if I can find a trout cruising a weedbed then I consider that I have found a trout I have a chance of interesting, however small.

Such a trout was a brookie, sliding silently past my position behind a tree, gliding effortlessly on a pair of white-tipped pectoral fins shining like newly varnished fingernails. The ambush had been set. My scud lay on the mud in the smoking room, ready to be lifted. But it never was, for just up-creek from me, the jagged shape of Diego, hidden behind the *colihues*, let out a yell.

'She took it! She took it! She took it!' Diego shrieked like some perturbed parakeet. 'But I took it right out of her mouth! Just as it was closing!'

Apparently, my brookie's big sister – with even flashier nail varnish – and lipstick Diego's scud didn't stick to – had been circling Diego's boots, dipping into silt and smoking that after-dinner cigar. She'd inhaled his mud scud, lying there on the table, in one big puff, watched it fly out again in front of her very eyes and decided to turn and politely leave the table, in quiet disgust. No rush. She was confused at the scud's bizarre table manners, rather than alarmed.

I still had eyes on my brookie that turned and swam away when another brookie almost twice its size – well over five pounds – suddenly appeared, uninvited, in her smoking room right in front of me.

Behind the screen of dry canes, I could hear the lonely clicks of Diego's reel slowly winding in his line.

'Is this your fish that's swimming past me?' I asked, watching the brookie disappear in and out of the deep shadows.

'Was my fish,' Diego sulked, 'the dirty rat.'

There were plenty of those around.

Arroyo Pescado

Alun Lloyd, my guide on the Rivadavia, is Welsh. Or rather, of Welsh descent. If he's trying to keep this quiet, the large 'Cymru' sticker on the back of his Jeep gives the game away.

His grandfather, Lloyd ap Iwan, was the only person in Argentina gunned down by Butch Cassidy and the Sundance Kid. Their *chacra* is just up the road from where I tend to rest my head outside Cholila. These days, their happy homestead is a cowshed. Let me tell you the tale.

Alun's grandfather was one of the original founders of the Welsh community in those parts. In 1865 he built an estancia thirty miles south-east of Esquel, about a two-hour drive south of the Rivadavia, in the middle of desert land. As this was the only trading place for miles, the enterprising Lloyd opened up a store, the Mercantile Company, serving passing coaches and travellers. News of its success travelled, too. Way north, to Cholila, just up the road from the Rivadavia, where Butch Cassidy, the Sundance Kid, Etta Place and other members of the gang had been farming for two years.

On the night of 28 December 1909, Lloyd was woken up by the noise of a torch being thrown through his bedroom window. He fired a few shots and managed to scare off the bandits, avert a robbery and put out the fire. But the next day, the gang returned. This time they overpowered him. During the looting, Butch Cassidy's spurs got tangled

up in a rug on the tiled floor. Cassidy fell over, giving Lloyd the chance to grab his pistol. But when he reached for the trigger he found there wasn't one. The weapon had been modified for the hammer to be 'fanned'. What with this and his burned hands from the night before, Lloyd just wasn't quite quick enough. The Sundance Kid walked in and shot him down with his Winchester .45 rifle.

The police eventually caught up with the gang months later on the Chilean border, but once again they were able to escape. Eventually, the Pinkerton Agency tracked them down in Bolivia where they finally gunned them down.

Planted in a shady oasis of Lombardy pines and firs is the late Lloyd's ranch house. Here flyfishermen are welcomed in the hall, where you pick up your ticket, standing on the same tiled floor that Butch Cassidy and the Sundance Kid had crossed to shoot him down. Just behind the estancia on the side of a rocky hill is Lloyd's tombstone, a plain brown slab stuck in the dust. It's visible just south of the road leading to the creek. Recently it's been surrounded with barbed wire to stop cattle knocking it over. You can't miss it as you make your way to the Arroyo Pescado – 'Fish Creek' – a six-mile-long silver vein that runs through the estancia and that has made this part of the world so famous – for flyfishermen.

Seemingly seeping out of nowhere, this cold-spring creek trickles idly through 20,000 acres of parched, treeless land of brush, rock and stone, creating deliciously crystal-clear ponds, one after another after another. Here is the finest sight-fishing for rainbow, brook and brown trout up to fifteen pounds that materialize out of fluffy clumps of wig-sized weed beds, morphing into nowhere, well rehearsed in commando

survival tactics. Opening in January and closing in March, the season is short. Only half a dozen rods are allowed, but I always get the place to myself and I only fish one place.

Alun, Michael and Benjamin – Michael's son and Central Patagonia's most pioneering guide – and I arrived in the last week of the season. We were the only people fishing that day. But we never moved from the first hundred yards. Here the creek widens, forming a pool a hundred yards long, bubbling with springs that form sandy bowls inhabited periodically by patrolling rainbows – on high alert. Exactly why they were like this was hard to tell, for not a blade of grass gave evidence of anyone having been there for months.

Trees once stood by this pool. But now they're just twisted bleached bones sticking out of the water, writhing up into the sky as if in agony. Every time I return, I expect them to have rotted away. I've been coming back for thirty years, and they're still there. I'm beginning to look bleached myself.

Perched high up on the end of tumbledown fencing at the far end of the pool, this is the best place to watch trout slip in and out of the long, dark shadows. Lift your eyes up from the cool of the creek and gaze across the vast, sun-baked aridity that surrounds you – the Andes in 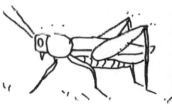 the background, distorted in a humming heat haze lifting off the sand, rock and grasshopper-grazed scrub – and the creek and its contents look totally out of place. Huge black clouds hanging over the mountains appear to head your way. You prepare for the mother of all tropical storms, but it never happens. When the clouds hit the heat, they think better of it and stay in Chile. Nothing stops the relentless trademark Patagonian wind, though. This arrives late in the day. But in my ringside seat on the fencing, I'm sheltered behind one of the only trees, a willow.

A monster rainbow appears out of nowhere. A curl of wind lifts its shape off the water and shatters it into invisibility. I have a tiny Rolling Ricky, the smallest nymph in my box, lying on the silt bed. A nothing, really. But a something to the trout, because of its size. It's the size of nothing. Nothing out of the ordinary. When I raise it in front of a trout, it doesn't raise suspicion. The guys from Montana, who come here when it's winter back on their own rivers, strip huge, ugly Woolly Buggers which, if they were dogs – and some of them are large enough to be animals – would be on the dangerous dogs list. But these flies are no danger to the trout. They are unceremoniously ignored. And the guys from Montana wonder why trout giggle.

Shallows two feet deep plunge off into a sunlit pool spread out like a beach towel, six feet deep. A second rainbow, longer than the first one, inches out from behind a branch on the bottom. I lift my nymph, lying long time frozen in the hot shafts of sunlight. The rainbow rushes it. Its mouth opens up like some huge tropical flower and sucks it in. My nothing is now something. Something heavy and unhappy on the end of my line. Last year the weed was soft and silky. This year, it's firm. My trout dives into the greenery and I'm struggling with a trout well over eight pounds, its head in a cabbage.

Alun arrives, wondering how I managed both to get my nymph so deep and to hold motionless for so long. I tell him I had to buy some lead shot in town.

'Hey, I got shot,' Alun tells me.

Seems it runs in the family.

Rio Carrileufú

From the minor to the major. The microscopic to the mammoth. The titchy to the titanic. The sublime to the ridiculous. Just as everyone who fishes the trout rivers of central Patagonia must have nymphs and dry flies tied on the minute side of small, so they must also carry around flies of such magnitude that they are best stored in the garage rather than a cupboard and transported around in a portmanteau rather than in a fly box.

I learned this one day when I found myself fishing with a guide from Texas, rather than with one of the local guides I'd been hiring. Dressed as if he was about to invade Poland, this guide had a chin I could have struck a match on. I offered to help him load the boat, but he scowled. I asked him about the fishing.

'Fella, if you catch anything today, you got luck tattooed on your ass.'

We didn't catch anything – and I chose not to fish with him again. But he taught me something.

'Fella,' he said, 'you flyfishermen fiddle about.'

I didn't understand what he meant, but I agreed all the same. (That day, under the warmth of his nuclear glare, I had decided to agree with his every word.)

'Always keep something big down here,' he said, slapping his pocket with such a crack that wildlife evacuated the surrounding *árboles del bosque.*

I promised I'd do just that.

I discovered that my guide preferred clients who spin-cast. This explained why he didn't have anything 'big' down there in his nether regions I could fiddle with. He was talking about flies, apparently. He believed flyfishers fiddle around with flies too small for the task in hand. His view was that when things get tough – and they were tough that day – the solution isn't to keep reducing the size of the fly until the trout breathes it in, like a minute particle of air, as I was doing. Sometimes the exact opposite is required.

To steal away a wild and woolly trout's attention when he's tucked under some bush, lying tight into the bank, or deep down in some scrape in the river, he believed the answer is to throw it something on the Grand Scale. Something that gets it revved up enough to want to grab it, involuntarily. A GTi fly. A Grand Theft insect.

And this is why the fly I am about to introduce to you is what it is, does what it does – and is called what it's called. And why, when the trout give you a hard time, you should always have one slapped in your pocket.

The big, bad, black Beastie is a whopper, there's no denying it. But for wild trout in areas of extreme wildness such as on the Rio Carrileufú – whose waters flow into Lago Rivadavia, which feeds into the Rio Rivadavia and polishes the sacred gravels of the Colehual – it has saved me from many a blank when trout with PhDs in entomology have poked fun at me. Indeed, it has resulted in me acquiring godlike status . . . when I whip it out.

So, what is this Beastie thing, other than something that raises the water level every time you slam it out there?

To all intents and purposes, it's a large beetle. (Not quite the size of a Volkswagen, but nearly.) Our largest is the stag beetle. In Argentina, it's the cicada. There are about 2,500 species of cicada around the

world, but I don't think the brownie lying in that pool under the toppled *colihue* tree on the Carrileufú had ever seen anything like a Beastie in its life before. A black sheep, perhaps – but not swimming. Did it feel it should have done? Or that it might be missing out on the munch of the century? Whatever, it snaffled it.

To tie, or rather to build my Beastie, you won't need an architect or planning permission. (Depending on where you live.) The design challenge is in the application of the necessary trickery required to keep such a large lump of materials afloat – otherwise you'd squirt out a pot of Gink each time you wanted to launch a Beastie. Regarding the design, my view is this: if the Queen Mary can do it, so can the Beastie. All it takes is a small amount of foam truths. Well, a lot, actually.

Stage 1: Snip barb and vice #6 long-shank D/E hook. Tie in a 10 cm long, 1.5 cm wide strip of black 2 mm closed-cell foam using thick black monocord thread as tying silk. Bind foam three-quarters of the way down to bend. Fold over and tie in doubled-up foam to bend, allowing it to extend beyond bend. Clip to separate strips.

Stage 2: Tie in a large bunch of peacock herl at bend. Wind monocord to eye. Wind herl to eye, forming a fat body. Fold foam strips, individually, to eye, covering top and sides of body. Tie in, leaving 4 mm extending over eye. Whip-finish. Clip.

Stage 3: Now trim head, rounding off corners. Wind on monocord 50 mm behind head, to segment body. Tie in a 4 cm strand of black Sili or rubber legs to form two pairs of 2 cm forward- and backward-facing legs either side of body. 50 mm behind this, tie in a 4 cm strand of black Sili or rubber legs to form two pairs of 2 cm forward- and backward-facing legs either side of body. On top of this, tie in a bunch of white deer hair. Points sloping back to form wing. Whip-finish. Clip thread. Clip deer hair butts close to body.

Stage 3: Now remove your Beastie from the vice and make sure all the whip finishes are well varnished – underneath and on top – and totally trouty snap-proof.

Having tied up your Beastie, there's only one stage left. Stuff it down into your pocket and just see if the trout aren't the only thing pleased to see you.

Lago Kruger

Laguna Larga, the 'big lake', isn't really that big. At least, not compared to some of the other lakes nearby. For a start, down the track, a left turn into the half a million acres of El Parque Nacional Los Alerces, the skinny Lago Futalaufquen is twenty miles long. Clearly, the Tehuelche Indians who gave the Laguna Larga its name didn't get out and about much. Or just wanted to frighten you off.

Here in Argentina's Patagonian central zone, there's a whole bunch of large lakes filled with cold, clean water and surrounded by natural forests of sinewy arrayanes trees the colour of cinnamon sticks, *colihues* and *alerces*. The Lago Rivadavia, Lago Verde, Lago Menendez and Lago Kruger are all big lakes, joined up by a string of glassy rivers that cut shaded corridors through breathtaking alpine scenery: the Rios, Arrayanes, Menendez, Frey, Desaguadero, not forgetting the Rivadavia and Carrileufú. There are no hosepipe bans in these parts.

So, where to start lake fishing? Answer: you start by asking around, beginning with friends. Your very best friends, like Diego Viganó, author of *Fly Fishing the Best Rivers of Patagonia, Argentina,* an exhaustive guide to all of Patagonia's dream streams, who was anxious to introduce me to this unique lodge 'strategically located to offer the very best wild trout fishing in Patagonia'.

We turn up the track just before you arrive at El Parque Nacional Los Alerces, as instructed; we take a right, open a gate, hang a left, open another gate, as instructed – and get nowhere. Nowhere being lost. It is time to make a phone call.

'I told him his place is impossible to find,' Diego says, slinging his mobile into the back of his Jeep onto Elmer, his Labrador dog.

'What did he say?' I ask.

'He said that's the way he likes it. He's coming to escort us in.'

Quitting a hectic business life as an international leather dealer, Andres Stewart and his wife Gisela bought 260 acres on the side of Laguna Larga and started building a lodge straight away. A place of great seclusion and unique privacy.

'I didn't want to die in Buenos Aires,' Andres says. Here, I thought, he could die and no one would find him.

This timber lodge made of cypress and Douglas fir (in the local style) has a reverse view. By this I mean that the view towards the lodge from the lake is just as overpowering as the view from the lodge over the lake towards the Andes. Inside are leather sofas that put their arms around you and hug, showers that cascade you with a thousand wet kisses and a drinks cabinet with no lock or key. No luxury or expense is spared to ensure you'll never want to leave. Except to go fishing.

That night, chef Paulo cooks our first meal. As I sit sipping at a health-giving beverage by a log fire, he is in the kitchen fussing over some fiddly fine sauce; I can't keep my eyes off him. Attired in an immaculate bleached chef's hat with a knotted 'kerchief around his neck below his goatee beard, he looks the ultimate professional. If the food tastes only half as good as he looks, we are in for a truly gastronomic experience.

'I hope you have a big appetite,' Andres says as Nene, the uniformed waitress, presents us with the first of four courses. 'The trout I'm going to find for you tomorrow certainly do.'

Next morning, we sling our gear into the back of Andres's boat, hook it up to his Toyota and bounce our way down the track in a cloud of dust, stopping only momentarily to open the occasional gate. Travelling south on Ruta 71, through El Parque, it is only thirty minutes to Puerto Limonao at Villa Futalaufquen where we launch our boat into Lake Futalaufquen. The fun part is yanking it across a short, sandy lakeside beach furrowed by rows of bronzed beauties, refugees from the Hosteria Futalaufquen, sizzling in sun oil in the Southern sun. In chesties, we look – well, weird.

The 70 hp, four-stroke *Silencio* purrs us up the lake, past the outlet of Rio Arrayanes to a short waterway called Estrecho de los Monstruos which connects Futalaufquen to Lago Kruger. The Estrecho de los Montruos, the Monster Straits, is exactly that. Here the pace quickens and the boat is sucked across some of the most eye-popping trout ground you are ever likely to see. A huge flat, with shallows and channels, streaked with weed beds, scored with gravel runs. Here at one time you could expect to return back to Limonao with at least a brace of rainbows over ten pounds. You would be lucky to do that now. But, gazing around at the landscapes and waters that surround you, how much luckier could you be?

At the end of Lago Kruger, where the Rio Frey pours into it, is a rickety pier, the landing point for visitors to the Refucia Lodge. Here we are greeted by Dalmiro, who appears out of a cloud of horseflies and pulls us ashore. Very quickly I learn that nobody says anything about flyfishing without looking at Dalmiro to check that what they are saying is correct. For, even though he can be no more than sixteen years old, Dalmiro is the resident expert around these parts – and he has a lollipop permanently sticking out of his mouth to prove it.

I soon realize that Andres has set me up. He's told the crowd that has gathered to welcome the flyfisherman from afar that I am England's flyfishing equivalent of David Beckham. A hard act to follow. But they do. They follow me all the way round the back of the lodge to a pool shaded by an ancient willow tree where Dalmiro wants to see if the English Expert can catch his pet trout. Clearly the only trout he has been unable to catch – all season.

He mumbles something to his friend, who is scaling the willow to get a bird's-eye view. Then he mumbles something to himself – or perhaps into his lollipop, sticking out of his mouth like a radio aerial, picking up the only network in the area. He is broadcasting; urging his friends to come and watch the English Expert skunk himself? Leaning up against the tree, motionless, he blends into the bark, perfectly. I am expecting a bird to land on his lollipop stick at any moment.

Even more people arrive and blend. All eyes are on a rainbow lying fifteen yards under a willowy canopy, in a wisp of water that circles off the main current and spins back on itself into the pool. I count five different currents at play that have to be transversed if I am to dead-drift anything to this trouty teaser. Dalmiro's eyes never shift from the lilac adversary, the lollipop stick pointing directly at its heart. His gaze shoots daggers at the pool's last remaining occupant.

I decide not to panic. But it's too late. I fiddle with my little nymph a little – a hare's ear with a copper bead head, on a #16. It will never take something as obvious as this, I think. I study the tips of my wading boots for a while, lifting my toes up and down. I straighten my belt and cough every now and again. But none of this takes Dalmiro's eyes, or those of his friend nesting in the tree above, off the trout. Andres appears and busily blends into a bush.

Then from nowhere another trout swings into the pool and sidles up against the bank next to me, as if joining the audience. Twenty – twenty-two – inches. It must be well over three pounds. The same size as the show-stealing trout at the head of the pool. All I have to do is drop my juicy bug on its nose. This I do. All the trout has to do is open its big mouth and snap it up. This it does. It can't believe its eyes, or its luck. And neither can I, as I feel the trout make off with my beady-eyed blob.

There is a huge commotion. A load of splashing; tons of yanking; huge waves smashing up against the shore. Dalmiro's eyes open up like two huge watery goldfish bowls. His jaw drops open. Momentarily a bend seems to appear in his lollipop stick, quickly straightening back up when Dalmiro regains control and slams his mouth back down on it again. Constant radio contact is resumed. I release the trout, as unceremoniously as I had caught it.

'*Entonces,*' my public relations officer, Andres, says casually, walking away with his arm round my shoulder, like a football manager escorting his star player off the pitch after he'd scored the winning goal. He is as relieved as I am. At least we'd put on a show.

'His first sardine,' Andres says, shrugging the whole episode off as an everyday occasion as Dalmiro unblends himself from the tree, looking around everywhere. Surely, in all that hullabaloo, it hadn't been his trout the Englishman had been tussling with? He really wasn't sure. Was it the excitement – or the Expert? Either way, his trout is no longer in the pool.

'Now let's go and do some real fishing,' Andres says, heading for the pier.

Dalmiro unties the boat and kicks us out into the lake, lollipop quivering. He wants to come with us. We can tell. He asks to see my fly box before we leave. He opens it, surveys it in milliseconds, and closes it with the same speed he'd slammed his mouth shut minutes earlier.

He digs deep into a pocket, pulls out a tin and hands me a locust. A black locust, looking as home-made as hell. Locust, grasshopper, farm animal – whatever it is intended to be, to a hungry trout it is Selfridges Food Hall strapped to a hook. It is another Chernobyl/Fat Albert Ant. I am ready for the dropper with the two-pound point and #20 nymph. It never comes. At last, I am in business.

I thank him and stick it on the sheep patch on my breast. Andres oars Diego and me, wearing my badge of honour from the Great Dalmiro, out into the lake, even bigger than 'the big lake'. Another lake devoid of other fishermen, full of trout lying waiting to pounce. Just off the reeds.

Andres steers a straight course down the south-west shore, a stockade of reeds barely bending in the stiff afternoon breeze fresh off the Andes. The trout, we are told, lie hard up against the shore, just at the end of a healthy cast. The air dances with damselflies. They dip and bounce off the glittering water surface.

'I should have brought my dapping rod,' I suggest to Diego, who is standing at the back of the boat, rod in hand, waiting for some action. There is nothing rising.

'Maybe you should chuck them something to rise to,' Andres suggests.

Dalmiro's Ant

Diego confirms that the pattern Dalmiro has given me is one of those 'ant things'. Or his version of one. It has strips of black foam sculptured to the shape of a buggy-looking thing, with two lengths of rubber legging criss-crossed in the centre of the hook.

'Shoot between the gaps in the reeds. Bring it back to you – in spurts.'

Spurt is the word. Pop-pop-popping through the breeze wave, it spits water out of its backside like a toy outboard. I am stripping it too fast, apparently, but not according to a mouth that opens wide and white to the sky and clamps down on its huge foamy chewiness, with the same determination that Dalmiro had demonstrated earlier, on his lollipop.

'You missed it. Slow down.'

It isn't my Ant that is racing now, it's my heart. I fill another reed gap with my gobstopper grasshopper and twitch it back, imagining Dalmiro is behind the wheel. What would he do? I am picking up his vibes. I am

on his wavelength. He is sending out signals. I can feel him at my side. 'Tweak,' he is bleeping. 'Now, wait, don't snatch your fly away from that black head that just pulled my Ant beneath the wave.'

This time, the fish is on. And it isn't going to get away. Although, launching itself head first into the reeds, it thinks for a minute it has. By the time it has run its course from one end of the reed bed to the other, Kew Gardens – or rather the Hanging Gardens of Babylon – is hanging off the end of the line. This makes the fish feel to me like it would bring the plaster off the wall if I were to have it stuffed and put in a case.

At the boat, Andres holds the speckled brown trout up to show me. It is over four pounds.

'Did you say *stuffed*?' Andre asks. 'This lake is stuffed with trout like him.' With this, he slips the hook and lets my trophy saunter back to its reedy kingdom.

'Let's just call it your second sardine?'

Rio Rosario

From Cholila to El Encuentro Lodge on the outskirts of Esquel, it's a three-hour drive through El Parque. Or two, if you travel a road that dissolves into dust as you pass through the modest country retreat of clothes magnate Luciano Benetton, the home of one hundred and twenty thousand sheep that produce five hundred tons of wool a year. That's some pullover.

At El Encuentro Lodge, where I had been staying for a few days, Michael's home beat is the Rio Futaleufú. It flows due west, through Argentine Patagonia to Chile. Broad and boisterous, it is best fished from a boat, although there are many willow-lined channels where you can fish from long, finger-shaped gravel islands in the middle of the river on tiny dries flicked between the branches. I'd been there a week, with Michael's son, Benjamin, as guide, but my stay was coming to an end and Michael had saved the best for last. A day on the Rio Rosario, deep in Welsh Patagonia. Mysterious waters situated below Nant Y Falls, four breathtaking waterfalls that spout out from Lago Rosario. Waters that hadn't been fished since Christmas. It was now the end of January.

On the Argentine–Chilean border, the Rio Rosario is an unassuming sliver of a creek, sliding languorously through scrub and forests of *lengas* and *ñires*, through land that has been farmed by the same family since the first Welsh colonists crossed overland from the Puerto Madryn on the east coast where they landed, finally settling by the Andes on the west in the 1880s. In Trevelin, meaning 'town of the mill' in Welsh.

At dinner on the night before our foray, Michael painted a picture of the terrain that we'd be fishing in this lonely part of Chubut that hadn't changed much in a hundred or so years: an estancia where the family and farm workers go up into the hills and hunt wild boar with a large variety of dogs of unknown breeds, some of them the size of pumas, tusk-scarred and stab-stitched; boars – and Chilean rustlers – that come down from the hills that they hunt down with Colt .38s. And anyone else they happen to find on their land who shouldn't be there.

'I'd better warn you,' Michael told me, 'we're lucky to be allowed to fish there. The owner, Mr Lewis, is suspicious about everyone. Be prepared! He's as wild as they come, and they don't come wilder. Trust me.'

His eyes opened wider and wider as he talked, as if he was trying to eject something that had flown into them. I could see the little blood vessels pumping away round the edges of his pupils.

'He scares the life out of me,' he went on, pouring me some more wine. 'I wouldn't want to put a foot wrong in his company. If you can call being with him "company". He's as distant as a planet, as cold as an iceberg.'

The room had gone quiet.

'Just one look at him – well, there's nothing easy on the eye about him. It's like looking into a cave.'

Now everyone was listening to Michael. Or rather, pretending not to. Everyone knew what he was talking about. Everyone was taking a heightened interest in the food on the plate in front of them. The atmosphere had changed; had gone chilly. Michael sensed it, too.

'So, anyone want to go fishing with Neil and me tomorrow?' he shouted down to the guides at the end of the table. Everyone became even more strangely preoccupied with what was on their plates.

I was in a hotbed of cold feet.

We set off at nine the next morning. Michael turned off the main road and bumped his Passat down an earthen track. I wasn't sure where we were heading. Neither was I certain if I was on the fishing trip of a lifetime, or a freight train to Crazy Town. The last thing on my mind was fishing.

We'd hardly set foot on 'Lewis Land' when a small man with a big hat, riding a pied horse, approached us sitting high up on a sheepskin saddle. He was flanked on both sides by a pack of wild dogs and two dubious-looking minders, one half Mapuche Indian, the other half Tehuelche, half wild beast. Both had Colt .38 revolvers stuck threateningly into stained leather holsters, distressed with age and use. The handgrips were wrapped round with what looked like Band-Aid.

As they approached, I leaned slowly across to Michael, never taking my eyes off the riders coming our way.

'If they aren't suspicious-looking, what do we look like?' I asked Michael. 'Is the small guy Lewis?'

'No,' Michael reassured me.

Whoever they were, they gave us the 'look' as they passed. The look you give someone when you're about to draw a gun, but don't.

Two of the dogs, one of them silver with sinister grey wolf eyes, the other with a recently healed gash in its side, stopped to bury their heads in a cow carcass lying a few yards ahead of us, and give it a chew.

'So, let's talk about the fishing,' Michael said, relaxing his grip on the steering wheel, trying to take my mind off everything that was going on around us. The impending doom.

'You'll like this creek. I'm taking you to a place where it runs through a forest. It's a series of deep pothole-like pools. Rainbows up to six pounds live there but no one seems to be able to catch them. But that Rolling Rocky of yours should do the trick . . .'

Michael cut himself short. A blue Ford Falcon had turned the corner fifty yards ahead of us. It stopped at a gate, waiting for us. When we got to the gate, Michael jumped out of the Passat and opened it. Just before he did he turned to me and whispered, 'It's Lewis. Out!'

By the time I'd clambered out of the car in my chest waders, Michael was already standing by the Falcon, talking. The passenger window was wound down enough for me to see a face blackened by the sun, a wispy, tobacco-stained moustache, eyebrows you could knit into a jumper and a gaucho beret that looked like it had been moulded onto the owner's head. This was Lewis, the unsettling settler from hell. Sitting behind the wheel next to him was a large woman dressed in black, eyeing me up and down.

I stepped forward and Michael introduced me. Lewis looked at me and growled something to Michael in Spanish. Michael nodded and turned to me.

'Señor Lewis says how honoured he is that such an expert fisherman from England is going to be fishing his river and how delighted he is that you came. He wishes you the very best of luck.'

As Michael talked, Lewis smiled at me warmly; a smile broad enough to reveal that whatever other despicable things he might have wanted to do to me, he didn't have enough teeth to bite me. With this, the satanic Lewis, his mysterious chauffeuse and the Falcon disappeared down the track.

'Was that really Lewis? *The* Lewis? Lewis the Lucifer?'

'That was him.'

'But he smiled at me. He was *nice*.'

'Well,' Michael said climbing back into the pick-up, 'a man never looks very threatening when he's with his Italian mother-in-law.'

Oh, the *vita* is *dolce*.

Rio Pico

Finally, a word about Michael's son, Benjamin Beale.

Fishing guides. They're good, bad, or lazy. Saints of sobriety. Or dirty drunks like my first guide in Montana, an Irishman. If you threw a petrol bomb at him, he'd drink it. Not that this dampened his spirit of adventure. Keener than red-hot mustard, he drove me up the wall. But not before he'd driven me halfway across the State, had me ploughing through marshes, trekking across rocks, pushing through rapids and climbing up cliffs at breakneck speeds. (One slip and your neck's broken.) If I didn't have a heart attack, I was hoping he would. And if he had I wouldn't have called an ambulance. I'd have written for one. Anything to get shot of him.

Love or hate 'em, the places my fishing takes me usually involve my needing a pointy finger. But, if you ever need a steering hand, take my advice. Don't look for a guide. Track down a pioneer. Preferably a member of one of the original pioneers in the area, like the Beales, who have been there longer than anyone else. This way, they have close relationships with the owners of all the best waters. With private access to the most exclusive of them.

Benjamin and I have fished together since he was knee-high to a pair of breathables. If his legs aren't in one or other of the rivers in the area, his ears are flush to the ground. So, when it comes to checking out new, unknown, untried, unfished beats, I'm not a flyfisherman, I'm a strip of litmus paper, dipping flies into unexplored streams to check out possibilities. If the fishing's not up to standard, we have a great lunch. If it's good, we still have a great lunch. I have the explorer in me, too. Pioneers find waters rarely fished; if ever fished at all. One of these places Benjamin took me to was Rio Pico.

Rio Pico is more than a river. It's an area. A bump on the side of Central Argentina on the Chilean border awash with trout-filled rivers, streams, ditches and lagunas. It's a slow half-day's drive south of Esquel, if you're in no hurry. But to get to there, Benjamin's wheels were spinning, dust was flying and records were being broken.

The Tres Valles (Three Valleys) Lodge is part of a 600-hectare estancia that stands on land once hunted by Mapuches and farmed by Tehuelche Indians. The Mapuches eventually chased the Tehuelches away, only to be slung out themselves when the Europeans arrived.

Things are a lot quieter now.

The property has tres owners. Bruno and Pascal are two of them; both French. To get there you turn off the Ruta 40 and head for the mountains. Overlooking the pastel-blue Laguna Vilchez, the snow-capped Cerro Conico and Desnudo mountains draw a picturesque curtain on Chile and beyond.

Kitted out in *bombachas*, *alpargatas*, a *facón* stuck down his *faja* – and a beret at just the right tilt – Simon Corti Maderna is both gaucho and manager. It was Simone's idea to open this five-star lodge constructed entirely of Oregon pine with *lenga* wood panelling. His wife, Guillermina, told me that it took forty workers two years to build. My room had a changing room, a lounge area and a bathroom with a showerhead the size of the moon.

Sitting on the end of my bed, I gazed across the *laguna* we were to fish after dinner. Streaked with snow and rock, the *cordilleras* looked like a rasher of bacon.

That evening Benjamin and Nico Fliess – a guide from El Encuentro who knew the area but wanted to know more – and I tripped over long shadows stretching across the lakeside. The surface flickered slightly in the last of the evening light. A fish of four pounds had swirled to take my damsel nymph cast into the shallows and pulled into a black hole.

Back at the fireside, Benjamin and Nico sat me down with a glass of Malbec. They had a story to tell me. I was sitting comfortably.

They had stumbled upon a place that was well off the well-trodden track. They didn't have cameras, only a cellphone which Benjamin passed to me. The picture was taken just before nightfall. But I could make out the shape of a rainbow trout Benjamin caught, most of it stretching out of both sides of the screen.

I goggled. Benjamin giggled.

'Eight kilos,' Benjamin said.

Sixteen pounds.

Volume up. Madonna sang 'Time goes by so slowly' to the sound of the tyres of Benjamin's Toyota thudding down relentlessly on tarmac. The road ended and we were on gravel, then stones, then rocks. Rock turned into sand, sand back to rock again. We started to climb. Then it seemed Benjamin's Toyota was driving up the side of boulders and banging back down again. We slowed. We quickened. The boulders turned to something softer. Grass, perhaps.

This was a journey I could only imagine because for the last forty-five minutes of it I couldn't see anything. I had been blindfolded.

Blindfold off, I could see where I was. Argentina, Chile – somewhere like that. Benjamin and Nico quickly raced me across scrub and marshland, skipping over nibbled grass, jumping over mossy pools. We were in a valley heading for a large blue flooded area.

I was soon to discover why such a place should be somewhere I would never be able to find or return to on my own. Pioneers need to be careful to keep their best locations best-kept secrets.

Just before we were about to sink out of sight, we arrived at a deep channel running through the soggy fenland we were squelching across. This is where the brook trout hole up.

More a ditch than a waterway, the channel was too narrow to cast across. I needed to chuck my fly – a woolly, black marabou-tailed bugger – directly upstream and let it drift past, hoping it would sink to the brook trout I was promised would be waiting deep-down. Brook trout like depth and darkness. They lie ready to ambush small fish. Flesh, not fly for the brookies here.

The ditch was only twenty yards long before it widened and shallowed. The sun lit up the flat like an operating theatre. The brookie boundary ends here. Starting at the top, I cast my way down, expecting a snatch at any time. But nothing. My fly wasn't getting deep enough and I began to wish I had that blindfold back on and was lying, eyes closed, face to the sun, catching up on lost sleep. Last night we'd fished late. We'd left at dawn.

'Let me see your fly box.'

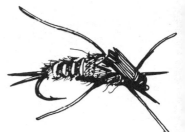

Benjamin picked out a large black stonefly nymph that had been so successful when we fished the Futaleufú that runs past El Encuentro Lodge.

'Knot this wool six feet from your fly and cast it as high up as you can.'

I let my lead-filled stonefly sink and drift down into the bowels of the mysterious passage, a subsurface cliff edge. The wool disappeared. I was getting the depth all right; I'd caught the bottom. But the bottom started to move.

The struggle was brief – and brutal. Brookies don't jump. They flex their shoulder muscles and dive deep and fast. Yanked to the surface, the brookie decided to return from whence it came and dig deep into the roots and reed stems. It broke off. The Law of Unintended Consequences. A lesson in hard reality.

Three more casts and I caught the bottom again. This time I decided this brookie wasn't going anywhere. My nine-foot seven-weight was going to earn its keep. It creaked a bit. The tip stabbed below the surface a few times but the knots held fast. I held on for dear life and between us we held the trout on the surface until Benjamin was able to scoop it out. A brookie of six pounds.

Minutes later, my rod was tested to even greater extremes. A third brookie grabbed my stonefly at the top of the ditch. But now we had a system. My 'horsing' was now accompanied by Benjamin's 'fleet of net' which was under the brookie before it had time to decide on anything.

Three was my total. Each with vivid viridian-green backs, flushed-red bellies and snow-white-tipped fins. The smallest six pounds. The largest, eight. Add up the two weights and I would have broken the world record set in 1915.

Was this place really only reserved for pioneers? I looked for footprints. Just one set. Hoof prints. The only sign of life in sight. And the last thing I saw for a while. It was blindfold back on.

To the strains of Johnny Cash's 'Dirty Old Egg-Suckin' Dog', we left the main road, me half covered by blindfold, my nose filled with dust. I could hear stiff grasses scrubbing the underside of the Toyota. Conversations suggested Benjamin and Nico were looking for tracks up hillsides rather than turnings on roadsides. My feet tattooed to the carpet ready for the next twist and turn, I was rocking and rolling. We hit something, with a bang. Blindfold off, I saw that we had stopped at a wire fence.

I followed Benjamin and Nico up a dry river bed that disappeared into thin air. Thirty minutes later, we arrived at a lochan circled by nine condors. We'd arrived.

No we hadn't. There was another thirty minutes to go.

Benjamin had tied a squirrel-tail streamer to the end of my line, with a large, black, deer-hair head. A leech wearing a niqab. Nico suggested I fish from a point, my back to a cliff face. The water shelved deeply away from the bank. Roll-casting my Islamic leech took some getting used to. But, third cast, there was a flash in the area of my fly, like a car passing by. But not a car, a lorry. There was a swirl, water washed over my feet and I was on the way down the lake, whether I liked it or not. It was me who was being played out.

Benjamin was squealing. This time he had a camera, not a mobile. And a fish to film of the same proportions that he'd caught on his previous visit.

Rod, line, leader were all of the correct proportion for a fish of this size, but not my hands. I could only just get my fingers round its tail end, its belly sunk into my palm. A pink-streaked hen rainbow with an emerald back, of seven kilos. About fourteen pounds.

Benjamin suggested we move upstream. Within minutes, I was moving back down again – at speed, skipping over rocks, slipping and skidding over gravels. My second rainbow was even bigger. And even more angry. Fortunately we both tired at the same time, but Benjamin's net wasn't big enough. He managed to get its arrow-shaped head in the mesh while I was happy to grab the tail end. Benjamin estimated the brute was nine kilos. Eighteen pounds.

A pioneer knows the value of his discoveries. He respects them. Two fish were enough. With the whooping and howls of happiness over, it was blindfold on and back to the lodge. A journey into silence.

I got to thinking. When I go fishing normally I like to know exactly where I'm going.

No more.

crested caracara
el 'carancho'

SEVENTEEN

Highlands and Islands
The Daddy Lang-Leegs

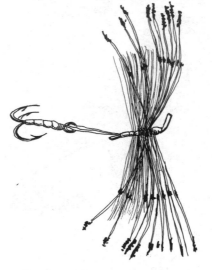

Hook 1: No. 16 Outpoint Treble
Nylon: 10 lb
Thread: Primrose yellow
Body: Pale yellow raffia
Hook 2: No. 10–12 dry fly hook
Thread: Black
Hackle 1: Large blue dun
Hackle 2: Short golden pheasant tippet hackle

Mr Mann's the Man

PARKAN DUBH IS A WINDSWEPT, salt-soaked croft on the Glenuig Estate, staring resolutely across the Arisaig Sound. Not exactly the Hebrides, but if the east wind blew any fiercer, it would be there in no time.

To get to the croft, you carry on past the Glenuig Inn, cross over a cattle grid and after a mile you'll see it. That August, when we rented it, hail and storm gusts clawed at the wood-panelled walls of our bedroom and played drums on the tin roof.

High tide coincided with supper, so Vincent and I fished from the rocks all afternoon. The walk from Parkan Dubh to the sea was a short one. You could see the rocks standing black and indestructible from the kitchen window. It was a downhill walk across a field sheltered from the weather, through a huddle of stone sheep pens, through an iron gate, over a wire and you're on the shore. The rocks were designed for fishing. They formed a long narrow peninsula. In front of this platform was the only bit of sand-bottomed coast reachable from the shore, the rest was a jungle of kelp. Behind you, cut out of the rock, was a backrest.

We ate pollock most nights, in candlelight in front of a driftwood fire. The room glowed as orange as a turnip. We were warm and cosy, but anxious to do some 'real' fishing.

In the telephone box at the Glenuig Inn, Vincent and I threw ten pences into the telephone box as fast as we could pull them out of our pockets. It was late evening and the light bulb had gone in the booth, but this didn't distract Vincent one iota. He was desperate to arrange some flyfishing, striking his way through a box of Swan Vestas like a demented Guy Fawkes, scribbling down the names and numbers of local guides.

Temperatures were dropping dramatically so we decided to hold Christmas Day on 25th September. We dug up a small fir and decorated it with silver paper, red wool and shiny things. For decorations, we hung beer cans on fishing line and strung them across the room, cutting Stars of Bethlehem out of Bacofoil and Kit-Kat wrappers. The wine poured, the fire roared, the candles sputtered, the chicken made do for a turkey. But Santa Claus doesn't bring sea trout down the chimney.

The next morning, we headed for Loch Shiel, a freshwater loch ten miles long, situated twelve miles west of Fort William. At Creel Cottage, Mr Mann had boats for hire, at Acharacle – pronounced, we guessed, 'Ack-Ar-Ackle'.

Mr Mann was quick to correct us.

'Hhh . . . aracle, Mr Patterson. Hh . . . aracle.'

The boat was ready for us, but he nodded at the waves licking at the bottom of his garden and across to the mountains where the sky rolled

up its lips and snarled. Not a day for the loch.

Mr Mann sent us along the coast to a small tree-lined lochan set high up in the hills at Glenborrodale Farm. A put-and-take affair where neither Vincent nor myself could find anything to take, no matter how much effort we put into it. Torrents of hail, plus special effects, soon had us cowering behind the dam. By late afternoon, I'd dug a deep, muddy trench in the bank where I had been marching backwards and forwards like a sentry on patrol, letting the wind inch a small nymph along the loch bed where I had reckoned the trout were cowering, too.

Back in Lochailort, at the Glenuig Inn, we told Mrs Millar how we'd got on. Her brothers hadn't caught anything there either, on their first two trips. On their third, the farmer appeared and threw in a bucket of pellets. The surface erupted with trout of all sizes. The next day, her brothers decided to bring a gun to a knife fight. They returned with a string of mackerel feathers and caught a rainbow trout of seven pounds.

After breakfast, the wind dropped and the sun came out. Mr Mann's boat was booked up, but we got one next door, at Dalelia, and a splendid boat it was, too. The Seagull outboard purred like a contented cat, musical ripples serenaded the hull and it was warm enough to fish in a jacket. But not for long. The heavens opened, an ugly wind hurled us down the loch and waves two foot high crashed over the side of the boat. When we'd managed to pull ourselves back to Creel Cottage, each taking an oar, we spent the rest of the afternoon fishing in Mr Mann's conservatory. He told us we had to learn the art of the dap before he took us out in his boat the next day. My heart thumped as we walked to the boat to get his rod and take it back to the warmth of his glass palace.

The rod was a seventeen-and-a-half-foot Viking telescopic. Clipped on the reel seat was a large Hardy Perfect reel charged with 20 lb backing, attached to a rod's length of 'Spinnaker' blowline dapping floss. Looped to this was two feet of 8 lb monofilament with a Daddy-Long-Legs – or Daddy-Lang-Leegs, as the Mann preferred to refer to it – at the point. The sun began to shine again.

The dressing of the Lang-Leegs is ingenious, ensuring that the tail of the Lang-Leegs trails realistically – and temptingly – through the crests of the waves. It also makes sure that when a fish leaps at it, there's no escape. A #16 Outpoint Treble makes sure of this. With this in the vice, thread a length of 10 lb Maxima nylon through the top of the eye, round the base of hook and back up through bottom of the eye. Bind down nylon with primrose yellow thread, tying in a length of pale yellow raffia to form the body as you go. Whip-finish, varnish. Remove and let dry.

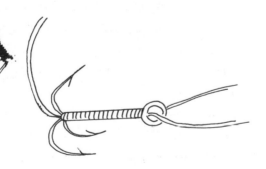

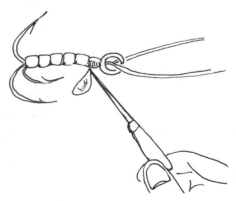

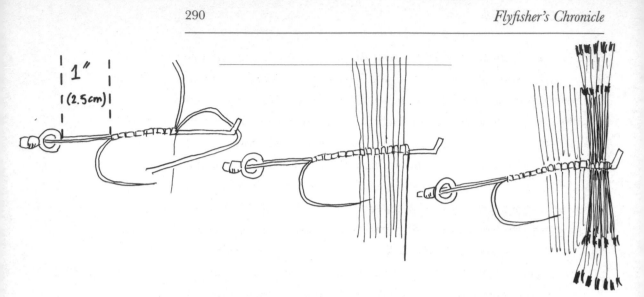

Now vice a #10 dry fly, up-eye hook, wind black thread behind eye and thread nylon through eye and bring back. Bind nylon tightly with thread. The treble should lie 1in. (2.5 cm) behind eye. Clip excess nylon, varnish and let dry. Finally tie in a large blue dun hackle two-thirds of the way down hook and wind towards the eye. In front of this, tie in a short golden pheasant tippet hackle by its tips and wind this towards eye. Whip-finish, varnish – and snip off hook bend with pliers.

Out in the garden, Mr Mann gave a demonstration. I watched the light-green floss blow magically across the lawn, lifting up between the trees at the end of his drive, the Daddy skipping like a ballerina, buffing up the gravels with its hackles. This was the nearest you can get to heaven with your heart still beating. I was spellbound.

The next morning we drove from Parkan Dubh to Creel Cottage with the sunroof open, arriving to find Loch Sheil a sheet of glass. The loch was now 'too calm' to dap, but Mr Mann pushed us out in a boat and we spent the morning paddling about flicking forlorn flies. At midday, the wind picked up and started to puff convincingly. It wasn't long before we saw Mr Mann walking down his garden to the loch in the direction of the jetty.

Grabbing the oars I rowed in his direction. We were in Mr Mann's boat before he had time to make room for us. I was given the shorter of the two dapping rods, with a large black and white fly, a Loch Ordie on the point. Vincent got the Daddy.

The art is to keep the rod as upright as a candle, and drop it at a

forty-five-degree angle, moving the tip in unison with the other rod, fifteen degrees from side to side. I was sweating with excitement, my arms electrified.

With my Ordie leaping around like a go-go dancer in a whoopsie bar, I was beginning to understand why people get so gushy about dapping. The first fish rose to my fly before I could compose myself. I panicked and struck immediately. No contact.

'Count to three, Mr Patterson, before tightening.'

I rose several others. One well over two pounds. Its monstrous head made me leap backwards, pulling the fly from its mouth. My strike was still too swift.

Vincent was much more controlled. He hooked a salmon parr that flew over our heads, such was the conviction he displayed with his 'tightening'. It dropped off before we could get a look at it.

But we were not alone on the boat. Far from it. Sandy, Mr Mann's snappy little West Highland terrier, was standing between us, hind legs clamped onto the floorboards, front paws up on the bow side, gazing out across the loch, focussed on my fly. He seemed inordinately keen on its every movement. I couldn't think why.

'Sandy knows how to do it, Mr Patterson,' Mr Mann nodded with a know-all wink.

I was about to hand Sandy the rod when Mr Mann went on to tell me to keep an eye on him. When Sandy sees a fish rise to the fly, he growls. When he gives a yap, strike!

'Mmm,' I thought. But right enough, a fish rolled on my Loch Ordie and Sandy started to growl. But he didn't get to yap. My strike was so fast, he never had time to. Instead he turned and growled at me. My next fish was the same. And the fish after that. Sandy was all growl, no yap. I was a trembling schoolgirl.

With my fly tripping nicely through a gentle wave, I could see Sandy shivering, transfixed with excitement, out of the corner of my eye. His locked-on gaze followed my fly's every move as it wafted from the right to the left, then back again; then lifting over a turning wave . . . then erupting in a cloud of spray. A switch was pulled. I held still. The growling began. A growl that turned into a whine. A lonely, haunting moan, like the distant toll of a church bell across water at midnight. I stiffened with anticipation, with fear, with dread, with nerves, with everything. I dared not make a move. Of any sort. (I think my heart stopped.) Then came the yap.

This time I was on cue. A parr the length of my finger lifted out of the water and landed in the bottom of the boat. I reached out to return it to the waves, but I wasn't the first to get there. At the snap of your fingers, Sandy had it in between his teeth. With a well-rehearsed toss of his head, he had the parr down the back of his throat, dispatched without further ado. So this was what all that high interest was about.

'That'll be hees tea, then,' Mr Mann said, smiling.

'Gnasher of Ak-Ar-Acle, eh?' I said, flicking my fly back into the wind, letting it trip away from the boat onto the tip of the foam-topped wave.

'Hh . . . aracle, Mr Patterson, please. Hh . . . aracle.'

EIGHTEEN

Outer Hebrides: Harris

The Goat's Toe

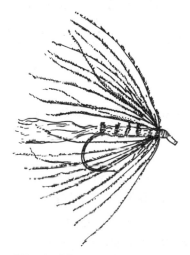

Hook: No. 10–12 heavy weight
Thread: Black
Tag: Red DFM wool, three times the length of a normal tag
Body: three strands of peacock herl
Rib: Excess DFM wool
Hackle: three turns of a large blue peacock hackle
(Stan Headley, *Flies of Scotland*; and this is how they hackle it at
Amhuinnsuidhe)

In Heaven with the Devil's Fly

THERE'S SOMETHING DEVILISHLY DEADLY-SOUNDING about the fly called the Goat's Toe. Long before I knew what it was or what it looked like, the name intrigued me. It sounded like something dark, satanic, full of foreboding; something . . . well . . . devilish. Something out of Dennis Wheatley, rather than a fly box.

When I first set eyes on the Goat's Toe, its appearance lived up to

293

its name. A shiny, steely blue hackle. A flash of blood-red lightning streaking down its body like an electric storm. Sinister, menacing – not resembling anything in the natural world – it was the fly from hell. Certainly not a pattern for the weak-hearted inhabitants of the still waters of the south of England. However, I tied some up, in case the opportunity should ever arise.

It was years before I got the chance to put one of them into practice – for you don't 'fish' the Goat's Toe, you 'practise' it. Like you do witchcraft.

Ian Scarr-Hall wafted into the room, camouflaged in tweed. As the new owner of the North Harris Estate, he was not at all as I had expected him to be. He is one of us. So much so that, long after I had started speaking to him, I was still waiting for him to make his entry in a Laird of the Manor-like way.

Ian may not have inherited the Estate, where he now lives, but he is not a new kid on the block. He has been fishing the Estate for forty-five years – ever since his parents used to rent a holiday cottage down the road – so he was well acquainted with what he was buying. More importantly, as a successful businessman, he had had the time to evaluate whether or not the fishing on the estate was still worth the investment. Clearly it was.

Since 2003, when the 55,000-acre North Harris Estate was acquired by the publicly funded North Harris Trust, Ian has been in the enviable position of being the owner of the sporting 'block' of the estate. This includes Amhuinnsuidhe Castle, perched by the sea, with towers, turrets and all the baronial trappings. A Victorian castle, it is surrounded by one of Scotland's most overpowering and formidable mountain ranges, overlooking the Kinlochresort estuary. Bat-filled belfries . . . a growling sea . . . waves beating salt against my bedroom window . . . at midnight! You can't imagine how my imagination ran wild. (Or maybe you can.)

Surely, here fish don't die of a heart attack at the sight of a Goat's Toe? Surely, here fish seize it with all the horror it inspires – as a matter of course?

In fact, this castle turned out to be heaven. There can be few places in the world that offer a wider variety of salmon and sea trout fishing in lochs. There are also three small and excellent rivers.

'Fancy coming fishing?' Mark asked. I had only just got my bag unpacked and I was bringing my tackle down to the fishing quarters. This is a pine-panelled room with outlines of huge salmon and sea trout drawn on the wall and photographs of past guests with grins almost as wide as the salmon they were parading. One, a twenty-three-pounder, had run its captor down to the sea.

'It's pitch dark!' I said to Mark.

'It's sea trout fishing. Let's go!'

Fifteen minutes later I was in a pick-up, in the dark; passing through a glen, in the dark; to a boathouse at the end of a stony track, in the dark; being rowed across a loch, in the dark; dibbling my fly from hell on a dropper, in the dark. What better fly to share my darkest moment?

Built at around the same time that Bram Stoker was walking England's east coast beaches dreaming up Count Dracula in the 1880s, it wasn't until the 1960s that the doors of Amhuinnsuidhe Castle were thrown open to paying fishing guests. Since then the Castle's previous owners have been, first, Sir Hereward and Lady Wake, then Gerald Panchaud, who was the owner when I first fished it. Now things have turned full circle for Ian, his love for the Estate reignited now that the name 'Ian Scarr-Hall' is on the door.

At this point I must confess that I've always had trouble with people with double-barrelled names. Not call-the-police trouble. Rather, with names – single, or double. In fact any name at all. Two names to remember doesn't make life any easier for me. Take the rods I fish with on the river down the track from my home.

I couldn't tell you exactly how many members there are in the syndicate, but there are a few. I know most of them, but not by name. However, I remember faces and I have a system that works for me. I call everyone 'Mate'. When they say, 'Hello, Neil,' I answer, 'Hello, Mate.' Easy.

Of course, I never forget my friend Mike's name. (See, I remembered it again.) One day we met one of the members who has been fishing the river almost as long as I have.

'Hello, Neil,' he said when we met on the riverbank. I said, 'Hello, Mate,' and started to go on. But he stopped me and said, 'Hey, Neil, we have been members of this syndicate for thirty years and you always call me Mate. Don't you know my name by now?'

I looked him straight in the eye, turned to Mike and said, 'Mike, tell him his name,' and carried on down the river. Mike turned to the man and quickly said, 'I'll see you later, Mate,' and hurried after me.

Now a lot of the rods in our syndicate have double-barrelled names. As I mentioned earlier, this makes it twice as hard to remember what they're called. One name is bad enough. Two? Well, forget it, which is exactly what I do. But with these members I have the perfect answer. When they say, 'Hello, Neil,' I just say, 'Hello, Mate-Mate.'

Of course it's a little different when I run into Randolph Scrivener who is well over ninety years old and still manages to fish without falling in. He has a perfect answer for this, too. He just sits outside the hut with a cigar and doesn't go anywhere near the river from the first day of the season to the last. He deserves all the respect I can muster. So, when he says, 'Hello, Neil,' I say, 'Hello, MISTER Mate.'

'I'll gi' ye a stalker to gae with you,' Kenny Morrison, the Head Honcho Ghillie at the Castle, told me when I asked if I could walk over the hill to the thoroughly far-off Loch Reedy. That spring, they'd taken a boat round the Sound and walked it through the heather to the loch.

The walk up the hill from Loch Voshimid to Reedy takes about an hour. At least, that's how long it took me, tripping behind Roddy up ahead of me, a long-poled landing net resting on one of his shoulders and a sack slung over the other. Like following a running deer, I watched him dissolve into something the size of a full stop. I arrived at Reedy swimming inside my shirt.

Reedy is one of the world's most desolate places where eagles, deer, even silence itself feel lonely. Long, slim and shallow as it is, I wondered why there was any need for a boat on this loch. One gust of wind blows you from one side to the other in minutes. Roddy invited me to step in.

The Silver Stoat, on a double hook on the point that balanced my Goat's Toe on the dropper, allowing for some deluxe dibbling, was catching weeds in the shallow water. I just had time to snip it off. Now I was dapping my GT and it had the effect I was after. A salmon appeared out of a hole in the weeds and, rolling on my fly, was greeted with a horror it had not expected.

Heading for the reeds on the far bank, taking the fibreglass boat and its contents with it, the salmon would have turned my leader into an Aran jumper of tangles had Roddy not oared me speedily back to the shore and ordered me out of the boat so that I could pull the salmon back to our shore, into his landing net – and the sack. Throwing this over his back, he slipped the net back into that groove in his shoulder and set off back over the hill and home. The salmon was on a slab at the Castle long before I returned myself.

Roddy is now head keeper. He ghillied me on my last day on my return visit in August – after a seventeen-year break. We fished Loch Voshimid, which Andrew Graham-Stewart calls 'one of the most reliable salmon angling lochs in the Hebrides'. Roddy knows this loch better than a resident brown trout. Certainly better than the visiting salmon. There are two kinds of ghillie. The ones that go backwards and forwards across a loch, as if mowing a lawn, hoping they might bump into a salmon. Then there are ghillies like Roddy, who make for where they know a salmon will be, if there is to be a salmon at all.

At the head of the loch, Roddy slid the boat to where the stream from Loch Weedy bubbles into Voshimid around large rocks.

'Put your fly there,' he said quietly, nodding towards one of the rocks, his hands on the oars holding the boat in position.

'There?' I asked, plopping my flies at the back of the rock.

'No, there,' Roddy said, nodding once more. A nod with the kind of accuracy that could land a spaceship on the moon.

Silver Stoat

My Silver Stoat plopped into a thin slit of current that slithered round the rock. My Goat's Toe was dibbling before it touched the water. But it hadn't dibbled long before the rod tightened into a sip of a swirl and I had a grilse. Without a sound, Roddy was pulling the boat back. With my fly exactly where he'd wanted me to put it, he'd caught that salmon before I'd made my cast. For Roddy, it was just a matter of going through the motions.

Innes Morrison is another ghillie I remember from my first visits. With Kenny retired, he is now the manager. He once ghillied me on Loch Scourst, in high winds. A gust whisked my dapping fly off the cream of a wave, sucking a snapping sea trout three feet up in the air after it.

'You should walk to Ulladale,' he said. A vacancy had appeared on one of the jewels in the Amhuinnsuidhe crown. It's a good walk to towering cliffs, dramatic scenery and wild, undisturbed salmon that guffaw at Goat's Toes.

But I never went. I kept my appointment with Roddy on Weedy. Machete-ing his way through reeds to get to where he'd seen salmon the day before, in thin water freshened by a trickle from the loch above, he left no salmon sanctuary unexplored, no lie unturned. I was Humphrey Bogart in *The African Queen* again.

Back for lunch at the hut above Loch Voshimid, we talked about our morning. The wind howled through gaps in the panelling. The only draught-free area was behind the no smoking sign nailed to the panels.

It was my last day. I stared at Loch Voshimid through a crack and wondered if it was possible to find a finer place to fish. Maybe Loch Ulladale? But a letter from Ian Scarr-Hall a week later confirmed that probably there wasn't. He wrote:

> The day after you left, I walked up to the head of Voshimid and hooked a salmon of 9lb which took over an hour to play out and land. Hooking it as I did, on the head of the run, involved having to scramble out of the stream and make a detour over the bank sides to find a suitable place to play the fish. After a number of exciting leaps, the line caught on a rock, mid-stream, at which point I thought the fish was lost. I returned to the river to endeavour to free the line and was eventually helped by the salmon which moved in a different direction and freed the line.

After seventeen years, Amhuinnsuidhe is still the place where my angling dreams come true. Even with the nightmare fly. By the sound of it, after forty years, it's still where Ian's dreams come true, too. Even though, for him, it's a reality. As I plodded across the moors that morning in Roddy's wake, I got to wondering: Is there anything we can learn from tackle manufacturers when it comes to selling our flies to discriminating trout?

At one time, the best-designed chest waders were made by a US tackle company. This was largely thanks to their patented 'stockingfoot'. No frills, they kept within a price bracket whereby anyone could afford the best – and this was the best part about it. But things changed.

I've been in advertising since I was eighteen and I could see it coming. This particular company became just another player in a category where other brands offered similar items at the same price. They didn't want their premium position diluted so they created a new category – the super-premium category.

To justify super-premium pricing, they 'added value' to their stockingfoots. Not one but five layers of Gore-tex, a pocket on the front (not just a flip-out inside), then two pockets, then two thermolaminated (yes, it's a word) zippered hand-warmer pockets, then a built-in patented retractor . . . what next – a compass, a torch, an alarm clock, GPS, a fishfinder, internet?

Before anyone knew it, this simple stockingfooted wader had kicked itself into its own super-sophisticated league, costing the same as a small car. But I haven't finished.

Recently I cast aside my top-of-the-range rod for a cheaper brand. Great design, and less than half the price of the one I had become so attached to. So, what do the manufacturers of this more economical rod do? They 'add value' – and up the price. Not to make the rod perform better or answer customer complaints (none from me), but to bring the rod 'right up to date' to meet (and this I love) 'changing conditions on streams' (eh?). And what are these futuristic additions? Twiddly bits. Better cork, a tweaked reel seat – and 'gunsmoke rings', the perfect smokescreen for a price hike.

Is this rod any better for being 'new and improved', now costing a good bit more? Not according to the salesman who had sold me my first rod, when I went to buy another and found it 'upgraded'. He threw it back on the stand.

To be fair to both companies – both great brands – all tackle manufacturers are the same. To put things into perspective, we're not in the 'Golden Age' of flyfishing – roughly 1952 to 1975 – when silk lines and bamboo changed to PVC lines and fibreglass, and finally carbon fibre. That was a time of genuine technical advancement, when real value was added.

Nope, we're in an 'Age of Tweaks'. A small change here and there is progress enough. Enough of a twiddle to claim innovation and justify progressing the price upwards. What I call 'the nudge'.

So, the point of my rant: How can we get even?

I have the answer. You learn from the manufacturers' marketing departments and fool the trout in the same way they fool us. By giving our flies that unarguable, irresistible 'nudge'.

In fact, this has been going on for some time, with little things being added to patterns to make them even more attractive to the trout. Red tags on northern grayling flies. Recently introduced flash materials incorporated into standard patterns. Holographic ribbing, rather than wire. Tungsten bead heads. The DFM-wool red spot on my Red Spot Shrimp, and so forth. In truth, we're all masters of duplicity when it comes to marketing our flies. I'll explain.

Every August I think of the salmon and sea trout I've caught fishing those lochs in the Outer Hebrides. In particular, the wild trout I've hoodwinked when fishing for salmon and sea trout – when I haven't been fishing for trout at all.

I think of the fly that accounts for the largest numbers and sizes of trout in the peat-stained lochs of North Harris and South Uist, where patterns need to be fashioned with feather and wool of a strong, hard colour. Like so many other flies that are thrown at the visitors, by the visitors, this fly originates from Ireland. It's that fly from hell, the Goat's Toe.

Earlier, I mentioned I was in marketing. I did the advertising for the Scottish Tourist Board, attracting tourists to 'Come early. Come late', to get the best weather. Meteorological records tell us that up north at the end of summer, the sun can shine the brightest. For this reason, trout don't come to the surface as readily as they do when the lochs are overcast.

But in bright weather and a good wave, a Goat's Toe will bring trout of the shyest disposition skywards to a powerfully tinted titbit. Even more aggressively when a Goat's Toe's brightness is given a 'nudge' – and the movement of a Bolshoi ballerina is dramatically imparted.

The 'nudge' comes in the shape of an extended tag. This, and an oversized blue peacock hackle with no supporting hackle tied behind, allowing colour to pulsate royally, in the disquiet and irritated roil.

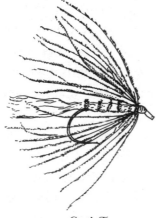

Goat's Toe

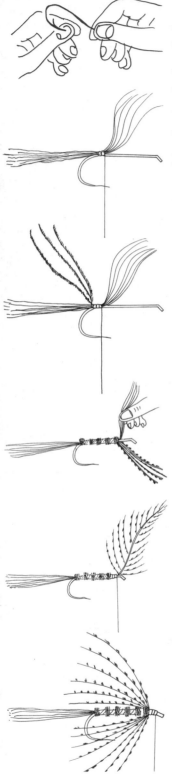

To tie, I run the point of a 10–12 heavy-weight hook across the nail of my thumb (not my toe) to check it's good and sharp. I then tie in black silk at the bend. I secure a strand of DFM red wool as the tag, clipping it so that it is three times the length of a normal tag. Don't clip the excess. Tie in three strands of peacock herl at the bend and wind to behind the eye. Rib with excess wool and secure. Optional: you can use the wool as the body material and rib with herl. Tie in large blue peacock hackle by tip. Wind 3–4 turns. Whip-finish and varnish.

Unlike some chest waders or fly rods, these simple additions don't give you more than you ask for or more than you need so that you can be charged more than you want.

Rather, they just might encourage the largest trout in the loch to progress upwards to examine your product – and buy into it. At really no extra cost to yourself.

With a boat on Lochs Scourst, Voshimid, Ladies and the romantically remote Ulladale awaiting me the next morning on the North Harris Estate, on my first night back at the Castle I couldn't sleep a wink. Lying there in the dark, staring into the early-morning hours, I thought back to my very first night at Amhuinnsuidhe, when I had also lain there, winkless, wondering what to do.

This time I decided to get up.

Now, here's the trick. Long before you get up to the lochs – and long before anyone gets up – there's the Castle Pool, right by the castle. No Land Rovers, no packed lunches, it's get up and go. Now, I don't exactly know which part of the two-hundred-yard slither of a stream that is sucked out of Ladies Loch down past the Castle to the sea, is called the Castle Pool. Perhaps none of the pools that fan out below mini-waterfalls has this name? Perhaps this is the name they give to the sea pool where a trawler-load of salmon await the climb back up the stream to Ladies and into the system?

For me, the Castle Pool is where a torrent of beer-coloured water with a creamy head gushes through a deep gorge you can jump over. Here the stream widens into a shallow pool where salmon lie on the far side under broom and birch waiting to jump, too.

Whatever they call it – and wherever the Caste Pool actually is –

there's nobody around at that early hour to ask. Or remind you that you're still in your slippers! For this pool is a three-minute stroll from your bed. Or, on your return, three minutes from the bacon, egg, the blackest of puddings and tea you can stand a spoon up in, awaiting you in the dining room at breakfast.

At 5.30 a.m., any salmon tucked up in this pool that makes a move is simply turning in its sleep. A salmon sticking its nose out from under the purple blanket of this early-morning stream doesn't look to me to be active. It is just rolling over in bed. Or so it seems. The occasional fish does leap out of his dreams, landing with a splash. This keeps you from dropping off, but I had found them hard to interest. It's just too early, I thought.

But then, I'm a trout fisherman, so I expect my fish to behave logically, which of course salmon don't. And anyway, surely I am only there for the silence and the solitude, not the fishing? To share a most magical time of the day – with myself?

I say magical, but on my first morning, as I emptied the contents of my fly box into the frothy dormitory, I decided it was going to take nothing short of voodoo to have a salmon sleepwalk its way to my fly and hook itself on the jaw-end of an ill-placed yawn. But this never used to bother me, for I always had the lochs to look forward to later in the day, when the salmon are more obliging.

But one morning, I pulled back the sheets with a quiet determination that had me jump out of bed with more vigour than the rowdiest of alarm clocks. I decided I was to catch a salmon before breakfast. And I did. In fact, I caught four. What happened? A change of fly, yes. But a little more than that.

I imagined I was in Iceland.

Shallow and slender, the stream that feeds the Castle Pool looks like so many of the waters I have fished at Laxá i Kjos. Streams where I saw in action for the first time an entirely different way of catching salmon on a fly. Most memorably, the salmon Jack Hemingway took using this method. A salmon I had spent all morning trying to interest with other things.

Let me take you back there again, to where I was taught to 'hitch' a fly when I spent a week with three of the world's 'riffle-hitch' experts. These were: Orri Vigfusson, founder of the North Atlantic Salmon Fund, whom we have to thank for the fact that there are still salmon in our rivers to fish (please donate generously); the late Jack Hemingway, who had just written the foreword to Art Lee's *Tying and Fishing the Riffling Hitch*; and John Hotchkiss, super 'Hotch-hitch specialist', leader of the party.

Man is one of a number of animals that make things. But man is the only one that depends for its very survival on the things he had made.

That simple observation lies at the heart of why we go fishing: we make something to catch fish – to eat. Flyfishing takes a bit more explaining, though. Especially if you go out of your way and travel all round the world to catch fish (using not one of the simplest of methods) just to put them back into the water again (and leave at the end of a successful day's fishing, gagging for something to eat). What strange creatures we flyfishermen are. Especially if we consider the situation we are in right now, with salmon.

These days, we can farm as many salmon as we will ever need. Once they are caged up, all you need do is net them out. It takes seconds. Yet, here we are spending millions of pounds protecting the wild ones. Those you can go a whole season without catching, for an astronomic price. (And perhaps even die of starvation as a result.)

The Take was a series of fishing films commissioned by Sky TV, produced and shot by a Norwegian production company. I was asked to script these two dozen, thirty-minute programmes; an offer I was more than happy to accept, mainly because they were not to be 'How to Do It', 'Fishing with the Expert' programmes. In fact, the film that pleases me most is the one where no fish appears at all. Virtually the whole film was shot inside a Laplander's tent, cooking up elk.

Although not all the episodes followed exactly the same format, most of them featured two flyfishers. One who knew what he was doing, the other who was doing it for the first time. All the films took the audience to different locations in the world; from as far away as Greenland, New Zealand and Cuba to as close to home as Norway, Sweden and Iceland, only a couple of hours' flight away.

In the Iceland films, shot at the Laxá i Kjos, I was both the writer and the inexperienced flyfisher. Salmon fishing has never really been my thing. I like to know why a fish takes my fly, not be amazed that it's actually taken it. I was, however, fortunate to be placed in the highly capable hands of Jack and Orri, who acted as my guides and mentors.

Spending all day with the son of Ernest Hemingway, your hero author, and sitting next to him at dinner for a week, you'd imagine there'd be lots of questions you'd like to ask about his father. But, strangely, talking about flies, salmon and the development of the 'riffle-hitch method' was much more fun.

I learned that the hitch is the knot you tie behind the eye at right angles to the hook, having secured the fly in the normal way. This makes the fly 'skitter' across the surface, forming a 'V' on the surface. It's this 'V' – and not the fly – that attracts the salmon. It was Lee Wulff who brought the 'Riffling Hitch' to everyone's attention, over fifty years ago. It was dubbed the 'Portland Hitch' after Portland Creek in Newfoundland where the tactic was developed. By mistake.

Way back in the days of gut-eyed hooks, salmon flies were expensive and hard to get your hands on. In Newfoundland, at least. To extend the life of their flies, Newfoundland flyfishermen would tie their flies on as normal, but they would then half-hitch the leader behind the fly's head so that the line was sitting at right angles to the hook. This took the strain off the gut eyes.

But very soon it became apparent that it also made their flies more effective, for it caused them to plane up head first, and then swim across the surface trailing a 'V' induced by the tension of the line and leader on the fly's elevated head. Allowing the fly to simply swim round at the whim of the stream's flow and current had salmon rising for their flies when they wouldn't look at anything else. The Newfoundland flyfishermen were dumbfounded. But why do the salmon take a fly when it does this?

Well, they don't. They take the 'V'. If, however, that fly is 'dragged', or 'stripped', which is what a good many anglers do when they think they're 'riffling', the salmon will come up and look at it, but they won't take it. However, a sweet, smooth-moving fly, riffled to hold in the current – and not drag across it – will be rewarded by a head and tail rise and the hook well and truly fixed on the tip of the salmon's nose. Every time. How can I be so sure that it's the 'V' the salmon takes, and not the fly?

To demonstrate that a fly's movement in the water can be just as much of an inducement as the shape, the size and the colour of the fly itself, the late Oliver Kite would fish a bare hook with just half a dozen turns of copper wire wound behind the eye so that it would sink, allowing him to lift it seductively in front of a feeding trout. In a similar way, I got rid of everything that makes the hooks of my riffle patterns look like a fly and I gave it a try. In fact, I got rid of the fly part altogether. The salmon kept coming.

Izaak Walton said, 'Angling may be said to be so like the mathematics that it can never be fully learned.' Now he may be right, but I finished all my maths at school years ago. I hated it, but I love fishing, and I believe there can be too much fuss and bother over flytying. If you want to fiddle about with tricky flytying procedures, rather than go fishing, then that's fine. I like to keep mathematics and fancy stuff out of it. I like to eliminate any finger-twisting flytying movements, not build them in.

It's an approach that has resulted in patterns I call *Volksfliegen*, or 'flies for the people'. Flies that have been 'designed', not invented. Flies that answer a particular brief, perform a particular job, pull off a particular stunt. Flies that are capable of being dressed by any angler, novice or professional.

So, in a search for a pattern that avoided the necessity of my having to half-hitch at the head – and, as it happens, having to tie a fly at all – I came across a riffle-hitch fly that is the simplest fly I know to tie. And, when the conditions are right, it's the most effective pattern I know.

To put this fly together (the word 'dressing' here is not appropriate as the fly, when finished, is as good as naked) I take a half-inch (1.25 cm) length of plastic Biro tube – and that's it. I could stop there. But I tie in a few stands of stoat (or squirrel) tail fibres at the head of the Biro tube, if only to make me feel I'm fishing a fly – and not writing about it. I may just add two Flashabou fibres or wrap a turn of silver lurex round the thorax to sex things up. But this is just me being flash. It's not necessary, for the most important bit of the tying is done with the dubbing needle. I prick a hole in the middle of the Biro tube and the fly is finished. Hello, the Riffler.

Back at the Castle Pool, the sun still hadn't risen above the sea. There were two salmon rolling in their sleep when I arrived. I was in no hurry and studied the movement of the current on the surface. I took my Biro tube and pushed my leader through the little hole in the middle of the tube and out the back. To this nylon, I attached a #16 treble and pulled the line taut so that the treble was hanging loose at the back. I don't stick the eye of the treble up the tube. Only when I'm putting it back in the box. I was fishing a nine-foot rod, with an eight floater.

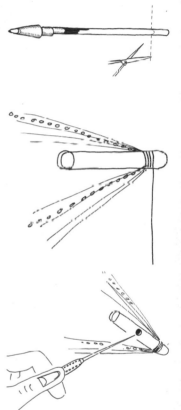

The first salmon lay six feet behind a large rock on the far bank.

Roll-casting fifteen yards, I let my fly hit the rock and bounce into the current below. I allowed my Riffler and line to drift for a few yards, then I raised my rod tip, adjusting my swing to retrieve the speed of the fly, preventing it from sinking or 'spluttering' against the current. The art of riffling a fly is similar to that of a racing driver taking a corner at high speed. He pulls the car round the bend, he doesn't skid. The driver is in control, not the car. When you riffle a fly, if you let your fly move too slowly – and there's excessive slack in

your line and leader – the fly 'spits'. Salmon don't like being spat at.

With the current holding my fly, I lifted my rod tip and let the Biro, mounted sideways, cut a hair's breadth of a 'V' in the surface as it glided towards the glide where the first fish had rolled. The sleepy nose of a salmon that was to wish it had never got out of bed poked out of the water. The first of four other salmon that wouldn't get to visit the lochs where I would be parking myself after breakfast.

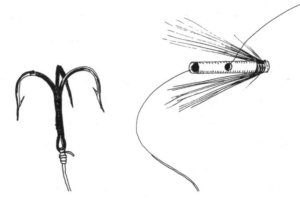

On our last night at Laxá i Kjos, it was pipes out all round for me and Jack Hemingway. I decided to ask him a question that for years I had wanted to ask someone who might know the answer. When you go to an historic house of some famous author or artist who once lived and worked there – Wordworth's Dove Cottage, or Jane Austin's house at Chawton in Hampshire, for example – just how authentic are they? Is that really the desk they worked at? Were those really the cups they drank their tea from? Was that really the bed they slept in, with that spectacular view out of the window? Were they really that tidy? I genuinely wanted to know.

Years ago, when I visited Ernest Hemingway's house in Key Largo, I had a picture taken of myself sitting on the terrace in a large, high-backed wicker chair, supposedly where Hemingway would watch the sun go down, glass in hand. Sitting there, I felt as close as I would ever get to my hero, be it only where we had both plonked our bums. Jack had mentioned in passing that he had moved with his father to Idaho from Florida. Now was my chance. I asked him if he could remember that yellow, high-backed wicker chair. He told me he did. His dad hated it. It was one of the few things they left behind when they moved. They only took the things they liked. He then went on to tell me what a terrible mistake they'd made selling the house. If they'd turned it into a museum themselves, they'd all be millionaires!

He went on to tell me that he'd once gone back and visited the house, now a museum, with a 'young lady' he was courting at that time. He'd never let on that the Hemingway whose house they were visiting was his father and that this was where he'd spent a good slug of his early life. Very soon on the conducted tour, things began to niggle Jack as the guide walked the group round the house, with everything immaculately laid out as if the Great Man had just popped out to the shops and they were allowed in to snoop about. The guide pointed to one room and told the group that this was where Hemingway had written *A Farewell to Arms*. And that this was where he would have his lunch. And this was where he kept his liquor. And then, opening a door to a room next to his study, the guide said that this was where Hemingway's children used to sleep. Jack couldn't take any more.

'No we didn't!' he shrieked. 'We had to sleep downstairs – next to the kitchen!'

The game was up. The museum was keen to keep the son of the Great Man happy. And, more importantly, keen for him to keep his mouth shut.

'They gave me my entrance money back, showed me the door and told me not to come back.'

The next day, Jack helped me put the fishing touches to my riffling lessons. Then, just before lunch, seeing Orri's Mitsubishi Colt GL, registration number UR 27 (presumably given to him on his twenty-

seventh birthday) parked outside the lodge, I decided it was a good time to interview him, as part of the film. We talked about all the great things that he and the North Atlantic Salmon Fund had done to raise the salmon nets in places where they were seriously damaging salmon stocks. After lunch, we went fishing. Putting everything that I had learned into action, I hooked into two silvery grilse, landing one and missing the other.

Back at the hut, I met Orri again and told him how happy I was with my one riffled salmon, expecting Orri's total to run into double figures.

'Nope, Neil,' he told me in his warmest Icelandic, 'I caught nothing this afternoon.'

'So,' I said in disbelief, 'that's why they call you the "Saviour of the Salmon"?'

NINETEEN

Iceland

Billy Dog

Hook: No. 10 Double Wilson
Thread: Black
Body: Flat silver tinsel
Rib: Silver wire
Wing: Goat or Icelandic Sheep dyed black,
four times the length of the hook
Throat: DFM Red cock hackle fibres

i.e. = Icelandic Experience

RIGHT UP TO THE MOMENT THE Toyota arrived to pick us up, I was up in my room, sitting on the bed, frantically tying up strange, long-winged flies. I had a fur and feathered bedspread.

'You been plucking chickens back there?' Ollie turned and inquired as I jumped aboard.

'No, goats,' I replied.

Norway, Monday. Iceland, Friday.

I had just returned from sea trout fishing, floating around on Lake Flakken near the Upper Namsen River in a belly-boat. Tippy-toeing through red and white polka-dotted toadstools in flippers to get to the water was like flyfishing in a Disney fairy story.

Elk Hair Sedge

A sea trout a little over two pounds spun up into the late-summer sunlight. It was caught on a small elk hair sedge at the very end of a two-dropper cast of elk hairs of various sizes. And caught on camera, to be broadcast in Scandinavia and on the Sky Sports channels in the UK. A famous fish indeed.

It was while I was fishing the Upper Namsen that someone told me that the most effective flies for the large, platinum-sided, sky-blue-backed sea trout of the Eldvatn in south-east Iceland were streamers with trailing wings and bodies with flash. A salmon fly called the 'Collie Dog' being the nearest thing.

Back in the good old days when people used what they had at hand to tie flies, they named their flies from the ingredients. This way the neighbours knew exactly what was catching fish. Landowners usually had a Border collie dog to round up their sheep and, it appears, to act as a portable flytying kit because it was sheepdog hair that was used to tie the very first killing Collie Dog fly.

With no pets in the lodge to clip, I christened my version the 'Billy Dog'. Billy goat hair dyed black was the nearest to collie dog hair that I had in my Portable Flytying Kit, a recently converted black plastic Muji toilet bag that was soon to become red hot. To start with, that is. Later, I managed to get my hands on some nice long and lively Icelandic sheep hair. Without the use of a sheepdog to round it up.

～

I shared the Icelandair flight with a German woman from Newfoundland forced to detour via Iceland due to an Air Canada strike (not a happy item) and Tom and Jerry (much happier items). The only German I knew was what I had picked up reading *War Picture Library* comics a long time ago, so our conversation was diplomatically brief.

At the squeaky-modern Reykjavik airport, with an oddball bi-plane hanging from the roof, a driver was waiting to fly Roll Cast – my companion on the trip – and me at high speed on the four-hour drive to the mystery river that Chuck, who had guided us in Alaska the year before, had recommended we visit.

'Crystal-clear river; perfect for sight-fishing.' That was the only insight we had. Crazy, now I come to think of it. But, do interesting things and interesting things happen to you. And they did.

The abbreviation 'i.e.', written out fully in Latin, is 'id est', meaning *that is*, or *in other words*. For me it stands for *Iceland Experience*, i.e. how the Iceland I experienced contrasted with the preconceived ideas I had before I went.

i.e. that Iceland is covered with thick, white ice. In fact, in my experience, it's covered with hundreds of acres of black, volcanic ash; i.e. that the air is pristine pure. In fact, in my experience, it's putrid with the nostril-awakening reek of sulphur and CO_2 gas making the road from Reykjavik heading east along the coast hostile and hallucinogenic. An acid trip of ever-changing land formations and weathers. No grass, just heaps of tube-shaped lava dumped like intestines coiled around the foothills of the Myrdalsjökull, the fourth-largest glacier in the area, whose ominous dark shape shadowed our every mile.

Resting on a highly volcanically active mountain massif, Myrdalsjökull erupts at intervals of forty to eighty years. Scarily regular, Roll Cast and I deduced. The volume of melted ice formed when it blows its top rushes across the outwash plain tsunami style. We learned the volcano last erupted, very powerfully, seventy years ago.

After Myrdalsjökull, foaming bleach-white waterfalls spew over rock-face crests into jet-black rivers. In the valleys below, snowflake houses with red, pink, emerald green and tangerine roofs scatter the fields like a tipped box of Lego bricks. The road winds through crevasses of peat, a maze of ditches and sphagnum bogs that fill a vast space, bacon-banding the view. A band of sky, a stripe of cloud and a layer of sienna and umber land fill the car window. A giant's golf course where no giant replaces the divots. A moonscape in the imagination. Jaws a-drop, we were travelling helter-skelter through a wild land of skies, mountains, glaciers and air-clear rivers the colour of tar. Iceland's impossible incongruity.

An unfinished volcanic road led to our brand new fishing lodge, i.e. our unfinished lodge, builder-filled to the tune of bang-bang-bang. The journey had taken longer than scheduled. It was evening when we arrived. Kirkjubæjarklaustur, easier to write than speak, was the reason for this. It was there where we had headed west rather than south, or perhaps east rather than north; not even the driver was sure, which was reassuring. Wherever, whatever, our journey wasn't via Route 1.

By now, the landscape, the place names, the improbability of everything had got to me. The landscape had put me in touch with all sorts of powerful feelings that I didn't know I had. I felt I needed to do something with them. Write poetry, write a diary, write home, write the whole thing off as some strange dream; all seemed good ideas. It was something to do with just wanting to create space inside my head – and extending this space onto a piece of paper.

Poised on the banks of the Eldvatn river system, the timber-framed lodge is situated on a lava field next to a recently built bridge. The name of the lodge I can't remember. I was unable to read it, let alone say it out aloud. I couldn't even pronounce it in my mind, so how would I ever be able to vocalize it? Or even remember a word with so many consonants and too few vowels, many of them joined at the hip. I don't think the people who owned the lodge could remember it, either. Every time they were forced to mention the place, it sounded as if they were clearing their throats. (I think they now call it the Eldvatn Lodge.)

We were greeted with the good news. The windows had just been put in.

The Eldvatn River, like everything else in Iceland, appears out of nowhere just when you don't expect it: from under a lava stream, called Skaftáreldahraun. It's is one of Iceland's larger sea trout rivers, with over thirty-two miles of fishing on the main river and tributaries and forty (unpronounceable) named pools. The sea trout are wild ice-age brown trout with 'the seagoing tendency', that grow very old and very big. To find yourself attached to one of ten to twenty pounds is to be expected. There are also big sea-run and resident char, resident brown trout and a few dozen salmon thrown in.

Our guide was Olafur 'Ollie' Sigurgrimsson, whose family farm the area. His mother, a handsome, fair-haired woman with a natural shyness (and total lack of English) was the cook. She greeted us in the best way she could, with a bottomless bowl of mushroom soup, smoked lamb, red cabbage and peas. A party of six Icelanders was resident in the other half of the lodge, the half where the windows had been put in the week before. Thor, the party leader, who delivered everything he had to say at booming God of Thunder level, told us they had been fishing from midday, spinning their way to dinner. They had taken two sea trout of four pounds, so there were sea trout in the system. And the lodge was fly only, i.e. you could spin if you wanted to.

There's no need for power stations in Iceland, the hot water just springs up out of the ground into the radiators and into your shower – gallons and gallons of it. What with the smell of sulphur and the disinfectant from my rods, reels, flies, and waders that had to be dipped in formaldehyde before I was allowed to bring them into the country, I woke on my first morning thinking I was in hospital.

The Icelanders had gone. With floor-to-ceiling wind and rain all week, yesterday had been the only day suitable for fishing. They'd spent the week shooting greylag geese.

Kippers for breakfast, i.e. cold marinated herrings, cheese and eggs. In the morning, we were to be fishing the Home Beat with a name that sounded like your mouth was playing the castanets: Steinsmyrarvötn, no less, meaning Stone Wetland Lakes, right next door to the lodge, in Ollie's family's backyard.

This was a creek that twisted through Patagonian-like grassland, but not the prettiest of locations. I found it hard to keep my eyes off the 1940s dredging crane that sat scuppered in the middle of the river. A one-spot beat, it was here where I pulled out just the one sea trout. My first, at four pounds. But only when I'd untethered the Billy Goat and replaced it with a Silver Stoat on a #14. Most of the rest of the time Roll Cast and I spent pulling one another out of the tar. Roll Cast got one leg so permanently glued into the liquorice goo of the river bed, I thought we would have to amputate.

Silver Stoat

Lunch that first day was going to change the whole pattern of the trip. I discovered haddock.

I'd fished for salmon in Iceland several times before, mainly earlier in the year at Laxá i Kjos in Iceland's south-west, an hour's drive from downtown Reykjavík, where I learned all my favourite ways of extracting salmon from rivers, the ways I fish with the most confidence. Tactics I

now prefer to use when the time comes – and it does every now and again – to address salmon in rivers in Scotland under the right conditions. In particular, on one of the longest rivers in Scotland, the Findhorn, located in the north-east, that flows into the Moray Firth on the north coast.

A salmon river designed by trout fishermen.

But these days, world-traveller anglers no longer talk about Iceland and salmon in the same breath. It's the brown trout they talk about now, in breathless admiration: the River Minnivallalaekur, Laxa Myvatn, Galtalækur, the trout beat at Tungufljot, the Rivers Litla, Jockla, Vididalsa, Vatnsa, Lake Heidarvatn and the huge area known as Arnarvatnsheidi, a vast highland moorland littered with lakes and interconnecting rivers, and whose name simply slips off the tongue. Occasionally, you'll hear talk of the sea trout.

At lunchtime, I talk about the haddock. And the Atlantic halibut.

To savour some of this, I was willing to give up two, even three hours' fishing to return to the lodge for lunch and the lady of the lodge's transparent, pinky-fleshed haddock, sometimes halibut, simmered to a state of total seduction, beyond temptation.

When the fishing is an hour or so's off-roading away, this was to become a problem when it came to maximizing fishing time. Making the most of lunch also had to become part of the schedule. But most Icelandic rivers close between 1.30 and 4.30 a.m. Eight hours' fishing is allowed – normally in two sessions.

On the week we were there, we fished four beats in all: the Upper Eldvatn, or the West River; the Upper and Lower East River; Melalækur; and the beat furthest away (and easiest to whisper without waking up the whole neighbourhood), Botnar, a series of pools turning off fast, powerful, rocky runs leading into long, deep, straight stretches of easy-flow, come-as-you-go, sea-trout-holding water, hopefully with sea trout coming rather than going.

White Leech

Botnar is a forty-five-minute, hair-raising journey leaping over black plastic hills and crags in Ollie's Toyota Hilux, which makes grabbing fistfuls of overhead hand grasps essential.

We made two trips to the Upper Eldvatn, or West River. Eldvatn means 'Fire Water', and I know why. Fishing it was like casting into a fireplace, flyfishing a coal mine. The riverbank was made up of dry, black tar. The riverbed resembled a Pirelli tyre tread. We fished it with large white rabbit-skin leeches, stripped through the pools and riffles. One day, we ended up at a waterfall that was gushing out creamy water, rather than twisting and tumbling it. A ten-pound sea trout had been taken here earlier in the season, but not today. I ended up fishing a gold bead head to a shoal of char with white-tipped fins, which were snacking on a large flat black rock.

Later, Ollie took us to two beautiful pools at the top of the beat. To get to it, he had to drive his Hilux over several steep-sloped humps, careering up one side, crashing down on the other side. One miscalculated inch and we would be swimming with the fishes.

The night before, a motley crew of Americans from 'Noo Joy-say' had taken a sixteen-pound sea trout from just below the waterfall, eighty-two centimetres long, with a forty-one-centimetre girth. It was the only fish the party took all day. He couldn't explain why, but Roll Cast bet me that this would be the only fish they'd catch during their stay. He also bet me the next day that I wouldn't be able to hook into the hen fish that had accompanied this sixteen-pound cock fish, which the Americans had spotted and reckoned would still be there. It was. But I managed to hook the bottom and lose the Black Woolly Bugger with a grizzle hackle palmered down the body which I tied up after lunch. The fly that had caught the monster, tied exactly the way those 'Noo Joy-say' boys had prescribed.

~

Just as the river we were fishing appeared out of nowhere, out of the ground and into the moorland, so did Joachim – out of the woodwork of the lodge into our Hilux and off fishing with us to Melalækur. Slight of build, this charming Portuguese Indian Roman Catholic from Goya, who had been a barrister in London and was now living in Paris, had just arrived from fishing in Ranga where he had extracted five salmon in one sitting – on worm. He was great company. We christened him 'Jock'.

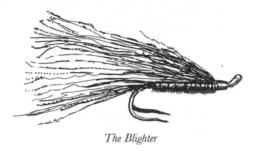

The Blighter

I had been up early that morning tying up chenille-bodied, silver-headed, marabou-tailed blighters on #10 Double Wilsons. I handed one to Jock, who went on to catch a five-pound sea trout, on a spinner, which he returned, i.e. knocked on the head.

At Melalækur, Roll Cast won the toss to fish the top beat lying above a challenging stretch where all the likely holes lay across strong, fast channels. Standing there, in a dark, dank, misty gloom, springs bubbling up around my feet, craggy rocks all pointing threateningly in my direction, I managed to extract a pound-and-a-half brown trout on a jungle cock-eyed marabou lure I'd tied up in the back of the Hilux, wondering how best to fish the stretch below Roll Cast.

Luckily, I didn't have to spend much time trying to work this out. Roll Cast hooked into a thirty-inch sea trout and I was there in a flash with the camera. I was on my way back to the car when Roll Cast started hollering again. This time he had a thick-set sea trout shaped more like a roach than a trout, estimated to weigh between eight and ten pounds. We settled for nine, on Ollie's recommendation.

I couldn't wait to get back to tie up the fly that had caught Roll Cast's fish and that had seemed so irresistible. A black rabbit zonker strip, a black chenille body ribbed with silver wire – and a bit of Flashabou to liven things up.

That day, the haddock took second place.

In the afternoon, Ollie put us on a huge expanse of deep water, with powerful current where the contours of the river bed changed at every step. The river water in Iceland is as clear as spring water; i.e. the water is totally opaque. With a black river bed, you step through clarity into darkness, straight into the unknown. You can see your foot as clearly as if it is right there in front of you in mid-air, but not what you're about to lower it onto. The water could be six inches deep, or six feet.

Roll Cast braved it, trying to get across the river to an island, but when he was halfway across he returned – a cloud even darker than the river bed was over his head.

That evening, it was time to complain.

The deal we had made with the outfitters was that we were to have two guides; one each. Every inch of water was new to us and, whereas you could have put either of us on a bonefish flat and left us to our own devices, as happy as sandboys, on Icelandic rivers that run over consolidated volcanic ash as vast and as unreadable as the Eldvatn, you needed not just someone to point a finger towards where a fish might lie, but also a shoulder to lean on as you were escorted in that direction.

In short, the river was dangerous.

Ollie listened. But 'Jock' stayed with us. When we arrived back at Botnar, we developed a new technique of exploring the river. Ollie was renamed 'Staff'. Not because we saw him as just someone we had employed to work for us, which I guess is what a guide really is. No, with a shoulder for each of us, 'Wading' Staff was going to be the big long stick to support us every time we had to cross a stretch of the river bed that looked like a tarmacked stretch of motorway after an earthquake.

On our way on the Paris–Dakar Rally to Botnar, I gave Roll Cast one of the flies I had tied up the night before using up the last of my vulturine hackles. These I tied onto the hook, Matuka-style, over a silver Mylar body, and strapped down with oval wire wound between the hackle fibres. With a silver bead at the head and a tuck of Day-Glo fluorescent red wool at the throat – its cheeks blushing with expectation. I was certain this was what the brawling brutes of Botnar were waiting for. I gave one to Jock, sitting next to me in the back of the Hilux. He went on to catch a magnificent hen sea trout weighing five pounds on a tube fly he fished with his spinning rod, which he knocked on the head.

Staff put me on a corner with safe wading in response, I assumed, to our 'Don't leave us alone!' plea. I hooked a salmon in an ice-blue run where an angry slug of water curled round a boulder and flattened out behind it. I had been eyeing up a couple of fish I'd seen moving below a pool a little further up, but Roll Cast got there first, extracting one of them at sixty-three centimetres, or seven pounds, on a Bloody Butcher on a #12 treble.

That night Jock had the top half of his sea trout cooked in butter. Roll Cast and I watched him swallow what he considered to be the best part. The head.

The next day, the wind had switched to the north and 8° C was the best the temperatures could manage. I had tied up a magnificent four-inch tube incorporating every possible bit of material I thought might result in me catching one of the sea trout I had come all this way to attach myself to.

Today we were fishing the lower part of the East River. I was happy here, skipping through magnificent pools, tempting glides and mouth-watering runs, but nothing wanted to share my happiness and make me even happier. Instead, I picked blackberries from the tundra for lunch, and mixed them with some yoghurt Ollie (mysteriously) had on his person, near his favourite spot where he'd caught his biggest sea trout ever, at fifteen pounds.

The wind was arctic. I wore my new fingerless gloves – a big mistake if ever I knew one. The mitten bit that was meant to flip over and protect the fingerless part kept flapping up and down like a Muppet's mouth, as if allergic to the back of my fingers. Useless. As a result, my hands froze and I christened the company that had persuaded me to purchase them 'The Fat Lot of Use Company'.

In the afternoon on the Home Beat, I wandered aimlessly, casting into arid swampland and marshes to find somewhere to fish. Staff eventually rescued me, helping me across the river to a long canal stretch. He suggested I fish it down. Not a scintillating stretch, by any stretch of the imagination, so I lay on the bank next to Staff watching Roll Cast's rod flash backwards and forwards in the sunlight as he worked his way round the lower beat, covering every black inch, tirelessly. His fly was in the air so many times, it went virtually viral.

Staff pulled my wrist closer to admire my watch. One with a red rim round it with the days in Spanish that I had bought from L. L. Bean for £45. We discussed how people attach so much importance to the watch they buy and wear, and how much stock they put in brand names.

I told him that I had met a fisherman in Norway with whom I had had a similar conversation. He'd bought a watch branded 'Tick', which he was delighted with until he met someone else with exactly the same watch branded 'Tock'. He wasn't happy for his brand to keep changing its name from 'Tick' to 'Tock' every six months, so he bought a Rolex. I think it's idle conversations like this on the riverbank that you call 'passing the time of day'.

After a kip, Staff took us lower downriver, to the Junction Pool where the water met the main river and widened out into a sea. It was like fishing an estuary. Roll Cast fell asleep instantly in the Hilux, but not for

long. A flock of sheep had escaped into a field of potatoes and Staff had
to round them up in his Hilux.

According to Staff, the river had more water in it than he and his
grandfather could ever remember. Dust, sand and ash were altering
the geography of the river, shifting holding lies and rearranging the
routes the sea trout take on their journey up the river. And all these loose
floating particles in the water don't increase a sea trout's contentment.
Indeed, if they get some in the gill, it sickens them.

This, we decided, was why we were catching fewer fish in the main
river and having the bulk of our luck in the side and upper streams.
We also noted that a relentless, driving wind wasn't helping the angler
standing midstream.

The Thug

Staff decided to investigate the lower regions, even lower down, and
headed to the coast. Crossing over a shallow volcanic seabed, the Hilux
got stuck for two hours, temperatures dropping by the minute. Staff's
uncle eventually appeared with his Nissan 'Thug', as I called it, which
whipped us straight out. If only the sea trout were as easy to extract.

By the time I'd finished tying up two Silver Stoats for Roll Cast, it was
well past midnight. Sitting there at the end of my bed, I realized that
I was enjoying the I.E. – the Icelandic Experience – more than I had
thought, i.e. I was starting to relax.

My black Muji kit was red hot again and I went on to tie up a fly I
christened The Thug. Big, black, bushy, and built up on a #12 long-
shank hook, this was a blunt instrument with a murderous disposition
containing every pound weight of my frustration.

The next day, it was colder, 4°. And I found a use for 'The Fat Lot of
Use Company' gloves. I put them on my feet. Too cold for fishing – but no.

On our way back to Botnar, I showed Jock my Thug. He shook his head, pulled out a fly box from his pocket and presented me with a beautiful, fully-dressed salmon fly with a gut eye which he planned using. A friend of his had tied it for him, a perfectionist in everything he did, but especially in his flytying, Jock went on to tell me, his eyes rolling. He had asked this obsessive friend of his how long he'd been tying flies and the friend had replied that he'd started when he was nine and five-eighths old, precisely. I duly handed the fly back to Jock, who went on to catch an eight-pound sea trout on a #4 Mepp which he returned, i.e. duly despatched.

Staff dropped Roll Cast and Jock on the pool where Roll Cast had fished on our last visit to these parts, where I had seen two fish moving and where Roll Cast had beaten me to it. The fish were still rolling.

I tied on my Thug and cast it upriver. The north-east wind, blowing over my left shoulder, was good for casting. With the rod pointing over to my left side, I wiggled the tip, pulling the fly back down through the shallow pool at the end of the run, gathering the line with my right hand as it went. The Thug rolled into white water below where one of the fish had turned. A fish swirled, but refused it. And again. And again. Addressing this trout was less like a seductive *pas de deux* and more like a bullfight, except that every time the sea trout charged the red cloak it stepped aside, so I switched to a Munro Killer for reasons I can't understand or explain.

Now, Icelandic sea trout hit your fly at a searing speed and take off downriver with the devil behind them. So, when my fish charged my Munro and took it, I thought I'd caught a rock. To start with, at least.

For other reasons that I can't explain, I 'trout-stuck' several times. Perhaps to check to see what the devil I had on the end of my line, for there had been no searing rushes to freedom involved here. Then, to check whether or not I really had a fish on the end of my line – and, if the latter, to get it to move, which it didn't – I 'strip-struck' violently two or three times like I would have done if a tarpon, and not a sea trout, had just engulfed my Munro Killer. Now things started to move. My fish went like the wind into the rapids, heading seawards. Then, unannounced, the rain came in on another wind and poured down in sheets, horizontally.

For twenty minutes it was like playing a fish while running up and down inside a car wash, stomping on squelchy sponges and chamois leathers, the boggy bank underfoot.

Still with the seductive smell of salty salvation very much in the fish's nostrils, I managed to turn the rod over my other shoulder and run the sea trout aground onto a strip of volcanic gravels. A dark-brown, speckled cock fish measuring seventy-two centimetres, filling the vacant space in my perfect week. The hook appeared to be embedded in the sea trout's neb, but it slipped out easily when the fish rolled down the gravels, back into the black. Nobody was there with a camera.

Back at the Hilux, talk was of other things.

Earlier that day, just before we'd started to fish, we'd noticed a jumbo jet circling overhead. This was unusual. On all the other days we'd fished Botnar we'd never seen any planes of any sort.

All morning the 747 circled around, disappearing for twenty minutes and circling back again. We were worried. We decided it was in trouble. The undercarriage was not lowering, or there was some similar technical problem.

Then, just as we were about to head off back to the lodge for haddock *en beurre*, the plane disappeared and didn't return. Even Staff was intrigued. Even more intrigued than he was to hear about my ten-pounder. Intrigued enough to phone the airport when we got back to the lodge. We couldn't wait to find out.

About ten minutes later, Staff came back with a broad smile on his face. The plane had landed OK.

We were relieved. It had just been burning off fuel so that it could land. It had a very heavy load aboard. So, what was the extraordinary weight?

'A film star,' Staff told us.

'A film star?'

'Well, a fish,' Staff went on.

'A star fish!?' We'd had enough intrigue for one day.

'No, a killer whale.' Now we knew he was joking. Except that he wasn't.

The fish was indeed a killer whale. A killer whale called Keiko, the star of the film *Free Willy*. Keiko was captured near Iceland in 1979 and sold to the Icelandic aquarium in Hafnarfjörður. Three years later he was sold on to Marineland in Ontario, where he first started performing for the public. In 1985, he was sold to Six Flags Mexico, an amusement park in Mexico City. In 1993 he got the starring role in the movie *Free Willy*. With filming over, Keiko was sold out and brought back from whence he came, to be returned to the sea.

'I thought you guys weren't too big on that sort of thing,' Roll Cast and I said to Staff.

'What sort of thing?' Staff said.

'Catch and release.'

TWENTY

Christmas Island

Sea Shrimp

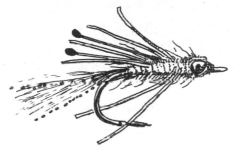

Hook: No. 6 saltwater hook

Thread: Lime-green

Weight: Bead chain. Metal or plastic, to desired weight

Beard: White or tan calf tail. Two strands of Krystal Flash

Eyes: Fly Eyes: nylon with black eyes on tips

Legs: Five White or khaki Sili legs

(to match colour of sand on flat)

Body: White or khaki mohair wool

(to match colour of sand on flat)

Fly Fishing at the Bottom of the Food Chain

IT WAS 6.10 A.M. THE CAB TO San Francisco airport was ten minutes late.

'What music do you folks like this time in the morning?' the driver asked us.

'Hawaiian,' Philip said.

'Silence,' I said.

We got Bach.

It's a five-hour flight to Honolulu. Then we had an overnight stay at the Sheraton on Waikiki beach. I spent the evening drinking Fire Hole beers watching Steve McGarrett, Danno and *Hawaii Five-0* lookalikes hula-whooping their longboats headlong into the waves, through weary, bloodshot eyes.

Our Aloha flight left at 7.30 the next morning. I had lost count of the time difference. Time was slipping away like a tsunami of lost sleep, going backwards. Which is why, I thought to myself, the planes seemed to be getting older and older as our journey progressed.

I was aching for sleep and silence. But in the States, everyone's got something to announce.

'In a moment,' the announcer announced, 'we will be serving breakfast, coffee . . . and a complementary screwdriver.'

To repair the wings, I thought.

I had just wrapped myself up in a blanket the size of a handkerchief to get some sleep when the passenger next to me asked if I wanted his.

'This is the last time you're going to feel cool for a week,' he announced. 'Enjoy!'

It was here I cut out.

Christmas Island is so very far, far away. Way beyond the fluffy clouds hanging on the Date Line, where cold air meets warm and shakes the plane about like a cocktail shaker. You don't strap yourself in, you bolt yourself down.

When you cross the Line, you lose an entire day. You leave on Wednesday morning and arrive Tuesday afternoon, yesterday. (Or is it tomorrow?) This explained why I was paying for six days, but on paper I was only getting five. I think. (But I'm still confused.)

Christmas Island is Cerebos City. Straw huts, with palms and salt scrub. Travel is slow as the tracks are scattered with a million immovable puffed-out booby birds. In the throat area, that is. Everywhere the land surface is paved with crabs, sidling about like Mandarin Chinese, their claws stuck down their sleeves. The sky is a-glide with frigate birds.

Once you've been garlanded with flowers, watched girls in grass skirts decorated with the shells of cowries dance the *ruoia*, eaten barbecued pig while
being serenaded by a gospel choir and gone shopping in the JMB Stores,
when it comes to entertainment on the island, there's nothing much more.

Go Like Hell, Bobby Delemo's Flat, Korean Wreck, Paris Flat, and
Smoky. The names of the places you'll be fishing sound like nightclubs
or film titles, so you can make believe there's a cinema. But I went for
setting the names of the fishing guides to music:

'You say Kareba, I say Katea. You say Tabaki, I say Teannaki. Ekenea
. . . Eceti . . . Ibbu . . . Otea . . . Let's call the whole thing off.'

One thing you can't turn off is the sea. In our little hut right next to
the beach at the Captain Cook Hotel, the soundtrack of *The Cruel Sea*
was on a loop. Lying face up, bleary-eyed in bed, the waves crashing
onto the rocks sound like jumbo jets taking off.

Waves filled with bonefish, rolling in the surf.

It was broken crockery that woke us up at 5 a.m., from Dan and N'ta's
hut next door. At breakfast, we discovered Dan had put aftershave in his
hair instead of conditioner.

If bonefish feed in pods, Christmas Island bonefishermen fish in
packs. And, as we were the only anglers who had booked our trips
directly, and not through some American outfitters who have been
taking the same parties out to the island for generations, when it came to
getting the best guides, Dan, N'ta (Anita), Philip and I found ourselves
at the bottom of the food chain. Direct-booking lepers.

Sardined into a wartime truck – or the *Ulua*, a banana boat version of
a Bluebird Bus – fishermen and guides are delivered to their allocated
fishing ground. There, parties split up, head off in various directions
and, well . . . disappear.

Standing ankle deep in an ocean the temperature of bath water, the sandy white flats in front of you stretch out to eternity, merging with the sky on the horizon. You feel you're inside a huge sky-blue beach ball. A ghostly space you share with toothy barracudas and leaping blacktip sharks, at the top of the food chain. And, somewhere down at the bottom of the food chain, bonefish. And little old you.

I didn't catch the name of our guide that first day and I didn't catch a bonefish, either. The Fat Jimmy Hendrix, the name I gave him, took us to a flat that looked like a reservoir in the middle of an aerodrome, a cobweb of white runways, where no bonefish landed, or were landed.

On the way back along the pine-lined road, we passed a field of rusting trucks. 'The only eyesore on the island,' Dan said. The UK transferred sovereignty back to Australia in 1958. 'And you left your junk behind.'

The next day it was a long drive to Korean Wreck, through a colony of Noddy birds that leapt aboard our truck like refugees at Calais. I was asleep in the back. I woke up covered in birds, thinking I was in a Hitchcock movie.

My guide, Eceti (meaning 'broken'), promised he would do all he could to break our blank. He started by telling us how the flat got its name. Apparently the crew of a Korean fishing boat got so fed up with the fishing, they wrecked their boat and went home, a story that did very little to raise spirits.

But bones swept in on the tide we missed yesterday. I was strip-striking into bone after bone.

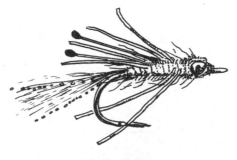

The Sea Shrimp

At the 'Which Fly?' competition, when you ceremoniously present your fly box to your guide, Eceti picked out one I called the Sea Shrimp tied on a slightly smaller than normal #6 hook. A simple tie. Bead chain

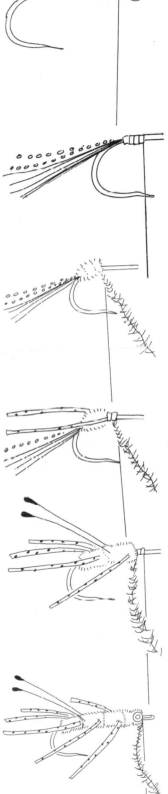

eyes of desired plummet qualities (or plastic, if the flat is only ankle deep) are secured behind the eye using lime-green tying silk. A pair of Fly Eyes, nylon with black bobbles on the end, is tied at the bend along with a small bunch of white or tan calf tail and two strands of Krystal Flash as a beard extending over the hook bend and three Sili rubber legs. These can be either khaki or white, to match the body which, again, is either khaki or white, depending on the colour of the flat. Always match the flat.

The body material I prefer is a length of mohair wool. This is tied in at the bend, after the Sili legs. Winding this wool to halfway up the fly, you tie in two more Sili legs and carry on winding. When you get to behind the eyes, tie in two more legs covering the roots with a turn of mohair. Winding the thread to behind the hook eye, you figure-of-eight the wool over the bead chain eyes and whip-finish behind the hook eye.

The Sea Shrimp performed better than any Tchaikovsky soloist. Then I caught a conch (unconsciously), the size of a cushion. Bouncing along the turtle grass, my Sea Shrimp went Crazy Charlie and attached itself to this eerie sea snail. Eccti told me a conch that size is ten years old. Despite pleadings, he smashed it open on a rock and ate it.

Now I know how he got his name.

N'ta (Anita) was Dan's wife. But he wasn't doing too great a job hiding the fact that he was having an affair. With Philip's large arbor.

'Listen to those ball bearings making love,' he'd say as Philip pulled off line. 'Sounds like the New York Philharmonic.'

'Nancy Sinatra's in there, too, Dan,' Philip added.

Every night, Philip made sure his rod was on the rack next to Dan's, so his reel could wind him up.

The Main Man, the hoochie-coochie of the guides, was Tyrone. Philip said Tyrone ticked every box in his Good Guide Guide. 'And he's got a good head of hair,' Philip added. He cost $65 extra a day. One morning, we booked him. But we didn't get him. That's living on the bottom of the food chain for you.

No Tyrone. Mixed up trucks. I sat in the yard, dozed off, waiting for a replacement. Then my guide arrived, Polaroid-free. If you've ever waded the flats sharing your Polaroids, you'll know it's like passing the hot potato, so we did more talking than fishing.

He told me a full moon is the best time for spawners and next week was such a week. Forty Yanks were invading. In landing craft. Not to mention the Japanese, who apparently just turn up with no rooms booked.

'It's bonefish Woodstock round here.' My blind guide blanched, visibly.

That afternoon, I got Matt with a hat made of straw of many colours. Matt the Hat. He liked standing around waiting for the bones to come to him. I found out later he couldn't move because he was desperate for a crap.

After an hour, a giant trevally of over fifty pounds crossed the flat at Gran Turismo speed. When it came onto the flat, the water level rose and jaws dropped.

We were picked up at 3.05 p.m. Things were ending earlier every day, so we fished the sea in front of the hut with a fly called the Chilli Pepper that Philip had bought in the store.

On Y-Flat the next morning, a truck arrived and Teannaki dumped a wagon of fishermen upwind of us, which spooked all the bones heading our way. It meant we had to walk half an hour to another flat. But at a drop-off I took a bone the length of my guide, Kareba's arm. An eight-pounder.

Back at the bus I had a word with Teannaki.

After lunch, 'Long Arm' Kareba and I were dropped off on a windy spit patrolled by the fussiest bones I have even encountered. The tide was rushing in. We only had an hour's fishing. I told 'Long Arm' that as we had been messed around and had lost a lot of time I was in no hurry to go. We had to swim back to the bus. Teannaki's Revenge.

On our last day, they winched me out of bed, into breakfast, onto a pick-up and into the catamaran pick-up to a place called London, half an hour away. We were off to Smoky Flat, a further half an hour away. Asleep, or awake – dead or alive – find yourself on the wrong side of the catamaran and the sun burns your face off.

My guide for the day was George, whom we picked up from the village on the way. We had to wait for him to get up, hanging around outside his hut, which he liked to call his 'apartment'. More a 'falling-apart' ment. It made *los baños* at Retiro bus station in Buenos Aires look like the banqueting rooms at Claridge's in Mayfair. When he finally appeared, he lay down in the catamaran and went back to sleep. Very reassuring, I thought, as I tried to picture the marvellous day we were going to spend together.

As in childbirth, I knew there was no going back. So I went to sleep next to him. When I woke up, the flats were filled with bonefish; there was neither an American outfitter nor any of his clients in sight. There was entertainment in the evening. And I hadn't lost a single day getting there.

When I woke up, I dreamed I was back in Cuba.

~

On the last evening of our stay at the Captain Cook, we sat on a rock on the beach to watch the sun go down.

Everything was packed and ready to go. The rest was folded up and left on the bed for the guides, who relied on the generosity of their clients to kit them out for the rest of the season. Wading boots, caps, shirts and shorts – and anything else we could give to the cause. Everything they stood in was stuff fishing guests had stood in once. It became a sort of competition to see who could be the most big-hearted. I saw one American guest hand his guide his flytying vice.

I left my old, ripped-up wading boots that had protected me from many an injurious scrape dished out from Cuba's cruellest corals. I was sad to let them go, for with them went many tales of wild wading. Scratches and scrapes hung from them like war medals, bringing back fond memories each time I unpacked them and put them back in my bag.

That last evening we all brought what was left of our duty-frees. This reminded me of early-days Cuba, where I had always thought that the 'Ron' in front of 'Bacardi' was the name of the guy who produced it. Ron Bacardi, like Arthur Bell, the whisky man. (Yes, it's a bit sad.)

We'd play this game to see who could make up an even more absurd name. Phil Smirnoff, Sid Croft's Original are just a couple I can remember.

But that night I had decided that I wouldn't be coming back to Christmas Island for a second time. I walked down the beach to where the surf stroked the sands and threw my empty bottle of Famous Grouse as far out to sea as I could, to where I knew bonefish had a bad habit of patrolling just out of casting distance at high tide.

It was time they took up another nasty habit.

Anyone who ties saltwater flies always needs to be on the lookout for materials that look like nothing much to the casual eye, but to a flytyer could be the essential ingredient in fooling unfoolable fish.

One such item in my box of bits and bobs is a parrot feather.

Back in the eighties, I wrote two TV commercials for the launch of a new magazine. The first featured Sir John Mills, who had recently won an Academy Award for Best Supporting Actor. The second featured Sir Ralph Richardson, who had received two Best Supporting Actor Oscar nominations and had been the first of his generation of highly

acclaimed actors – that included Laurence Olivier and John Gielgud –
to be knighted. In my commercial, I wanted him to be dressed up as a
tramp and to lie on a park bench covered with newspapers. Famously,
he agreed.

We were invited round to Sir Ralph's house in Chester Place, London,
overlooking Regent's Park, to discuss the script. But, first, the location.
Rising, statesmanlike, from his chair, Sir Ralph walked to the window,
stroked his chin and dropped his head in the direction of the bench on
the other side of the road from his house. That was agreed on. Next,
wardrobe. We were led up a flight of stairs to a large room with built-in
wardrobes on all sides except for the window side. There was a chair, a
full-length mirror and, in a large Victorian cage hanging from the ceiling,
a parrot. Sliding open the wardrobe, Sir Ralph pulled out a brown trilby,
placed it on his head at an angle and stared, apparently into space, waiting
for approval. But not from us. He pulled it off. It wasn't right.

Hat after hat was put on and taken off. All pleas for approval addressed
seemingly into the middle distance from whence authorization was
required. The coat was next. More doors were thrown open and all
manner of overcoats paraded for approval. But, again, not from the
director or the writer, but from someone in that middle distance.

It gradually became apparent from which direction Sir Ralph was
looking for this approval: the direction of the parrot, who was observing
every move with enormous interest, nodding excitedly at certain
moments. It was this gesture that the eminent actor was taking as a 'yes'.

The dress was agreed, the director was led downstairs leaving the
scriptwriter alone with the most influential unit of the whole production
so far, the bird. One feather protruded out of the bars. How could I
refuse this new addition to my box of bits and bobs? A parting gift that
ended up as part of a rather ingenious fly which parted company from
the end of my line. And which – unless it has unhooked itself since – is
still swimming around in the Gulf of Mexico, an elegant piercing in the
lip of a rather large saltwater fish.

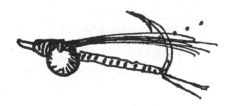

TWENTY-ONE

Alaska

Ted's Improved Nothing

Hook: No. 2–4 salmon hook
Thread: Black
Tag: Green hair
Body: Silver tinsel
Wing: Brown hair
Head: Peacock herl

Call in the 'Litmus Twins'!

IT WAS A TIME WHEN THE Japan Airlines flight to Osaka stopped at Anchorage to refuel, and you were the only one to get off. A time when you'd never see another flyfisherman on the Copper River. You were the only one there. But no longer.

Now JAL flies to Osaka direct. And fishermen from lodges all over the Bristol Bay area are airbussed in and line up to fish for the same rainbows you had set your heart on catching as you rolled through the clouds in a Beaver in a nervy, buckled-up dream.

On my first flight to Anchorage, the 747 was empty. One person in First, half a dozen in Club and twenty in Economy. All of them Japanese, who immediately after take-off rested their heads on folded arms on the tray they'd flipped down in front of them and went to sleep. Soundless for the entire eight-hour-fifty-minutes flight.

I chose to watch the movie. *Jagged Edge*, volume down low.

I got some sleep, assured that when I got off the plane my rods would be getting off with me. They had allowed me to take my rod tube into the cabin. Thinking back, it's remarkable they let me do this. My rod tube – or rather 'tunnelling' – was drainpiping I'd bought in the local builder supply yard, big enough to take eight rods and two wading sticks. To make it portable, I had drilled two bolts into the side and attached a strap I'd taken off my French wicker fishing creel.

At Anchorage, Roll Cast and I booked into the International Airport Hotel, ordered a prime rib and sat drinking Moosehead beer under the biggest moose head I'd ever seen, hanging on the wall. We were in bed at ten and up at seven to catch a cab to Anchorage, only to find all the fishing stores closed. At two o'clock, a Ryan Air – 'The Tough Get Going' – Beech 1900, 13-seater bush plane screamed us over a volcano that had erupted just two months before. This large puff of hot ash was front page news in the *Anchorage Daily News*, but didn't get into the aircraft engine.

It was a forty-five-minute flight. Ted Gerken was waiting for us at the airport at Iliamna, which is perched on the side of Lake Iliamna, a pool of black and limitless space. In Anchorage, the weather had been warm, 'hot' even. At Iliamna temperatures were several degrees below, but Ted's welcome was as warming as his big grey beard.

Opened in March 1977, Iliaska Lodge is run by Ted and his wife, Mary. Their original acquisition had amounted to an odd collection of buildings in desperate need of repair, huddled together on a narrow strip of land that jutted out into Lake Iliamna, and standing in the full face of whatever the forty-ninth State threw at it, weatherwise. To transmute these tumbledown shacks into one of America's premier catch-and-release flyfishing lodges was a blood-and-sweat tribute to determination, set against a backdrop of unparalleled natural beauty.

The population of Iliamna is half native, half white. The native population is predominately Yupik Eskimo, with some Athabascan Indian and Aleutian Eskimo. There is no segregation. The indigenous people and whites intermingle round a central airstrip and a floatplane pond called 'the Slop Bucket'.

Ted had been a US Coast Guard career officer, rising to the rank of Commander before retiring in 1975 to be a fishing lodge owner and bush pilot, with a commercial pilot's licence with instructor's and instrument ratings.

At that time, his staff totalled thirteen. Guides, pilots, maintenance men, cooks and room attendants. He had two pick-ups, a truck, ten boats with outboards scattered round in various locations, two Cessnas and a de Havilland Beaver on floats. You ask him why flying out from there costs so much, not forgetting to add in all the food, insurance and licences – and accounting for the fact that everything has to be flown in, which costs 'a little and a half' – Ted is quick to put you at ease.

'Don't worry, fella. You'll get your money's worth.'

Our room for the ten days was like staking-out inside an orange box. All wood, wood and more wood. In fact, the whole of this corrugated, sky-blue tin-roofed lodge, standing to attention in the acid-green tundra on the side of the purple Iliamna Lake, was like being in an orange box. And they said psychedelia was only to be found in California.

But the mattresses were like falling backwards into clouds. The sheets and blankets like the lining of a womb.

Safely unpacked and down in the lounge, my fellow flyfishermen broke the bad news. And in no way gently. State law forbids alcohol in the area. The system is, you share your duty-frees. Now, had I known this before I left, I'd have doubled, even trebled my Famous Grouse stock. Fortunately, everyone else had come well prepared and it wasn't to be too long before my Grouse turned into a Wild Turkey.

The mountains, the lake, the sea of tundra, the views that surrounded us emptied the mind like someone had pulled a cork, gripping our thoughts, compelling our imaginations. That first evening, the sight of the sun setting would have made Turner throw his paints out of the window in despair.

We all met in the sitting room, with its bearskins, and muskrat pelts pinned on the walls at an artistic angle, along with frames of flies, photos of salmon of a size that only swim in your dreams, and barometers that Ted couldn't pass by without giving each and every one of them a tap with his finger, just to check.

Before dinner, Ted gave us his well-rehearsed introduction talk. A forerunner of all Health and Safety decrees. A creepy talk about the etiquette and style, the routine, the dos and don'ts and . . . the coastal grizzly bears code.

'We have a stalemate with them,' Ted told us, in basso profundo. 'If you see one to talk to, back off slowly, saying "Hello, Mr Bear", to let the bear know you know he's there. "Nice to see you on the river this afternoon. Fishing has been fine today. We were just leaving. You're welcome to take our place and fish here if you insist. You just carry on, Mr Bear. You have the place to yourself."'

His pace quickened.

'The last thing you do is run!'

Our heart rates quickened, too.

'You are not a food item,' Ted reassured us. 'Quicken your step as you go. But don't run. When you think you're far enough away, now's the time to run – like hell! – remembering the top speed for an adult is forty miles an hour, so make sure you're far enough away.'

The room had fallen silent. We were all trying not to focus on the sound of the wind whistling through the corrugated metal roof.

'One last thing. If there's a bear about and you've a fish on the end of your line, snap it off. And don't climb trees. Bears do it faster. I've seen them scale sheer-sided cliffs. They'd find a grip on that window behind you.'

We all turned round to look at the widow and tried to imagine this actually happening. When we turned back, Ted was gone.

After dinner of whitefish in butter, Roll Cast and I headed for bed. We both woke up at 2 a.m., asking one another if we were awake. Roll Cast got up and killed time. He unpacked and repacked his bags again. Everything he has is put in its own separate plastic bag. He's expecting rain.

At 5.30 a.m., Ted comes crashing up the stairs.

'OK, you guys. Reveille! Time to get up, it's 5.30.' He then chuckles to himself with a grizzly snarl. 'Silence. All I get is silence.'

After breakfast, it's down to the tackle room and into chest waders, pick-up bags, Roll Cast's plastic bags and all the plastic bags holding plastic bags. We wade out into the lake, where the Cessna 206 is parked, strapped down in case the wind picks up. Our pilot was Reuben, our guide, John. Inside, it's a tight fit in chest waders, in plastic bags, in everything.

'Buckle up!' and we're off.

Lower Copper

The engine is ear-shattering on take-off, but that's the price you have to pay to be kept reminded the propellers are still whirring. We splashed down on Lower Copper Lake, boarded a small flat metal skiff and hummed up the Lower Copper, as clear as glass, tumbling over high-polished gravels, gliding through narrow bear-high marsh grass channels. I hadn't stepped out of the skiff before I could hear Roll Cast howling. He'd taken a six-pound rainbow, first cast. His #6, seven-foot-six inch rod bent into a perfect parabola. As dynamically curved as his smile, inverted.

The moment I balanced my nine-foot-three-inch Hardy Richard Walker Superlite reservoir rod in my hand, with a lead-tipped weight forward line, I knew it wasn't going to be a day of intense sensitivity. From that moment on until the day we left, I never managed to abandon the feeling that I was fishing with nothing less than a telegraph pole with all the understanding and compassion of the Russian Steppes.

My largest rainbow that morning was five pounds. It just about managed to make my tackle creak. Any other rod would have leaped around like an athlete over a crossbar. But I was happy with the 'creak'. It was some feat for a rod you would need to run over with a tractor to extract a squeak, let alone a snap. In the afternoon I borrowed John's Windsor and my life changed. I took a rainbow of four pounds with a lipstick skid mark the length of its side.

Upper Copper

We woke up at 5.30 a.m. to a wild storm, the wind whisking the lake to cream. Ted looked out of the window after breakfast and delivered his verdict.

'We hang out in the lodge for an hour and see how things develop.'

When word went around that it was safe to fly, I looked out of the window and wondered, 'How safe?' But Ted was our pilot, flying with his old friend and co-pilot, 'Uncle Bill' Ryer. Enough reassurance required to take the bumps out of the bounces as we rocked from side to side over waves, the engine humming like a washing machine on spin programme. En route I bit the first bit of skin off a finger.

When we landed on Fog Lake, ricocheting off one wave onto another, spin-flapping across the larger ones, finally coming to rest on the crest of a foaming nine-inch wave that attacked the floats like a wild, rabid dog, my digit had been sculpted into something of a shape that would not have been out of place in the Anchorage Museum of Modern Art.

In truth, I felt seasick.

The Copper River lies just across from the lodge, left hand down a bit. It follows westwards out of the mountains, separating Lake Iliamna and Lower Cook Inlet and Kamishak Bay. The river starts in among snow-laden gullies and ravines tucked into the upper slopes of the Chigmit Mountains. From here, the water trickles and splashes downhill, over ledge and gravel into a system of small lakes interconnected by a gently flowing stream. Four miles further on, the river plunges over a forty-foot waterfall, winding its way through miles of spruce standing tall, cottonwoods lining the bank, backed up by alders, stunted birches, willow and shrubs and grasses.

The Upper Copper is a short beat, so we spent most of the morning fishing the first bend and a little below. We didn't move far. Here, there's a deep hole and Ted insisted it was stuffed with rainbows.

I walked it up, fishing wet. Then I twitched a Vermont caddis as, every now and again, the pool would erupt with fish rising to nothing, for no reason. No hatch, just a flare-up.

Behind me, Ted was putting up a rod: his #3, seven-foot-six-inch Thomas & Thomas named the Baetis. Fifteen minutes later, he was beaching a six-pound rainbow just down from me. Hand-landing it, he put his rod away and didn't fish again all day.

With bears patrolling around behind us, I was happy to stick close to Ted. Sensing this, he offered me some 'twitching' instructions. He sensed I was twitching all over.

'Here. Give your caddis some life. Cast it straight across from you. Holding the rod loosely in your right hand, gathering line with the left – elbows out from your side – you wind in the line figure-of-eight style, rocking the rod in an upwards motion held in between your index finger and thumb, on the ball at the base. Got it?'

Hemmingway Caddis

He made me check that the Hemingway Caddis I had changed to was well oiled and the line greased so that my fly skidded gradually across the surface. I soon discovered just how many trout there were in that pool.

After lunch, he took me to the next pool down, with a deep hole of turquoise water at the head. Fish were lying under the far bank pitted with dark, ultramine-blue holes on the other side of some shallow flats scattered with brown and yellow pebbles. I twitched up two rainbows to five pounds. One of them snarled at me, brandishing a set of teeth like the radiator of a Dodge from Detroit City. With his first-hand bear experience, I asked Ted to make the fly extraction.

Back at the first pool, the fish were still rising, to nothing. I managed to catch one. The largest fish of the day, topping well above the six-pound mark.

I asked Roll Cast if he had his camera with him.

'It's in one of these plastic bags, somewhere,' he said, slapping his jacket all over, like a Scotsman trying to find his wallet.

Bending down and releasing my fish-of-a-lifetime, I decided it was quicker and easier to store the memory of it in my mind.

Upper Upper Copper

Our pilot was Jim, our guide, Greg. For some reason Jim always had me sitting up front next to him.

'To keep an eye on you,' Greg later suggested.

I watched Jim check every switch, as if it was his maiden flight. A careful pilot, he had his eye on everything.

'Buckle up,' he said, turning the Cessna head first into the wind. Twenty-five minutes later he landed the bird on Fog Lake, like a feather. I didn't even feel it touch down, which is how, I decided, the phrase 'duck down' got its name.

It's a long, winding trip in an aluminium skiff to the waterfall at the head of the Copper. With tufts of jet-black hair shooting out at all angles on either side of his peaked cap, Greg is a quiet guide. But over the outboard we wouldn't have been able to hear much of what he was saying even if he'd screamed like blue thunder.

Reports from the Copper had been mixed. The water was high, but not coloured. The run of salmon, essential to the whole ecosystem, had been poor. The numbers of salmon entering the spawning beds upstream were not going to exceed, let alone equal, the twenty-two million sockeye salmon that had escaped the nets of Bristol Bay and entered the Kvichak River the year before. For this reason, the big rainbows had not been following them up. Indeed, by all accounts, the Copper had not fished well this season and Roll Cast and I were hard pushed to catch the half a dozen small fish we managed to poke out of the holes on our way back down.

Crème Delight

We had been fishing eggs. Babine Specials and Crème Delight patterns. I found one good spot on a corner in shallow water before a wide riffle opened up. I eked out several rainbows in among the spawning sockeye, like flicking the pips out of a grapefruit.

At lunch, there was entertainment. I was sitting on the side of the skiff repairing a leader when there was a splash right next to me. I jumped and found myself staring into the eyes of a little head, creased in a mixture of desperation and embarrassment. A ground squirrel had lost its grip and fallen out of the tree into the stream. Scratching its way up the side of the skiff, it jumped in and leaped for terra firma, in a cascade of droplets.

Greg asked if he could fish behind us. Two casts in, he had a fine rainbow right behind Roll Cast. Then another. Roll Cast and I were out of the water and standing over him in seconds, ready to learn the killer technique.

At a distance, it looked like he was fishing not one egg pattern, but two. What we'd mistaken for the second egg was a strike indicator made out of the same material used to tie our egg patterns.

With a clench knot, Greg attached two strips of polypropylene wool – one white, the other daylight fluorescent orange – to the end of his leader. Once done, he then dipped it in silicone and rubbed in Gink floatant or muscilin line dressing, drying it thoroughly. This process is done religiously. More of a ceremony than communion.

'It has to be,' Greg told us. 'It'll ruin your day otherwise.'

With the wool at the end of the line, he then attached two feet of seven-pound monofilament at a 90° angle to the leader. Six inches up from the point, he clips on a small piece of shot and, at the end, a #12 egg pattern.

He doesn't cast it far, just off the end of his rod. We found out very quickly that rainbows lie at the sides of the channels where the sockeyes like to travel in the slacker current and where they eventually lay their eggs. One mend is enough to keep the float unhindered from a bellying and bulging reel line.

Roll Cast and I were now fishing with renewed confidence – and effectiveness. We immediately started to catch fish. In fact, at the end of the run, at the end of the day, I hooked into a trout the size of which I can only imagine. I never got to see it. The monster hooked itself up and with a bang and a swirl it careered downstream, my little Princess reel spewing out line as it headed for the rapids, turned, opened up the spinnaker and started to head off back down to Iliamna Lake.

Greg was quick to react and came floating downriver with the skiff, Roll Cast riding shotgun. Pulling me aboard, rod held high, we all set off on the current, the engine purring, my Princess screeching, in hot pursuit.

We were just about over him when he rocketed off once again, for the last time.

Over dinner that night, Roll Cast and I got to thinking that this wool is a little crude and unreliable as a floater. How about those foam earplugs we were stuffing into our ears to stop ourselves being deafened as we flew about the skies?

Our 'Egg-plug' was to change our whole trip.

Return to Lower Copper

Rain had made it difficult for Ted to choose destinations. He had planned to fly the whole lodge (except Roll Cast and me) to Volcano after silver salmon that had populated the area, but the wind and impending storms put paid to all of that. And not for the first time.

'Volcano doesn't exist. It's only a dream,' one of the Tennessee doctors who were sharing the lodge with us huffed, heading off to Newhalen with the others.

This was the day when Roll Cast and I realized we weren't guests, we were barometers. Ted was starting to use us to check places out. Sometimes new haunts, but today it was to be the Lower Copper, not one of the prime beats at the moment. However, things can change, dramatically. The big rainbows weren't there yet, but they might just arrive, so off we set. The A-Team, or rather the 'Egg Team', was back in business, earplugs and Egg-plugs at the ready.

When we got there, there wasn't a big fish in sight. Not even a teeny-weeny one. The water was swollen and unrecognizable. We couldn't even find the spot where Roll Cast had caught his first six-pounder, first cast, first day.

I got myself stranded in water too deep to wade and had to be rescued. I was carted off rather unceremoniously by the guide, by the scruff of the wading jacket. I was taken to a shallow gravel bank where I rigged up our new Egg-plug rig and a tiny Crème Delight egg pattern.

The rig had hardly hit the water when there was a Gadarene rush, not to my fly, but to the Egg-plug, the swine! This quickly disappeared beneath the surface in a huge boil of water and sound of gnashing molars.

Once I got my Egg-plug back and moved further downstream, it dipped under the surface, just as it should do, and I pulled in a fish that was a cross between a chub, a barbel and a grayling.

'A sucker,' John enlightened me.

'It's us who are suckers. Coming here!' Roll Cast said.

On my way back to the Cessna we passed tree trunks that looked as if they had been chopped down with a hand axe. The axe was a beaver's front teeth. But it was the young alders standing a foot high and looking like they'd been felled by one swipe of a machete that were to rip the waders of one of the Tennessee Boys up on Upper Talarik.

Rub up against one of these and neoprenes are no-nos.

Upper Talarik

Roll Cast and I discovered the Upper Talarik on our second visit. Mainly because it hadn't really been discovered before.

Ted had worked us out correctly, as we had discovered on our last trip to Lower Copper. He'd cottoned on that we weren't in Alaska to fill our boots with fish. We came to fill our lives with adventure. And what could be more adventurous than being the first people to fish new water? Especially if we were to be the first to fish it. Even more especially if we were to discover that water was boots-full of fish.

Our sixth day in, Roll Cast and I had settled into the rhythm of getting up every morning, not to go to work, but to go to work on a pod of fish. One or two procedures, new to us, were beginning to become standard, as if we'd been doing them every day of our working lives. Formalities like carrying a briefcase, wearing a tie, or catching a bus were exchanged for carrying a fishing rod, wearing chest waders and catching a Cessna.

One everyday thing in particular had taken on a new importance: making sure you had a handkerchief, clean or otherwise – but never wet. Forget this and leave your handkerchief on the bed, or in a pocket of the trousers you wore last night for dinner, and your day could be ruined. How else would you be able to wipe the mist off your sunglasses, dry your trout-slimed hands, blow away that sniff that had mysteriously developed as a result of waking up in below-zero degrees and fishing in degrees well above it? Or, as once happened, alert the guide that you were up to your chin in water.

I'd invented one or two systems to make changing tactics more efficient. Roll Cast and I were only using two methods of addressing trout. One, by Egg-plug. The other, the 'No Egg-plug' technique: a simple lead shot on the leader, where the 'outrigger technique' is adopted, ticking your egg fly along the gravel to a waiting rainbow, already sighted.

Different conditions, depths and current speeds dictate the choice of method. The change needs to be made swiftly and simply, thus my system. On my wading jacket there's a brass ring above the chest pocket, on the right-hand side. If I'm not using my Egg-plug, and want to fish a dry fly, I simply fold up this rig and let it hang there on the ring for when

I need it. This rig consists of a six-inch length of heavyweight twenty-pound monofilament looped at both ends, which I loop onto my leader point. Onto this tough section I clip shot on and off in various sizes and amounts according to the depth of the run I might be fishing. I then follow this up with nine inches of six-pound tippet material to which I attach my egg.

With all these loops, rigs, lead shots and weights hanging all over me, George, our guide, gave me the hairy eyeball when I climbed into the Beaver.

'Where d'ya think you're going with all that, Neil?'

I had the answer.

'I've a one-way ticket on the first freight train to Crazy Town, George. Where you going? Now buckle up!'

The Talariks (there are two, an Upper and a Lower) are George's new beats. We were the first guests to fish with him there. George had been up there so often, it was like going home for him. He talked about nothing else. Way past the Newhalen, down Lake Iliamna, heading for far-off Igiugig, for Roll Cast and me it was like leaving Planet Earth.

The Upper Talarik is a good hour's walk from our splashdown in Duck Pond. Here, you either like the surroundings, or you don't. Either way, there's lots of it, and nothing else. Tundra times two. A treeless wasteland of sphagnum and calliergon moss, tufted saxifrage, pasque flowers, diamond-leaf willow. Blueberries and cranberries sparkle out like tiny moons in this astronomy of biology. A foot-tall pine with a trunk a foot in diameter is a hundred years old.

'Don't pick those berries up one by one,' George instructed us, bending down and taking a handful. 'Graze on them, like a cow. Like the bears do.'

The tundra's vastness and self-similarity affected our perceptions of distance. Looking across at the sky on the horizon was the only way to gauge the distance we had come. It seemed we had not advanced at all. Underfoot, everything was a springy, bouncy bog, the terrain getting meaner and meaner the closer to the river we got. We were leaping over peat ditches, tippy-toeing our way across streams and over tussocks.

Over a ridge, we hit a marsh. Even George slowed his step. Indeed, he didn't step at all. He hovered. We attempted to do the same. Hovering in #10 chest waders, Nijinsky-style. Tricky. George had practised this many times.

Picking our way through the squishy-squidge behind George in a smirr of rain, we weren't sure who was helping whom for every time George sank up to his waist in marshland, he couldn't have got out on his own. Yet he must have done in the past.

To cross some of the trickles of streams on the way, Roll Cast and I were up to our waists in water in places, too. Luckily, none of us was up to our waists at the same time. An hour in, we got to solid ground and followed paths where small firs had been either felled by beavers, or simply pushed carelessly to one side by bears.

'Them beaver dams is the reason for all those bogs we have to negotiate.'

The Upper Talarik feels like home for George. For Roll Cast and me it was like the middle stream on the River Kennet where we fished together back in England. A small stream, with deep holes and long shallows that can be reached from the bank with a rolled-over flick. Roll Cast was in his element.

We had both reduced our tackle to what we could fit in our pockets. Or, in my case, hang from the rings of my jacket. It didn't take long to set up our tackle on a gravel bar by a small pool.

My first cast, my Egg-plug dipped under like it was supposed to do and there was a massive rush in the downstream direction and plug, egg, line, the lot disappeared round a corner fifty yards down before I had time to acknowledge something was hanging on the end.

After this, the fishing didn't get any easier. Made trickier when George left you on your own and your eyes were on constant bear watch.

Surrounded by tundra, without even a hillside to break the line between land and sky, nowhere was where we were.

'But we're not alone,' George said to comfort me. 'Round here, bears appear out of nowhere.'

Roll Cast had spent a good hour after a rainbow he estimated at between six and seven pounds that was exercising in a run below where a braid ran into the river. Having had his tiny egg refused a hundred times, Roll Cast decided to up the stakes and put on something a little more substantial. A double egg pattern George called an 'Iliamna Omelette'. The rainbow took it immediately, as if served up on toast.

On our way through a jungle of alders to another pool, we had a scare. George, who was leading the way, suddenly swung round with a look of fear and signed to us to stop in our tracks. I almost leaped into Roll Cast's arms. And he, into mine. There was a rush to do an Arms Deal. Here was our first bear encounter, we thought.

In fact, it was a large porcupine that came ambling out of the bushes following a beaver track.

On our way back to the lodge, our pilot, Reuben, swooped over the Upper Talarik in the Cessna. It was tiny and there wasn't any sign of salmon that usually hug the sides of the streams like a red dye.

'Wait until you see the Lower Talarik,' George said, already feeling homesick.

Lower Talarik

Ted flew us down the coast in the Beaver, with George hanging on in as our guide, again.

'Time for you to discover the Lower Talarik, fellas,' George said, happy to be going home. 'We've christened you two the 'Litmus Twins'. Test this one out. Let's see what you make of it. No one's fished it yet.'

Back at the lodge, any mention of 'Lower Talarik' incites a frisson of excitement in the eyes of all the guides. George was planning to set up a camp there the week after we'd gone, rods staying overnight in the region. We were told that the Lower Talarik is one of the most productive sites – when you hit it right on the button. But when is that time? And where's the button?

The Lower Talarik is a creek, a rod's-length wide. A short stretch of shallow, fast-flowing, crystal-clear water that runs parallel to Lake Iliamna, running from the little lake we splashed down onto, before crashing into the hungry pounding waves of Lake Iliamna, waiting there to swallow it up. There is only a narrow gravel bank between the two.

It's this little run-off, five hundred yards in length, that the sockeye that come out of the Lake have to negotiate to get up into the Talarik system. It's a bleak, unforgiving spot that promises nothing. Except that, if you get it right, the rainbows that follow behind the salmon up this creek are bigger than the salmon themselves.

This was enough to encourage Roll Cast and me to shrug off the fact that for the first two hours we had only caught a couple of striplings. Roll Cast had taken off to litmus-test a canal stretch at the other end of the splashdown lake, which turned out to be equally unproductive. I had joined him.

When we returned to the creek, a blinding, driving rain, coming at us from behind, was there to welcome us. We decided to have an early lunch – caribou hamburgers and a sausage jammed into a roll laden with mustard, mayo, green relish and ketchup, with a cup of George's radioactive coffee and the tying and retying of hood straps in preparation for the afternoon.

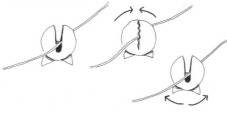

George encouraged us to fish a heavier leaded rig on a shorter leader, twelve feet long. Eight feet of this was a leader tapered down to fifteen pounds, then nine inches of twelve-pound tippet. Above the knot, he clipped on a 'Water Gremlin', a lead shot with wings you can clip on and off.

With a mighty wind howling off the Lake at our backs, one turn of the rod tip was enough to shoot this rig to the far side of the creek. With the rig landing at two o'clock upstream, I made downward mends, following the bowed reel line round with the rod tip until the rig was parallel to the gravel on the bank. Then, if nothing was attached, I heaved the rig upstream again, taking one step down, following the cast through. This is the way you work the Lower Talarik. A gentle rhythm. Should you tire of this mechanical regularity, and wish to dream off across the wasteland, you can switch to automatic pilot.

Out in the Lake behind me, scarlet sockeyes were rising and falling in the waves, waiting their turn to leave the sea. Having fished the creek a couple of times and only having taken three rainbows to three pounds, Roll Cast and I decided to put our heads together. Shouting over the crashing sea behind us, we started to wonder what sea trout would do in a situation like this. We decided that they would be lying in the first pool up from the lake. At my first cast, my drift came to an abrupt halt. I thought I'd wound round one of the small rocks, but when the quiet waters of the pool opened up and belched out thirty inches of solid, angry silver I realized that this was what I was attached to.

My high-octane fish belted back downstream, leaping twice more before it yanked me, George and Roll Cast off the end of the gravel bar, over the gravels that separated the braid from the lake, and into the four-foot waves rolling onto the shore of the lake.

I watched my monster, no longer powered by the downstream flow of the creek, holding its side-on position in the waves, lifting up and down in front of me at eye level. It was like watching it swimming around in an aquarium. Even better, mounted in a glass case. Now the fun was getting it to the shore.

As the waves receded from the gravels, George would run forward and try and grab it while I ran back to try and horse it in. It was as if we were watching the event on film, with the footage being wound on and then rewound, as both George and Roll Cast rushed forward as the waves went out, then back again as they came back in. This went out and in, on and on, as if on a loop.

George finally got a hold of it – a silver cock fish with the early signs of a vicious kype – and I grabbed hold of him, giving him the hug of his life.

'Beats anything a bear ever gave me,' George said.

Thirty inches long, with a sixteen-inch girth, it was a rainbow of almost ten pounds. It was half an hour before I had it in me to fish again, I was so overcome. I just gazed out across the sea, the wind pounding on my face, my heart pounding deep down there in my chest waders in the wildland of the skies.

I hadn't been fishing for five minutes before my rig shuddered again and I had another fish, a fraction smaller than the one I'd just returned to the sea. It tail-walked its way towards the outlet and off back to the Lake, and off the line. Three casts later, I was attached to a third silver-plated rocket filled with spitting anger. This fish I managed to land, discovering that it was even bigger than my first.

At five o'clock, sitting in the tundra waiting for Ted to splash down, we got chatting.

'Bears love them cranberries. But they don't digest them,' George said, pointing at a heap of bear droppings sitting next to me. It looked like someone had collected a bowl of berries and tipped it over.

The wind now was a gale. I was starting to get anxious. Earlier, I'd watched a Cessna taking off from the Slop Bucket and it had almost grounded on the far shore when a gust caught it on take-off. At the snap of a finger, the gale turned to wind, turned to draught, and Ted breezed in, drooping out of the sky like thistledown.

Back at the lodge, we handed our report to Ted over barbecue ribs and scallops rolled in bacon with garden peas.

'A-plus. Could do better,' we reported.

'Let's see. Tomorrow we're taking you to Gibraltar.'

Gibraltar

The Gibraltar River runs out of a lake of the same name, just across the lake from the lodge. A hop, skip and a bump in a Cessna.

When we arrived, John pumped up an inflatable and we headed off the six miles downstream towards the Iliamna Lake. John would race us from one spot to the next, dropping one of us off at a likely location, then punting the other a little further down. Then he'd sit in the middle of us on 'bear watch', to make sure we didn't get carried away on the current, or in the claws of a grizzly.

It was hopping, skipping and jumping all the way.

The day sparkled with sun lighting up one of the most spectacular corners of the wilderness. To top this, I was catching a rainbow at every cast, my Egg-plug spending more time under the water than on top of it. At the end of a short stretch I had taken sixteen rainbows averaging two pounds. I was fishing off the top of my head. Wading out, wading back in again, wading without thinking. I was swept away by the wonderfulness and rhythm of it all – and further away from John and Roll Cast. Almost swept away by the river, it was time to reintroduce myself to my partner and guide. I followed a bear track, trying to find them, hoping that there was just the track and not the bear, too.

Just as I was setting off, another angler appeared out of the bush, out of nowhere. The only other fisherman I was to meet the entire trip. He hollered after me:

'What they taking?'

'Eggs,' I told him.

'What size?'

'On twelves, fourteens.'

'Where are they?' he shouted, wading out into the river, water up to his chest.

'You're standing on them.'

~

The inflatable was barely big enough for three, although John assured us it could take five. Sloshing down rapids, water pouring over the sides, I had my arm round Roll Cast, who had a grip on my jacket. The whole balancing act was made slightly more interesting due to the fact that I had studs on my boots, so I had to pirouette on the canvas raft bag to make sure my feet didn't slip onto the rubber and rip the raft bottom open and scupper the whole caboodle.

That night, after dinner, Ted donned his woolly hat, cleared his throat to silence the room and started reciting by heart 'The Shooting of Dan McGrew', a poem by Robert Service, 'The Bard of the Yukon': an eerie tale that takes a good fifteen minutes to narrate and had us gripped to our seats as if fisted in a grizzly's claw.

> Were you ever out in the Great Alone,
> when the moon was awful clear,
> And the icy mountains hemmed you in
> with a silence you most could hear;
> With only the howl of a timber wolf,
> and you camped there in the cold,
> A half-dead thing in a stark, dead world,
> clean mad for the muck called gold;
> While high overhead, green, yellow and red,
> the North Lights swept in bars?
> Then you've a hunch what the music meant . . .
> hunger and night and the stars.

Then we were sent to bed.

Iliamna River

There were rumours that the arctic char on the Iliamna River were stacking up on top of one another in their multitude, the ones on top happy to take a dry fly. But these were only rumours. Time to call in the 'Litmus Twins'!

Roll Cast and I made sure we were well stocked up with flies without names from the selection for sale in the dining room, hoping we had a Ted's Improved Nothing or two in there somewhere, for we were off to the Iliamna, running fresh off the snowy-capped Chigmit Mountains at the far east of the Lake.

As we flew along the Lake through crystal-sharp glacial air, down Pile Bay with Lonesome Bay on our left, we began to get the feeling we were really getting away from a place we'd come to . . . to get away from it all.

The flight to the Iliamna takes an hour. As we powered up the river past pine forests dripping with freezing snow, stabbing at the fog circling all around us, the icy air stung our ears. We'd arrived in a metal world. The mountains were glaciers, as hard as iron. A steely blue sky tried to slice through the mist. The cold had a razor-sharp edge. We were glad we'd taken heed of the advice to bring warm clothing. Watching us huddled together at the end of the skiff, feeling as though ice was forming inside us, white sheaths wrapping around our bones, Chuck, our guide, laughed.

It's a cold, cold river, inches from being as frozen as we were. A bald-headed eagle followed us for a while. A bear, standing in the icy river up to its waist, saw us approach and leaped up a sheer-faced bank. A wall, four feet high.

The river is cut into sections. Long reaches of sandy bottom with stretches of stones all the colours in a box of paints. Yellows, reds, blues, ultramarines and turquoise. Then long reaches of classic, glacial river run grey, clay-bottomed and featureless. Here is where the arctic char hang out in their hundreds.

The rule is: Don't go near the water. It's too cold. We were breathing in the frost in the air, hissing on the warmth of our lungs.

The fishing style is simple enough. Floating lines, cast down and across and let your fly trail. The char like to chase silver clouds of fry, at high speed. To keep warm, we concluded. They smash in, head-butting anything that moves. In effect, the highly recommended Ted's Nothing is nothing more than a super-accelerated moving target. I assume his *Improved* Nothing is a revved-up later model that breaks all the speed records. Apparently it's nothing like his unimproved Nothing, so they tell me. You see, I saw nothing of his original Nothing, so how would I know if it had been improved or not? So, if it's nothing like his Nothing, what's it like?

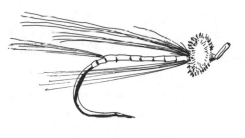

Ted's Improved Nothing

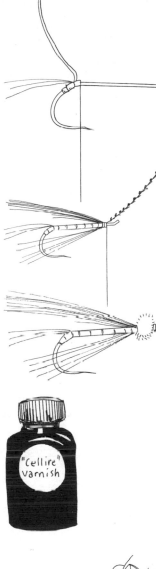

If anything, his Improved Nothing is a souped-up Polar Shrimp. A Polar Shrimp with nothing fancy added which, if nothing else, is an improvement. But I can't be sure, because when Ted said to me before we left, 'Try my Nothing today,' I thought I had nothing like it in my fly box filled with unmade flies, so he handed me a fly I guessed was his Nothing, or the Nothing he had improved. Anyway, I fished it and it did the trick, so there's nothing more I can add except, here's how it was tied.

The hook is a #2 or a #4 up-eyed salmon hook with wispy green hair making up the tail. The body is silver tinsel, the underwing is wispy green hair, the overwing wispy brown hair and the head peacock herl. The whipping is varnished with black Cellire. See, there's really nothing to it.

My first char on Ted's Improved Nothing was seven and a half pounds, according to measurements and Chuck's little calculator. With dark green and silver flanks, pink lip-gloss daubs, it had white trailing edges on its fins. A handsome fish. Uncharacteristically, it sneaked up slowly behind my Nothing and wolfed it down ever so softly. When we made contact it immediately swapped its carpet slippers for running shoes, slipping into lead-filled snowshoes when it got to the corner just downstream from the run where I'd hooked it. Here it sank to the bottom of a pool, sulking, its nose tucked away in the stones.

After twenty minutes of yanking and pulling, Chuck signalled to raise my rod tip and the char swung round into his net. Chuck doesn't stand for any sulking. He had it dispatched and filleted before I'd reeled in. We were to have it for lunch.

Bit by bit, the fog lifted to reveal the spiky-topped mountains, sprinkled with frost, that surrounded us. Temperatures rose and I found

myself peeling off much of the clothing I had layered on that morning.

Lunch was my char. Chuck had a little stove set up in the raft. He chopped the char into cubes, rolled them in breadcrumbs, dill and parsley, melted some butter in a pan and cooked the char cubes until they were a dark orange colour and a bit crispy. Sitting in a garden of wild Alpine flowers, among snow-topped mountains set against a shiny blue sky, listening to the music of Chuck's whistling billycan, I was, strangely, reminded of Julie Andrews.

The stretch of river in front of us was no more than a foot deep. Char were lined up side by side, nose to tail, like an airport car park. They looked easy meat. But they were far from it. Unlike the char in the run we'd fished before lunch, when they stopped showing an interest in a fly, that interest wasn't renewed if you presented them with a different one. We moved further upriver to a pool strewn with stones of all sizes, black against the sand.

'Those aren't stones,' Chuck said. 'Those are char.'

I raced my Nothing over them and got something first cast. My line went snap. A golden crowned sparrow in a bush behind us summed it up: 'Oh . . . dear . . . me . . . oh . . . dear . . . me,' it sang, sorrowfully.

If nothing else, on the Iliamna I'd learned how to spot a char in a glacial stream. You look for grey against a grey background.

Newhalen River

That evening for dinner we had Artichoke Dip and Crackers as an appetizer, followed by Halibut Caddy, Teriyaki Steak, Moose Pot Roast, Fettuccine, Baked Squash, Cioppino with Alaskan Shrimp, Scallops and Crab, Roman Salad, Summer Marinated Salad, Asparagus Marinade, Fruit Tray, Angel Biscuits and Peach Pavlova followed by coffee and, of course, a Grouse turned Turkey.

After dinner at Iliaska Lodge, you don't go to the cinema or switch on the TV. With the lights still on outside, you switch onto the idea of going fishing again. Just down the way, in the Newhalen River. You jump in a truck and you're off to the sockeye disco, in the light of the midnight sun.

We had fished the Newhalen once before. In an emergency. Ted had tried to fly the Cessna to the No-Name River, but it was nowhere to be seen in the fog. He lifted us up high above the clouds where we circled for near on an hour. Unable to find a hole to drop down into, Ted decided to go for Option 1: he tried to splash down at the Iliamna River. But same again. So it was Option 2: fly back to the lodge, pile into a truck and head off to somewhere local. Somewhere with a name and no fog: Newhalen.

Newhalen is an enormous expanse of river near civilization. In parts, it's where the locals dump their old cars. In other parts, it's where the Rainbow King Lodge dumps its stranded clients.

The part we were taken to was where the sun shone brightly. So brightly, we were in shirtsleeves. We wanted to get pictures of salmon jumping and, hopefully, pictures of salmon on the ends of our lines. We nearly broke two rods, and Roll Cast almost lost one of his. A sockeye took his fly at great speed. The line wrapped round his rod and pulled it out of his hands. I rushed across, chasing after the fish. We found the rod on the riverbed. Roll Cast stood on one end of it, I lifted up the other with my foot. When he picked it up, the salmon was still on the end of the line and I took a picture of Roll Cast with a fish, both of us in fits of hysterical laughter.

A bear gave us a bit of bother at lunch, but he seemed more interested in a group from Rainbow King Lodge and headed off in their direction, with purpose. He crossed a 1 in 4 cliff edge of sand and shingle at top speed to get to them. We got the hell out. But the best was yet to come.

We were out deep wading and Roll Cast hooked a salmon which took off in my direction, heading straight at me two feet above the water surface. Belly-flopping to avoid a neb-to-nose collision, it drenched me in a shower of spray ending up down the front of my waders. But, like that sockeye, I digress.

That night, Roll Cast and I were the fastest to tackle up and the first to get to the head of the pool, at the 'Rock', and perhaps one of the best runs of salmon in the world. They were there in their thousands upon thousands. Here salmon throw themselves out of the water to greet you, jockeying for position to be next in line to find themselves at the end of yours. I had a salmon knocking on my fly every cast. I was taking three-to-ten-pound salmon on a Polar Shrimp with a flowing white hair wing, orange seal fur body and red cheeks. I'd have red cheeks, too, with a hairstyle like that.

Polar Shrimp

But is this the most fun you can have in the world? Strangely, perhaps not, for the hard part isn't hooking them, it's hooking them where you're supposed to hook them, in the mouth. Salmon were being caught on every side, literally. We were told when retrieving not to pull too fast in case we snagged them.

By midnight, we'd had enough. On our way back we heard someone shout: 'Bear!' We looked to where fingers were pointing. Gerken fired two pistol shots in the air, but the bear wasn't at all interested in us. He was making his way towards a group who were occupying the place we had vacated at the 'Rock'. Sniffing the air, the bear looked mean and hungry and quickened his pace. It was a sight to watch: a line of twelve burly men slowly backing away towards the boats and away from the finest salmon fishing in the world.

'Whatever aftershave those guys use at Rainbow King Lodge, I don't want it,' Gerken joked as we passed the group, frantically pushing out their boat, grizzly in hot pursuit for the second time.

The night's fishing had drawn blood from my left index finger, when a salmon had grabbed my fly and the line sliced into it just below the joint . . . added to the gash where it had got caught up in a whirring reel handle . . . added to the nail that got nibbled off on a bumpy flight . . . added to where I'd taken the skin off the tip . . . one nervy take-off.

Back at the lodge, the Tennessee Boys had returned late from Volcano, after spending a day going after silvers and Dolly Varden. Eleven rods had taken two hundred and fifty salmon.

'You guys would make better dentists than doctors, the way you extract things,' Jorn, the Norwegian in the party, announced, with a shout of laughter.

The funny thing was, Jorn had been at the lodge all week and this was the first time anyone had heard him say anything. Let alone shriek like a clapped-out starter motor.

Moraine

Apart from the River Kvichak, way down at the west end of Lake Iliamna, Moraine is the furthest Ted takes you. Situated in the Katmai National Park, this is the beat everyone in the lodge has been talking about, and not just because there's only been one party there in the last ten days, although this is a lot to do with its attraction. No, the real charm is that Moraine is largely unknown, untouched – and unpredictable. And it's where the guides go and fish on their day off.

It was a jarring flight and for the first time I used my earplugs as they are intended to be used – to stuff in your ears. But I kept my eyes open. With a view of forests set against mountains, the approach across the lake is spectacular, which might explain why the splashdown lake is called Spectacle Lake. As we flopped down we skimmed over the head of a bear on sentry duty at the side of the lake.

'You scalped that one!'

We climbed out into the bleakest terrain yet. Hard, unfriendly tundra land. The presence of a grumpy bear gave a little edge to the short walk from the lake, over a ridge, and down a slope to the river, just above a cliff.

'Ted reckons that was the bear that cut a hole in the cooler box when we camped here last week,' Greg, our guide, remarked as he pumped up the raft. I decided to take some photographs, but soon concluded there was really nothing to photograph.

Greg pulled us over to the other side of the river in the raft, delivering us onto a gravel bar on a bend lying in the shadow of the fifty-foot cliff. The sun opened up and stayed out all morning, displaying the soft side of mean old Moraine. But not for long. A lashing wind whipped us raw, freezing us to the bone.

'Put up a six-weight.' Greg recommended. 'Here, if there's a wind without a home, it snuggles itself down on the river and sleeps restlessly.'

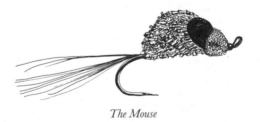

The Mouse

To warm things up, I pulled out my 'mouse', sculpted in deer hair whipped onto a Moby Dick hook, with leather ears, a tail and whiskers. I slammed it across the river under the far bank. A rainbow trout lying there must have thought it was Christmas and pounced on it immediately. Greg was taken aback. This was the first time he'd seen a trout taken on a mouse. I was taken aback, too. I thought the pattern was invented in Alaska.

After this, we powered upriver heading for a stretch that looked like it was running through a Scottish moor. There was a fish rising below a pool so I tied on a small Hemingway Caddis. The fish turned out to be an arctic grayling that upped his huge sail fin and let the current rush him downstream, making me climb a cliff, passing my rod from one hand to another to get round alders and birches on the way down. We finished up in a fast run with me standing several yards above him, perched rather precariously on a cliff face, unable to reach down and release him. One way or another, I got the grayling back to the pool where we started, winding my way round trees and rocks. It was like unravelling a knitted scarf, but it was well worth the effort. Greg was waiting with his tape measure. It was nineteen inches long.

We ended the day just above the estuary, where the Moraine runs into Kukaklek Lake. Here, standing on a high bank, we watched a slow, steady stream of sockeye wind their way upstream relentlessly, like pilgrims. Behind us, twenty-five miles of nothing; just moss, lichen, grass and mountains tipped with snow. It was hard not to keep turning back and looking at the view and pinching yourself.

We spent the last hours spotting the rainbows in among that conveyor belt of sockeyes. They were harder to spot than I would have imagined. It wasn't a matter of simply looking for silver fish among gold fish. The sockeye were still fresh and as silver as any rainbow. So how could we tell the difference? By their movement. The rainbows swing backwards and forwards, as if rounding the sockeye up. Look for the sheepdogs in the flock of salmon and those will be the rainbow trout.

To entice the rainbows away from the sockeye, we cast egg patterns beyond the silver stream of salmon that showed no interest, for they have other things on their minds. But not the rainbows.

I thought my first one was a sockeye on account of its size, but it turned out to be a thirty-inch rainbow.

After this, I sat on the bank just watching the sad procession of sockeye making their way upriver to procreate and die. To multiply and subtract.

Temperatures dropped even lower. The wind picked up and started to blast into my teeth. I was beginning to wish it would pick me up and dump me back in the raft and take me back to the pick-up point and home. Then Roll Cast fell in, soaking his waders, his clothes, his everything.

I couldn't resist it.

'You should have packed yourself in a plastic bag,' I shouted to him.

TWENTY-TWO

Islamorada

Rabbit's Hat

Hook loop: Half an inch of 30 lb monofilament

Hook: No. 3/0 circle hook

Thread: Orange monochord

Eye: Self-adhesive (optional). Bead chain, or eyed
dumb-bells, to desired weight

Tails: Orange hackle and calf hair and six
strands of gold Krystal Flash, at bend

Wing: 2½ in. strip of natural wild rabbit pelt, at bend

Neck: Orange Glo-Brite fluorescent floss. Coat with epoxy

Dinosaurs on Fly

WHEN I BOARDED *FLY DIPPER*, TIED up at the Lor-E-Lei bar,
Islamorada, Captain Bob Branham looked at my seven-
weight fly rod and smiled.

'Cute!' he said, shaking his panda-eyed face. 'The fish out there are
so big they can tear a man's arm off.'

I looked at his rods resting on the weathered planks of the dock.
Twelve-weights with great reels cut out of blocks of prime-grade
aluminium. You'd need two hands to lift them.

'If ya' hook a tarpon, that rod of yours will sure explode.'

Nature was in a big sulk. Dodging waterspouts and electric storms,
the powerful Johnson V4 boomed us across a vast ocean to Channel 5,

to Craig Key. My vertebrae rubbed together like walnuts. Soon we were staked on a flat, on a picket line, in a queue, half a dozen skiffs in front of us, waiting. Long Key, Duck Key, Grassy Key, all the way down to Key West, the Marquesas Keys and beyond, tarpon have been passing these spots for millions of years. Once every million years, I began to think.

We'd passed a Colombian family anchored in a boat upcurrent from a viaduct. They were floating live mullet back towards any fish that might be waiting there. They watched us pass with suspicious eyes, lifting their gazes to the sky to yell at an Immigration and Federal drug-smuggling spotter plane.

We might cover a hundred and fifty miles in a day, at speeds of fifty knots. An hour into the ocean, twenty miles into the back country. Maybe across the Gulf of Mexico to Jack's Bank, poling across the flats, the skiff slicing through thick turtle-grass like a razor blade. Birds flew out of the mangroves near a small key a hundred yards away. Mainly Roseate Spoonbills.

Our wake washed over Shell Key, where all the big fish had been taken by the early fly-rodders, so that it was now overfished and useless. We watched an old bone amble across the marl, in no hurry, like an elderly man in the park. He'd seen everything, taken everything, been caught-and-released by everyone and their daughter. But that was years ago. He had taken so many flies in his time the inside of his mouth was like a kitchen colander.

A lemon shark patrolling the drop-off eyed him as he passed and turned away. The sun blazed down. Sweat poured into my eyes bringing with it Factor 15 and sting.

The 100 lb shock tippet I had wound round my forefinger looked like telephone cable. The forefinger of my other hand was wrapped round the bend of a man-sized 3/0 Tiemco circle hook as if I was about to pull a trigger.

A tarpon comes rolling out of the sun across the flat, lifting out to gulp. I place my rabbit fur streamer in front of it, let it drop and lift it up slowly. The fly is engulfed by a mouth that opens up like some stainless-steel kitchen gadget with complex levers and hinges.

The fish is up in the air, just like you see in films, shaking its head, bending double. Out pops the fly, like you read about in books. Then down again, showering the skiff in a thousand pearls, as in dreams. The rod doesn't have time to explode.

That day, on my first tarpon trip, I remember wondering: If everything about the Silver King comes in XXL size, what constitutes the 'finer points' of tarpon fishing? For isn't it understanding these 'finer points' that rewards the expert?

Since then I've discovered just how different a day's tarpon fishing can be from the images that loom large in magazines and DVDs. Now, when I close my eyes and think of the tarpon experience that has left an indelible impression on my mind, I no longer see big sky, big sun. In fact, I don't see anything. I see big blackness. And I'm shivering.

What happened?

An alarm clock is ringing.

It's 4 a.m. Philip and I stumble around in the dark. Blind men, picking up one another's tackle, putting on one another's clothes. The flat's an hour away. If Bob makes *Fly Dipper* go any faster, we'll lose our hair. The chill will remove our noses.

An American is to blame. George Anderson, fly-shop owner in Montana. He'd come up with the idea that tarpon are mysterious in more ways than one. In particular, in the way they move. But in order to witness this you had to get up at a mysterious time. What could be more mysterious or sweeter than just before dawn? After a night of whiskey sours?

We arrive at the mysterious flat just before sun-up, shivering, silent —
and surrounded. Tarpon snuffle about on the surface. The tide whooshes
in. At sunrise, a flat is no different from a carp lake. The enchantment is
the same. You go soft-footed and silent. There's a real sense of drama.
Voices aren't raised until the darkness is torn away. When this happens,
it's a magical moment. Like ripping the wrapping paper off a birthday
present.

'What's that?' I ask, pointing to where a silver sea suddenly flattens.
Tarpon, war dancing, following one another head to tail in a circle,
forming a daisy chain. Are they angry we've found out their secret hour?

'It's not what they're doing,' Bob says, 'it's what you do about it.' But
it's too late. My fly lands in the middle of the circle. The water explodes.
The fish are gone.

'*Outside* the ring!' Bob says. 'Jumping a tarpon is good. Making them
jump out of their skin, no good.'

Tarpon fishing is beset by all sorts of pitfalls they don't tell you about
in brochures. Like how do you land a tarpon over a hundred pounds?

Bob had poled Philip and me to where a channel cuts between two
flats. Twenty feet down, bonefish patrol the drop-off.

'Tarpon,' Bob whispers.

They look tiny. The lead fish lifts to my fly. Every inch it lifts, it puts
on another pound. When it reaches the surface, it is over a hundred
pounds. This time, I remember to 'strip-strike'. The tarpon heads for
the flat with Bob after it, engine on.

'Why do tarpon take such small things?' I ask.

'Elephants eat peanuts,' Bob replies.

Another tarpon jumps mid-channel, going the other way. It's five feet
long.

'Glad we're not attached to *that*!' Philip jokes. But we are. Our tarpon
has turned and is heading to the other flat. The line hadn't had time to
pull round and point in the new direction.

Back on that other flat, Bob jumps into a chest-high sea. Using a tiny
trout net, he paddles across the flat towards the tarpon.

'He'll never get *that* . . . into that,' I think, just as Bob is getting that's
head into the hairnet. Flopping around like Pete Doherty on stage, the
demobilized dinosaur rolls into Bob's arms, anaesthetized. A net result.

Bob goes for the 100 lb tarpon with a trout net.

Tides don't always run in your favour. But low tide doesn't mean no fishing. It means a different kind of fishing, like fishing in tiny spaces. Like in a bathroom. In the mangroves. It's here, in clearings two rod lengths square, that tarpon of all sizes go baitfish bashing in the rooty tangle of alleyways.

'How can you cast in here?' Philip asks. Bob points into the sky. 'You cast . . . up there.'

Philip and I are terrified a squeaky foot will give our position away. Not a problem shared by Bob. Rather than the coy, Bob prefers to appeal to the curious side of a tarpon's nature and starts stamping on his platform as hard as he can – and revving up *Fly Dipper*'s engine. Immediately, five tarpon appear out of the mangroves.

'*Cast!*' Bob screams. One steeple cast and Philip has his fly inside the mouth of an inquiring tarpon. With no room to 'trout-strike', even accidentally. One 'strip-strike' is enough. Three leaps later, the tarpon is up into the mangroves. One more cast and Philip has another. It leaps into the air straight into the skiff. A tarpon in the boat is worth two in the bush.

The next day, Bob, has a different plan on our second low-tide morning. We head for the edge of a reef where the ocean sweeps onto a flat no deeper than a flooded lawn. Trying to keep our balance, standing with waves lifting the anchored skiff and smashing it back down again, is a circus act. I'm holding Philip's legs.

A tarpon takes his fly. A thirty-pound baby curls in the air, scattering the other six in the pod. Then there is a ten-foot swirl.

' Shark!' Bob yells. Philip's tarpon is in the jaws of a shark the length of the skiff, in knee-high water. Not a scale left to prove he had been attached to anything. The shark has taken the lot.

'Not quite,' Philip says.

The ultimate insult. The shark has spat out the fly I lent him.

But even with all your tactical ducks in a row, with tarpon fishing – as with so many things – nothing can beat a little magic.

~

I'm on my next foray. I'm with Lord Shoreditch, my good friend, Steve Edge. Today Steve is wearing a crimson and blue Maharishi kaftan. A shock of blond hair sticks out either side of a white cap with an orange peak, like the mane of a crazed horse. A hand stuffed into a black motorcycle glove grips a fly rod.

Everyone's looking at him standing there on the dock. I'm looking at him, thinking: What if this skinny blond kid from the East End – Shoreditch's 'lean boy' – finds himself attached to a fish of enormous size? With scales the size of his palm? What if this creature from prehistoric times, one of the oldest to still roam the planet, should take his fly? A Silver King, that leaps six feet in the air and rattles his gills at you, making the sound of nuts and bolts being shaken around in a rubber bucket? That crashes back down into the sea, showering the boat with foam and fury? On a fly longer than one of his fingers?

Whatever happened, I had to be there. But right now I was waiting for someone to say something. And they did. Under their breath. In Spanish.

'*Eso es pescador?. . . O mago?*' one of the guides asked me as they watched my boat partner make his way to Bob's *Fly Dipper*, tied up, ready and

waiting at the mooring. Is this a fisherman? . . . Or a magician?

Yesterday, Steve and I had spent the morning a mile out at sea, in water ankle-deep, waiting to ambush jittery bonefish as they were lifted out of deep, blue channels on a rising tide and rushed onto shallow water, their bellies scraping on the marl. Covered with yellow turtle-grass, these 'flats' are huge dinner tables. Crab, shrimp and various seafood combos are served up, twice daily.

But today, Steve only had flies for tarpon. This was a fish he had never caught. The Big Daddy of the Flats. Leaping and jumping, a tarpon this size is like having Kylie Monogue, live – on the end of your line.

Rabbit Hat

Arriving at the skiff, Steve presented his tarpon fly to Bob. Four inches long, bound up with rabbit fur, tinsel with googly eyes, it was dressed on a hook you'd use to dispatch a salmon, rather than attract it.

'I think I'll have a hat made out of it,' Steve said. He wasn't joking.

My long-nosed Rabbit Hat had hooked itself into a tarpon well in excess of a hundred pounds the previous day, several other smaller 'poons during the week. As always, it was tied on a circle hook, a juicy #3/0.

When it comes to tying it, the first thing I wind on after the thread is a short thirty-pound line. I use this to form a small loop, about half an inch (1 cm) long at the bend, to stop the materials that will be hanging off the back of the hook wrapping themselves round it. Next, I tie in a small, short bunch of orange calf tail and half a dozen strands of gold Flashabou. Finally, on top of all of this, I tie a 2½ in. (6 cm) strip of natural wild rabbit fur. Not bleached, not dyed, straight off the pelt. With all of this bound in securely at the bend, I tie in a ginger hackle. This should be lying just above the hook point.

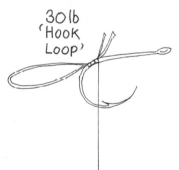

30 lb
'Hook
Loop'

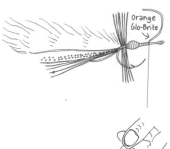

Now I wind on a length of orange Glo-Brite fluorescent thread and build up a slim body that tapers back to the bend to form a head, covering up where I had secured the rabbit and tail materials. Here, on either side of the hook, I stick on two self-adhesive eyes.

Finally, the gluey part. I cover these eyes and the whole length of the body with a thin coat of epoxy. No need for bead heads for weight. Because it's weighty and invisible, epoxy is one of the best weights you can get your hands on. Although it's tricky to get it off, if you get it on your hands.

The tarpon flat was an hour away. Bouncing us over waves, my teeth merrily clacking away as if I was in the Arctic, *Fly Dipper* came to a sudden halt. Bob had spotted a barracuda lying black on a white flat.

Which one was the fastest? Steve, jumping up onto the front of the skiff with his spinning rod, or the barracuda, turning for a moment like a gun turret, then shooting itself skywards to savage Steve's floating plug, pop-popping through the spume, a character out of *Looney Tunes*?

With teeth like those of the mother-in-law from hell, we were glad to return that 'cuda to the sea. But not before I got it to grin to camera.

I was admiring an osprey in a dead mangrove when I spotted the tarpon. It shone like a large silver salver as it twisted in the sun, chasing the small baitfish that feeding tarpon corral in the mangrove roots and gobble up like peanuts. Bob had seen it, too. He was poling in its direction.

It was Steve's turn up front. With nothing but baitfish on its mind, Bob was able to get *Fly Dipper* to within yards of the tarpon. Three false casts and Steve had his fly landed in front of its nose. Perfect.

The thrill of fishing the flats is that the action happens right in front of your very eyes. The tarpon quickened its pace to catch up with Steve's fly. Then . . . lights, camera, action . . . the monster's mouth opened up like a huge white tropical flower sucking in Steve's monster confection.

A tarpon's mouth is a dustbin lined with sandpaper. Having no teeth, tarpon crush their prey. To pull the hook home takes not one, but many violent yanks at the line – with your bare hands. Once set, if the tarpon decides to make off for Miami, the line slices off your fingers in the rush. Unless you happen to be wearing motorcycle gloves.

Now, Steve understands animals. He'd been brought up with them as part of the family. His father was an animal trainer. Snakes, lizards – he used to sit next to a chimpanzee at mealtimes. He had tried to tame an iguana on the beach that lunchtime. But first you have to catch it. He'd come close.

Tarpon throw themselves in the air, twisting like Olympic high jumpers. They skim across the surface like surfers. Steve's tarpon was five feet long. A heavyweight versus a lightweight. Steve realized he wasn't going to win the battle by conventional means. His only chance was to fight a battle of wits.

Right now, Steve was anticipating when the tarpon was going to jump next, ready to lower, or rather, 'bow' his rod to the Silver King and have slack in the line to prevent it tightening and snapping. To stop it leaping, he kept the rod tip in the water, moving it from left to right; turning the tarpon's head this way and that, disorientating it. Bob was no longer anxious.

Thirty minutes later, the tarpon was at the boat. But how to get it in for a photograph? This wasn't to be. Near eighty pounds, the fish was too big for Bob to lift out of the water.

'Blimey, mate. It's bigger than me!' Steve yelped as, with a flick of its tail, the tarpon moved slowly away, turning into the current like an articulated lorry pulling out of a service station.

'Thanks, baby,' Steve said, hugging Bob and giving him a huge kiss. 'That was magic!'

No, the fly was magic. This is the miracle of minimalism.

FIN